W9-BLZ-664

The
Paradiso
Files

The Paradiso Files

Boston's Unknown
Serial Killer

TIMOTHY M. BURKE

Steerforth Press
Hanover, New Hampshire

For information about permission to reproduce
selections from this book, write to:
Steerforth Press L.L.C., 45 Lyme Road, Suite 208,
Hanover, New Hampshire 03755

Library of Congress Cataloging-in-Publication Data

Burke, Timothy M.
   The Paradiso files : Boston's unknown serial killer / Timothy M. Burke. — 1st ed.
     p. cm.
   ISBN-13: 978-1-58642-140-3 (alk. paper)
   ISBN-10: 1-58642-137-9
   1. Paradiso, Leonard J., 1942– 2. Serial murderers — Massachusetts — Boston —
Biography. 3. Murder — Massachusetts — Boston — History. I. Title.

HV6248.P28B87 2008
364.152'3092–dc22

                              2007042576

FIRST EDITION

I dedicate this book to my dear friends
George and Terry Webster. I wish there was more
I could have done to ease your pain.

Contents

Paradiso Files: Time Line

- -

JANUARY 1967	Doreen Kennedy is assaulted in Saugus, Massachusetts.
JANUARY 5, 1970	Florence White is abducted from the Combat Zone and taken to East Boston, where she is assaulted.
SUMMER 1971	Jennifer Lawson is assaulted aboard the original *Mala Femmena* in Boston Harbor.
LATE SUMMER, 1972	Patti Bono is assaulted near Pier 7.
SEPTEMBER 28, 1973	Connie Porter is assaulted by Paradiso in Andover; she had been hitchhiking and he picked her up.
JUNE 27, 1974	Lois Centafante's body is discovered near the Governor Edwards Bridge in Revere.
SEPTEMBER 27, 1974	Leonard Paradiso is convicted of assaulting Porter. He is placed on parole pending appeal.
NOVEMBER 16, 1974	Kim Benoit's body is discovered in Florida, Massachusetts.
DECEMBER 27, 1974	Kathy Williams's body is discovered in a rest area in Andover.
MARCH 2, 1975	Holly Davidson's body is discovered in Methuen, Massachusetts.
JUNE 29, 1975	Melodie Stankiewicz's body is discovered in Salem, New Hampshire.
JULY 1, 1975	Paradiso begins serving his sentence for the Porter assault.
SEPTEMBER 17, 1976	Paradiso talks with fellow inmate Tony Pisa in prison.
OCTOBER 1976	Candy Weyant writes to the parole board.
MAY 10, 1978	Paradiso is released from the Salem House of Correction and placed on parole.
AUGUST 11–12, 1979	After the Milano wedding, Marie Iannuzzi is murdered.
SEPTEMBER 13, 1979	Candy Weyant reports her Buick LeSabre stolen.

DECEMBER 24, 1979	Paradiso talks to Pisa about the Iannuzzi murder.
MAY 3, 1980	Paradiso buys another boat, a 26-foot Chris-Craft, and names it the *Mala Femmena*.
EARLY JULY 1980	Janet McCarthy is assaulted near Candy Weyant's home in Revere.
JULY 26, 1981	Paradiso claims the *Mala Femmena* has been stolen.
AUGUST 18, 1981	Paradiso files for bankruptcy.
OCTOBER 1981	Joan Webster vacations in Ellsworth, Maine.
FALL 1981	Robert Bond is arrested and charged with the murder of Mary Foreman.
THANKSGIVING WEEK, 1981	Paradiso's bankruptcy finalized.
NOVEMBER 28, 1981	Joan Webster disappears from Logan Airport.
NOVEMBER 30, 1981	Paradiso is treated for an injury to his left finger at Lynn Hospital. He beats a guard dog the same day with a lead pipe.
DECEMBER 18, 1981	Paradiso calls Pisa and makes a statement about Webster.
DECEMBER 25, 1981	The Websters make a public appeal for information about their daughter's disappearance.
FEBRUARY 1982	The *Boston Globe* publishes a story about the unsolved murders of Basilisa Melendez and her two children.
LATE FEBRUARY 1982	Kathy Leonti calls the DA regarding the murder of her sister, Marie Iannuzzi.
MARCH 2, 1982	Paradiso is served with a subpoena to appear at the grand jury. He takes a cross-country trip that lasts six weeks.
MARCH 5, 1982	The grand jury begins to hear evidence on Marie Iannuzzi's murder.
JUNE 28, 1982	Paradiso is indicted for Ianuzzi's murder.
JULY 6, 1982	Paradiso is arrested. He is returned to Charles Street Jail to await trial for parole violations.
DECEMBER 13, 1982	Robert Bond is convicted of murdering Mary Foreman.

JANUARY 5, 1983	The DA receives a letter from Bobby Bond regarding his conversations in jail with Paradiso.
JANUARY 10, 1983	The DA talks to Bond.
LATE JANUARY, 1983	Bond passes a lie detector test. The DA learns that Paradiso talked with Pisa, too, about Webster and Iannuzzi. Janet McCarthy comes forward.
FEBRUARY 1, 1983	Patti Bono comes forward.
EARLY MARCH, 1983	The DA talks to Pisa.
MARCH 30, 1983	Paradiso writes to his friend Sammy.
APRIL 1983	The police search Candy Weyant's home. The DA meets with Joan Webster's parents.
EARLY SUMMER 1983	The DA calls in the FBI.
LATE SUMMER 1983	The FBI finds Paradiso's ex-girlfriend Charlene Bullerwell.
SEPTEMBER 26, 1983	The sunken *Mala Femmena* is found in the harbor.
OCTOBER 1983	Paradiso's replica gun is found in the harbor.
NOVEMBER 1983	Paradiso's motion to change attorneys is approved.
JANUARY 1984	The DA receives a letter from Paradiso.
MARCH 15, 1984	The prosecution's petition to include testimony from Bono, Porter, and McCarthy is denied.
JULY 9, 1984	Paradiso's trial begins.
JULY 21, 1984	Paradiso's verdict is read.

Prologue: Harvard Medical College, 1849

It was late fall and a pleasant day for a walk from Boston's Beacon Hill down the narrow cobblestone streets toward the Charles River. Not far from the muddy banks sat the original site of Harvard Medical College. Adjoining the medical school, the new Charles Street Jail was undergoing construction, taking form in the shape of a large stone crucifix. In the inner recess of Boston Harbor, flat-bottomed skiffs and three stately clipper ships lay comfortably moored in the calm water, their sails and riggings tightly secured to their masts in anticipation of winter. The scene evoked a Fitz Hugh Lane oil painting.

A tall, thin man with a black stovepipe hat walked down State Street, past the site of the Boston Massacre toward Faneuil Hall, the birthplace of the American Revolution. He momentarily considered the possibility of a meal at Durgin Park restaurant, but the waitresses there were too rude for his liking. Besides, there was the matter of a debt to be collected.

On Thanksgiving weekend 1849 Dr. George Parkman, one of Boston's wealthiest citizens, disappeared without a trace. Three years earlier Parkman, a Boston Brahmin, had donated the land upon which his alma mater built Harvard's first medical school. He was well known and respected within the city's elite; his friend, ornithologist James Audubon, even named the Parkman wren in honor of the physician. When Parkman didn't return to his home at 33 Beacon Street late that November evening, his family offered a large reward for information as to his whereabouts.

Days later, a second Harvard physician and professor named Dr. John Webster was arrested and charged with the murder of Dr. Parkman. Parkman had loaned Webster a sum of money that went into default. Parkman was last seen walking toward Harvard Medical College, where Webster lived and taught chemistry. Parkman's body was never found. Only bone fragments and a section of a jawbone were recovered from a furnace in Webster's laboratory at the school.

The landmark case *Commonwealth of Massachusetts v. John Webster* was presided over by Chief Justice Lemuel Shaw, the father-in-law of author Herman Melville. Prior to the arrest of John Webster, the law required proof to an absolute certainty that a person had been murdered through identification of the corpse. Because Parkman's body, the corpus delicti, was never found, his death couldn't be proven with absolute certainty. The prosecution was required to establish that Parkman had been murdered by using circumstantial evidence to prove the jawbone came from his body, and that John Webster was responsible for his murder.

The Webster trial of 1850 was a sensational case, with thousands of spectators attending the proceedings. For the first time, a jury was allowed to hear expert testimony that the false teeth found in the jawbone recovered from Webster's furnace matched the teeth made by a dentist for Dr. Parkman. More important, Judge Shaw's jury instructions changed the requirement for conviction from "proof to an absolute certainty" to "proof beyond a reasonable doubt"; this would become the new standard for every future criminal case in the country.

More than 130 years later one of the most celebrated murder cases of the 1800s would emerge as a key piece of the puzzle in the investigation of another murder case. On Thanksgiving weekend in 1981, a Harvard University graduate student named Joan Webster disappeared without a trace from Boston's Logan Airport.

This is the true story of a serial killer who murdered Joan Webster and other young women, but has yet to stand accused of, let alone be held accountable for, many of his crimes.

1: The Combat Zone

Prior to 1970, Boston's Scollay Square was the city's unofficial red-light district. The former home to bars, burlesque shows, and bawdy houses, the square was razed by city officials intent on localizing the burgeoning porn industry into the newly formed Combat Zone section of Boston.

A four-block area bordered by Chinatown and the theater district, this "adult entertainment zone" centered on Washington and Tremont Streets, between Boylston and Kneeland Streets, extending to Park Square. The Combat Zone received its unlikely moniker from the large number of local military officers who frequented the strip clubs, porn shops, and prostitutes in the area.

Violent, crime-ridden, sleazy, and drug-infested, the Zone attracted dozens of soldiers, sailors, hookers, students, pimps, tourists, police, and businessmen alike. Home to the Pussy Cat Lounge, the Intermission Lounge, the Sugar Shack, the Two O'Clock Lounge, and the Naked Eye, as well as a slew of peep shows, nude dance clubs, and bars, the Combat Zone was the new epicenter of Boston's seamy underbelly.

At 2 AM the bar doors closed and the drunken patrons emptied onto the streets. The rabble would then find their way to the late-night Chinese restaurants adjoining the Zone — places like the South Seas Restaurant, which featured after-hours beer euphemistically named "cold tea" as well as hot-and-sour soup, General Gau's Beef, and Strange and Slippery Chicken.

Outside the restaurant, the street scene continued to play itself out with hookers soliciting the recent evacuees from the nearby 663 Club and other bars and strip joints. Throughout the area, prostitutes from sixteen to sixty plied their trade under the watchful eye of pimps as well as police. The action was wide open; there were no limits in the Zone.

Florence White was a runaway at the age of sixteen. A street child with an innocent smile, she stood alone on January 5, 1970, turning tricks on Harrison Avenue, just opposite the South Seas Restaurant.

It was cold that night, and traffic was slow as Lil' Flo surveyed the scene from her corner perch. A light snow was beginning to fall, blending with the white fabric of her coat and matching boots. Silently watching her breath disappear into the night air, she stared straight ahead as a newspaper page pinwheeled across the street. Behind her the stench of stale urine wafted from the doorway. Nearby, an outdoor speaker blared remnants of the recent Christmas past as Bobby Helms sang "Jingle Bell Rock."

"Yeah, that's me, dancin' and prancin' in the frosty air," the girl sang as she listened to the music, wishing she were home.

A Zone regular who'd left her mother and dropped out of school at fifteen, Flo had been seduced by the life of easy drugs and random sex. It all came too quickly for a girl running from an unwanted past. Pimped out and drugged up, she was well accustomed to making and receiving propositions when the pale green car pulled up alongside her curb just before two in the morning.

"Youse need a ride home?" the lone driver asked the girl with the innocent smile.

"Yeah, are ya goin' out tonight?" she answered sweetly into the thin air.

The driver smiled in agreement and summoned her to the passenger's side with a tilting nod. White kicked the sidewalk snow from her midcalf boots as she walked toward the front of the car and peered in the windshield. The streetlight above her highlighted the image of a woman-child as she glided past the illumination of the headlights and reached for the door.

She shuddered from the cold leather seat beneath her short skirt as she closed the heavy door behind her. The girl glanced across the seat and smiled at the potbellied driver.

He looks Italian or Jewish, she thought as the man threw the car into gear. The driver turned his unsmiling face toward her as he pulled out into traffic and reached into his leather coat pocket.

"Youse coming with me," the driver said as he brandished a silver gun and reached across the girl's body to lock the door. There was a sudden rush of fear in the girl with the innocent smile. The driver held the revolver beneath the dashboard, pointed the shiny barrel at her breasts, and spoke once again without emotion.

"Youse coming with me, bitch."

2:The Corner of Cottage and Webster Streets

The pale green car passed quickly through traffic from the Combat Zone toward the Callahan Tunnel. The dark, cavernous passage beneath the waters of Boston Harbor had opened in 1961. It was named for Lieutenant William F. Callahan, son of the first chairman of the Massachusetts Turnpike; he'd been killed in Italy shortly before the end of World War II. The tunnel carried one-way traffic from downtown Boston to East Boston and Logan International Airport.

The mismatched couple shared a fear-induced silence as their car snaked past the other occasional night-owl motorists, eventually approaching the tollbooths at the end of the tunnel.

"I wish Sugah was here. Sugah would protect me," the street hooker said softly. Several miles away her pimp had just begun searching for Lil' Flo on the empty streets outside the South Seas Restaurant.

"If youse says another word, I'll fuckin' kill ya. Youse hear me?" The driver pressed the cold steel of the muzzle against her left temple.

The girl with the innocent smile nodded in panicked agreement as she whispered a Hail Mary to her God.

The car rolled through the deserted tollbooth, turned toward East Boston, in the direction of Maverick Square, and a short distance later stopped at the corner of Cottage and Webster Streets. The large man with the potbelly parked the car, ordered the teenager outside, and directed her toward a three-story brick house with a gray door.

"Just get the fuck upstairs," the man hissed as he motioned with the gun toward a narrow stairway leading to the top floor.

There was nowhere to run, no one to help, and no one to protect her. She was alone, more alone than she had ever been. Inside the dirty and disheveled two-room apartment, the man put the silver gun to the terrified girl's head again. She closed her eyes and asked God to forgive her for being bad.

"Get your fucking clothes off, bitch, you're gonna suck me off." He pushed her into the center of the room and made a call on his phone.

"Yeah, I got me one. Get the fuck ovah here," Lil' Flo heard him say.

Before she was naked, another man appeared at the door.

"You're gonna do him too, honey," Potbelly said, pointing to his groin and laughing.

"Oh, that's good, bitch, now get rid of those boots," the newcomer said as he undid the front of his pants.

Shivering from the cold, the girl stared at the hunting rifles in the rack on the wall and did what she was told. Potbelly's callused hands clumsily groped her body as she stood naked in the center of the room.

"You see those guns, don't you?" he said as he fondled her and then pushed her to the musty couch. "You say one word to the fuckin' cops and you're dead." He brought the thick lips of his mouth to hers.

She screamed briefly in pain as he entered her. The first punch to her face made her bite down hard on her tongue. The second and third ground her teeth into the right side of her mouth. The rush of pain passed quickly and silently as she stared at the ring on her left hand, sobbed softly, and thought of her mother.

Potbelly's bulk engulfed her small body as he wrapped his fingers around her throat. The smell of his skin and lust hung in the air. She felt nauseated as she watched the second man reach to turn the volume up on the ancient Philco radio positioned on a nearby table.

There was no one there to hear her as the eerie sounds of Led Zeppelin's "Whole Lotta Love" drowned out both her cries for help and the rhythmic slapping of the big man's body against hers.

"Get the cunt's money and the diamond ring off her finger," Potbelly said to the second man as he rolled off the girl with the innocent smile and began to gather his scattered clothes from the floor.

Lil' Flo instinctively pulled her thin legs up to her chest and wrapped her arms around them as the second man approached.

"Give me that fuckin' ring," he barked, and the girl complied.

She started to cry again as the second man stood before her and pulled his soiled black pants down to his knees.

"Oh look, the dirty little whore's cryin'," he laughed as she retreated farther into the sticky cushions of the musty couch.

"The little bitch must feel really bad she ain't gettin' paid to suck my dick," the second man mocked as he angled his body toward her face. "This is gonna feel really good, ain't it honey?"

When he was finished, number two turned to Potbelly.

"Whadda ya wanna do with the bitch now? We can't just let her go."

Potbelly smiled and waved a switchblade in the air.

"She ain't gonna say nothin', are you bitch?" Potbelly said menacingly as he reached into his pocket and removed four round-headed bullets.

"You see these, honey? I got one waitin' here just for you. If ya sez a word to anybody, youse dead meat. She's nothin' but a little whore. No one's gonna believe her," Potbelly told the second man, then turned back to the girl. "Get your shit and get the fuck out of here."

She grabbed her white coat and matching boots from the threadbare rug and ran to the door naked. She dressed at the bottom of the stairs and went quickly outside into the cold January night. It was still snowing, and the side of her face ached. Tears streamed from her eyes as she stood alone shaking in the dark. She didn't care about herself or the money. It was her mother's engagement ring they had stolen from her. The ring was all that remained from a distant memory of an abandoned life. In her child's mind she knew at that moment what she needed to do.

Lil' Flo glanced back at the dark brick building with the gray door at the corner of Cottage and Webster Streets. She wiped her tears with the bloodstained sleeve of her white coat and headed toward the police station. Maverick Square and District 7 were just five blocks away.

3: Suffolk County

"That's the man that hurt me, oh my gawd, that's him," Florence White said as she thumbed through the plastic-covered three-ring binder of mug shots. "He took me to Cottage Street. He said he would kill me if I told you." Tears welled in her eyes as she spoke. "He took my mother's engagement ring. It's all I had. Look, you can still see the marks on my neck and my face. He did that to me."

"Are you absolutely sure he's the one?" asked Detective Ed Mahoney, the man with the badge and the reassuring smile.

"Yep, it's him, I know it's him. He had a switchblade and a silver gun and those funny-lookin' bullets. He's the one that raped me."

From hundreds of suspects' photographs at District 7, the girl had selected just one. It was Leonard J. Paradiso, a local mob wannabe with a sadistic temper. The youngest of six children, Paradiso was born in Italy on December 8, 1942. He was twenty-eight years old, large-framed, potbellied, and the current occupant of 31 Cottage Street, a three-story brick house with a gray door.

Known as Lenny "the Quahog" throughout East Boston and the North End, Paradiso was a fish merchant who'd earned his peculiar nickname selling clams and shellfish at the Feasts of the Saints in the insular Italian sections of Boston.

A truancy and discipline problem early on, Paradiso dropped out of school in the eighth grade and was sent for two years to the Lyman School for Boys, a reformatory. He later joined the merchant marines and was discharged for being AWOL. Seemingly outgoing and friendly, he'd apparently been psychologically wired early in life to hate women. Paradiso married in the mid-1960s; his wife divorced him two years later for cruel and abusive treatment.

Based on Lil' Flo's identification, the police applied for a search warrant for the house with the gray door at the corner of Webster and Cottage Streets.

On January 11, 1970, Lenny "the Quahog" was arrested for the kidnapping and rape of Florence White. Inside his two-room apartment, the detectives found a fully loaded silver .38-caliber revolver, a switchblade knife, hunting rifles on the wall, and bullets matching the description Flo had given. The serial number on the revolver had been obliterated, making the weapon untraceable.

As the detectives led the handcuffed Quahog out the gray door to their waiting cruiser, he turned to Mahoney and, with his best East Boston linguistic calling card, told him, "Youse fuckin' guys got the wrong fuckin' guy."

Ten days later Paradiso's case was "bound over" from the East Boston District Court to the Suffolk County Grand Jury for indictment.

Suffolk County is the geographic center of eastern Massachusetts. Lying alongside the Atlantic, it comprises the cities of Boston, Revere, Winthrop, and Chelsea. Bordered by Essex County on the north, Middlesex on the west, and Norfolk to the south, Suffolk County is also the center of criminal activity in the commonwealth. The Suffolk County Grand Jury sits five days a week to hear evidence on the region's major crimes. The jury consists of twenty-three citizens chosen at random from voter registration lists who serve for a period of time ranging from three to six months.

The grand jurors' responsibility is to determine whether there is "probable cause" to believe that a crime has occurred and that the person charged committed it. A majority vote is all that's needed to charge a suspect. If probable cause is found, a "true bill" of indictment is returned, and the defendant is arrested and arraigned on the specified charge. It's that simple. If probable cause is not found, the true bill is not returned and the case is dismissed.

The assistant district attorney assigned to Florence White's case spoke bluntly to the detective as the two men sat in the District 7 booking area talking between the ebb and flow of the station's daily arrests.

"Listen, Eddie, you and I both know if this girl comes into the grand jury and testifies about what happened to her, this Quahog guy's all done. It doesn't matter if she's a hooker or not. No one rapes and beats the shit out of a sixteen-year-old like that."

"I know. You shoulda seen her, her white coat covered with blood. We got pictures of what she looked like. It's just a matter of getting her there. She's a street kid," the detective added. He pulled Lil' Flo's black-and-white likeness from the manila folder.

"Shit, look at her. Man, he did a job on her. This grand jury will indict a piece of toast. This bastard's looking at ten to fifteen years in Walpole minimum." Quickly the DA added, "On the other hand, if she doesn't show up, we're toast."

The older lawyer raised his hand to his forehead. "Tell me this guy's not out on bail?"

"He made bail in district court. The judge said he was a lifelong member of the community and set bail at just a hundred bucks personal recognizance."

"Are you kidding me?" the DA asked incredulously. "Who was the judge?"

"Turn-'Em-Loose Bruce," the cop retorted.

"That figures," the lawyer said with a grimace. "Look, I'm sorry, but the quickest I can get you into the grand jury is on February 5. That's only two weeks away. Just make sure she's here, will ya?"

It was late January 1970, and the marks had just begun to fade from the girl with the innocent smile's face and neck. As she crossed Tremont Street in her white boots and coat, she stopped in front of the Two O'Clock Lounge. Staring back at her through the plate glass window was a poster touting the club's featured stripper.

She's very pretty, Lil' Flo said to herself. *I bet she's nice.*

MISS RIO DEL GRANDE, the sign read, FRESH FROM NEW ORLEANS, FOR YOUR VIEWING PLEASURE. TWO SHOWS NIGHTLY.

A silver tiara topped an enormous fall of thick dark hair, which hung down to the top of the stripper's large, tassel-covered breasts. An arched finger beckoned seductively from her black-gloved hand. The stripper's dark eyes stared blankly into the crowded street as the girl slowly passed by.

Maybe I could get me a job there someday, she thought with a child's mind. *Then everybody would be looking at me.*

Straight ahead, a familiar figure wearing a full-length fur coat and a fedora with a peacock feather came striding toward her. It was Sugah, her pimp. The tall man pointed to the girl and fixed his eyes upon her. She sensed something was wrong. Lil' Flo waved and anxiously smiled her smile as the pimp approached. Sugah wasn't smiling back.

"Yo, Lil' Flo, somebody been lookin' fo' you." A silver toothpick dangled from the corner of Sugah's mouth as he spoke. "Big ol' fat dude. Say he gotcha diamond ring and the green he snatched from ya."

The girl knew he would hurt her. She sensed she had done something wrong as Sugah placed his right hand on her breast, leaned forward, and closed his long, thin fingers around her.

"Don't chu be seizin' up no trouble for me, girl. You hear me plain?" he said as the woman-child's face grimaced in pain. "Ain't no good gonna come wid you talkin' to them policemens."

As Sugah tightened his grip, he whispered into her ear with whiskey breath, "You jus' go 'bout your business. That's all. You takes the cash and the ring back from the fat man. You hear me, bitch?"

The girl with the broken smile nodded obediently. And with that done, Sugah walked away.

— — —

On February 5, the Suffolk County Grand Jury convened to hear evidence in the case *Commonwealth of Massachusetts v. Leonard J. Paradiso.* Three of the charges against Paradiso carried life sentences.

Florence White never appeared.

The grand jury was continued for a month to give the District 7 detectives a chance to locate the state's only witness. Without her cooperation and testimony, there would be no prosecution.

On the next scheduled date in early March, Detective Mahoney appeared before the assembled members of the grand jury and gave them the news.

"You can't find the girl?" the DA asked.

"No," answered the cop. "I spoke to her mother. She said her daughter hasn't been home for a long time."

"She's a prostitute?" the prosecutor asked bluntly.

The detective didn't answer. He felt he owed the girl with the innocent smile that much. "She's never home. She hangs in the Combat Zone," he said softly.

"Why don't you outline what happened in this case?"

Mahoney nodded, straightened himself in the dark blue leather chair, and began to read somewhat woodenly from his police report.

"Sometime around two in the morning on January 5, Florence White was offered a ride home by an unknown man that looked either Italian or Jewish with a potbelly. He pulled a gun on her and told her she was going with him. She was only sixteen."

Mahoney raised his head from the report, paused briefly, and then continued reading.

"The defendant took her to a two-room apartment in East Boston. The place had guns on the wall in a rack. He called another man on the phone, put a gun to her head, and made her undress and then he raped her. He showed her a switchblade knife and told her he'd kill her if she talked. He took some money and a lady's diamond ring from the victim."

There was a collective sinking feeling as the detective looked up from his report into the eyes of the twenty-three jurors. They were intent on what he was saying and clearly wanted to help. The cop and the jurors both wished desperately that he'd found the girl.

The detective knew instinctively what the next question was going to be.

"She identified him, but now she's refused to testify, is that it?"

"Yes," said the detective without hesitating.

"Is the defendant still in custody?"

"No, he's out on bail." Mahoney hesitated and briefly looked at the police report before he offered the rest of his thoughts. "She called me a month ago and told me she met Paradiso in the Combat Zone again. He gave her the ring and money back. I tried to get her to testify. She never called back."

The detective didn't bother explaining to the jurors, but it was the law of the streets. It's just the way things went in the Combat Zone. The cop knew it. He understood it. He hated it, but he understood it. The young street hooker was a victim once again. Alone and vulnerable, with no options, she had been reached.

At least she got her mother's diamond ring back. Maybe that's all she really needed, the cop silently thought as he left the stand.

The grand jury deliberated briefly and returned a "no bill" on the charges of rape and kidnapping. Leonard J. Paradiso was indicted for possession of a switchblade knife and removing the identification number on a firearm. He was arraigned in early April.

On May 28, 1970, Lenny "the Quahog" pled guilty to the two charges in Suffolk Superior Court and was given a fifty-dollar fine.

He was a free man.

4: Boston Harbor

Jennifer Lawson met Lenny Paradiso through a mutual girlfriend.

It was midsummer 1971, and the Red Sox were already in third place, fifteen games behind the division-leading Baltimore Orioles. Rod Stewart's "Maggie May" topped the music charts on that steamy day. The air was dead on Atlantic Avenue in the North End of Boston as the couple sat outside the Jib Restaurant talking. There was no breeze, only heat.

"Ya wanna take a ride on my boat?" Paradiso asked the young woman as he wiped the beads of sweat from his broad forehead with the meaty backside of his right hand. Quiet, with languid eyes and a disarming smile that women seemed to like, the large man employed them fully as he extended the invitation.

The young woman had seen him at the Jib a couple of times before. Lenny had bought her a drink and seemed friendly, even safe.

"Where do you keep it?" Jennifer asked as they headed to Lenny's car en route to a nameless pier.

"It ain't far," Paradiso told her. He pulled from an empty parking lot near the Jib and steered them in the direction of the shoreline.

The boat was a nineteen-foot day-tripper comfortably bobbing in the mild wake of another passing cabin cruiser. The registration beneath the running lights on the bow read MS 9 LP. At the stern, an oversized Italian flag hoisted atop a white pole and hung over a handmade wooden nameplate that read MALA FEMMENA.

"What's *Mala Femmena* mean?" Jennifer asked.

"It's Italian for 'evil woman,'" the owner responded without elaboration.

Two heavy braided ropes tethered the small pleasure craft to a tall black piling. A white gull perched atop the piling kept a silent guard pending the boat owner's arrival. With a small cabin area belowdecks that slept two, the vessel provided a comfortable jaunt into the murky waters of Boston Harbor.

On board, an eight-track tape deck blared the voice of a woman singing Italian songs as the boat pulled from shore and headed due east. In a matter of minutes the shoreline faded from view as the craft headed to the quiet outer reaches of Boston Harbor.

"Who's that singing?" the young woman asked as she draped her hand over the side of the boat and felt the cool spray on her bare arms and legs. She smiled at the captain as she removed her shorts and T-shirt to reveal a modest bikini beneath.

"It's Connie Francis," Paradiso said. He stared at Jennifer and poured a bottle of Narragansett beer in large gulps down his large throat. "Her birfday is jus' four days after mine," he added with a peculiar sense of pride.

"Oh, I loved her in *Where the Boys Are*. I think she played Angie," the young woman said, squinting from the sun as they headed out to sea.

"She's a Pisan, jus' like me. She shoulda never changed her name from Franconero. Her father made her done it," Paradiso explained.

"Oh, she really has a great voice," the young woman said, though the Italian words meant nothing to her.

"Yeah, I love her, too. She ain't like the rest of dem," the Quahog said between swallows as he began to sing along with Connie. He knew all the words to the song by heart and sang on key, as if he had years of practice.

> *Femmene comm'a te,*
> *Nun ce hann a stà pe n'ommo*
> *Onesto comm'a me . . .*
> *Femmena,*
> *Tu si' na "Mala Femmena" . . .*

"That's so pretty. What's she saying?" Jennifer asked as Lenny cut the engines of his boat in the choppy waters and dropped anchor two miles from the Boston skyline.

"Connie sez she ain't gonna be an 'evil woman' to her man. Ya know, like fuckin' wid everybody else behind the poor bastard's back," Paradiso offered.

There was an unwelcome edginess to the man's voice as he used the word *fuck* for the first time. Jennifer thought about saying something, but let it pass. *Maybe it was just the beer,* she thought.

"That's why I named my boat *Mala Femmena*. I done it for Connie. She ain't like the rest of dem," the captain said, apparently making the subtle distinction between Madonna and whore.

"Women are evil. They just use ya and fuck ya over," the skipper added to his female guest, who suddenly turned her face away, realizing for the first time she had made a mistake in boarding the *Mala Femmena*.

As he spoke, Paradiso drained the residue from another Nasty Gansett beer and turned to face the young woman. He pulled the white T-shirt off his body, exposing a similarly colored, pasty expanse of flabby skin covered with thick chest hair. Without hesitation or comment, Paradiso undid the front of his shorts, pulled them down to his ankles, and kicked the collection off to the side with his Docksider shoes.

"What the hell are you doing, Lenny?" the frightened young woman said as she realized there was no place to go.

"Youse gonna suck my cock and then yer gonna fuck me," Paradiso said rather matter-of-factly. He opened a small hinged compartment next to the helm of the boat and produced a silver gun. "If youse don't, I'll fuckin' kill ya right here."

As the boat swayed to the rhythm of the swelling waves, the naked man with the gun directed the young woman in the bikini toward the bed inside the small cabin belowdecks.

"Get the fuck down there," the captain ordered, gesturing downward and toward his right side with the barrel of the silver gun.

As she passed by him, she pleaded, "Lenny, Lenny, please, please don't do this." With a swipe from his left hand directed to her head, the Quahog drove the young woman's body forward, down the three steps and into the cabin. He ripped the bikini from her body, threw her onto the narrow bed with the tiny seashell-patterned bedspread, and raped her.

Above them, the sounds of Connie Francis's "Who's Sorry Now?" played on the eight-track as Jennifer prayed the fat man with the hairy chest wouldn't kill her.

When it was over, Paradiso left her naked in the cabin quietly crying. She could hear him grunt as he hoisted the anchor and the engine began to turn the propeller shaft. She felt the boat heading off toward an uncertain destination. Too afraid to speak or move, she stayed below, praying to live, quietly awaiting her fate. After an eternity, she heard the engine wind itself down and felt the boat jolt against the wooden pier. Bare feet padded toward her.

"Get the fuck outta here," Paradiso said as he threw the young woman's T-shirt and shorts at her feet. "If youse sez a word about this I'll fuckin' kill ya. You come out here on the boat alone wid me. Showin' me your tits like dat. Youse got what you deserved. Youse jus' a fuckin' whore, jus' like all the rest of dem."

The next day Jennifer Lawson left the city of Boston and moved to the West Coast. It would be more than ten years before she told anyone what had happened to her on that warm day in the summer of 1971.

Lenny Paradiso was still a free man.

She was a North End girl, very Italian, very pretty, with long dark hair, olive skin, a warm smile, and straight white teeth. Patti Bono walked into the Jib Restaurant on a breezy warm night in late summer 1972 and smiled at all her friends seated alongside the long mirrored bar.

Everybody knew Patti.

The Jib was a popular local hangout, nautically situated on the waterfront just off Atlantic Avenue, less than half a mile from downtown Boston. In the corner of the bar Patti saw the Quahog seated alone at a table meant for four. She had known Paradiso since grammar school.

The Quahog stared at the young woman a little too long, running his thick tongue along the outside of his upper lip.

Effervescent and self-assured, Patti briefly waved to Lenny and then walked to the bar, where she ordered a Tanqueray and tonic with two limes. Paradiso watched her ass in her tight jeans, momentarily closed his eyes, and then moved his right hand under the red-checked tablecloth into his waiting lap. She stood at the bar talking with her friends, watching the Red Sox lose another one while the man with the hand in his lap continued to stare at her. The 1972 major-league season had opened with a players' strike. The Red Sox played only 155 games that year, winning 85 and losing 70. Detroit played 156 — one more than the Red Sox. Detroit won eighty-six games. It was a bad year for the Sox. They finished half a game behind the Tigers, who won the American League East Championship.

Suddenly Lenny was standing behind her. "Hey, Patti, can I talk ta youse for a minute," the Quahog asked, pointing to an area away from the bar, out of earshot from her friends.

"Sure, Lenny. How are ya?" She moved away from the bar.

"I ain't doin' too good. I got me some chest pains right now. I needs ya to give me a ride home. Would youse do that for me, Patti?" the Quahog asked as he placed his large meaty right hand in the middle of his chest.

"Sure, sure, Lenny, but I don't have a car. I walked here from home," she replied as the Red Sox finally scored.

"I got my car wid me, youse can drive me home and then take my car, and I'll pick it up later, okay?" the Quahog said, feigning another bout of chest pain.

"Okay, just let me tell everyone I'm gonna drive you home, and that I'll be right back," Patti said innocently as she began to turn toward her friends seated at the mirrored bar.

"No, no, no. Don't do dat," Paradiso said hurriedly as a fat hand reached for the pretty girl's arm. "I don't want nobody makin' a fuss. I don't want none of dose guys knowin' I got a problem wid my heart."

The girl from the North End paused momentarily and then just as quickly discarded her fear. She knew and trusted Lenny.

The mismatched couple left the Jib that warm night and climbed into Paradiso's pale green car. Patti started the engine and looked briefly across the seat at her passenger.

"Where do you live, Lenny?" she asked.

"Youse gotta go ta South Boston. Go past James Hook and Company, get on Northern Avenue, and then head toward Pier 7," the Quahog said as he took his thick-fingered hand away from his chest and began to stare at his chauffeur.

The pair crossed the Fort Point Channel Bridge as Paradiso directed her on each right- and left-hand turn until the last narrow street ended, and they could go no farther. They were at a dead end. The shimmering expanse of Boston Harbor lay straight ahead as they silently sat at the end of desolate Pier 7. Directly across from the pier, Logan Airport's lights hung just beyond the harbor's farthest edge. Every ninety seconds another flight roared overhead.

"Okay, Lenny, cut the crap, where do you live," Patti demanded, staring into the empty darkness of the harbor.

"Wait, wait a minute, I gotta pee," Paradiso said as he left the parked car while a seemingly suspended 747 slowly glided past overhead.

Gawd, I don't know how I get myself into these situations, the apprehensive girl said to herself as a stream of urine resounded from behind the parked car. When the sound ended, the passenger's-side door opened and the familiar face entered the car again.

In an instant the years of grammar school, Sunday school, first communions, and a life spent within the same tightly knit Italian community ended as Paradiso lunged at the young woman, grabbed her neck with his left hand, and punched her face with the other. As she screamed in pain, he reached into the glove compartment with his right hand, removed a silver gun, and held it hard to the side of her head.

"Youse gonna do what I say, bitch, or youse gonna wind up in the fuckin' water and no one's ever gonna find ya. Youse gonna suck my cock. Ya hear me, ya fuckin' bitch?" Patti knew Paradiso would kill her. Her breath came in short gasps. This was real. In the dark, alone and vulnerable, she now knew what true fear tasted like. It was amazing how quickly her mind worked. The thought of her family calmed her as she spoke.

"Lenny, Lenny, wait, you don't need to do this. I've had a thing for you ever since we were in the eighth grade," Bono said as she fought for her life with her words.

"You're full of shit, you never liked me," a pathetic Paradiso whined.

"No, Lenny, it's weird. All this time, I thought you never liked me. Remember that harbor cruise we all took in high school. Remember I tried to get you to dance with me? We all sat at the same table. Then that big fight broke out and some guys got locked up. Remember that?"

The longer she talked, the more emotional connections she made.

Lenny looked at her. Clearly he wanted to believe.

"Look. Here's my phone number. I mean it. Call me. Call me for this Saturday," the young woman said, her performance worthy of an Academy Award.

"You know you're really a sexy guy. You know that? You really are."

The terrified young woman leaned toward the Quahog, gently placed her hand on his right cheek, and kissed his lips. She pulled back from the kiss, looked warmly and deeply into his dark, dead eyes, then leaned forward and kissed him once again.

She wasn't sure which of her lines had worked, but he lowered the gun from her head and his body went limp. It wasn't until then that she realized she was bleeding from below her left eye. She wiped the blood with her hand and made Lenny promise her he would call her that weekend.

Paradiso drove Patti Bono to her home that evening in summer 1972 and promised her he would call the next Saturday.

Patti ran upstairs to her bedroom and locked the door. She washed the tears from her face, vomited uncontrollably for half an hour, and then called a male friend from the North End.

The next morning three of Billy Fopiano's crew went to Paradiso's home on Cottage Street in East Boston and sat outside waiting for him to leave for work. When the Quahog walked out of the house with the gray door, the three goons beat the shit out of him.

"If you ever come back to the North End, you're a dead man. For real, you fuckin' puke," the hardest of the three said as he placed a worn work boot hard to the midsection of the prone Quahog, who lay moaning and vomiting on the ground.

Lenny was still a free man.

The Greyhound bus terminal in Boston's Back Bay was a dismal port of entry into "America's Greatest City." Dirty and full of exhaust fumes, the terminal attracted an odd assortment of characters through its revolving brushed-steel doors. Along with the regular mix of students and other travelers, the terminal was a melting pot of drug users, con artists, prostitutes, and "chicken hawkers" on the prowl for vulnerable young women.

Lenny Paradiso enjoyed the bustling activity of the bus station. There were lots of women to see and occasionally talk to. His ready smile and easygoing demeanor belied the anger that raged just beneath. The bus terminals, as well as the airport and train stations in the area, all provided the predator with a ready source of opportunities to meet young women.

Lenny watched the scene and waited patiently, like a hawk circling for prey.

Connie Porter stepped off a bus from Hartford, Connecticut, and into the dingy terminal hoping to catch the next bus to her parents' Andover home. She had hopped a 5:30 PM Greyhound for the two-hour ride after wrapping up her shift at Fairfield Connecticut State Hospital, where she worked part-time. She'd arrived in Boston just late enough to miss the 7:30 PM bus home. The next bus wasn't leaving until 11 PM, and the nineteen-year-old art major, anxious to start her weekend, didn't want to wait around.

Tall and thin with long straight hair, she walked past the service counters, glancing at the silver-and-blue baggage storage lockers lining the walls, then stepped out onto busy Stuart Street, hoping to find a ride. As a struggling college student, she couldn't afford the twenty-five-mile taxi fare to Andover. Impulsive and headstrong, she decided to hitchhike home.

Walking the few blocks to the Boston Common, Porter stuck out her thumb, hoping a sympathetic motorist would pick her up. She hurried down Charles Street, a stretch of blacktop separating the grassy, tree-lined common from the more pristine, flower-studded Boston Public Garden. At the end of the street, a cabdriver came to her rescue and took her to the traffic rotary near the Museum of Science in Cambridge, just a few miles away.

She thanked the cabbie, quickly closed the cab's door, and turned to face oncoming traffic. Almost immediately a car pulled up beside her. It was about 8:15 PM when a driver in a red-and-white windbreaker offered Porter a ride. Lenny Paradiso pulled his white Chevy Caprice to the curb near the Museum of Science in the early-evening hours of September 28, 1973, and asked the young hitchhiker where she was headed.

"I'm going to my parents' house in Andover," she replied quickly.

"I can only take you to the Route 93 on-ramp," Paradiso said, smiling broadly.

It's dark out already, I've got to get home, she thought. "Okay, that's fine," she said before jumping into the car.

Dressed in a pink sweater, red plaid shirt and blue jeans, Porter slid into the passenger seat beside Paradiso. Placing her red carryall on the seat between them, she eyed the burly, dark-haired driver and smiled in appreciation for the ride. Paradiso smiled back and winked.

"Oh, I love that song," she remarked as Roberta Flack sang "Killing Me Softly" on the radio.

Paradiso reached to turn off the silver radio knob as he put the car in motion.

"Hi," he offered, "my name's Lenny."

"My name's Connie."

"Hey whaddya know. Connie, that's my favorite name. Jus' like Connie Francis," Lenny told the girl.

As the car lurched forward into traffic, Porter could detect the faint smell of alcohol on the driver's breath. She didn't care. They were only going a short distance. She would be home in less than half an hour. By the time the pair reached the top of the on-ramp, Paradiso had agreed to drive the pretty brunette to her parents' home.

Heading north on Route 93, the Chevy moved slowly up a highway still busy with commuters leaving the city for the weekend. The conversation was pleasant at first, just casual chit chat about Watergate, the Middle East, and Porter's job as an intern in the occupational therapy unit at the hospital. The teenager gradually relaxed as the car blended into the flow of traffic heading north. Then she sensed a change in the driver's questions.

"How 'bout chu, do ya drink or do any drugs?" Paradiso wanted to know.

"No," she responded quietly.

"What about sex?" the driver asked as he stared at her body.

The teenager fidgeted uncomfortably in the passenger's seat as she unsuccessfully tried to steer the conversation to another topic.

"What do you do when you get loose?" the driver persisted.

Porter stumbled through the conversation, telling him simply she liked to travel.

"Would youse ever have sex for money, like those hookers in the Combat Zone?" he asked, staring at her eyes.

"No way," Porter mumbled, now feeling more uncomfortable than ever.

"Yeah, I used to go down to the Combat Zone all the time," Lenny continued. "You should see all them fuckin' hookers walking around half naked." Paradiso's jaw tightened as he spat out the words *fuckin' hookers*.

Porter cringed at his use of the word *fuck*.

"There's a shitload of them out there every fuckin' night. Them broads is always down there trollin' for tricks," the driver said in a voice now low and guttural, while his eyes darted from the girl to the road ahead and back. "The fuckin' cops don't do nothin' 'bout it, neither," he added.

There was a pause as the girl struggled to respond. She felt helpless, her mind blank. The noise from the tires spinning over the roadway was the only sound between them when suddenly she heard him speak as if she weren't there: "I got me a girl now, but I got a bad back, too."

He paused. "That's like been a problem for the two of us. Sex ain't so good wid us. Youse know what I mean?"

Porter listened uneasily and stared straight ahead, motionless, afraid to respond.

Traffic on Route 93 was heavy that night, slowed by construction that kept cars moving at a crawl. *Andover is just two exits ahead,* Porter thought as the Chevy sedan edged into the right lane and unexpectedly headed toward the Wilmington exit.

"This traffic's too fuckin' slow," Paradiso said, feigning exasperation. "I know a shortcut." He took the ramp at exit 40 and headed south on Route 62.

"Wait, wait, you're going the wrong way," the teenager said in a panicked voice.

"Relax, relax, honey, I know where I'm goin'," the driver said. He smiled at her blankly and then, just as quickly, turned his face away.

Paradiso's "shortcut" eventually took them to Route 495, just a few miles from Andover. Porter felt relieved to see the big green signs for the major roadway looming ahead.

Maybe he was right and did know a shortcut, she thought.

Paradiso entered the highway and once again headed toward Andover. Within moments, he had changed his mind.

"I gotta find me a gas station," Lenny told his passenger as he steered the big car into the right lane, turning off 495 and onto Route 133 toward Andover.

"No, no, this isn't my exit," the girl said as they began the ride down the darkened road.

Straight ahead a pair of headlights flickered in the distance.

As the car approached, Paradiso could make out the outline of a police cruiser in the darkness. He instinctively gripped the steering wheel tighter and cleared his throat. His breathing quickened, and a thin bead of sweat broke out in the middle of his forehead. He glanced back and forth from the road to the rearview mirror, keeping the cruiser in sight until the red taillights evaporated into the night.

Lenny continued slowly down deserted Lowell Street, reaching under the seat with his left hand to touch the smooth, cold metal of the .38-caliber Smith and Wesson.

Paradiso briefly turned to look at the girl, wondering if the bitch had seen the cop's car. Her face was barely illuminated by the glow from the dashboard lights, but he could smell her fear.

"It don't fuckin' matter if she did see 'em, I own the bitch now."

Nothing mattered now. Paradiso's eyes turned back to the road and momentarily closed. He knew at that moment he was going to kill her. He needed to find a place to do it.

Connie Porter watched the driver's eyes darting from side to side, as if searching for something known only to him. She thought about her family as the car passed by the tall maples that lined the sides of the macadam and hid the stars on the moonless night.

When he came to a small dirt road, Paradiso pulled the Chevy off the pavement and across the brown entrance and into the woods beyond.

"I gotta take a leak," he announced.

Connie couldn't breathe or talk when Paradiso didn't stop the car near the edge of the highway. The Chevy continued down the dirt path and into a sea of empty darkness. The headlights barely lit the two thin fingers of brown dirt and the tall grass that lay ahead. She could hear the grass swish as the car passed above.

The girl closed her eyes as she heard the car's tires slowly grind to a stop. Paradiso said nothing, shifting the car into park, turning out the lights, and sitting motionless, staring straight ahead. For the first time she could smell his cologne. She wanted to gag, and began to breathe through her mouth. It was at that moment Connie realized she was going to die tonight.

Without warning Paradiso grunted and turned to open the driver's-side door. Simultaneously the dome light flashed on, and the teenager could see the enormous bulk of his body as the Fat Man left the car. Just as quickly, the door closed and the interior of the car went dark once again. Connie could hear the sounds of a zipper and then a stream of urine coming from in front of the car. Fear paralyzed her as Paradiso opened the driver's door and reentered, reaching toward the console.

"Come on, let's go," she pleaded to Paradiso.

As she spoke, Connie reached to open the passenger's-side door, knowing there was no place to go.

"Hold on. I wanna light my cigarette," the driver replied as he turned to face his passenger and then angrily said, "Shut the fuckin' door, and lock it."

When the girl hesitated, Paradiso reached across her body, pushed the lock down, and, as he withdrew his hand, grabbed her breast.

This can't be happening to me, Connie thought as she frantically struggled to open her door and push the heavy, callused hands away from her body. She was no match for the Fat Man's overpowering strength as he grabbed her neck and pushed her head forward beneath the dashboard.

"Come here, baby, come here," the stranger murmured as she tried to free herself from his powerful grip.

In a state of frenzy, the terrified girl began screaming for someone, anyone to help her.

"Shut up. Shut up, or I'm gonna fuckin' kill ya." Connie managed to blindly unlock her door and slide feetfirst out the open passenger's side onto the ground.

"Come here, ya fuckin' bitch. This is all yer good for," her assailant said as he grabbed his crotch and slid across the seat.

As the girl tried to get her footing, Paradiso suddenly loomed above her, grabbed her by the hair, and began to shove her back into the car. When she tried to fight him off, the Fat Man threw her back to the ground and slowly, methodically, began to kick her in her shoulders and back. As she lay helpless and writhing in pain beneath him, Paradiso spread her legs with his foot and crashed to the ground on top of her.

"Now you're gonna get it, you fuckin' whore," Paradiso said as he brought his mouth close to the defenseless girl's face, staring at her with his dark, dead eyes.

Connie could barely move under his massive weight as she continued to scream desperately.

With his left hand around her throat, Paradiso began punching the teenager in the face over and over with his massive fist. Between each punch he screamed into the silent night, "Shut up you fuckin' bitch, shut up."

As he punched, Paradiso dug his thumb into Connie's windpipe, causing her to gasp for air. Even when she could scream no more, he kept hitting. "You're gonna ball me, understand? You're gonna fuck me." Paradiso quickly moved his hand from her throat to his belt and unzipped his pants.

"Look, you don't understand," the desperate woman lied as she gasped, still struggling to breathe, "you don't understand, I'm pregnant."

And just as suddenly as it began, the frenzy ended.

Paradiso loosened his grip on her, and Porter, exhausted, managed to wiggle free from his grasp, quickly backing away up a tiny knoll.

Then something strange happened.

A faraway light momentarily illuminated Paradiso's twisted, contorted profile just as he extended his hand and calmly said, "I ain't gonna hurt ya. It's all right. Let's be friends. Here, shake."

8: Ames Pond

The cruiser had nearly made it past the hidden dirt roadway off Lowell Street when Paul Enos said to his partner, David St. Jean, "Whoa, back up a second. There's somebody else's tracks across our tire prints in the dirt. Someone's been down there. Let's take a look."

"Sure," St. Jean responded. He backed up the cruiser and turned sharply left onto the dirt road. "But it's probably just a couple of kids making out."

There was an aura of apprehension as the cruiser wound its way into the darkened woods leading to Ames Pond.

The Andover police frequently got calls to the site to break up keg parties or roust kids parked near the water's edge. To make it easier to patrol the isolated area, the two officers would spin their tires across the entrance to the unpaved road, leaving visible tire prints from their cruiser in the dirt.

If another car pulled in after the officers left, the new tires would cross the artificial barrier the cops had made, signaling to the two patrolmen that someone had driven down the road while they were on patrol elsewhere. As they slowly made their way toward the pond that night, Enos and St. Jean could make out the reflected taillights of a car parked in the roadway ahead.

"Looks like you might be right," Enos told his partner. "It's probably just a couple of lovers."

Connie Porter saw the lights spinning in the distance as she hovered in and out of consciousness. Her legs and back ached as she cowered from the large man extending his hand toward her. Her head throbbed and she wanted to vomit. Droplets of blood had gathered under her nose and eyes. She could taste the warmth of blood in her mouth. Her face was swollen, her clothes in disarray. She saw the eerie silhouette of the Fat Man turn his back to her and then suddenly disappear. Dazed and frightened, the girl wondered if the bright lights drifting toward her were from the beyond.

Am I in heaven? Did I die? Connie thought.

The glow seemed to get brighter, somehow closer. Then she heard the faint sound of a car's engine. The sound was muffled and seemed far off. Connie stumbled off the knoll where she had sought refuge and headed out of the darkness and into the light.

As their cruiser came closer to the parked car, the officers could see it was a white Chevy Caprice, the same car they had passed a short while earlier on Lowell Street. The license plate read MASSACHUSETTS 446 D. With the lights from their cruiser illuminating the area, the two men saw a large white male with dark hair, dressed in a red-and-white windbreaker, standing near the passenger's-side door.

As they stopped the cruiser, their headlights caught something else: the figure of a woman directly behind the large man. Her clothes were disheveled and her jeans grass-stained. She stumbled toward the headlights, blood smeared across her lips, streaming from both sides of her mouth.

"Please, please, get me out of here and keep him away from me," she screamed to the officers.

The silence of the night air was punctuated with the desperate shrillness of her voice.

"He choked me and hit me, he tried to rape me, oh my God, please help me," the girl cried between gasps for air.

Stunned, Enos and St. Jean, now out of their cruiser, ordered the large man to put his hands on the roof of the Chevy. As St. Jean approached the suspect, Paradiso turned his face to the young officer and nonchalantly began to speak.

"I picked her up like that. She told me two kids had beat her up and robbed her."

"Bullshit," Porter yelled back. "You tried to kill me, you were gonna strangle me."

While Enos placed the girl in the backseat of their cruiser and called for a backup, Paradiso calmly zipped up his pants and buckled his belt. As St. Jean approached the defendant to handcuff him, Paradiso smiled at the young officer and began to speak softly out of the hearing of his partner.

"I got me a bad back. It's killin' me. Can youse cuff me in front and let me sit in my car till the uddah cruiser gets here?" Paradiso asked.

"If you fuckin' move toward that front seat, I will put one of these bullets in your head for the big dirt nap. Now put your hands behind your back," St. Jean said evenly as he quickly handcuffed the large man.

When the backup cruiser arrived, Paradiso was transported to the Andover police station. There he was booked, fingerprinted, and allowed to make a phone call from the station pay phone. Five minutes after he hung up, an unidentified caller dialed the Andover station and threatened to "blow the fuckin' place up" if Paradiso wasn't released from custody.

"You fuckin' clowns got no idea who you're dealing with," the nameless voice on the other end of the call warned and just as suddenly hung up.

Connie Porter was taken to a nearby hospital, where she was treated for multiple contusions to her face and neck, her spine and ribs. The hyoid bone in her neck was bruised. Droplets of the girl's blood were found on the large man's clothing. Traces of seminal fluid containing sperm cells were discovered on a portion of the victim's clothing.

Under the floor mat on the driver's side of Paradiso's car, the officers found a large buck knife. A blackjack was tucked into the crevice of the driver's seat. A loaded .38-caliber Smith and Wesson, its serial number obliterated, was stuffed in a holster under the seat. Hidden in the glove compartment was a paring knife and extra ammunition for the gun.

In the trunk was a machete.

At his arraignment in Lawrence District Court the following Monday, Paradiso appeared with his attorney and was released on bail in the amount of one hundred dollars.

Paradiso's trial started in September 1974, a year after his arrest. The judge was Ruth Abrams, a bookish maven of tremendous intellect. She had purportedly read every case decision ever written in Massachusetts and had served as a prosecutor in the investigation of Albert DeSalvo, the "Boston Strangler." Years later, Abrams would become the first woman ever appointed to the Massachusetts Supreme Judicial Court.

This was one of Abrams's first jury trials.

Paradiso's defense centered on the contention that he'd found Connie Porter in her beaten condition when he stopped to relieve himself near a dirt road off Lowell Street. Paradiso told the jury that when he first saw the girl lying on the side of the road, she was crying. She told him two kids had robbed and beaten her. He explained that he put her in his car, intending to take her to a hospital or the police station, and instead of backing out of the dirt road, he drove forward 460 feet to the spot where the police later found him. When the victim suddenly left his car, he continued, as he tried to turn around, and followed her just as the police arrived.

Paradiso also denied giving Porter a ride up Route 93 and offered the alibi defense that he had been at his girlfriend Candy Weyant's home at 212 Crescent Avenue, Revere, earlier that evening. Paradiso testified that he'd left Weyant's home and driven from Revere to the Scarlet Pub, a Lawrence bar, where he was drinking with another woman until shortly before the police arrived at the scene of the assault near Ames Pond.

The defense called Weyant as a witness; her testimony corroborated Paradiso's presence at her Revere home earlier that evening.

Paradiso's second alibi witness was Frances Melillo, a longtime friend. Melillo confirmed that she'd been with Paradiso at the Scarlet Pub, just north of Andover. She even offered the name of the waitress who'd served them drinks that evening. In a surprise move, the prosecution called the waitress as a rebuttal witness.

The waitress denied seeing either Paradiso or Melillo in her bar the night Connie Porter was attacked near Ames Pond.

On cross-examination of Melillo, the assistant district attorney asked Paradiso's alibi witness, "Did you testify in district court at the probable cause hearing?"

The defense attorney immediately objected to the question, and the court excluded it before it was answered. The judge admonished the jury in a lengthy instruction to disregard the prosecutor's inquiry.

Massachusetts law prevents a prosecutor from making any reference to whether defense witnesses testified at an earlier proceeding. Specifically, Massachusetts General Law, Chapter 278, section 23, provides, "At the trial of a criminal case in the Superior Court, the fact that the defendant did not testify at the preliminary hearing, or did not offer any evidence in his own defense, shall not be used as evidence against him, nor be referred to or commented upon by the prosecuting officer."

Once the judge instructed the jury to disregard the question, Paradiso's lawyer requested a mistrial. This would have effectively ended the prosecution against Paradiso on the basis of double jeopardy: A person cannot be tried twice for the same crime. The charges against him would have been dismissed.

The court denied defense counsel's request and continued with the trial.

Judge Abrams sent the case to the jury after closing arguments and allowed them to return a verdict. Paradiso was found guilty of assault and battery and assault with intent to rape. At his sentencing, the prosecutor asked the court to impose a sentence of fifteen to twenty years at the maximum-security prison in Walpole.

Under Massachusetts sentencing guidelines, Paradiso would have to serve at least two-thirds of the minimum sentence imposed before becoming eligible for parole. With a fifteen-year minimum, Paradiso would not have been eligible until he had served approximately ten years in a maximum-security facility.

After listening to the arguments of both counsels, Judge Abrams imposed a ten-dollar fine for the assault and battery on Connie Porter and a six-to-fifteen-year sentence on the conviction for assault with attempt to rape.

The judge then "stayed" the implementation of the sentence with the consent of the defendant, placed him on probation for the interim, and reported the case to the appeals court for their review.

Despite his conviction by the jury, Paradiso remained a free man for the attempted rape of Connie Porter.

Ten months later, the appeals court rendered its decision on Paradiso's case. During that same time period, from September 1974 through July 1975, four young women would be murdered and left on the side of the road.

9: Florida, Massachusetts

Several weeks after his September 1974 conviction for the attempted rape and beating of Connie Porter, Lenny Paradiso went deer hunting with his friends.

Although he was on probation while he appealed his conviction, the Quahog was still able to travel anywhere in the state. Lenny packed his Day-Glo orange hunting coat, with a matching fur-lined Day-Glo orange hat, and drove from East Boston to the small town of Florida, in western Massachusetts. Located ninety-four miles northwest of Boston in the Berkshire Mountains, Florida was an isolated rural community of fewer than six hundred people.

When Paradiso and his small group arrived at their destination, the hunters gathered at a local motel for a photograph. Outside the lodge, Paradiso smiled brightly for the camera as he stood holding his shotgun in front of a neatly printed, large white sign on the roof that read SUMMIT MOTEL.

It was hunting season for Lenny Paradiso.

On November 16, 1974, the body of sixteen-year-old Kim Benoit was found discarded alongside River Road in the town of Florida.

The girl had been strangled and dumped down a small gully next to the roadside. Her body rested supine against a small maple tree, with her left hand inadvertently pointed back toward the killer. A passing deer hunter discovered her that morning, not far from the Summit Motel.

Missing for several days, she'd last been seen in the nearby town of North Adams. A partially smoked cigarette near her body was the only evidence found at the scene.

Sixteen-year-old Kim Benoit's murder remains unsolved.

Six weeks after the discovery of Benoit's body in the Berkshires, another young woman's body was discovered in the town of Andover, not far from where Connie Porter was assaulted.

Located in Essex County, on the southern banks of the Merrimack River, the small town of Andover is bisected by two major highways, Routes 93 and 495. Bordered by the towns of Methuen and Lawrence to the north, Andover is situated twenty-three miles geographically north of Boston, but light-years from the Combat Zone.

The sleepy little bedroom community wasn't Mayberry, but it had little in the way of violent crime. There was the occasional larceny, an operating under the influence of alcohol or kids smashing a mailbox, but for the most part life was very tame in Andover. The attack on Connie Porter in September 1973 was an aberration, or so the thinking went.

On December 27, 1974, the naked body of Kathy Williams was discovered in a rest area in Andover, just off Route 93, tauntingly dumped about a hundred yards from the Massachusetts State Police barracks.

The sixteen-year-old Williams had last been seen alive leaving the 663 Lounge at 2 AM the same night. This notorious bar was located at 663 Washington Street in the Combat Zone — just a few blocks from the South Seas Restaurant on Harrison Avenue, where Paradiso had abducted sixteen-year-old Florence White in January 1970.

Kathy Williams was known to frequent both the 663 and Good Time Charlie's, where she solicited patrons for sex. A pretty street hooker, she'd been strangled and beaten so badly, her nose was broken in several places. A butterfly tattoo adorned her abdomen.

Her murderer has never been apprehended.

Williams wasn't the only young prostitute taken from the Combat Zone while Paradiso was on probation awaiting the results of his appeal.

On March 2, 1975, the body of Holly Davidson, twenty-two, was discovered on Route 495 in Methuen, just north of Andover. Like Kathy Williams, Davidson had been strangled and was dumped naked on the side of the road.

A street prostitute, Davidson worked out of the Sugar Shack bar in the Combat Zone. Her body was found approximately four miles from the site where Connie Porter had been assaulted eighteen months earlier, and four miles from the Andover rest area where the body of Kathy Williams was discovered. Like Williams, Davidson had a butterfly tattoo.

Holly Davidson's killer has never been apprehended.

Boston homicide detectives, together with Andover and Methuen police, conducted an investigation into both murders without success. The two killings were dubbed the "Butterfly Murders" by the media and police alike. The similarities between them momentarily intrigued the public, but the cases quickly faded from view without resolution.

On June 24, Leonard Paradiso received notification that the appeals court had reached a decision on his appeal of his conviction for the attempted rape of Connie Porter. The Quahog wasn't happy. His appeal was denied and he was going to jail. The court set the date of July 1 for Paradiso's surrender to the authorities at Walpole prison.

Paradiso had one week of freedom before he began his six-to-fifteen-year sentence.

Five days later, the partially nude body of Melodie Stankiewicz was discovered five miles north of Methuen in the shallow waters of Captains Pond, a remote area of Salem, New Hampshire. Stankiewicz had been savagely beaten and repeatedly stabbed.

Stankiewicz was last seen alive on June 27 in the Combat Zone. She was observed leaving the 663 Lounge on Washington Street with a dark-haired, large-framed man.

Melodie Stankiewicz's murder has never been solved.

Two days after the discovery of Melodie Stankiewicz's body, and ten months after his conviction for the attack on Connie Porter, Lenny Paradiso was finally incarcerated at the maximum-security prison at Walpole.

He wouldn't be there long.

10: Norfolk Prison

Six weeks after he was incarcerated, Paradiso was hospitalized in the prison infirmary for gastric ulcers. Four months after his incarceration, the Quahog was transferred from the maximum-security institution at Walpole to Norfolk prison, where he was evaluated and found not to be a sexually dangerous person.

The Norfolk correctional institution is a medium-security prison located in its namesake town approximately twenty-three miles southwest of Boston. Hailed as the first "community-based" prison in the country, Norfolk housed more than a thousand inmates. The prison held both short-timers as well as the vast majority of the "lifers" and other long-term inmates in the state. Most inmates had jobs.

Just over a year into his sentence, Paradiso began working at the auto school on the prison grounds. He gradually became friendly with another inmate by the name of Ralph "Death Row Tony" Pisa, a lifer serving a sentence for murder.

Within the prison community, Pisa had acquired a considerable reputation as a jailhouse lawyer. Amid the carburetors, mufflers, and exhaust pipes, Paradiso frequently sought Pisa out to discuss his appeal.

"The fuckin' bitch enticed me. What youse expect. She wanted it and I jus' fuckin' give it to her," the Fat Man said to Pisa as the two sat talking in the garage of the auto school at Norfolk prison.

"I read your file, Lenny. The girl was all beat up. You had just been on top of her choking her when the cops pulled up," Pisa responded, rolling his eyes skyward. He didn't have a law office and there was no secretary to screen his calls, but Pisa had an idea of the day-to-day business of dealing with clients who were in denial.

"Yeah, well, if da bitch wasn't around to testify there woulda been no case, right?" the Quahog said, attempting to demonstrate his legal acumen.

"Well, that's not exactly true, either." Pisa tried to explain the doctrine of fresh complaint to his attentive student. "If she told the police you raped her, even if she didn't testify, the cops could still use her statements to them as evidence of what you did. They could still convict you."

"That don't seem fuckin' right ta me," Paradiso whined. "How they gonna believe some bitch who ain't even at the trial?"

"Ya fuckin' dummy. It's called circumstantial evidence. The cops don't always need to have a witness to prove ya done something," Pisa said to the Fat Man, then adding a twist even more remarkable. "The cops can prove you killed somebody even if they don't have the victim's body."

"No fuckin' way, man, youse can't do that," an astounded Quahog said as he leaned closer to his mentor.

"Listen to me, ya fuckin' knucklehead. There's this famous old case from back before the Civil War. It's called the Webster case. And it's all fuckin' true. A Harvard professor was tried for killing some rich guy in Boston," Pisa began as Paradiso sat staring, openmouthed.

"The Harvard professor's name was John Webster. He owed this rich guy some money. They got into a fight and Webster killed him and burned the guy's body up. Only a chunk of this guy's jawbone was ever found. The cops never found the rest of the dead guy's body and they still convicted the Harvard professor for murder. They hung his ass thirty days later."

"No fuckin' way, man. I ain't comin' back to this fuckin' place again. Next time there ain't gonna be no fuckin' witnesses, 'cause there ain't gonna be no bodies," the Fat Man said as he began to clench and unclench his powerful hands. "I'll fuckin' bury 'em or put 'em where the fuckin' crabs will get 'em. When the crabs get ya there ain't nothin' left, I seen it happen."

"Lenny, you're just fuckin' sick. Ya know what, man, you're just too fuckin' sick," Pisa said as he turned from the Quahog and slowly walked away.

Shortly after Paradiso began work at the prison auto school, another inmate broke his hand during a physical confrontation. The incident prompted a request for Lenny's transfer out of Norfolk to be "nearer to his family." Over the next several months Paradiso's girlfriend, Candy Weyant, organized a letter-writing campaign requesting his transfer to the Deer Island House of Correction in East Boston.

Just before Christmas 1976, Paradiso's request for a transfer was approved, and he was moved from Norfolk prison to the Salem House of Correction (not Deer Island, as Weyant had hoped). Shortly afterward, his request for one-third parole consideration rather than the statutory two-thirds was approved by the parole board.

Within two months of his transfer, Lenny was placed on a weekend "furlough" plan allowing a twelve-hour release from jail to visit his family. For the remainder of his incarceration, Paradiso was granted furloughs nearly every weekend for up to sixty hours of unsupervised time outside the jail's walls. On May 10, 1978, Paradiso's incarceration ended. He was released from prison and placed on parole.

Lenny Paradiso was a free man once again.

On the weekend of his release, the Quahog was welcomed home by his friends and family. Paradiso celebrated his return to the free world and a brand-new start on life with a "coming out" party. Just over a year after his release from jail, Paradiso would become a suspect in the murder of another young woman. The victim lived in East Boston. Her name was Marie Iannuzzi.

As the Quahog enjoyed his freedom that weekend in May, another celebration was being held four hundred miles away in upstate New York. Joan Webster, a pretty, dark-haired interior design student, was graduating from Syracuse University. After a year in New York City, Webster would attend Harvard University for her graduate degree.

Unknown to each other, the lives and deaths of the Harvard graduate student and the girl from East Boston would be forever intertwined.

King B's Auto Mart was a low-end, anonymous used-car lot located just off the Lynnway in the blue-collar city of Lynn, Massachusetts.

Cash was king at King B's. Quick talking, fast dealing, no questions asked, and no honest answers given were the golden rules. Red, white, and blue triangular pennants flapped overhead in the early-morning breeze as Lenny and his girlfriend, Candy Weyant, pulled into King B's parking lot. It was one day after the Fourth of July weekend, 1978. The two bargain hunters parked their ride and then began to survey the selection of "Manager's Specials" placed closest to the small, windowless sales office.

"I like the yellow one, Lenny," Weyant proclaimed as she directed Paradiso's attention to the two-door Buick LeSabre.

"Let me go inside and Jew 'em down," the Quahog grunted as he briefly examined the price tag scrawled in white soap on the yellow Buick's windshield. "I know I can fuck with dem on the price." Lenny smiled to the bleached blonde as he sauntered toward the dealer's office.

Ten minutes later the happy buyer walked out of the office fifteen hundred dollars lighter, with title and car keys in hand. The new owners were so pleased with their purchase at King B's, they returned five weeks later and bought another car for Candy, a red Cadillac Coupe DeVille.

In late February '79 Lenny bought a third car, from Muzi Motors in Needham. It was a Chevy Caprice. Two weeks later Candy's red Caddie was "stolen" and later discovered burned to a crisp in Machias, Maine, sixty miles east of Ellsworth.

Lenny and Candy promptly filed a claim with Liberty Mutual for the stolen red Caddie, and were paid $3,162.

In mid-March 1979 Lenny and his parole officer, Victor Anchukitis, stood talking near the Commercial Lobster Company located on Pier 7 in South Boston. "I just got me a job as a sales rep for a seafood company," the Quahog began.

"What's the name of the outfit?" the PO asked as the Fat Man shifted the fat roll of hundred-dollar bills, courtesy of Liberty Mutual, in his right rear pant pocket.

"It's Lee's Seafood outta Saugus. The guy owns it is one of Red Milano's kids. I need ta get me a travel permit ta go out west and drum up some business for 'em," Lenny explained, shuffling his weight from one large foot to the other.

He looked down at the crumpled socks around his ankles, one blue, one black, and then quickly turned his face back to read the PO's response.

"When ya leavin' and when ya comin' back," the PO asked nonchalantly.

"I just got me some new wheels. It's a Chevy Caprice. I wanna leave the end of March and be back here in 'bout three weeks," the Quahog announced as his supervisor rubbed his broad forehead and slowly nodded his approval.

"Thanks, Vic, let me know if youse needs ya any lobstahs," the con offered with a smile as he lumbered toward his new wheels and sped away.

— — —

Two weeks later Paradiso's cross-country trip began with a short trek from Boston to the Bronx, with next-day stops in Baltimore, Memphis, Oklahoma City, Amarillo, Gallup, Lake Havasu, and temporarily ending in sunny downtown Los Angeles. Lenny's '74 Chevy Caprice made the left-coast turnaround, headed back to Vegas, crossed through Utah, and then rolled over the Rockies into Grand Junction, Colorado.

In Colorado the Quahog spent the next four days touristing the sights around Denver. He never made any business contacts for Lee's Seafood and gradually made his way back to Boston. Two months later Lenny's new ride, the cross-country Chevy Caprice, was stolen.

Lenny promptly filed a claim with his insurance company.

"We got an invitation to the Milano kid's wedding," Candy Weyant told her boyfriend shortly after he returned from his "business" trip to the West Coast.

"Oh yeah? When the fuck is it?"

"It's the middle of August. The reception's gonna be at the Ship Restaurant in Saugus. It sounds like a lot of fun, can we go, Lenny?" Candy asked meekly.

"All they want is some fuckin' money outta me. They know I didn't make no fuckin' contacts for 'em out West," Paradiso wheezed as he turned and walked away.

On August 11, 1979, Candy and the Quahog drove the yellow Buick LeSabre they'd bought at King B's to the Milano wedding reception in Saugus. Three weeks later, the Buick was reported stolen from outside Weyant's home in Revere. It was never recovered.

The pair promptly filed a claim for the stolen Buick with their insurance carrier.

12: The Pines River

In the early afternoon of the day following the Milano wedding, anglers on a passing fishing boat observed a young woman's body on the banks of the Pines River, directly behind the abandoned Conley and Daggett's lobster pound.

The sight of the lifeless form in a bright red dress on the rocky shore was morbidly surreal. Overhead, the shrieking caw of seagulls reflected their obvious distress at the intrusion into their quiet domain. Saugus police were notified of the discovery and immediately responded to the scene, together with representatives of the Essex County DA's office.

The unidentified victim was estimated to be between eighteen and twenty-five years of age. She was dressed in a red Danskin bodysuit with a matching skirt; a paisley-patterned black scarf was knotted tightly around her neck. The scene was photographed extensively, and a search of the area was conducted for evidence. None was found.

The young woman's body was ultimately removed from the scene and transported to a local morgue awaiting identification. Local media outlets were notified, provided a description of the body, and asked to broadcast a plea for public assistance.

Barbara Iannuzzi was heading home in her car when she first heard the news on the radio.

According to the announcer, a young woman in a red dress had been found strangled in a Saugus marsh. The mother immediately thought of her youngest daughter. Marie had worn a red dress to a wedding she'd attended the day before with her boyfriend. The fleeting idea was incomprehensible to the older woman. She had just spoken to Marie the night of the wedding, when the twenty-year-old called to say she was staying overnight at a friend's house, and would stop by the following day to celebrate her father's birthday. It couldn't possibly be her sweet Marie, Mrs. Iannuzzi thought as she followed the narrow road to her home in East Boston.

Marie never did stop by her parents' home to wish her father a happy birthday. As the day progressed, they became increasingly worried. Around one thirty that Sunday afternoon, Marie's boyfriend, David Doyle, called the Iannuzzi residence to inquire about Marie.

"The last time I saw her was at the wedding," Doyle told Marie's sister, Jean. "I was wondering if anybody heard from her."

When Jean said the family was concerned that Marie hadn't shown up for her father's birthday, Doyle suggested they call the police. No one ever did. The day passed slowly into evening. No one heard from Marie.

Early the next morning, August 13, Mrs. Iannuzzi and her daughter Jean heard a second news report about the woman found dead in the Saugus marsh. They immediately drove to the Jeffrey's Point triple-decker in East Boston that Marie shared with Doyle.

Unexpectedly, Doyle's mother answered the door, placing her hand over her mouth as she said "Oh my God," and beckoned them inside the cramped third-floor apartment. Doyle was still in the bedroom getting dressed. Frantic with fear, Jean recounted the description given on the radio and screamed, "Tell me where my sister is. Tell me you heard from her!" Emotionless, Doyle turned away from the Iannuzzis, said nothing, and left to brush his teeth.

Just before noon on the same day, two police detectives knocked on the Iannuzzis' front door and asked the gathered family if Marie wore a wedding ring and had a scar on her left knee.

The reality of Marie's death came one step closer to the Iannuzzi family when they said yes to both questions.

Marie's father, brother-in-law Tony Leonti, and boyfriend David Doyle were asked to accompany the detectives to view the young woman's body and possibly make an identification. The group somberly left their home, hoping against hope that the nightmare would end.

It didn't.

At the hospital morgue David Doyle pulled back the white linen sheet covering the body and paused as he gazed downward at the face of the beautiful young woman now devoid of life's color. Purple strands of bruising encircled her neck. He placed the sheet back without saying a word.

It was Marie.

13: East Boston

Christmas Eve 1979 was rainy, windy, foggy, and cool at just below fifty degrees.

Death Row Tony Pisa was on furlough from the Bay State halfway house for the holiday weekend. He had driven with his wife and son that afternoon to visit attorney John Cavicchi at the lawyer's home in East Boston.

Ten years earlier, Pisa had been arrested for the murder of George W. Deane, a security guard last seen in the company of Pisa and a friend. Deane's body was discovered the next day with three bullet holes in his head, fired from the victim's gun. Pisa was subsequently convicted of first-degree murder and given the death penalty.

Pisa was fine-boned, small in stature, dark-haired, savvy, and hardened by his years of incarceration. He was also nobody's fool.

Pisa had been represented by Cavicchi for seven years and occasionally referred him to other inmates at Norfolk and Bay State in need of representation. Following his conviction for Deane's murder, Tony Pisa became the first inmate to earn his bachelor's degree from Boston University while incarcerated.

Pisa spent hours reading in the prison law library and soon became adept at drafting motions and briefs in criminal law. Cavicchi recognized Pisa's talents and frequently hired him to do research. On December 24, Pisa and his family brought gifts to the Cavicchi family, thanking them for their support over the years. It was a happy, pleasant afternoon spent talking in the kitchen with Cavicchi and the lawyer's mother and brother.

It was approximately 4 PM and approaching darkness when another shadow crossed the threshold of the Cavicchis' doorstep, a visitor whose face was familiar and whose speech was grammatically flawed.

"Hey, John, I got youse a bucket a lobstahs and clams," the Quahog said to the lawyer as he lifted the catch onto the kitchen table, silently desperate for a nod of approval. "I jus' wanted ta t'ank ya for what ya did this summer wid dat Iannuzzi thing," Lenny explained to the unresponsive lawyer.

There was an uneasy silence as the large man surveyed the scene and then smiled broadly as he spotted Pisa.

"Hey, man, what the fuck youse doin' here?" Paradiso asked. "Shit, I ain't seen you since we was together in Norfolk. I didn't know youse got out."

"Hey, Lenny, watch the language, okay? There's women and kids here," Pisa responded. "I'm out on furlough from Bay State. Just home for Christmas, but thanks for reminding me that I'll have to go back."

"Oh, sorry, sorry 'bout that, ladies," the Quahog said, smiling sheepishly again. "My ol' lady woulda slapped my face if she heard me talk like dat."

The large man placed his hands together apologetically, slurped the offered drink loudly, and quickly said his good-byes. As he waddled stage left, Lenny turned to Pisa and said, "Hey man, come outside wid me for a sec. I wanna show ya my truck."

Pisa reluctantly headed for the door, sending a baleful look toward his wife as he left the warmth of the Cavicchi kitchen. Outside, he could see the Quahog's truck parked on the wrong side of Wordsworth Street.

Figures, Pisa thought as the two men stood outside the door, paying limited attention to the stated reason for their exit. Eventually, Paradiso turned the conversation from the mundane to the more serious, and then to the deadly topic of murder.

"I got me some problems with the cops," the Quahog began. "They been hasslin' me over this Iannuzzi murder. They been trying to pin it on me. I been waiting for them to go to the grand jury. They ain't done nuthin' yet."

"I can't help ya. I'm not a lawyer," Pisa said without emotion.

"Yeah, but Cavicchi can. Just tell him ta take it easy on me with the dough. I got short money. It's a easy case. I need a lawyer like him," Paradiso said as he shuffled from one foot to the next in front of his truck, clenching his thick hands into fists.

"You're gonna have to peddle a lot of fish to get a good lawyer," Pisa said to the Quahog as he began to feel the cold from the winter night. "I can't make you any promises. I'll see what I can do."

"Listen, this ain't no joke. I fuckin' killed her, okay. I killed the Iannuzzi broad. I need representation. It's an easy case. They got no fuckin' witnesses. Just ask him ta take it easy on me with the fuckin' money, will ya?"

It suddenly got a lot colder for Pisa as he stood openmouthed, speechless. When the conversation ended, the two men turned away without shaking hands and walked in opposite directions. Pisa returned to the warmth of the Cavicchi kitchen and stared at his wife as "Silent Night" played in the background.

"Oh, did Lenny leave?" Cavicchi's mother asked. "He's such a nice Italian boy."

"No, Mrs. Cavicchi, he really isn't such a nice Italian boy," Pisa responded without elaboration.

Shortly after his return to prison, Pisa received a call at Bay State from Paradiso.

"Hey man, youse jus' forget what I told ya at Cavicchi's house Christmas Eve," the Quahog said. "I had me too much ta drink. Youse jus' keep ya fuckin' mouth shut. Youse got a family out here. Youse jus' fuckin' remember that."

The same day Paradiso threatened Tony Pisa, Lenny met with his parole officer outside a turquoise-and-coffee-colored trailer, inconspicuously planted within a rusted six-foot chain-link fence at the entrance to Pier 7. Bright red-lettered signs on each side of the makeshift office housed within the forlorn wharf at 290 Northern Avenue announced COMMERCIAL LOBSTER COMPANY to an uncaring world.

Overhead, three striped buoys were somehow suspended in midair from a power line, marking the presence of lobsters, crabs, and shellfish for sale, wholesale and retail. There weren't many takers.

"Hey, I jus' wanna tell youse, I got me a new roommate. He's a Lynn firefighter. His name's Peter Brandon," Paradiso told his PO as the two men stood talking outside the trailer shortly after Christmas.

"Okay, where you living?"

"I'm living wid him at his apartment at 100 Magnolia Street in Lynn. It's right offa the Lynnway," the parolee told his supervisor.

"And what are you driving these days?"

"I'm gonna get me another set of wheels at King B's. My uddah one got stole a coupla months ago and the 'surance ain't paid me squat yet," Lenny said as he spat a large roil of phlegm onto the muddy crushed-stone driveway.

"Just keep your nose clean," the older man advised, watching the Fat Man scribble out his recent take from the sale of clams, littlenecks, and crabmeat shipped from Maine.

"Hey, Vic, youse know me, I always do the right thing. I'm thinkin' 'bout buying me a boat, too. I got me a place ta keep it down here next ta the pier," the former convict explained.

"Where you getting the money for that?"

"Looka here. In the last t'ree months I done me 463 gallons a shucked clams at thirty bucks a gallon. That's seventeen large. Then I done 378 pounds a crabmeat at three and a quarter a pound, that's twelve large, and then I got me 150 bushels a littlenecks at thirty bucks a bushel, that's anuddah four large," the Quahog said as he quickly did the math on the back of an envelope.

"Just keep me posted," the PO said as he checked the penciled scrawl.

"Yeah, I need me anuddah travel permit ta go down ta Florida and make some contacts to sell my stuff down there, too," the fish peddler pleaded, simultaneously holding the stub of the eraserless yellow pencil as well as his breath.

"I'll see what I can do," Anchukitis told the con without further elaboration.

On New Year's Eve a travel permit was issued to the Quahog. Three days later he boarded an Eastern Airlines flight to Miami.

During the next month, Lenny toured Miami, Palm Beach, and Key West, charging $5,735 on his brand-spanking-new Carte Blanche credit card. He never paid the company back a dime. He bought jewelry at the Marco Polo Hotel and gifts at Pearl's Gifts, the India Boutique, Sunset Giftware, and the Golden Rainbow. Lenny made a run for clothes at the Big Man, Tall Man store and dined at the Blue Seas Hibachi and Piccolos restaurants. He rented a car from Avis and quickly put 1,770 miles on it.

Paradiso never made any business contacts in Miami.

When he returned to Candy's home on Crescent Avenue in late January, Weyant opened a savings account in trust for her boyfriend at a bank in Maverick Square and deposited two thousand dollars into it.

15: Winthrop Avenue

Six months after Lenny's trip to Miami, a dark-haired young woman wearing Roman-styled sandals and a brightly colored summer dress stood hitchhiking at the entrance ramp to Route 93 in the North End of Boston. Janet McCarthy had just left the Café Pompeii, planning to meet some friends at a dance club in Revere. With less than a dollar in her wallet, hitchhiking seemed a reasonable alternative to the MBTA commuter train.

It was the second week in July and Don Zimmer's Red Sox were out of town playing the Milwaukee Brewers as Lenny followed the play-by-play on the car radio.

"Youse guys suck," the Quahog remarked as the home team trailed in the early innings.

He wheeled the yellow Caddie slowly down Hanover Street, past the hustling street vendors, and headed toward Mike's Pastry. Mike's was a North End favorite with a dozen small wrought-iron café tables and chairs that fronted an open bakery with wide glass display cases. Each of the tiered shelves beckoned to the street with row upon row of half-moon and elephant ear cookies, rocky road fudge, raspberry macaroons, fresh ricotta and fruit pies, and decorated cakes of every size for every occasion.

Paradiso considered stopping for an espresso and one of the chocolate chip cannolis, but glided by and made the turn toward Salem Street. Straight ahead, the driver spotted the teenager with the sleeveless dress.

The girl smiled warmly as she spotted the car slowing down to take a look at her. She pointed her thumb outwardly from her thin thigh as she tried to peer inside the driver's-side windshield.

"Where youse going?" the Quahog smiled in response to the hitchhiker as he pulled the sedan to the curb.

"I'm headed to the clubs on Revere Beach. I wanna go dancin'," Janet said to the large-framed man in the barracuda jacket.

"Hop in, I'll take ya there." She opened the door and slid into the front seat.

The Caddie rolled up the ramp to the expressway and onto Route 93, heading toward the Tobin Bridge to Chelsea and beyond to Revere, past Suffolk Downs racetrack and onto Winthrop Avenue.

The driver never identified himself to his passenger as he began the usual questions about drugs and sex.

"Ya wanna smoke some pot?" the unknown man asked as the young woman turned to stare at his profile.

"No thank you," Janet answered, growing suddenly uncomfortable with the man seated next to her.

"Do youse have a boyfriend?"

The young woman hesitated, trying to anticipate where the conversation was headed. *He's probably gonna ask me about sex next,* she said to herself.

Janet was right.

"Do youse two do it much?" the driver asked nonchalantly, as a growing sense of uneasiness, bordering on panic, pervaded her mind.

She stared at the road ahead and simply shook her head no. McCarthy knew she had made a mistake by accepting the ride.

"I know me a shortcut," the driver said as the Caddie turned off Winthrop Avenue onto Webster Street and then quickly left onto Crescent Avenue toward the familiar gray home of Paradiso's girlfriend, Candy Weyant.

The chubby driver glanced briefly at his girlfriend's car parked outside the gray house and said nothing as they went down the hill on Crescent toward a broad expanse of darkness. Less than half a mile from Weyant's home, he pulled the Caddie into an isolated area between a six-foot-high white cement wall and a marshy swamp that seemingly went on forever.

There was no one within screaming distance.

"I gotta take me a piss," the large man said as he opened his door and went to the front of the yellow car. The familiar sounds of urine hitting the ground filled the otherwise silent night.

I need to get out of here, the girl said to herself as she surveyed the desolate area surrounding her. She opened the passenger's door just as the driver returned.

"Where the fuck youse think youse goin'?" the man, suddenly enraged, asked as he grabbed her neck and punched the terrified girl in the face with his huge left hand.

The pain seared through her. A second punch and then a third landed, driving her to the edge of unconsciousness. The big man smiled a cruel smile as he grabbed the top of her dress and yanked it down, exposing her breasts. Lenny took momentary advantage of Janet's stunned condition to fondle her while she struggled to push him away.

Time accelerated wildly. *He'll kill me. I know he will,* her mind screamed as she looked into Lenny's cold, dead eyes. Determined to live, she kicked wildly at her partially opened door.

Panic-stricken, Janet fought her way free and managed to fall out of the passenger's side of the car onto the broken pavement. Screaming for help, she pulled up the top of her dress and quickly made her way to the seawall, climbing up and over it as the stranger in the car sped away.

In front of her, the headlights from the traffic rushing by on Winthrop Avenue loomed ahead.

With the emptiness of the endless marsh behind her, she staggered out of the darkness and into the first lane of traffic. Her legs were cut and bruised, her face was swollen, and her mouth was bleeding. Janet covered her eyes with one hand as she frantically waved for help with the other. She stood by the side of the road, screaming for help from the stream of cars passing by. The bright lights of one of the cars blinded her as it pulled slowly to the side of the road.

The girl with the Roman sandals and the torn summer dress thought she was finally safe.

She wasn't.

"I had my hand over my eyes," she would later tell the Revere police detectives.

"Then what happened?" one of the cops asked.

"I opened the door of the car and screamed to the guy who stopped, 'Somebody tried to rape and kill me.' I took my hand away from my eyes and looked at the driver, and oh my gawd. Oh my gawd, it was him. It was him."

"Jesus, what'd you do then?" Detective Billy Gannon asked the tearful girl.

"He just laughed at me and says, 'What happened?' Like he didn't know what I was talking about. Then he started to laugh and just drove off."

"You're one hell of a lucky young lady. Ya know that?"

"I know I am. He woulda killed me. I know he would have. He had this look in his eyes. Like something I've never seen before," Janet explained, her hands trembling.

"I want you to look at these mug shots and tell me if you recognize anyone, okay?" the detective said. She thumbed through page after page of suspects previously arrested in the city of Revere.

The hitchhiker from the North End couldn't make any identification.

Lenny Paradiso's picture wasn't in the selection. He had never been arrested in Revere.

The Quahog was still a free man.

16: Bankruptcy Court

Two weeks before the July 1980 assault on Janet McCarthy, Paradiso once again met with his parole officer at Pier 7. Lenny sauntered to the end of the wharf, where he proudly showed the PO his latest purchase, a twenty-six-foot Chris-Craft boat moored between the pier and the rusting hulk of a dilapidated hundred-foot barge. Lenny christened the cabin cruiser with the same name he'd used for all of his other boats: the *Mala Femmena*.

"Yeah, I had me the Coast Guard come down and 'spect it. I took me out a loan from the credit union. They stuck me for eight large," the fish peddler told his supervisor, who smiled apprehensively, wished Lenny good luck, and wondered how the parolee could pay off the loan while making just three hundred bucks a week.

During the span of the next year, Paradiso charged more than five "large" on his Amoco credit card. He paid them nothing. Early in 1981 Paradiso and Weyant charged more than twelve hundred dollars on Lenny's Zayre's credit card at different stores on the North Shore of Boston. Candy signed off on several of the charges as "Mrs. Leonard Paradiso." Mr. Leonard Paradiso paid Zayre's nothing. Ten months later the company wrote the account off.

In April 1981 Candy's latest Chevy was reported stolen from in front of Lenny's newest address on Ocean Street in Lynn. Weyant promptly filed an insurance claim. Two months later the Chevy was found submerged in Boston Harbor.

In early May 1981 Paradiso placed a notice in the *Bargain Hunter's Guide* advertising the sale of a twenty-six-foot Chris-Craft boat in "excellent condition." The *Mala Femmena* that Lenny had bought a year earlier for "eight large" was offered for sale at "ten grand." The boat's insurance was about to run out the same week. In the same edition of the *Bargain Hunter's Guide*, Candy listed her most recent purchase, a 1979 Cutlass, for sale at seventy-eight hundred.

A month later Paradiso called a lawyer in East Boston and made an appointment to file for bankruptcy. Lenny renewed the insurance on the *Mala* the same week.

On July 26, 1981, Lenny Paradiso reported the *Mala Femmena* stolen from Pier 7 to the Coast Guard, state police, metro police, and Boston police. The same day he claimed the boat stolen, Lenny filed an insurance claim with Liberty Mutual.

Two days later, on July 28, Paradiso once again listed the *Mala* for sale in the *Bargain Hunter's Guide.*

In September 1981, two months after he'd claimed the boat stolen, Paradiso canceled his boat insurance policy in a rage because his claim of loss for the *Mala Femmena* hadn't been paid yet.

During Thanksgiving week 1981, Paradiso appeared in federal district court and finalized his petition for bankruptcy. Under the pains and penalties of perjury, the Quahog was required to list all of his assets and all of his liabilities.

Lenny failed to mention the insurance claim for the stolen *Mala Femmena* as an asset.

17: Logan Airport

It was the Saturday of Thanksgiving weekend.

On November 28, 1981, Eastern Airlines Flight 960 out of Newark touched down at Boston's Logan Airport shortly after 10:30 PM in a raw wind.

On the plane Joan Webster, a second-year graduate student at Harvard University Graduate School of Design, grabbed her coat, purse, and brown leather totebag, filled with textbooks, and waited in the stuffy cabin for the plane to empty.

It had been an uneventful hour-long flight as Joan chatted with other passengers about the holiday spent with her parents in her home in Glen Ridge, New Jersey, and the architectural program she was enrolled in at Harvard. She was, her family would later say, in a buoyant mood, excited about a design project she was working on with two of her classmates.

The weekend had been a flurry of activity for the pretty brunette.

After a Thanksgiving dinner at the retirement home where her grandmother lived, the family went to New York City the following day to see *The Pirates of Penzance*. Joan loved New York with its lights and excitement. Most of all, she loved Broadway. It was a passion developed from two years of living in Manhattan while working for an interior design firm. She had moved to Boston a year ago, when she was accepted into the master's program at Harvard.

Constantly surrounded by the friends and family she adored, Joan was a bundle of energy and enthusiasm, busily moving about, engaging and involved.

As the youngest of three children, Joan always tried to keep up with her older siblings, Steven and Anne. Unlike her brother and sister, she was not particularly athletic, but she occupied herself in many other ways. She threw herself into fund-raising events, baking butterscotch brownies by the dozen, was a camp counselor, and worked for two summers as a nanny. She developed a love of horse racing, gleaned from her paternal grandfather, who often took her to Aqueduct and Belmont. Her boundless enthusiasm was infectious, and her passion for poetry and music — especially that of Joni Mitchell — soon earned her the nickname "Joni."

Joan found her real calling when she took an art class in high school and realized she had a flair for design. At Syracuse University she was on the team of architectural students who designed the Kuwaiti embassy in Washington, DC, winning praise from the chairman of the design department, who called her one of the best students the school had ever had.

Lying across her bed in the house where she grew up, Joan immersed herself in her architectural textbooks. The course work at Harvard was demanding. She was worried about her studies.

The project she was working on with two fellow Harvard graduate students was of particular concern to Joan. She had decided to leave New Jersey after a cocktail party planned for that Saturday night. She needed to get back to Boston that evening because of a meeting she had scheduled early Sunday morning to discuss the project with her colleagues, she told her parents.

The news didn't sit well with Terry and George Webster, who wanted their youngest child to return to Boston by car the next day with her older sister, Anne, who worked in the Boston area. When Joan insisted, the couple gave in. After the cocktail party at the home of family friends, her parents and Anne drove her to Newark Airport, handing her twenty dollars to take a cab from Logan Airport in Boston to her dormitory in Cambridge.

Wary of her daughter becoming the victim of a mugging, Terry cautioned her to remove the gold charm bracelet she was wearing on her wrist. Joan took off the bracelet, filled with charms from years of childhood travels, and slipped it into her purse. With no way to know that she was saying good-bye to her parents and sister for the last time, Joan stepped into the airport terminal to board her Boston-bound flight.

Once in the air, Joan settled in, chatting with a priest from East Boston and a couple sitting nearby. She hummed "Poor Wandering One" from *Pirates of Penzance* as the flight droned on. When the jet approached the swatch of runway that cuts into Boston Harbor, an enormous red glow filled the eastern sky. A fire was burning out of control in the city of Lynn, just eight miles north of Boston. The conflagration ended sixteen days later; it had destroyed eighteen buildings and damaged eight others.

The raging inferno would be forever known as the Great Lynn Fire. Only one Lynn firefighter didn't respond to the emergency callout that night.

By the time her plane touched down that Saturday night, Joan was exhausted. Dressed in the same black suit and red paisley shirt she had worn only hours before to the cocktail party, the attractive young woman stood by the baggage claim area with her Chesterfield coat slung over her arm, waiting patiently for her dark plaid Lark suitcase.

She grabbed the bag, stuffed with a weekend's worth of clothing, as it slid past on the luggage carousel, walked out of the terminal into the chilly night air, and simply disappeared.

18: The Lynn Marsh Road

The phone call sent an ominous chill down Terry Webster's spine. It was the morning of Tuesday December 1.

"Mrs. Webster," a worried voice on the other end of the line said, "has Joan come back to Boston yet?"

The caller was David Duncan, her daughter's boyfriend. He related that he had not seen Joan since she'd left Cambridge more than a week earlier to return to her parents' home for Thanksgiving break. He stated that Joan was supposed to attend a meeting with her fellow students the day after her return to Harvard on the twenty-eighth.

"She never showed up," he said. "There's a pile of notes stuck on her door at the dormitory. I don't think she's come back yet."

Terry Webster put down the receiver and immediately picked it up again, this time frantic with worry. The day became a long blur of anxious phone calls, first to her husband George's secretary, to find out when George's plane was due back from a California business trip, and then to Joan's sister Anne, who had just returned to her home in the Boston area on November 29.

After the call with Anne ended, Terry called every hospital in Boston. She called Joan's friends and colleagues at school, her pals in New York, and finally the police at Harvard University. No one, it seemed, had any idea what had happened to her daughter.

When the Harvard University Police went to Joan's dorm room in Perkins Hall to begin their investigation, Anne was already inside speaking to her mother on the telephone. Anne told them she'd last seen Joan as she walked down the ramp to board the one-hour flight from Newark to Boston. Frightened by her sister's disappearance, she was also angry that no one seemed to take it seriously.

"My sister just wouldn't take off without telling anyone," she told the campus officers. "Something happened to her, I just know something's happened to her."

By the time George Webster returned from California that night, there was a Glen Ridge, New Jersey, cruiser parked outside the family's home and an officer sitting at the kitchen table. An executive with ITT, George knew that "Joni" would never have accepted a ride from a stranger to her dorm room at Perkins Hall.

"She is very independent," Terry Webster told the officer. "She isn't the type to call when she got back to Boston."

She also wasn't the type to take off without notifying anyone, Joan's mother assured the cop.

Afraid to think the worst, the couple considered every possible explanation for their daughter's disappearance. Despite their efforts, there was no logic to apply and no rational reason why Joan was suddenly missing from their lives. The next morning the frantic parents took a flight to Boston, determined to find their youngest child.

But in Boston on December 2, the news wasn't any better.

The Boston police took a missing-person report and promised to conduct an investigation, but referred the matter back to the Harvard University Police. With more than forty colleges and universities in the Boston area, police receive hundreds of reports annually about missing students who later show up wondering what all the fuss was about. Unless something turned up to indicate foul play, the cops told the couple, there was nothing more they could do.

The weather the next morning was bleak and rainy as Revere native Anthony Belmonte walked near the embankment of the Pines River in Saugus, Massachusetts. With the shape of a coiled snake, the Pines River meanders through the thick marshes of Saugus as it slowly makes its way to the Atlantic Ocean.

The river flows easterly, eventually making its way under a narrow causeway to the Point of Pines, a lonely spit of land that separates Revere from the cities of Lynn and Saugus. The desolate paved causeway, referred to by natives as the Lynn Marsh Road, is one of the main routes of travel between Revere and Lynn.

As Belmonte walked along the river's edge, a light drizzle spilled from the sky, coating the sea grass that hunkered down along the shoreline. It was a chilly, wintry day made even colder by a brisk northeast wind coming off the sea.

A fisherman by trade, Belmonte was on the southbound side of the Lynn Marsh Road, opposite the old Connolly and Daggett's lobster pound, when he saw a wallet partially hidden in the tangle of grass. Picking it up, the fisherman turned it over, brushed off the wet sand, and looked inside. Within the wallet was a woman's driver's license, her personal papers, and an ITT phone card imprinted with a telephone number.

"If found, please call this number," the card read.

In Belmonte's other hand, the radiant face of a young woman with long dark hair smiled from the license.

Belmonte returned to his home and immediately dialed the number on the card. He anxiously explained to the secretary who answered the phone that he'd found the card in a young woman's wallet. The secretary in turn said, "Yes, yes, we know, she's missing. Please give me your name and address."

Within minutes a Revere police cruiser arrived at his home and Belmonte directed Officer Joe Marshall back to the site where he'd found the wallet. Almost immediately the pair located a red leather pocketbook in the same area of the marsh. Inside was a checkbook belonging to Joan Webster.

Joan's wallet and pocketbook were six miles from Logan Airport.

For the Websters, the discovery was ominous. It was five days since Joan had last been seen, and the unearthing of the wallet and purse did nothing to dispel their fears. They now knew something terrible had indeed happened to their daughter.

The idea she had been kidnapped was still too hard to comprehend. Joan would never take a ride from a stranger, and it was unlikely she would be abducted from busy Logan Airport. It just didn't make sense, but then, nothing made much sense anymore.

At the marsh, Saugus police cordoned off the area where the purse and wallet had been found.

On December 3 another chilly breeze blew in off the coast as several scuba divers from the state police suited up along the banks of the Pines River. Dressed in shiny black gear, they were on hand with dozens of officers from different area departments to begin an intense search for additional clues. Search dogs and boats had also been brought in. Uniformed officers walked in grid formation across the wet marshland, looking for anything that would yield a clue to Joan's disappearance. If the swampy marshland held any secrets, it was not about to give them up easily.

Nearby, a small team of Boston-area television and news reporters gathered to watch the search. Their daily reports would later dominate the local news, topping the Reagan administration's plans to increase the gas tax and a fatal mine collapse in West Virginia.

With the discovery of the wallet and purse, the *Boston Globe* and *Boston Herald* began to run almost daily stories on the disappearance of Joan Webster. The bold headlines — "Search Continues for Missing Harvard Student,"

"Grad Student Still Missing," "No Leads in Disappearance," "Joan Webster Hunt Goes On" — drew the public's attention to the Websters' plight.

After two days of searching the marshland without success, investigators looked to other avenues for help in the case. Over the next three days they questioned more than a hundred people, many of them passengers on the Eastern Airlines flight Joan had taken.

Police scoured the passenger lists of other arriving flights, hoping that one of the 720 people who'd flown into Logan on the evening of November 28 would have something to add to the case. None did.

The case, cold from the start, was growing even colder.

As the brief December days stretched on without news, the Websters felt engulfed in perpetual darkness. After nearly a week in Boston, they decided to return to their New Jersey home and wait while the police did their job.

By the time the couple was ready to leave, a raging snowstorm had dumped more than ten inches of powder on Boston's streets; winds over forty miles per hour were wreaking havoc with flights out of Logan.

Exhausted and eager to return home, the couple scrapped their plans to fly and instead drove through the blinding snowstorm with two officers from Glen Ridge who had been assisting the Harvard police. It was a terrible ride made more difficult as the group repeatedly spilled over the details of the case, trying to spin what little information they had into a logical explanation for Joan's absence.

The whirl of the next few weeks melded into a blur of raw emotion for the Webster family as the holidays closed in with no word of Joan. Shortly before Christmas, the Websters sent a tape recording to Boston's local newspapers and the area television and radio stations imploring their assistance in finding their daughter.

Their plea produced not a single clue to her whereabouts.

19: Bay State

It started out as just another day for Tony Pisa as he and one of the staff members decorated the Christmas tree at the Bay State correctional facility.

It was a cold day, a temperature near freezing made to feel much colder by forty-mile-an-hour wind gusts. Outside, the drifting snow blanketed the brick halfway house for inmates on the backside of their sentences.

Pisa's birthday had fallen the day before, but he wasn't celebrating. On the television, the news mentioned the missing girl from Harvard University and the request by police for information on her disappearance. The father of five children, Pisa heard the news and thought about his life, his sentence, his children, and what he would do if one of them were missing.

As he hung the lights on the Christmas tree, Pisa began to sing the words from "I'll Be Home for Christmas" to himself. *Just like Bing Crosby,* he thought. In the adjoining room, one of the pay phones was ringing.

It was Lenny Paradiso calling for Pisa.

"Hey man, how youse doin'?" a cheery Quahog asked.

"Fine, what's up," Pisa responded coldly, remembering the conversation between the two men around Christmas Eve two years ago at attorney John Cavicchi's house in East Boston.

Lenny's really not such a nice Italian boy, Pisa reminded himself as he waited for Paradiso's response.

"Hey, what was that case youse used ta tell me 'bout at the auto school. Ya know, the one where they fuckin' hung the guy. Tell me 'bout that case again, will ya?" Paradiso said, his tone becoming considerably darker.

"I told ya, it happened in 1850, right around Thanksgiving. It was a famous conviction based on circumstantial evidence. It's the Webster case." Pisa's aggravation silently grew.

"Did youse say the 'Webster' case?" Paradiso responded with surprise.

"Yeah, John Webster was the last person seen with the victim. They found him guilty even though the cops never found the victim's body."

"How could they try him without the fuckin' body?" Paradiso asked, outraged at the thought of the possible injustice to the accused.

"I told ya, they found a piece of his jaw, and the cops used that to identify the missing person," Pisa replied.

"Well, like how many uddah cases there been where dey don't find no body?" Paradiso inquired.

"None that I know of. What the hell do you wanna know about that old case for? They found the fuckin' body in your case," Pisa said, recalling the Iannuzzi girl's name and Paradiso's confession from two years back.

"They ain't fuckin' found her body yet. All they'se got is the bitch's pocketbook," Paradiso responded with a flourish of sudden anger.

There was a pause as the pieces slowly began to fit together for the jailhouse lawyer. "Oh my God, Lenny. Are you — did you have somethin' to do with that missing coed?" Pisa asked. "Did you kill the Webster girl?"

For the first time Paradiso spoke Italian as he told Pisa, "*Tu stazitto*. Shut your mouth."

"Hey you fuckin' asshole, you called me, I didn't call you," Pisa said as the image of Lenny and the young woman on a deserted road passed through his mind.

"Yeah, I know. Youse been cool. Just keep youse fuckin' mouth shut," Paradiso warned. "Remember youse is in there and I'm out here. Say Merry Christmas to youse family for me. Ya know what I mean, Tony?"

There was a pause and then a single click as the receiver went dead.

"What's the matter, Tony, you look like you seen a fuckin' ghost," a staff member said as Pisa returned to the Christmas tree.

"Nothin', just thinking 'bout my family I guess. I got a furlough for Christmas Day. I can't wait to be home and have dinner with my wife and all my kids." Pisa said, as he began to count the number of days left inside the walls.

20: White Christmas

Bing sang about it, people dreamed about it, Santa needed it, but Christmas Day 1981 didn't bring it. It wasn't white. There was no snow. It was rainy and foggy.

A mild weather front had moved into the Boston area the night before the holiday, bringing gusty winds and temperatures topping forty-five degrees. The same day, the *Globe* and *Herald* ran a personal appeal from Joan's parents, asking the public to provide any information they might have about her disappearance. The local TV stations carried the story as well.

Tony Pisa read about the missing girl in both newspapers with a tortured interest. He carefully placed them on his kitchen table and took a walk outside into the thin morning mist with his wife. When he returned to his home, Pisa read the story in both papers again. Later that day he sat at the dinner table with his five children, said grace, and wondered how the missing coed's family was spending Christmas Day. The image of an empty chair at the Webster family table passed quickly through his mind as he smiled at his seated children.

I got three more years to serve, he said to himself, dispelling any notion of talking.

Earlier that day, in another town not far away, a large delivery truck had pulled up to a small gray house with the name BURKE imprinted on a sign suspended from a lamppost in the front yard. Inside the shuttered front window, a brown-haired child watched as the workmen carefully positioned a metal ramp up to the front door.

The child called to his father to come look. Together the young lawyer and his two-year-old son watched the deliverymen as they carefully maneuvered the new piano with its huge red ribbon down from the truck and up the ramp into the house.

"Merry Christmas," the lawyer said to his wife as their son clapped his hands in anticipation of his mother playing "I'm Dreaming of a White Christmas" on her new piano.

On TV an early-morning news story brought the smiling image of a dark-haired young woman who had disappeared from Logan Airport a month earlier. The child looked curiously at the picture of the missing coed as the reporter told the sad story.

The two-year-old pointed his tiny right hand toward the screen and spoke the word "Mommy" as he stared at the reflected image, and then turned back to look at his mother.

"God, that missing girl looks just like you," the lawyer said to his wife. He turned to the child to explain, "No, honey, that's not Mommy. It's another young woman. She's lost. They can't find her."

"Her lost?" the child asked innocently.

"Yeah, 'her lost,'" the father repeated softly as he gently touched the child's hair. "But don't worry, honey, somebody will find her."

At Christmas dinner in Glen Ridge, New Jersey, Nat King Cole's "Christmas Song" played as Terry Webster tearfully listened. She momentarily thought of Joan at the words "tiny tots with their eyes all aglow." Terry knew she needed to be strong for the rest of her family. She wiped her eyes before anyone could see her and then carefully laid out a place setting at the table for her missing daughter.

21: False Leads

In the days following the Christmas holiday, George and Terry Webster returned to Boston to join a group of Joan's friends who had organized a search for the missing graduate student. Armed with a stack of flyers bearing her photo, the group scoured Cambridge and Boston, tacking up MISSING posters with a picture of the vanished coed on hundreds of signposts and subway stops. To the continued despair of her parents, the search proved fruitless.

The year 1981 ended with no word on Joan's disappearance.

The New Year would bring Michael Jackson's "Thriller" to the top of the charts, the Falklands War to the front pages, and the untimely deaths of Princess Grace and John Belushi. For the Websters, the year began as hopelessly as the last had ended.

In the middle of January police announced they would take the unconventional step of calling in a hypnotist to extract more information from witnesses who'd seen a suspicious white taxicab near the site where Joan's belongings were found on the Lynn Marsh Road.

"We're hoping the hypnosis will bring things out. Things that they don't realize they know," the Saugus police sergeant told reporters, who by now had become enthralled with the story of the missing Harvard student. The hypnosis sessions produced few results. Any clues gleaned from the taxi witnesses led nowhere.

The following day Terry and George Webster stepped in front of the bright lights of television cameras to offer a fifty-thousand-dollar reward for information on their daughter's disappearance. That same day, the Saugus police received a telephone call from a woman who wouldn't give her name.

"There's a man I know who might have something to do with Joan Webster's disappearance. About twelve years ago, I was in a bar in the North End. This guy told me he was having chest pains. He asked me to drive him home. We went to someplace in South Boston. He pulled a gun on me and said he would kill me. His name's Lenny Paradiso. He lives in East Boston," the unknown woman said as she hung up.

"Who was that?" the duty sergeant asked the young dispatcher.

"I dunno, she wouldn't leave her name. She said she knew somebody who might have somethin' to do with that missing coed. Probably just another prank call," the dispatcher said as he jotted the information into an obscure daily journal.

The offer of a reward yielded a response to the Essex County DA from three juveniles who claimed to know Joan's whereabouts. Their claim provided another bitter heartache for the Websters. The three were arrested and charged with trying to sell false information.

The reward spurred more false leads.

Saugus police received another anonymous note that Joan had been murdered, her body placed in a sleeping bag and sunk in the waters of a nearby pond. Divers were immediately dispatched and conducted a full search of the murky waters. They found nothing but shopping carts strewn on the pond's bottom.

The mystery deepened during the first week in February, when a New York City employee of Greyhound Bus Line discovered a small plaid Lark-brand suitcase with a luggage tag listing an address in Glen Ridge, New Jersey.

It was Joan's.

The Lark bag had originally been stored in the bus terminal in Boston, then shipped to New York and placed in long-term storage there. Police were able to determine that Joan's suitcase had been placed in a thirty-day storage container at the Boston bus terminal sometime between Joan's arrival at 10:35 PM on November 28 and 9 AM the following morning. Her suitcase was shipped to New York City after being left unclaimed for over a month.

The new information about Joan's suitcase only brought many, many more questions for the Websters and the police.

There was no apparent connection between the discovery of Joan's wallet and handbag on the Lynn Marsh Road in Saugus and the recovery of her suitcase in New York City. With each revelation came another round of news reports and speculation in the press, as well as the public. The mystery of Joan's disappearance had become a household phenomenon throughout the metropolitan area surrounding Boston.

Despite the discovery of Joan's suitcase and the reward offer, the case remained as bleak and cold as the raw New England winter.

It would be early springtime 1982 before a young prosecutor, intrigued by a call from the sister of another murder victim, would begin putting the pieces together.

22: The Boston Globe

The youngest of twelve children, he had grown up poor, the fifth son of a potato farmer. Blue-eyed and Irish Catholic, he was an unrepentant altar boy, quietly challenging the status quo of a limited future in the small town where he was born.

He excelled in school and sports, going years without missing a day of class. He loved music and books, once saving enough money from a paper route to buy a grocery store edition of an encyclopedia, reading every page of each volume from A to Z. Knowledge provided a measure of certainty and control over a chaotic existence.

When the time came for college, he packed a single bag and hitchhiked to Syracuse University, searching for another life that he knew existed but had yet to find. He met his future wife washing dishes for meals in her sorority house. She was struck by his drive to achieve and convinced him he would make a great lawyer.

His first job after law school was working in the Suffolk County District Attorney's office.

It was February 1982, and the first time the assistant district attorney had ever met the reporter from the *Boston Globe*.

Jeremiah Murphy was old school. A navy veteran who graduated from high school in '44, he boarded a train the following morning to serve his country. Murphy knew and loved the Boston political scene. Of average height and build, he had been a city beat reporter and columnist for more than twenty-five years when he met the young attorney. Wearing his trench coat and armed with a tan spiral notebook and number two pencil, he was obviously Irish and open-faced with a touch of sadness to his smile.

"Tell me a little bit about this case you're working on," the man in the rumpled raincoat said to the lawyer. "I want to do a piece on it for tomorrow's column."

The DA had been assigned more than twenty murder cases, but he knew immediately which one the reporter was asking about. It wasn't an "assigned" case. It was a triple homicide that had been relegated to the scrap heap of unsolved cases.

The case had already been passed from one lawyer in the Homicide Unit to the next, and then to the next. Each had taken a shot at solving it, finding the missing link, taking the one additional witness statement that would put it all together. Finally cataloged as "cold" and filed in a three-drawer steel cabinet, the case was already two years old when the young lawyer first discovered it. The file was a tattered slate-gray case jacket containing police reports, lab tests, and photographs that lured him in, shocked him, and made him want to puke with rage and horror.

A pretty Hispanic mother of three children had been raped and stabbed more than thirty times by an unknown intruder. Her two young children hid in their bedroom listening to their mother's screams until the killer came for them. The killer pulled them out separately from beneath their beds with the Mickey Mouse sheets, dragging them down the hallway to where their mother lay dead, naked on the floor. The killer then slit their throats after he had stabbed each of them in their childs' hearts.

Thrown against the wall where their mother was silently waiting, three bodies lay akimbo, a tangled, blood-soaked heap of death's final embrace. A crime of unspeakable violence, random and horrific, the only living witness a six-month-old baby left untouched in a crib not far from the family Christmas tree.

The lawyer told the reporter he'd become obsessed with the case after reading the file. He felt, irrationally, the case had been hidden there all this time, dormant, brooding. Waiting just for him to find it and solve it. For reasons known only to him, the case consumed his waking hours and thoughts.

He began to go to the triple-decker house on Jacobs Street in Dorchester to visualize, to sense, to feel, and to understand what the killer and victims alike knew and saw. A single drop of blood, discovered on a brown bag that covered a brightly wrapped Christmas present beneath the tree, provided the only link to the killer's identity.

The lawyer explained he had gone back to the house at 12 Jacobs Street with the homicide detectives on too many occasions to count. Each time he stood near the stained floor of the now empty apartment, holding the forty photographs taken of the scene that night, placing his mind's eye in the same location as the camera's lens.

The two men spoke for more than an hour about the case, the lawyer's family, his motivations and thoughts.

"It was a grotesque seduction of my mind," he tried to explain. "I was driven, compelled, and somehow moved by this unexplainable force to solve this horrible mystery." He looked directly into the eyes of the reporter and said, "I know it sounds weird, but I know I am the only one who can do this."

The older man listened impassively, making nodding motions with his head as he wrote.

"What's the telephone number here for your office? I want to add it to the story, maybe somebody out there will give you a call," said the reporter, pencil poised.

The lawyer gave him the number and watched as he scribbled it down hurriedly, stood up, said his good-byes, and cracked open the wood-framed door with HOMICIDE UNIT written on the frosted glass. As he started to leave, the older man turned back and faced the lawyer still seated at the cluttered desk.

"Ya know, kid, you really shouldn't do this to yourself." He paused momentarily as if he was trying hard to get it right before he said it. "In a strange way, it's sorta like the Red Sox. If ya care too much, they'll break your heart every time."

The reporter smiled briefly, added a wish for good luck, and passed through the door and out of sight.

In his mind, the lawyer felt a sense of relief for the first time in months. He knew someone was going to call.

- -

Jeremiah Murphy's column about the triple homicide ran on the front page of the metro section of the *Boston Globe*.

The headline screamed "An Obsession to Find a Killer." Beneath the bold print was Murphy's byline. The story ran from top to bottom along the left-hand side of the page. It was a Saturday; tens of thousands of readers in the metropolitan Boston area would see the story.

Somebody was certain to call.

The lawyer stayed up all night to buy the early edition of the paper. They were being sold outside a movie theater in Newton Corner, a suburb of the city. When he arrived, hundreds of newspapers were neatly stacked and wrapped with thin tan twine. He paid the man for two copies and read the first paragraph beneath the unlit marquee of the theater building. Directly above him, the signboard advertised the two currently featured movies, *On Golden Pond* and *Death Wish II*.

As the words unfolded, the DA felt embarrassed by the frequent mention of his name and the written expression of his inner thoughts and emotions. Despite his hesitation he knew the article might help solve the case. He read the entire column quickly. It seemed he did so without even breathing. Then he went back to the top of the page and began to read the story again for content. Murphy's writing style was direct and blunt.

> Everything changed for Suffolk County Assistant Dist. Atty. Tim Burke last September when he was assigned to prosecute murder cases. He was checking the unsolved murder cases, when he came across the newspaper photographs of Kenneth, 3, and Johanna Rodriguez, 4, and that is when the long ordeal began.
>
> The two children and their mother, Basilisa Melendez, 25, had been found butchered to death, and those words are the only accurate description, in their first floor apartment on Jacobs Street in Dorchester on Dec. 5, 1979 and their murder remains unsolved.

The lawyer stood transfixed alone on the quiet sidewalk as he read on. Murphy's words melded into his own mind. The reporter had taken the lawyer's thoughts and told the story of the triple murder to anyone willing to read. Murphy chronicled the life and death of the three victims and the quest for their killer. He made his plea, relying on the power of human emotion to inspire someone to make a phone call.

But that all happened two years ago on a poor street in Dorchester where mostly blacks and Hispanics live. So after a day or two the story dropped out of the newspapers, because it didn't have the old standby elements of prominence of the people involved and possibility of sex and the presence of mystery. The case was unsolved despite many hours of police work.

Now it was almost two years later and the manila folder was on Burke's desk and he kept coming back to the photographs of the two kids smiling. That is when he started waking up at night, and thinking about those kids, even though he knew that you can't get emotionally involved in a case. He would lie in bed and think about the evidence in the case and try to put the puzzle together. This is when he started making trips out to Jacobs Street to look again at the three decker where the kids and their mother had been killed. Now a single day does not pass when he does not think of those children.

It has been going on for eight months with Burke, and he said the other day, "this case is driving me crazy. You can't just come into a house and butcher a mother and two little kids and just walk away. There has to be some accountability. There has to be some justice. If only somebody saw something that day. If only somebody would call us and tell us."

So Tim Burke continues his lonely ordeal, the long vigil that has turned into an obsession. A defenseless mother and her two innocent little children were horribly murdered and nobody knows why and by whom. Three people are dead and more than two years have passed since that awful day in Dorchester. The public has inevitably forgotten, because other subsequent murders have taken their place and a few of the stories stayed in the papers for weeks. Now most people have forgotten about a young mother and two little children. But Tim Burke hasn't forgotten and continues to wake in the night and try to put the puzzle together. He desperately needs a phone call from someone who saw something on Jacobs Street in Dorchester on that terrible day. His number is 725-8701.

The telephone call will cost you a dime, but it could lead to the butcher of children.

The young lawyer was stunned when he finished the story. He ignored the sounds of the morning traffic as it passed anonymously by. The images of the children obliterated everything else as he thought about their bodies askew in the corner of the apartment.

He had never fully understood the path he had chosen when he became immersed in this case. It all became very clear to him at that moment. There was no turning back. Jeremiah Murphy's story defined him as a person. The telling of the murders publicly established his responsibility to the two innocent children and their mother. He was more certain than ever that someone would call. It was only a matter of time.

He quietly closed the newspaper and began the wait.

- -

The Monday following the *Boston Globe* story brought a renewed sense of interest in the triple homicide.

Nearly everyone standing in line at the courthouse coffee shop asked about it, wondering aloud what they could do to help. Prosecutors, defense lawyers, judges, court officers, and clerks alike inquired of the lawyer, as if in unison, "Has anyone called yet?" Even "Jimmy from Southie," the elevator operator, asked the lawyer, "Hey, did chu hear anythin'?" He told them all no one had called yet, but he knew they would.

Three Boston homicide detectives were waiting for the DA when he returned to the cluttered desk and the day-to-day press of his caseload that Monday morning.

He called them "the Three Amigos with Irish Accents." It seemed they were always together. The three detectives shared a lot in common, including the triple murder.

"Buenos dias, muchachos," the lawyer offered with a failed attempt at an Irish brogue.

Detectives Tom Cashman and Mark Madden smiled upward as they sat in the two brown fake-leather chairs opposite his desk reading the *Boston Globe.* Sergeant John Doris stood near the room's only narrow window. He had bad knees. It hurt to sit.

"Ya done good, kid," the older men chimed together as they reached to shake his hand.

They were men of few words. Fatherly in appearance and seasoned with years of investigative experience, there wasn't much they hadn't seen. The trio brought the young lawyer under their collective wing because he shared their feeling about the case.

Cashman had been one of the first at the scene that night, arriving within minutes of the discovery of the three bodies. He later found the killer's blood on the Christmas package beneath the tree. He told the lawyer he wanted to cry when he saw the children and their mother, but couldn't do it in front of the younger officers at the scene. The detective bit the inside of his lip as he told the lawyer one of the uniformed guys left the house to go outside and vomit.

The homicide detectives liked the fact the *Globe* had breathed new life into the case, but they took the story in stride. They were hopeful, but realistic.

They worked each case with or without media fanfare. They were impervious to the mind-crushing emotional gamut of murders. They had seen too many. They knew and understood the stench and reality of death. Their lives revolved around the sudden finality of a life ended before its time. They understood that age and youth were no barrier to death, nor race or wealth, nor position or status. They knew that when death came for you, you went. It really was that simple.

The Three Amigos with Irish Accents enjoyed the moment, said their good-byes, and left the lawyer to await the call.

He sat at this desk and told himself it was just a matter of time.

Each day followed the next, and then the next. Time passed without a word. The lawyer frequently found himself blankly staring at the black phone in the left-hand corner of his desk, imagining it was ringing. There were times when he swore he could hear the phone ring. He would turn down the ever-present music from the nearby radio and pick up the receiver to hear nothing but a hollow dial tone. Each day when he returned from court he would automatically ask if anyone had called on the triple.

With the misguided confidence of an unrequited lover, the lawyer waited for the call that never came.

The reality slowly began to settle in that no mysterious witness was going to suddenly materialize and solve the triple homicide. The DA had just returned from lunch at the Steaming Kettle across the street from the courthouse when his secretary waved and pointed to the phone.

"You got a call, they're on hold," she said, smiling. "It's someone who wants to talk to you about the article in the *Globe*."

He could see the blinking yellow light flashing on the base of the phone as he entered the office. The radio was playing as he reached for the handset. He simultaneously turned down the volume and thought, *I stopped believing too easily.*

He carefully placed the phone next to his ear. "DA's office, can I help you?"

"Hi, Mr. Burke? My name is Kathy Leonti."

It was a young woman's voice, tentative, soft, and unsure, somehow searching to connect personally with the stranger on the other end of the line.

"I don't quite know where to start. I read the story about the two kids and the mother that were murdered," she said haltingly. "And, and, I wonder if I could just talk to you about my sister's case. She was killed two years ago. Nothing's happened on it yet. It's still unsolved."

The breath he was holding slowly eased out as the lawyer realized the young woman wasn't calling about the triple.

"Yeah, sure, why don't you tell me what happened," he said, trying to be polite without revealing his disappointment. He reached for a yellow legal pad and began to take notes as he listened impassively.

"She was only twenty years old," the voice on the other end of the phone began. "She went to a wedding and then a reception at the Ship Restaurant in Saugus. She and her boyfriend had a fight. He left and then afterward she got a ride to a bar in East Boston, near the airport, and then she left there some time after midnight."

The young woman's voice faltered as she began to cry between each spoken word. "They found her the next day. She was strangled and raped. Somebody killed her and just dumped her body on the rocks near the Pines River in Saugus."

There was a pause followed by a long, deep sigh as she slowly gathered her composure and continued.

"She was beautiful, and now she's dead and nobody seems to care anymore. Her case is two years old. That's when I read the newspaper article about that other case you had and decided to call you."

"Did you say they found her body in Saugus?" As he spoke, the lawyer realized he wouldn't be able to help the young woman. Saugus was Essex County. If the murder had occurred there, it was beyond the jurisdiction of the Suffolk County DA's office. Any help would have to come from another county prosecutor. In a way, it was a relief not to have another case added to his current files.

"Yes, they found her in Saugus, behind some lobster pound," the young woman added quickly, not realizing her answer would end the conversation.

"I'm sorry. I am very sorry about your sister, but that's out of our jurisdiction. Saugus is situated in Essex. That's another county, you're gonna have to contact them —"

The young woman interrupted him. "I know, I know. I've already talked to them and they've tried, but nothing's happened. All I'm asking you to do is take a look at her case, that's all, would you please, please help my family?" she implored.

There was a quiet desperation to the plea that appealed to the young lawyer. He wanted to help, but he felt torn by his commitment to the triple. He felt he would somehow be cheating the mother and her two children to divert his attention. As the DA listened to the young woman, he realized for the first time no one was going to call on the triple.

Maybe the triple's a lost cause, he said to himself. *Maybe I can help these people instead. Maybe that's what led her here.*

There was a pause as the lawyer briefly thought about his options on the jurisdiction issue. "Whereabouts in Saugus did they find her body?"

"It's on the Lynn Marsh Road, right near the Pines River. Why?" the girl with the soft voice answered.

"Because there's this old statute that says you can prosecute a murder case in either county if it occurs within a certain distance of the border between the two."

"Okay," the girl said without understanding what she was agreeing to.

"Do you know what cubits and rods are?" the lawyer asked.

The young woman seemed excited but puzzled. "No, what are they?"

"Well, a rod is an ancient measure of length from the Old Testament. Under this statute, if the murder occurs within one hundred rods of the county border it can be prosecuted in either place. A rod is sixteen and a half feet. So a hundred rods would be 1,650 feet. That's what we have to work with," the lawyer said as he quickly did the math on the yellow legal pad.

"Okay," the female voice said uncertainly.

The DA hesitated momentarily and added, "I'll get the investigative report on your sister's case from one of the troopers I know and we'll take a ride up there and measure it. That's all I can do for now, okay?"

"Thank you so very, very much," the young woman said. She began to cry once again.

"Oh, I'm sorry, one last thing. What's your sister's name?"

"Her name is Marie Iannuzzi. She was so pretty. We loved her very much."

The lawyer spelled out the victim's name, took a callback number for the family, and hung up.

Where the hell is the Pines River? he wondered.

25: The Cardinal's Nest

Immediately after his conversation with the soft-voiced girl, the DA called the state police at Logan Airport.

"Hey, Drew, what're ya doin' tomorrow?" the lawyer asked without explaining.

Drew was Andrew Palombo, a trooper assigned to the detectives' unit at the airport and one of the lawyer's best friends. They had met a couple of years earlier when the lawyer was doing a wiretap investigation with the state police's Major Crime Unit.

Drew was easy to describe, but hard to define. Six foot four and 240 pounds, he had a trooper's internal moral code wrapped inside the fabric of a Hell's Angel exterior. Ask anyone who knew him when they'd last seen him in uniform — no one could tell you. Ponytailed, earringed, and square-jawed, with deep-set dark brown eyes and a low, soft voice, his uniform of the day was denim blue jeans, rust-colored cowboy boots, and a black leather waistcoat.

Women loved him. Creeps feared him. Drew was a good guy.

Drew loved his Harley and referred to himself as "just a swamp Guinea from the lower end of East Boston." But he ran much, much deeper than that. There was a compassionate side to him that he kept hidden. Drew had a thing about men who hurt women. Maybe it was something out of his past, or maybe it was because he was the father of four daughters, but he was a walking, talking restraining order for domestic abuse cases. You could sell crack and he'd arrest you. If you beat your wife or child, well, he'd arrest you, too, but it would hurt.

Andrew Palombo was the kind of guy you'd want on your side in a fistfight or a gunfight. He'd been in plenty of both. Everyone called him Andy. The lawyer made it Drew to set him apart from the crowd.

"I just got a call from a woman whose sister was murdered two years ago up in Saugus," the lawyer explained. "I promised her I'd go up there and take a look and measure how far it is from the Suffolk County border. Wanna come?"

"Don't you have enough to do?" Drew responded. "I thought you were working on the triple homicide. Did anybody call yet?"

The question was an unwelcome reminder that the lawyer's mind should be somewhere else. He answered matter-of-factly, "No, nobody called. Anyway, I've got some time. My next trial isn't for another week. So I thought I'd go up there. Her name's Marie Iannuzzi. It happened in August of '79. Can you get the file and any photographs and pick me up tomorrow? It should only take an hour or so."

"The Essex DA isn't gonna like you digging into one of his cases, even if it is two years old. You know that, don't you?"

"We're just gonna take a look, that's all. If he tells us to butt out, we will. I told her sister I'd do it. It's not gonna be a problem," the lawyer responded as he thumbed the tattered gray file of the triple.

The next morning was chilly but sunny, without a cloud in the sky. Drew was driving a new silver Jaguar X12 with three bullet holes in the driver's-side door. They made a tight pattern. Recently seized from a drug dealer, the Jag was now being used by the state police as an undercover vehicle.

It was a great cover.

"How do you always manage to get these cars?" the DA asked his friend as he slid into the leather seat.

"Ya see the holes in the driver's door? They're mine. The dope didn't wanna stop, he was holding three keys of coke and an automatic. He let five rounds go and killed the engine of my unmarked. It's the third one this year. The job sent someone out to investigate the shootin', but they decided I was better off keeping the Jag. Probably figured I'd be less likely to crack it up or somethin'," the trooper told his friend as they pulled away from the rear of the Suffolk County Courthouse.

"Well they obviously made the right decision," the lawyer retorted. They wound their way down New Sudbury Street and through the Callahan Tunnel toward "Easta Bost."

"I got the reports and skimmed through them last night," the trooper said.

"What'd ya find out?" the lawyer asked as the X12 passed through the tollbooths, over Chelsea Street, and into Easta Bost.

"She was last seen leaving the Cardinal's Nest. It's a local watering hole on Maverick Street here in East Boston. She was found the next day behind some lobster place on the Lynn Marsh Road in Saugus. Time of death was probably around one or two in the morning. No rape kit. She was strangled with her own scarf and left on the rocks of the Pines River," the trooper related.

There was a pause in the flow of conversation as the driver momentarily thought of his four daughters.

"She was a very pretty girl. Kinda sad," he added as he handed the lawyer the thick, dark brown file containing the police reports and the crime scene photographs.

"Any mopes in view?" the DA asked.

"Yeah, her boyfriend, of course. They had a fight at the wedding. He wound up leaving the reception. Some of the witnesses said they saw some scratches on his hands later on. The other mope is some guy she got a ride with from the wedding reception to the Cardinal's Nest. Unfortunately, the second guy was with his girlfriend. She's his alibi."

"Great. No rape kit. Two suspects and neither one quite fits the bill, right?" the lawyer deadpanned.

"You got it," the trooper said as they pulled up next to the Cardinal's Nest. "That's why the case has gone nowhere for more than two years."

"That's okay, we'll figure it out," the lawyer responded enthusiastically.

The two men stepped from the bright sunlight outside into the darkness of the Nest. It was midmorning, but it could just as easily have been midnight inside.

The dive was your typical beer-swilling, shot-doing hangout, with a sticky checkered linoleum floor and a ceiling fan to stir the smoky air. The Cardinal's Nest was East Boston's answer to Cheers. On the glowing, multicolored Wurlitzer in the corner, Tony Bennett lamented about leaving his heart high up on a hill in San Francisco.

The two men spoke briefly to the bartender, who knew nothing, then stepped back out into the brilliant sunlight and headed to the Lynn Marsh Road.

It was a short ride.

The former Conley and Daggett's lobster pound was now the Atlantic Lobster Company.

A place set apart on the causeway from Revere to Lynn, the pound was a ramshackle, weathered-gray shingled flop of a building on the northbound side of the Lynn Marsh Road. You could drive by three times a day and never notice it. Multicolored buoys and fish netting on the exterior provided muted nautical atmosphere to any interested passersby.

A small dirt parking lot in front of the structure provided access for the public to buy lobsters and seafood wholesale. A narrow unpaved road trailed off from the parking area, snaking back behind the building to a secluded area overlooking the Pines and Saugus Rivers.

Hidden from the highway, marked by PRIVATE PROPERTY and NO TRESPASSING signs on a chain-link fence, with tall sea grass lining the banks of the river, it was a perfect place for a murder.

The trooper and the lawyer pulled into the lot, parked the Jag, and walked directly down the unpaved road behind the wood-framed structure. Holding the photographs of the original crime scene, the two navigated toward the river's edge. They positioned the eight-by-eleven glossies before them as they walked, providing a now-for-then view of the murder scene.

Each picture brought them closer to the location where Marie's body had been discovered.

"Hey, can I help youse fuckin' guys?" asked an angry voice from just inside the doorway to the rear entrance of the lobster pound.

A shadow cast across his face masked his identity, but the man's tone made it obvious he wasn't happy with the strangers' presence. He was stocky, about six feet tall, with dark wavy hair. Large-framed and dressed in rough-hewn work clothes, the unhappy camper consumed the width of the door.

Drew produced his silver badge from beneath the black leather jacket, turned to the man, and said brusquely, "Yeah, state police, we'll be right with ya, asshole."

The man quickly disappeared from sight.

"This is where they found her body," the lawyer said as he looked down at the large rocks on the riverbank and then back to the photographic likeness for comparison. The picture had been taken from the same place where the two now stood and showed the young victim's partially nude body strewn lifeless on the shoreline. The two men stood motionless for several minutes as they examined the scene, imagining the moment of death years earlier.

"I think the killer's been here before. I mean to this place," the prosecutor told the trooper as he surveyed the secluded area overlooking the river.

"Ya think he knows about this place?" Drew asked, looking back toward the building and hidden roadway.

"Yeah, I do. It's not random. They didn't just coincidentally wind up here. The killer's got to be familiar with this location. He had to have known about this place before he brought her back here. He brought her here to kill her," the DA said as he closed his eyes.

"Ya think so?"

"Yeah, I do. This is his environment. This is where he's comfortable."

"So do ya wanna get involved in another murder case? Ya got enough time?" the trooper with the ponytail wanted to know.

"Maybe. How far d'ya think it is from here to the Suffolk County border?"

"Hey, I'm not Noah, and I'm not building an ark. I don't even know what a cubit is. But I do know it's gonna be close to 1,650 feet from here to the middle of the Pines River. We gotta have jurisdiction if you wanna do the case," the big trooper said as he looked back toward the skyline of Boston. "I'll come back tomorrow and measure it exactly just to make sure it's within that statute you talked about."

"Good, let's do it," the DA said. "The case shouldn't be that hard."

The two drifted back toward the Jag, talking over the case.

The frequent calling of seagulls passing overhead pierced the sounds of the traffic on the Lynn Marsh Road. Theirs was a mournful sound in a mournful place. It was high noon as the lawyer stood on the passenger's side of the car, waiting for the trooper to unlock the doors.

"Hey, Drew, didn't they find the missing Harvard girl's pocketbook and wallet somewhere around here?" he asked as he looked blankly across the shiny metal roof of the Jag.

"Yeah, it was somewhere near here, but I think it was on the southbound side of the Lynn Marsh Road. Saugus PD has the case. My job sent some of our divers to do the river, but they never found anything else. Why?"

"I don't know, idle curiosity I guess," the lawyer said as he listened to the seagulls and looked across the road toward the marshy grass of the Pines River.

The trooper and the prosecutor returned from their trip to the Lynn Marsh Road that sunny afternoon and headed to the attorney's office on the sixth floor of the courthouse. The lawyer turned on the radio as they began the tedious process of reviewing the Iannuzzi case file.

As the two men sat in Room 603, Burke's mind drifted back to the mother and two kids on Jacobs Street. The image of the two children being dragged down the narrow hallway to a certain and brutal death flashed through his mind.

"How can someone do that?" the lawyer asked his friend, pointing to the gray file on his desk.

"You mean the triple?"

"Yeah."

"I dunno. There's a lot of sick people out there we're never gonna be able to understand. Our job's catchin' 'em and putting 'em away. You gonna solve it?"

The lawyer didn't respond as he placed the dark brown manila folder of Marie Barbara Iannuzzi's murder investigation on the cluttered desk next to the tattered file of the triple. Like two large bookends, the brown and gray files dominated the landscape of legal briefs, memos, and motions scattered about the desk.

— The DA opened the Iannuzzi folder and gave half the papers inside to Drew. The two men sat quietly listening to Bertie Higgins sing "Key Largo" on the radio as they began to read. The lawyer thought briefly of Bogart's line from *Casablanca:* "Here's looking at you, kid," as the image of the young woman's smiling face appeared and just as suddenly disappeared.

"Ya ever watch old movies?" the lawyer wanted to know.

"Just murder mysteries," the trooper said with a large smile.

There were thirty-six neatly typed, single-spaced pages detailing the investigation conducted by the Saugus police and the Essex County District Attorney's office.

As they studied the reports, the two men visualized the flow of the case and the role each actor had played. They read every word, sentence, paragraph, page, and inflection over and over. The detectives initially assigned to the case had done a thorough job of interviewing witnesses in an attempt to make sense out of a senseless crime.

The case file consisted mainly of written statements taken from Marie's family members and guests at the Milano wedding and reception. They told an inconclusive story of confusion and uncertainty. Two primary suspects emerged from the list of numerous possibilities. The two "mopes in view" were Marie's live-in boyfriend, David Doyle, and Leonard Paradiso, a family friend of the groom.

Shortly after Marie's body was identified, a detective from the Saugus PD and a trooper from the DA's office interviewed the witnesses at the Cardinal's Nest who were at the bar on the night of her murder.

"Okay, Drew, listen to this," the DA said as he began to read from one of the pages.

"The cops interviewed Christine DeLisi. She was a friend of Marie's. DeLisi told them she saw Marie drinking at the Cardinal's Nest with a 'large-framed, dark-haired' guy sometime after midnight the night she was murdered. DeLisi said Marie looked 'gorgeous' that night."

"They ID him?"

"Yeah, they did. She told them Marie left the bar with the same guy. Just before she left with him Marie told DeLisi, 'Wait right here. Don't leave without me. I'll be back in a half hour.' The guy was holding the door waitin' for Marie while she's talkin' to DeLisi."

"Who was it?"

"Four days later they take DeLisi to District 7 in East Boston. They give her eleven photographs to see if she can ID the guy. All the photographs of the guys look alike. Ya know, dark hair, stocky build, same facial structure," the lawyer explained as he held the identification report in his right hand.

"And who'd she pick out?"

"It took DeLisi about ten seconds to pick out this guy Paradiso."

"Yeah, I got the reports on him." Drew held up four pages from the file. "Initially, no one seemed to know or be willing to say much about Paradiso. His nickname's 'the Quahog.'"

"What the hell's a quahog," the lawyer from upstate New York wanted to know.

"It's like a big clam. It tastes just like a piece of a Goodyear tire on a hot summer day. Don't they teach you nothing in law school?"

"I probably skipped class that day."

"Well, he's got a record from eight years ago. It doesn't say for what, though. Anyway, he's got a solid alibi. Paradiso was interviewed a couple a days after the murder. He told 'em he was with his girlfriend, Candy Weyant, at the Milano wedding and later at the reception." Drew put the police reports back into the brown file.

"How did he wind up at the Cardinal's Nest with Marie then?"

"Apparently everybody got invited back to the groom's house in Saugus. According to Paradiso, Marie gets drunk and causes a scene at the house by flirting with one of the Milano's sons. So the Milanos ask Paradiso's girlfriend to give Marie a ride to East Boston, which she does and drops her off at the Nest," Drew explained.

"Where's Paradiso?"

"He stays at the Milanos' house. When his girlfriend comes back, they leave, and on their way home they find some stuff in the car they think belongs to Marie. So they stop at the Cardinal's Nest and Paradiso goes inside to give it back to her."

"What was it?"

"Just some papers, a notebook."

"Okay, so what happens next?"

"Paradiso leaves her there at the bar and gets back in the car with his girlfriend, and they drive to his apartment on Princeton Street in East Boston. When they start to get out of the car, they find a set of keys wedged between the seats. So they go back to the Nest a second time. This time Paradiso's inside the bar a little longer. He told the cops he gave Marie the set of keys and leaves just as Marie is heading out the door."

"So where's Paradiso's girlfriend?"

"His girlfriend's parked right outside the Nest waiting for him. He tells the detectives he walks outta the bar with Marie. She heads up Maverick Street and that's the last he sees of her. Paradiso says he and his girlfriend ask Marie if she wants a ride home and she tells them no, she's meeting someone else."

"So where do Paradiso and his girlfriend go then?"

"They're driving the girlfriend's Buick. It's a yellow '73 LeSabre. After they leave the Nest, they head back to Paradiso's apartment, where Weyant stays for about half an hour, and then she drives her car back to her home alone in Revere. Paradiso tells Saugus when Weyant got home she called him to let him know she had arrived safely," the trooper with the ponytail related without emotion.

"How far is the Cardinal's Nest from his apartment on Princeton Street?"

"Maybe a mile. Probably less."

"And how far is the Nest from the girlfriend's house in Revere?"

"She lives on Crescent Avenue. So it's maybe ten or fifteen minutes, depending on the time of day."

"And how about Marie, do any of the reports say where she was living?"

"Yeah, she was living with her boyfriend at Jeffrey's Point in East Boston. It's only a couple of blocks from the Nest," Drew said.

"Did these guys interview Paradiso's girlfriend?"

"Yeah, one of the guys from my job was with the Saugus detective when they interviewed Paradiso and Weyant. It was Carl Sjoberg. He was assigned to the Essex DA's office."

"Do you have her statement?"

"It's right here. They questioned her two hours after they spoke to Paradiso. They went to where she was workin' at Northeast Petroleum in Chelsea. And she confirmed everything Paradiso said to them earlier."

"Really?"

"Yup. She told 'em that on the way home from the Milanos', they found Marie's papers on the seat in Weyant's car. They drove to the Nest, parked the car, and Lenny went inside. She says he was only in there a couple of minutes and when he came out, he told her Marie was still inside drinking. When they got to Paradiso's apartment, it started to drizzle. After they parked, Weyant pushed down the seat to get an umbrella and Paradiso found a set of keys wedged between the seats. So Weyant said they drove back to the Cardinal's Nest, Lenny went back inside for a brief time, and when he left the bar Marie was with him," Drew recited from the police report.

"What does Marie do?"

"Weyant told them Paradiso asked Marie if she wanted a ride, but Marie mumbled something about going somewhere to meet someone and walked off toward the front of the building and down the street."

"Does she confirm the rest of Paradiso's story about going to his apartment and then callin' him when she got home that night?"

"Almost verbatim."

"That's a pretty good alibi, don't ya think?"

"Real good. Who's the other mope?"

"It's her boyfriend, David Doyle."

'What's his story?"

"It ain't pretty. He's a user. Got a temper. They interviewed three or four people who all confirm that Doyle had an argument with Marie at the wedding and left her there alone at the end of the reception. I guess that's why her family blamed Doyle for Marie getting killed," the lawyer suggested.

"Did you read the interviews of her family?" Drew asked.

"Yeah, a couple of 'em said he never cried when he went to identify her body at the morgue. They told the cops he just looked at her and threw the sheet back over her face. They said two of her sisters went to the apartment at Jeffrey's Point to pick out clothes for her wake; Doyle had already packed up all of her belongings. And there were three dark brown spots of what appeared to be blood on the steps leading up to the apartment," the lawyer related as Drew's expression changed.

"Really?"

"There's more. At the wake Doyle supposedly had scratches on his hands. First he said a cat had done it and then he claimed he got into a fight during the wake at a nearby bar. He never even went to Marie's funeral. He winds up gettin' arrested in Newark, New Jersey, the same day stealing luggage from a baggage carousel." The lawyer shook his head from side to side.

"Holy shit."

"I'm just warming up. Apparently, Doyle was jealous of some other guy Marie was secretly seeing."

"There's a motive," Drew interrupted.

"It gets better. One of Marie's sisters told the detectives Doyle grabbed Marie by the throat and choked her a month or so before she was murdered. Her sister said you could see the marks on Marie's neck. Marie moved outta their apartment for a while because she was afraid of Doyle. She moved in with her friend Christine DeLisi."

"The same Christine DeLisi who saw Marie leave the Cardinal's Nest with Paradiso?"

"One and the same."

"Damn it, I thought you said this case was gonna be easy. No wonder it's almost three years old."

"Ya want more?"

"Pour it on."

"There's a statement Doyle's supposed to have made to a friend of his. A druggie by the name of David Dellaria," the DA told Ponytail.

"Wait a minute. Aren't you prosecuting a guy by the name of David Dellaria?"

"One and the same. I got him for robbing and beating the crap out of a sixty-five-year-old woman in East Boston."

"See what happens every time you turn over one of these rocks? Something crawls out from under it. So what did Doyle tell Dellaria?"

"Doyle supposedly told him that he 'did what he needed to do, and Marie got what she deserved.'"

There was a pregnant pause before Ponytail said, "Nice. You sure you wanna do this case?"

There lawyer offered no immediate response.

The more they read from the police interviews in the brown file, the more uncertainty there was about who killed Marie. It was a familiar game of homicide Ping-Pong with no clear-cut means, opportunity, and motive for either suspect. Each layer of information brought more questions. Each answer led to another series of doubts and more reservations.

"Ya know what, Drew? I'm not gonna have to just prove that one of these two mopes murdered Marie. I'm also gonna have to prove that the other one didn't."

"Just another easy case, right?"

"Yeah, it's got *reasonable doubt* written all over it," the DA said as Judge Lemuel Shaw's landmark definition from the Webster case of 1850 passed through his mind.

28: The Usual Haunts

Over the next two days the lawyer and the trooper met in their usual haunts to review the case and discuss their thoughts. There was an uncertain back-and-forth over which of the two mopes in view was more likely to have committed the murder, with the scale tipping decidedly in the direction of Doyle. Yet the statement from one witness at the Cardinal's Nest raised a recurring question in Weyant and Paradiso's alibi.

The prosecutor read Christine DeLisi's statement out loud for the hundredth time.

"This may be the key to the case," he said to the trooper sitting across the cluttered desk from him. "Why the hell would Marie leave the bar with Paradiso for half an hour? She didn't know him that well. Everybody who saw her that night said she looked dynamite. She's not gonna go parking with some big slug who's practically married to Weyant. She wasn't leavin' for the night with him; she was goin' somewhere and then comin' back. She told DeLisi she would be right back."

The trooper waited for the end of the lawyer's sentence before quickly responding. "What about Doyle? What makes you think he didn't do it? If you believe Weyant's story, Marie leaves the bar and walks around the corner. She goes down Maverick Street and outta sight. Doyle could've killed her sometime later on and then dumped her body in the Pines River. Hell, the two of them lived just a couple of blocks away from the Nest. Maybe she left the bar, walked home, and they got in another fight."

"Okay, so let's say Doyle killed her. Tell me why she winds up behind Conley and Daggett's lobster pound? What possible connection does David Doyle have to the Pines River and the Lynn Marsh Road?" Another volley in the homicide Ping-Pong match.

The trooper eyed the lawyer, paused, and pointed at him with a large finger. "I'm listening, but you can't get around the fact that Doyle had a fight with Marie that same day. He's a druggie. Maybe he's jealous. Maybe he's got another reason to want to hurt her again. How you gonna explain to a jury that Marie went to stay with Christine DeLisi for five days because Doyle grabbed her by the throat and choked her? DeLisi said she saw the marks on Marie's neck from where Doyle grabbed her."

After a pause the DA replied, "Look, Drew, anything's possible, but Paradiso's alibi is just too, too perfect. He knows someone is likely to have seen Marie leave the bar with him. That's why he admits to walking outta there with her. There's a kernel of truth in every lie. He's smart. He takes certain facts that are true and works them into his alibi. The problem is, Paradiso doesn't know what Marie told DeLisi about waiting for her and coming back in half an hour. I don't think the bastard went back to his own apartment with Weyant. I think he drove Weyant home and then came back to the Nest a second time alone and somehow convinced Marie to leave and go somewhere with him."

This time Drew didn't respond.

"Don't you think it's just a little odd that Iannuzzi, who had just spent the entire day at a wedding, would be carrying around papers and a notebook and a big ring of keys? Then she would all of a sudden forget all that stuff in Weyant's car? And how come Weyant doesn't see them on the way back to the Milanos'?" the lawyer asked. "I just don't understand why the hell she winds up behind the lobster place."

"Hey, I don't know why she's there, either, but I do know you're gonna have one hell of a hard time convincing twelve people Paradiso killed her. Not with all of this crap about Doyle in the background."

The DA nodded. "Did they ever search the car Paradiso was driving that night? It'd be tough to get a search warrant now, almost three years later."

"No, it was never searched. They didn't have probable cause at the time of the murder, plus it was Candy's car."

"Well did anyone ever pull Paradiso's parole records and the arrest reports on that case he had back in the 1970s?" The lawyer quickly added, "What kind of case was it?"

"I don't know. I think he beat up some hitchhiker."

"Male or female? Ya know, we really should try to find out more about it."

"The *we* means *me*, right?"

The lawyer nodded, paused for a moment, then said with a measure of finality, "I think we oughta start doing a time line and get as much information on both of these two mopes as we can. We oughta start a John Doe grand jury investigation so we can subpoena some of these records. Then we can just bring everybody in and let them tell their story to the grand jury. That's the only way we're gonna end this Mexican standoff."

"How the hell is that gonna help solve this thing?"

"None of the witnesses were under oath when they gave their statements to the police. They can still lie in the grand jury, but at least we'll have them under oath. Besides, I'll be able to cross-examine them and evaluate their testimony and it'll all be recorded by a stenographer. Both Doyle and Paradiso, plus Paradiso's girlfriend, will have a chance to testify. They can all explain where they were and what they did. If nothing else it would bring the case to a head," the DA told his friend, trying to convince them both.

"That sounds good in theory, but you've got two possible suspects. The transcript from the grand jury is gonna create an excellent blueprint for some defense attorney to point the finger at the other guy."

"What's the alternative? We do nothing, right? And some mutt walks on a murder. Is that what you wanna do?"

"You're nuts. You know that? You're friggin' nuts." Drew grinned. "Let's do it."

29: The Registry of Motor Vehicles

The following day the DA drafted grand jury subpoenas for every witness mentioned in the large brown case file. He subpoenaed Paradiso's records from his arrest by Andover police in 1973, his prison records from the Massachusetts Department of Corrections, and his parole records from the parole board. Requests for information were sent to the Registry of Motor Vehicles as well as the telephone company and various credit card companies.

The lawyer then used the thirty-six pages of Saugus police reports to begin a draft of a minute-by-minute time line for the twenty-four-hour time period leading up to Marie's death and the week following the discovery of her body. He marked a map of pertinent sites in East Boston, Revere, and Saugus with red flags to show their locations and routes of travel and, then drove from place to place until he knew the way by heart.

"Hey, Drew, guess what happened to Candy Weyant's car a month after Marie was killed?" the lawyer asked Ponytail as he sat at his desk staring out from between the brown and gray files.

The big trooper hated it when the lawyer knew something and he didn't.

"Weyant called the Revere police and reported her Buick LeSabre stolen on September 13. She told them it disappeared from in front of her house."

"Are you kidding me?" the trooper asked, trying hard not to sound surprised. "Ya think they did it because they were afraid Saugus PD would get a search warrant?"

"Dunno. Ya know that check we ran on all of Paradiso and Weyant's car listings? I went through all of them, and guess what? Are you sitting down for this? In three years, they reported eight cars and two boats stolen for insurance claims. They were paid more than forty grand for them."

"That's a lot of money, and a lot of stolen cars."

"I know. They claimed three of the cars were stolen right out in front of Weyant's house in Revere," the DA explained.

"So maybe the car Paradiso's driving the night Marie was killed was 'stolen' as a part of their scam and not to hide evidence," the trooper mused.

"I don't think it's a coincidence, Drew. Paradiso was interviewed. He knows he's a suspect. Maybe he's worried about Marie's blood being found in Weyant's car."

"That's gonna be tough to prove, but at least it gives us something to think about. How many cars did you say they reported stolen?"

"Eight cars and two boats in four years. Then he bought another boat. It's a twenty-six-foot Chris-Craft. Paradiso named it the *Mala Femmena*. Drew, you speak Italian. What the hell does *Mala Femmena* mean?"

"It means 'evil woman,'" the trooper answered.

"Nice name. That fits doesn't it? Somebody that's got a bad attitude toward women," the lawyer said, only half in jest. "Anyway, I got a call from the parole board, too. They got the subpoena and they're gonna be sending Paradiso's records over to me tomorrow."

"Give me a call if you get anything interesting." Ponytail left Room 603 and headed to the bank of elevators, where the kid with red hair and a worn Red Sox cap stood holding the brass doors open.

– – –

A week later a thick tan envelope was placed on the DA's cluttered desk with the rest of the day's mail. It sat there innocuously enough, MASSACHUSETTS PAROLE BOARD stamped on the upper left-hand corner.

It was a mother lode.

The parole board's file contained all of the observations and conversations Paradiso's parole officer, Victor Anchukitis, had had with the subject over the past four years. The DA began with a careful read of each entry for the first two years of Paradiso's parole. They were placed chronologically, outlining the parolee's communications and weekly contact with his supervisor.

When he came to Anchukitis's entry for April 2, 1980, the DA stopped reading. His mouth went dry and he began to sweat. Neatly typed and sparsely stated, one paragraph in the parole officer's report did what nearly three years of investigation couldn't.

The lawyer read the paragraph over and over to himself. He understood now for the first time why Marie was strangled and left on the rocks in that particularly lonely place near the Pines River.

He picked up the phone and called Drew.

"Holy shit, Drew," the lawyer began, "listen to this: 'PO spotted subject at the old Conley and Daggett's on the Marsh Road in Lynn. Subject took PO on a cook's tour of how the operation goes. Subject makes deliveries at the Company, has been doing business there for quite a time.'

"Drew, Paradiso killed Marie. That's his connection to that place. He made deliveries out back there. He knew all about that secluded area behind Conley and Daggett's. That's why he took her back there. He got her in his car at the

Nest and brought her there and raped her and strangled her. It was Paradiso, not Doyle."

"Holy shit. Man, holy shit."

— — —

Two days later David St. Jean, the Andover police officer, called to tell the DA that the reports from Paradiso's arrest in 1973 would be sent to his office immediately.

"I remember this case," the Andover cop began as the attorney took notes. "I'll never forget it," St. Jean went on, as his voice thickened. "He beat the crap out of this girl he picked up hitchhiking. He tried to rape her, too. She fought him off. He was tryin' to strangle her just as we pulled up behind him. I can still remember his license plate number. He woulda killed her. I know he woulda."

The lawyer said nothing as the cop continued.

"The bastard had a Smith and Wesson hidden underneath the front seat of his car. I was a rookie then. He wanted me to cuff his hands in front of him. He was tryin' to convince me to let him get back in his car and sit down. He told me he had a bad back. If I ever let him do that, he woulda gotten the .38 and killed us, too."

There was a brief pause before the cop from Andover spoke again.

"We had him dead to rights, but the bastard had an alibi. He told us he had 'just found the girl like that.' Then at the trial, he brought in a couple of women to testify for him. One was a bleached blonde. They made it really tough for the jury. They came damn close to walking him."

There was another moment of silence as St. Jean gathered his thoughts.

"I hope you understand you're dealin' with a really sick bastard here. This guy is pure evil."

30: Indictment Number 038655

In early March 1982 the first witnesses were called before the Suffolk County grand jury in the case *Commonwealth of Massachusetts v. John Doe*, the investigation into the murder of Marie Barbara Iannuzzi. The inquiry was held in a solemn, windowless room with twenty-three dark blue leather chairs facing the prosecution's table and the adjacent witness stand.

Completed in 1937, the "new" courthouse was a project of FDR's Works Progress Administration during the Great Depression. The sixth-floor grand jury room had gracefully withstood the passage of time. With fifteen-foot ceilings, dark mahogany wainscoting, and thick blue wall-to-wall carpeting, it had been a witness to every murder and rape investigated in the county for almost half a century.

Unknown to the prosecutor, the name of Leonard Paradiso had echoed throughout the same room twelve years earlier when he'd escaped indictment for the kidnapping and rape of Florence White.

This time, more than twenty-five individuals would be summoned to appear before the grand jury over the next four months on Marie's case. The DA met with each of them beforehand, explaining the procedure and eliciting a summary of his or her expected testimony. As he did, he searched their faces, their eyes, and their voices for any expression or emotion indicating deception or dishonesty.

Each witness then came before the grand jury, was sworn to tell the truth, and testified about the death of Marie Iannuzzi. It was a rambling, often frustrating, time-consuming procedure. Witnesses' testimony was somewhat predictable, but at times confusing when they spoke clearly against or in favor of one of the two suspects.

On the last day of the proceeding, Paradiso and Weyant sat huddled together, quietly conversing on a heavy wooden bench located just outside the entrance to the grand jury room. A lit Camel cigarette hung languidly from the corner of Lenny's mouth. Its smoke circled upward above the pair.

Across the wide expanse of marble floor, on an identical bench, sat David Doyle, alone, and seemingly very small.

The thought had already crystallized in the lawyer's mind that Paradiso was a stone-cold killer and had indeed murdered Marie Iannuzzi. The DA scanned the room quickly as he tried to decide which person to call as the next witness. It was an easy call. He walked across the marble floor to the couple seated on the bench, extended his right hand toward the heavyset man in the double-breasted suit, and introduced himself.

"Hi, I'm Assistant District Attorney Tim Burke."

"Youse got the wrong fuckin' guy," the Quahog said as he rose, slowly placing his large callused hand around the lawyer's.

It was a grip of death. The lawyer knew it instantly. It felt as if a malevolent electrical force coursed, unchecked and uncharted, through his body. The strong fingers and broad palm were warm and moist with anxious sweat. He stared into Paradiso's eyes as the man exhaled a half breath of smoke into the musty air. The scent of stale cigarettes and cheap cologne lingered about him.

The larger man seemed to be measuring the lawyer's strength as they stood motionless, temporarily connected, breathing the same air. After a perceived eternity of silence, Paradiso abruptly withdrew his hand, looked beyond the lawyer, and nodded toward Doyle. "That fuckin' kid over there done it," he said in a low, guttural voice. *That fuckin' kid over there* would become the next witness, as Leonard "Lenny the Quahog" Paradiso exercised his Fifth Amendment privilege and declined to testify before the grand jury.

The DA walked back across the marble floor, introduced himself to the young man seated alone on the heavy wooden bench, and read David Doyle his Miranda warnings. Doyle waived his rights and calmly walked into the grand jury room. Over the next hour he told the jurors, between bouts of tears, that he loved Marie, that he was an admitted drug user, that they often argued, sometimes violently, but he hadn't killed Marie.

Doyle explained he never cried openly at Marie's wake, but wept uncontrollably when he was alone. After Marie's death, he told the jurors, he'd tried to overdose and wanted to die because she was gone. He'd gotten his scratches in a drunken fight during the wake, he added. Depressed over his loss, he could not face her family at the funeral — he knew they blamed him for Marie's death. He explained that he had been up all night after they found her body and needed something to do, so he packed Marie's clothes. Doyle answered every question put to him. He was a willing witness, convincing, sincere, and forthright.

At the end of his testimony the grand jurors knew in their hearts and minds that David Doyle wasn't Marie Iannuzzi's killer.

On June 28, 1982, the Suffolk County Grand Jury returned a true bill on indictment number 038655, charging Leonard J. Paradiso with the first-degree murder of Marie Barbara Iannuzzi.

31: Revere

In the late afternoon of Tuesday, July 6, 1982, four Massachusetts troopers prepared to visit the home of Candy Weyant at 212 Crescent Avenue, Revere. They were armed with a warrant to arrest Leonard Paradiso for the murder of Marie Iannuzzi. Andrew Palombo was among them. The trooper with the ponytail carefully placed the arrest warrant in the pocket of his black leather coat and called his friend from the state police barracks at Logan Airport.

When the phone rang, the lawyer was standing in the kitchen of his home pouring boiled spaghetti into a copper colander. It was a familiar voice on the line.

"Hey, Tim, we're just about ready to go up there now and pick him up." Drew paused. "What the hell music is that you're playin'? Sounds like you're goin' to a funeral."

"It's Irish. It's 'Danny Boy.'"

"What the hell is 'Danny Boy'?"

"It's a song. It's about a father saying good-bye to his son. The son's goin' off to fight in a war. The father's afraid he'll never see him again," the lawyer responded quickly. "Have you got enough guys?"

"You Irish guys are whacked, ya know that?" The trooper laughed. "Yeah, there's four of us. We're gonna go to his girlfriend's house again. That's where he's been staying."

"Be careful, Drew. He's capable of anything," the DA said to his friend.

"So am I," Drew replied. "Gotta go. I'll call you when we find him."

The city of Revere was a close-knit blue-collar community, predominantly Italian, located five miles north of downtown Boston. Home of the nation's oldest public beach, it was named after Paul Revere, the silversmith and horseman made famous by Longfellow's poem. Bordered by the Pines River on the north, Easta Bost to the south, and the Atlantic Ocean eastward, Revere and its beach featured a seemingly endless strip of honky-tonk.

Roast beef sandwich shops, biker bars, used-car lots, liquor stores, clam shacks, tow yards, fast-food joints, nameless nightclubs, amusement park rides . . . Revere Beach had it all. A couple of miles away you could bet on the dogs at Wonderland Racetrack or on the horses at Suffolk Downs. Not far from the two tracks you could catch a ride at the Wonderland MBTA station or go dancing at the famed Wonderland Ballroom.

Candy Weyant and the Quahog lived less than a mile from Wonderland.

The two unmarked Ford Crown Victoria cruisers rolled out from Logan Airport, heading north up Route 1A past Suffolk Downs. They exited at Revere Beach onto Winthrop Avenue, continuing toward the quiet residential neighborhood surrounding Crescent Avenue.

"Ya need ta remember this guy we're arrestin' is a killer, okay. He may not go easy," the man with the ponytail and the two-day growth announced to his passenger. The young trooper dressed in his pressed and starched blue uniform simply nodded.

It was a study in contrasts as Drew in his black leather coat and scuffed cowboy boots spoke to the newbie with a spit-shine polish on black midcalf boots.

"He's got access to guns. He's capable of anything. Consider him armed. Two guys at the back door, you and me at the front door. If he makes a move for a gun, shoot him."

"Sir, yes sir," the rookie with the high-and-tight blond crew cut replied, swallowing hard and staring straight ahead.

Drew thought about the Irish song as he spoke to his younger companion. "Look at me, kid. This is real-life shit here today, okay? This ain't the academy. I plan on goin' home tonight, and I plan on makin' sure you do, too. Just do what I fuckin' tell ya, okay?" Drew glanced away from the steering wheel long enough to make eye contact with the recruit. There was a strength to his voice that reassured and calmed the younger trooper.

This guy's got balls, High-and-Tight thought as he mouthed, "Yes sir."

"And don't fuckin' call me *sir.* It's Andy," he said, wheeling the unmarked Crown Vic off Winthrop Avenue and onto Crescent.

Straight ahead and two blocks away was a dark brown Chevy Blazer with Massachusetts plate number 371-FII and a matching brown speedboat hooked behind it. Water dripped from the stern, forming small puddles that traced the outline of the nineteen-footer. Affixed next to the Blazer's license plate was a white bumper sticker with red and green lettering: EVERY GIRL NEEDS A BIG ITALIAN GUY.

The Blazer was parked in front of a small, dark gray, two-and-a-half-story wood-framed house with the number 212 positioned above a picture of a smiling black Labrador retriever. The name WEYANT was printed beside the happy Lab.

Drew called the plate number into headquarters as the unmarked car made a slow pass by the Blazer and boat, then circled the block while the other cruiser remained out of sight down the street. As the first cruiser made the turn back onto Crescent Avenue, a voice crackled over the radio, "Andy, that's your boy. It's his Blazer. We got more backup if you need it." The dispatcher waited for a response.

There wasn't one.

Drew turned to the two troopers in the adjacent cruiser, gave the thumbs-up sign, and the two vehicles accelerated quickly down the block and just as quickly came to a stop, one behind, one in front of the Blazer and boat. Without a word, the two troopers in the second cruiser went to the rear of the dark gray house with their hands in the ready position by their sides.

At the same time, Drew calmly walked past an elderly man weeding a nearby patch of parched earth and up the front steps of the house. He placed his right hand on the automatic beneath the thin leather coat and said in a loud, clear voice, "State police, open up." He could feel the sweat begin to form on his forehead.

The bleached blonde who answered the door spoke briefly to the two troopers and called upstairs to a second-floor bedroom for Lenny. On the kitchen table a spaghetti dinner was about to be served. The smell of sweet basil and garlic filled the hallway adjoining the front porch.

On top of the refrigerator, an ancient Philco played Connie Francis singing "Where the Boys Are." High-and-Tight stood at the ready, pondering the irony as Connie belted out, "Someone waits for me."

Minutes later, heavy footsteps thundered down the stairs as the large-framed man pushed aside the screen door and stepped outside.

"Are you Lenny Paradiso?" the man in the ponytail and leather coat asked.

"Yeah, whose the fuck are you?" the Quahog responded.

"I'm Trooper Andy Palombo," Drew responded quickly as he flashed his silver badge. A sense of calm came over the trooper. For the first time he felt truly in control.

"You're under arrest for the murder of Marie Iannuzzi. Let's go," Drew added as he reached for the back of the Fat Man's arm.

The Quahog glanced briefly at the bleached blonde, and then at the fair-haired High-and-Tight, weighing his chances . . . and thinking better of it. He slowly brought his hands down toward his sides, clenched his fists, and said, "I got me a bad back, cuff me in front will ya?"

"Okay, we'll do that for you," Drew responded as he reached for his cuffs and briefly thought of Lenny's arrest by the cops from Andover. He placed the heavy metal on Paradiso's thick wrists behind his back and turned to the newbie.

"If he moves, shoot him," Ponytail instructed as Lenny blanched.

As he led the handcuffed defendant down the stairs, Drew recited Miranda word for word. Shortly after he got to the part about "If you can't afford an attorney, one will be appointed for you," Ponytail turned to face the Quahog.

"You don't seem too surprised to see us," he said.

"I've been waiting for youse guys for three years," Paradiso replied.

Twenty seconds later, near the cruiser parked on Crescent Avenue, the Quahog turned to the trooper with the long hair and the cowboy boots.

"Youse got the wrong fuckin' guy," he whined.

Drew wasn't convinced.

There are moments in each life when the real becomes the surreal and the ordinary becomes the outrageous. The serene becomes the storm, and the beginning becomes the end.

Such a moment happened for Lenny the Quahog on a warm evening in early July 1982.

32: The Arraignment

"You're never gonna convict him with this evidence. You know that, don't ya, Tim?" Paradiso's attorney and the prosecutor were on the seventh floor of the courthouse in Pemberton Square. "That winning streak of yours is about to end."

The DA simply smiled in response as the two lawyers briefly shook hands outside the first session of the criminal court. Paradiso was scheduled to be arraigned that morning.

The defense attorney was short, with a stocky build, a round face, and owlish glasses. Jimmy Cipoletta was his name. He'd grown up in Revere, where he had attended high school with Candy Weyant. Cipoletta knew his way around a courtroom and had a younger brother on the state police. He was a good street lawyer and a perfect fit for Lenny.

"I'm gonna be asking for Paradiso to be held at Charles Street on $150,000 bail," the DA announced as the two made their way toward the double swinging doors.

It took the defense lawyer all of three seconds to come up with a response. "This is a weak case. I can't believe you indicted him. None of the Connie Porter case evidence comes in during this trial. David Doyle's gonna be on the stand for three days explaining why he tried to strangle his girlfriend and never went to her funeral. We got a good alibi with Candy Weyant and all you've got is the fact that my guy used to deliver quahogs to the place where Iannuzzi was killed. Hell, didn't you know Doyle worked a mile away from where she was found. No jury's gonna put my guy away for life with that kind of evidence."

There was a momentary pause as the reality of the weakness of his case hit home. The DA smiled thinly, as if he already knew about Doyle's previous place of employment.

"Am I missing something here?" the defense lawyer wanted to know as they walked into the courtroom.

Seated at the prisoner's dock, and dressed in a short-sleeved, white-on-white shirt with dark blue pants, Paradiso stared at the prosecutor and mouthed the words "fuck youse" as the two lawyers stood at the podium's microphone.

"What can we do for ya today, gentlemen?" Hizzoner asked as the large courtroom grew very still.

It was showtime for all the clerks, court officers, defense attorneys, prosecutors, and defendants whose cases had yet to be called. There was an energy about the place — the uncertainty and excitement that attach to any murder case.

"Good morning, Your Honor. It's good to see you." The defense attorney smiled. "I'm here on an arraignment with my client, Mr. Paradiso. The DA wants him held. He's looking for $150,000 in bail. I'm requesting that he be released on seventy-five hundred cash surety."

"What do you say, Mr. Burke," the gray-haired judge asked as he stared out over the rim of his glasses. "Is there any history of defaults on the defendant's record?"

"No, Judge, there isn't, but there's a prior history of a similar offense in 1974. He's still on parole for the attempted rape of a nineteen-year-old girl he picked up hitchhiking. The new charges against him carry a life sentence. I am asking the court to have him surrendered for violation of his parole. I believe he's a risk to flee if he remains out on bail. As you know, there's no statutory right to bail for a murder case," the DA added quickly. "In this case, the defendant was the last person to have seen the victim alive. She was a twenty-year-old woman who had previously been at a wedding reception, at which the defendant was also present."

"What was the bail in the previous case?" the judge asked both lawyers.

"A hundred bucks," Cipoletta said.

For the next several minutes the two lawyers argued over the risk of flight, Paradiso's parole status, and the lack of prior defaults. After each positive comment by Lenny's lawyer, Paradiso would smile at the prosecutor, nod in agreement with his attorney, and then extend the middle finger of his right hand downward to the side of his leg.

"Your Honor, my client is a thirty-nine-year-old owner of a wholesale fish business. He has a conviction in 1974 and has been on parole for four years without incident. He has been granted permission to travel throughout New England, Canada, and the western and southern states for his wholesale fish business, without incident. Although he was a suspect in this investigation, there was no attempt to flee. His girlfriend's father is a retired naval officer and is willing to post the deed to his real estate, which has no mortgage."

"They won't take real estate, Mr. Cipoletta," the judge reminded Lenny's lawyer.

"I just want to add that throughout this investigation my client has maintained his innocence. There are no statements, no confessions, and nothing on record to indicate Mr. Paradiso is going to flee or has confessed to this crime."

When the two lawyers had exhausted their energy, as well as their arguments, the judge turned his attention to the clerk seated in front of him, and without further comment to either side said, "I am setting bail at seventy-five hundred dollars cash."

Before the judge could finish, Lenny smiled warmly and once again mouthed "fuck youse" to the DA.

The Quahog had more than enough money to make bail.

"And please remand Mr. Paradiso to the custody of the Charles Street Jail, where he is to be held on a parole surrender violation," Hizzoner continued, letting the air out of Lenny's tires.

— — —

The DA was headed back to his office when he spotted his mentor standing by the bank of elevators on the sixth floor of the courthouse.

"Tim, do you have a moment?" the first assistant district attorney said to the young prosecutor.

The two men walked silently down the narrow corridor and through the wood-framed door marked PAUL K. LEARY on frosted glass. He gestured to the lawyer to have a seat and said softly, "I just read the grand jury transcript on the Iannuzzi case. The Essex County DA called. He's not real happy you took their case to the grand jury here in Suffolk County."

"Mr. Leary," as he was known throughout the DA's office, was a kind, quiet, dignified, and religious man. In the five years he had known him, the young lawyer had never heard Mr. Leary swear, let alone raise his voice. The first assistant was prone to using antiquated expressions like *Jiminy Cricket* or *Jeepers creepers* when he felt the rare need to spice up his dialogue.

Today was different.

"Jesus Christ, just what the hell are you doing, Tim?" Mr. Leary continued, his voice rising twenty decibels.

"Mr. Leary, we've got jurisdiction. We measured it. The victim's sister called me and asked me to take a look at the place where Marie was killed. The case was three years old. It was dead in the water. I dug up some stuff on Paradiso. Where he worked. What he's like. He's the killer, I know he did it. It fits his pattern. He tried to rape and strangle another girl in 1974 —"

"You still shoulda called the DA's office in Essex and told him first before you went to the grand jury here. Besides, it looks like an awfully thin case. You've got no eyewitnesses and no admissions from Paradiso that he did it.

How you gonna prove it? And none of that stuff comes in from the '74 case either," the first assistant told the young DA.

"I know, I know. I just heard the same thing from Paradiso's lawyer," the prosecutor responded dejectedly. "At least the judge held him on the parole violation."

"Look, Tim, I'm not trying to be critical, but sometimes you get too emotionally involved in these cases. You spent over a year chasing Whitey Bulger with the state police, and we got nothing to show for it. No arrests, no indictments, not even a single interception of a conversation with him. Bulger's still out on the street. The DA took a lot of heat on that investigation."

"I know he did, but every wiretap we put in place was compromised. Someone tipped Bulger off every time we had one of his places bugged."

The first assistant leaned forward and smiled. "Look, all I'm sayin' is that you need to take it a little slower. I give you a free rein here, but you can't be goin' out on some wild goose chase that we're not gonna be able to prove. Besides, I thought you were working on that triple homicide."

The older man's voice wavered at the end. He knew he had struck a nerve.

The young lawyer sat silently trying to gather his thoughts to respond.

He couldn't.

Crestfallen from his conversation with Mr. Leary, the lawyer returned to Room 603, where the radio always played, and stared at the tattered gray folder. The Commodores were singing "Oh No" as he opened the file, closed his eyes, and once again tried to visualize how the triple murder had been committed. Pictures passed through his mind one after the other, like freeze frames from a horror movie.

The grainy "film" began outside the house on Jacobs Street, where a broken wooden screen was propped beneath the open bedroom window, lace curtains lifted by the cold December breeze. The DA could see an unknown man with a knife inside the house. The baby in a crib. Two young children hiding. Their mother, fighting desperately to save her family. A hand over her mouth. The stranger reaching for the knife. The piercing, unheard screams. The sound of footsteps coming down the hallway, closer toward the children. Their final moments, knowing they were about to die. A package under the Christmas tree with a drop of the killer's blood.

The lawyer went over the information piecemeal, trying to understand how the killer's blood had been left at the scene. How could he trace that drop of blood back to its source? The killer had to have been injured during the murders. All the victims had been stabbed with the same type of knife. No murder weapon was found at the scene. The intruder had to have killed the mother first and then the children.

Could Basilisa have hurt her assailant? How? Maybe she got the knife from the killer and turned it on him. More likely she had the knife first, and he took it from her after he was cut. That must be why the killer bled the drop of blood on the Christmas present beneath the tree. Basilisa must have cut him.

That explains his blind raging fury — why he stabbed her so many times. If Basilisa cut the bastard bad enough, maybe he went to a hospital. Maybe the killer went to a hospital, the lawyer repeated silently.

The thoughts came one after another until his eyes opened wide and he spoke aloud to no one but himself, "Wait a minute, one of the neighbors the cops interviewed went to the hospital that night. He had a cut on his arm, too. That can't be a coincidence. But the guy said he was in another part of the city when he got hurt."

It was another exercise in homicide Ping-Pong. The lawyer weighed and sifted the information until his brain actually hurt.

"The welfare checks were delivered in the mail earlier that day. The bedroom was ransacked. The killer broke into the house to steal the money. It's the neighbor. He lives a couple of doors away. That's why he has to kill the kids after he kills their mother. He's afraid they'll be able to identify him."

The DA wanted to scream as the possibilities began to unfold before him.

"The baby in the crib was only six months old, too young to identify the guy. That's why he doesn't kill the baby."

It all seemed so simple, so basic. How had he missed this scenario nine months earlier, when he'd first found the tattered gray file? The lawyer's mind shifted to the neighbor's statement about being injured elsewhere in the city. Maybe he'd jumped to the wrong conclusion.

It was early afternoon the following day when he called the Homicide Unit in South Boston.

"Hey, John, what the hell was the name of the guy that lived a coupla doors down from the triple on Jacobs Street? The one that told us he got the cut on his arm somewhere else the same night?"

"Gomes, Antonio Gomes. Why, ya got somethin'?"

"Yeah, I'll tell ya what I'm thinkin'. I'm thinkin' maybe I should contact all the hospitals in Boston and find out exactly how many other people were treated for a knife wound the same night of the triple," the young prosecutor said, searching for a measure of approval in the older detective's voice.

"Okay, what's that gonna buy ya," the man with two bad knees said skeptically.

"If I can narrow it down to a few possible suspects, that might give me probable cause to get a search warrant for a sample of Gomes's blood, compare it with the blood on the Christmas package." He was struggling to recall the constitutionality of forcing a suspect to provide a blood sample. He knew it was rarely done.

"I don't think we ever did anything like that before, did we? But man, that would be incredible if you can get a search warrant for his blood," Doris said with renewed enthusiasm.

"Well, the law against self-incrimination applies only to oral statements made by a suspect. Gomes can refuse to answer questions about what he did or where he was, but the law says he has to produce a sample of his own hair, or his handwriting, so why should it prevent me from being able to get a sample of his blood?"

"Kid, I gotta tell ya, ya never cease to amaze me. Where the hell did ya dream that one up?"

"I was out runnin' last night. I always think better when I'm runnin'," the DA explained.

Rejuvenated by the possibilities, the lawyer quickly drew up a list of all of the hospitals and clinics in the metropolitan Boston area. He quickly addressed a letter on the District Attorney's stationery and sent it to the keeper of records for each facility. The letter requested the medical records of each person treated for a stab wound on December 5, 1979, the night of the triple homicide.

Massachusetts General Hospital, Beth Israel, Boston City, the Brigham, the Deaconess, Tufts New England, the Faulkner, the Baptist, the Leahy Clinic, the Carney, the Lynn, Saint E's, Lawrence General, Quincy City, Newton Wellesley, Children's Hospital, and Mount Auburn got their letters, as did all the smaller clinics and treatment centers in the Boston area.

It took more than a month to get all the responses.

34: The Steaming Kettle

"Let's take another ride up to the Pines River, Drew." The DA and his friend stood finishing their chowder in the cramped quarters of the Steaming Kettle.

This particular "chowdah" was a hometown classic, served piping hot in a plastic bowl, with a plastic spoon and a cellophane bag of tiny oyster crackers that when released floated daintily atop. The "Kettle" was located kitty-corner to the courthouse, across Tremont Street, adjacent to Boston City Hall. Its floor-to-ceiling windows afforded an open view of the broad expanse of brick yard that fronted the Government Center MBTA trolley stop and City Hall. Outside, above the doorway, a huge golden kettle percolated real steam into the sky as it beckoned passersby inside. The Kettle was the daily mixing pot for the courthouse regulars during their lunch hour.

Drew nodded, agreeing to the lawyer's suggestion. "Any particular reason you want to go back there?"

"Yeah, frankly, I just don't think it's a coincidence that the Webster girl's pocketbook winds up across the road from where Iannuzzi was killed."

Drew gulped a large spoonful of chowder. "Whoa, where the hell did that come from?"

"I'll tell ya. Right after Paradiso's arraignment, I pulled his entire criminal history. There was an old case, back about twelve years ago. I got the police report and the minutes from the grand jury. The Quahog picked up a girl in the Combat Zone and raped her. Her name was Florence White. She wouldn't testify against him. The grand jury didn't indict him, but it still tells me there's a pattern to this guy."

"She's a hooker, of course she's not gonna go to the cops."

"Exactly, that's what Paradiso thought. He made the mistake of letting her go, thinking she wouldn't go to the police. He learned from that mistake. That's why he was gonna kill Connie Porter. The Andover cops said the same thing. If they hadn't caught him in the act, he woulda strangled her. She woulda been just another unsolved murder."

The trooper leaned closer, weighing each word carefully.

"Drew, I don't think Iannuzzi was the first or the last for him. There's a common theme to all of these women. It's the same thing with the Porter girl. Once he has them in his car, he's got control over them. Whether it's a hitchhiker, or a hooker from the Zone, they all become vulnerable once he gets them in his car." The lawyer paused and then continued cautiously, testing his theory out loud for the first time.

"I think he's a serial killer."

Drew didn't react.

"Okay, what if you're right, what the hell does that mean for the Webster girl?" the trooper finally responded in a calm voice.

The lawyer hesitated again. "I know it sounds weird, but Paradiso has a psychological link to Conley and Daggett's. He killed Iannuzzi there in August '79. Two years later, nothing's happened on her case. He thinks he's beat it. Webster disappears in November '81. Three days later they find her wallet on the Lynn Marsh Road. It's almost like he wants to be caught. He's leaving clues behind for someone to put together. Why, of all places, does Joan Webster's handbag wind up on some deserted causeway directly across from the lobster pound?"

Before the trooper could respond, the DA turned to face his friend.

"I think he killed her, Drew. I think Paradiso killed Joan Webster."

"Hey, didn't the first assistant tell ya not to be goin' off on another wild goose chase?" the trooper said, trying to protect his friend. "Why don't you just focus on the triple?"

There was an uneasy strain to the conversation as they both struggled to fill the sudden dead air between them.

"Can you at least get me the reports on the Webster investigation so I can take a look at them? And I *am* focused on the triple. I just sent out a request for medical records on the case. I wanna find out how many other stabbings there were in Boston that night."

"Okay, I'm sorry. I'll take care of getting the reports on Webster. We have some of them at our office at the airport. I'll talk to my sergeant about getting the rest of the reports from Saugus."

"Is Carmen Tammaro still in charge of the detective unit at the airport?" the lawyer asked. "Didn't he grow up in the North End? Maybe he knows Paradiso."

"You know 'Carmenooch.' He knows everybody," the trooper answered. "If he doesn't know Paradiso personally, he'll know someone who does. I'll talk to him when I get back to the office."

The two men shook hands beneath the huge kettle outside the restaurant and headed their separate ways. The lawyer returned to his office just as Sinatra was beginning "Summer Wind" on the radio. He lingered there, listening, until a phone call interrupted his thoughts. It was Carmen Tammaro.

"Hey, Carmenooch, don't you have any Irish troopers left at the airport anymore?" the lawyer asked.

"You're young enough, Tim. You can still take the state police entrance exam. The job needs some more smaht lawyers," the head of the detective unit said, laughing. "Are you still running every day?"

"Yeah, it's a struggle, but I've been doin' about thirty-five miles a week. The marathon is only nine months away. How 'bout you?"

"Naw, twenty-six miles in one day is too far for me, but I'll look for ya at Heartbreak Hill."

The two men had met a couple of years earlier when a drug mule by the name of Thomas Barnes Preston from Marshfield, Massachusetts, tried to transport a suitcase with two hundred forty thousand dollars in cash through an airport security checkpoint. When asked whose money it was, Preston told the trooper he didn't know. Carmen called the prosecutor to find out what could be done before he let Preston board his flight to Miami.

"Let the mule go, but seize the money and I'll file a petition to have it forfeited as the proceeds of a drug sale," the DA advised the head of detectives. Three months later the courier disappeared and a superior court judge ordered the cash forfeited as laundered drug money.

Recently promoted, Carmen Tammaro was just over six feet tall, handsome, with salt-and-pepper hair and a bright smile. His personality endeared him to everyone who met him. He blended well with both sides of the law enforcement equation. Born and raised in the North End of Boston, Carmen was known and respected by the Anguilo crime family that operated from within the narrow streets of the Italian community. He knew everyone in the North End — if he didn't know you, you didn't live there.

A tough street kid who was no stranger to the cops or the courts, Carmen spent his early years accompanying his father with his pushcart to the open-air market on Blackstone Street. Melons, fruits, tomatoes, vegetables, candy, and cookies were the order of the day for the elder Tammaro, a strict disciplinarian who worried his son would be led astray by the lure of the streets. At sixteen Carmen was taken into custody by Boston police for a fight that led to a near riot on a moonlight cruise ship in Boston Harbor. When the boat docked at the pier, the police wagon was waiting, and so was his father.

"You heard what Judge Forte said the last time you were in court," the elder Tammaro said to his son. "The judge told you the next time you come back to his court to bring your toothbrush. He said you're goin' to jail. I'm not gonna let that happen to no son of mine."

One week later Carmen Tammaro was enrolled in the Cardinal Farley Academy in upstate New York, a rigid military school run by the Christian Brothers of Ireland. It was a turning point in his life.

"Andy said you're interested in the Quahog," Carmen offered without being asked.

"Is there any background about him that could help us?"

"Yeah, he grew up in the North End around the same time I did. Everyone called him the Quahog because he used to sell fish from a little pushcart during the Feasts of the Saints. No one trusted him. He wasn't too smart as I recall. Sort of a *deez* and *doze* kinda guy, ya know what I mean? Ya never really knew what he was thinkin'. He was kinda timid, believe it or not, soft-spoken, low-key." The head of the detective unit paused for a moment, then added, "There was somethin' that happened awhile ago you might be interested in, though. The word around was that Lenny grabbed a young woman from the North End and supposedly pulled a gun on her. I heard she was very pretty and very smart. She talked her way out of it. Believe it or not, she told Lenny he turned her on and as soon as she said that, he couldn't get it up. He let her go."

"Really, that's kinda weird," the DA responded.

"Yeah, she was also very connected, apparently. Some of the mob guys paid Lenny a visit and 'spoke' to him. They barred him from living in the North End. I think it was Billy Fopiano and a coupla other guys. The Quahog's lucky he isn't on the bottom of Boston Harbor with a pair of cement slippers and a log chain necklace," Carmen stated matter-of-factly.

"Do you think she'll talk to us?" the DA asked, writing as quickly as he could.

"You know how things are in the North End, she may be reluctant to go public," the detective replied. "Let me ask around, see what I can come up with."

"Thanks, Carmenooch. If anyone can get her to talk, you can."

"Anything I can do to help, you know that," he responded. "Is he out on bail?"

"No, I got his parole revoked. He's being held at Charles Street."

"Good, that may make it easier to convince her to talk," the detective said. "Lenny's probably a lot safer in Charles Street Jail than he would be back out on the street now that Fopiano's guys know he killed another woman. They're not going to be happy with him after they booted him outta the North End. Everybody's got a code, y'know."

"Let her know that there's no plea bargaining in this case," the prosecutor told him. "If we convict him, he's goin' to jail for the rest of his life."

"Listen, I read all the reports and I talked to Andy. Iannuzzi is no easy case. You could indict the boyfriend and probably get a conviction on him easier than you can Paradiso," Carmen said with half a laugh.

"You're right," the lawyer said. "The only problem is, the boyfriend didn't kill Iannuzzi, Paradiso did. If this girl from the North End talks to us, I'll file a motion to have all of these women testify at trial to show that there's a pattern to Paradiso's conduct, sort of a behavioral fingerprint."

"That would be a first," remarked the detective. "I'll get back to you in a week or so. Keep up the running."

"Thanks again, Carmen. I'm actually goin' out to run right now."

35: Electrophoresis

Only one person in the city of Boston was treated for a stab wound on the night of the three murders at 12 Jacobs Street: Antonio Gomes, who lived at 24 Jacobs Street.

One of several suspects in the triple homicide, Gomes arrived at the emergency room at Boston City Hospital at approximately 7 PM on the night of the murder. He was treated for a stab wound to his right forearm and a badly bruised right hand. Gomes told the doctors he had sustained the injuries during a fight at an MBTA trolley stop in Jamaica Plain; he was holding his five-year-old son, he added, when the incident happened.

Two uniformed Boston police officers, Ronnie Erickson and Frank Evans, reported to the hospital upon notification of the stabbing. Arriving at BCH shortly before 10 PM, neither officer was aware of the triple homicide earlier that evening. They took a brief statement from Gomes, who seemed surprised to see them.

Gomes told them a black man with a large knife stabbed him in an attempted robbery. He gave the officers uncertain answers and was anxious to leave the emergency room, saying that someone was picking him up. The officers went to the location where Gomes said the assault took place, but were unable to locate either a weapon or any blood. Later that evening, the two officers heard a news broadcast about the murders and notified homicide detectives about their encounter with Gomes at BCH.

The next day three detectives from the Boston police went to Gomes's home and questioned him about the previous night. Sergeant Bob Bird, together with Detectives Jay Green and Warren DeLauria, spoke to Gomes and his girlfriend Donna Dailey in the living room of Gomes's home. His story differed from what he'd told the uniformed officers at the hospital only hours earlier. This time Gomes said a white man had attacked him in a racial incident.

When questioned about the three murders, Gomes told the detectives, "If you want my ideas on this thing next door, I'll tell you right now those Puerto Ricans are all fucking each other. They're doing their relatives and everyone else."

Two days later the same three detectives returned to Gomes's home and talked to him once again about his injury on the night of December 5. Gomes removed the bandage and showed the detectives the wound. "See, it's only a scratch, that report I made to the police? It never happened. I cut myself."

A minute later Gomes changed his story again.

"I didn't cut myself. I had a fight with my girl and she stabbed me," he told the detectives, nodding in the direction of his girlfriend, Donna, standing nearby. Then suddenly, as the detectives listened, Gomes blurted out, "I hate those fucking people anyway. Now get the fuck out of my house."

The investigation of Antonio Gomes essentially ended that day with the slamming of the door behind the detectives as they walked down the front porch steps of 24 Jacobs Street. It was three days after the murders. A short distance away, a young father struggled as he made the final funeral arrangements for the burial of his family.

Thirty-two months later it all seemed clear to the prosecutor. In hindsight, he knew it wasn't a coincidence that Gomes had been the only person in the city treated for a stab wound that night. Gomes's proximity to the victims' home, his contradictory statements about his injuries, his remarks about hating "those fucking people" — everything led the DA to believe Gomes was the killer. It was like the unveiling of a portrait. What was hidden was now seen. Knowing who committed the crime, however, was very different from being able to prove it beyond a reasonable doubt. A jury would expect much more than just conjecture on a case of this magnitude.

It was early August 1982 when detectives Mark Madden and Tom Cashman walked into the Homicide Unit and asked for the prosecutor.

"Tim, we just got your call about the search warrant for Gomes's blood. You actually think the judge will order him to give us a sample?" Cashman asked as the two men sat across from the desk with the two large files, one gray, one brown.

The detective turned to his partner. "I don't think we ever did that before did we, Mark?"

"No, I don't think we ever did," Madden replied. He smiled at the assistant district attorney and added, "I liked what you called it, a 'vampire' warrant."

"Yeah, I think we got a shot. I spoke to the forensics people at the FBI, they have this new thing they can do with the enzymes and proteins in your blood. They can tell you what the different ones are in your system. Everybody's different," the DA explained. "The FBI's test results have never been introduced in a Massachusetts court, so we'd have to show that their procedure is scientifically reliable before a judge would allow it."

"What's it called?" one of the Amigos asked.

"Electrophoresis. We sent them the bag from the Christmas package to test. They told me the enzymes in the blood on the bag are really quite unusual.

They're only found in 1.2 percent of the population," the lawyer continued. "I have the affidavit drafted to support the search warrant. The doctors are all lined up to do it if the court approves. You guys ready to go?"

There was an electric aura as the three made their way upstairs to the judge's chambers. The stoic jurist pointed to the overstuffed leather chairs surrounding his desk and visually examined the two detectives as they anxiously listened to the prosecutor describe what they were asking the judge to do.

"Let me get this straight, you want me to issue a search warrant for a sample of this Gomes fella's blood to compare with the crime scene blood, is that it?" the man in the black robe said sternly as he began to read the attachments to the application for the warrant.

"Yes, Your Honor, that's exactly what we're asking you to do," the prosecutor replied as the words *another wild goose chase* reverberated in his mind.

Damn it, I should have told Mr. Leary I was gonna do this, the DA thought without changing his facial expression. The elderly judge read each of the fourteen pages attached to the warrant, adjusted his glasses, ran the narrow palm of his right hand over his balding pate, and then read them all again. He took forever.

"Well, I must say this is a highly unusual request, Mr. Burke," the judge intoned flatly as he grimaced at the cops and then the lawyer. "I've been a sitting judge now for well over twenty years. I don't think I've ever quite seen the likes of this warrant."

The DA's mind raced as he considered what his options would be if the warrant was denied.

"However, you have established sufficient probable cause for me to issue the search warrant and that is exactly what I am going to do," the judge continued as he signed on the bottom of the page. "Good day and good luck to you gentlemen."

With that flourish of the pen, the Gomes case became the first in Massachusetts to use electrophoresis to target a killer.

Outside the judge's chambers the three men took turns congratulating one another and shaking hands. Suddenly, Cashman's face went ashen as he turned to the prosecutor. "What'll we do if we get Gomes's blood and it doesn't match?"

The question had a sobering effect as the trio walked silently down the stairs and into the lawyer's office, where they sat without a word, trading looks.

On the radio positioned between the brown and gray files, Jimmy Buffett sang about sponge cake and searching for a lost shaker of salt.

36: Boston City Hospital

"I called BCH. They're all set to take a sample of Gomes's blood and send it to the FBI laboratory for comparison with the blood on the Christmas package," the lawyer told the Three Amigos the next day as they sat in his tiny office on the sixth floor of the courthouse.

Boston City Hospital is the busiest inner-city hospital in the state. Located just off the South East Expressway on Albany Street in the South End, it maintained the largest trauma unit in New England. Many a potential murder became just another serious assault and battery because the victim was lucky enough to get shipped by ambulance to BCH. Gomes had visited BCH on the night of the triple nearly three years earlier. The perp didn't know it yet, but he would be returning there that morning.

"He's gonna think he can talk his way out of this," John Doris said as the trio discussed their options.

"We'll just let him talk," Cashman responded. "He's gonna wet himself when he finds out we got a vampire warrant."

"Call me as soon as the doctor takes his blood," the lawyer said as the three detectives left the office and headed to Jacobs Street.

The trio pulled the dark Crown Vic close to the curb and walked quickly up the stairs to the porch of 24 Jacobs Street. Madden knocked on the door twice, waited, and then knocked again. Four doors away, the unshuttered windows on the porch of 12 Jacobs Street reflected the morning sun back toward the three men as they stood staring at the scene of the murders.

"Yeah, whattya whant?" a woman with rollers in her hair snarled. She opened the front door of the modest house just wide enough for Madden to see a man with a goatee standing some distance behind her.

"Good morning, ma'am. Is Tony home?" Mark Madden said as he held the door with one hand, the warrant in the other, and carefully placed his large black-leather-bound size 11 foot in the door opening.

"Yeah, Tony, it's fer you," the woman screeched loud enough to be heard four doors away.

"Antonio Gomes?" Madden asked as the door opened and the man stepped toward him.

"Yeah, that's me. What the fuck ya want?" Gomes sneered.

"I've got a warrant from the superior court ordering you to provide us with a sample of your blood. We intend to compare your blood with blood evidence seized from your neighbors' home the night they were murdered," Madden answered, pausing long enough to watch the pupils dilate in Gomes's eyes.

Time stood momentarily still as reality settled into the mind of the man with the goatee.

"I want you to come with us to Boston City Hospital. That's what I want, Mr. Gomes. You can do it the easy way, or you can do it the hard way. What's it gonna be?" Madden added without emotion.

There are a few moments in a cop's life that he dearly wishes he could capture on film. This was one.

"I gotta pee first," Gomes said.

"Not right now'" Doris answered as he reached for his cuffs. "We don't want ya gettin' lost."

37: 24 Jacobs Street

It had been two months since the judge in Courtroom 808 issued the search warrant for the blood sample from the resident of 24 Jacobs Street. Every day the three cops and the DA waited and wondered if they had the right suspect. And each day the Three Amigos would make their way to the sixth floor and ask the prosecutor if he had gotten the test results back from the FBI laboratory in Quantico, Virginia. Each day they were met with a "not yet" from the lawyer and then the requisite discussion about their case, their blood evidence, and their likelihood of a conviction. At first the wait was easy. They knew the test would take time. But the longer the process dragged out, the greater their anxiety grew.

It was midmorning in early October when the manila envelope addressed to the DA was unceremoniously left on top of his heavy metal desk by the letter carrier. Postmarked with the insignia of the Federal Bureau of Investigation, it had the weight and texture of importance. The lawyer noticed that his hand was surprisingly steady as he dialed the Three Amigos, waiting for their arrival before opening the sealed tie string flap.

When the moment came, the DA carefully unfolded the letter inside and slowly read the contents to his small audience.

"The FBI electrophoresis test results matched the sample of Antonio Gomes's blood to the drop of blood left at the scene on the Christmas package," the DA told them.

"Oh my God, it was him. It was him," said one of the Amigos. "I'll be damned. He's the son of a bitch that killed the mother and her kids."

— — —

On October 8, 1982, Sergeant John Doris and Detective Tom Cashman returned to Jacobs Street and arrested Antonio Gomes for the murders of Basilisa Melendez and her two children.

It felt good to be able to do something toward resolving the case.

The detectives took Gomes to Area B headquarters in Roxbury, where he was booked, printed, photographed, and given his Miranda warnings. With each step, Gomes sneered and smirked his way through the process with a sense of bravado that came from nearly three years of avoiding detection for an unspeakable crime.

The kid was a punk.

John Doris was a quiet, stoic man. There wasn't a whole lot of pretense or fluff to him. Doris said what he thought and he meant what he said. The Boston police had been his life for nearly twenty-five years. He was just under five foot ten with straight, swept-back silver hair, clear blue eyes, two bad knees, and six children. Two of them wore the same badge as their father. Doris loved his God, his wife, his family, the job, and golf, usually in that order. He never brought work home or home to work. Doris had a great memory for conversations. His mind was better than a Memorex tape.

"Okay, Tony, I just read your Miranda warnings. Is there anything you wanna tell me about the night of the murders?" Doris asked.

"Yeah, man, ya got it all wrong," Gomes began, smiling contemptuously as he spoke. "I worked till two in the afternoon. A couple of my friends picked me up and we drove to my house on Jacobs Street. My girl, Donna, wasn't home, so I walked over to my mother's house and watched TV, right up till the six o'clock news come on Channel 5. So I was there at my mother's the whole fuckin' time."

Gomes told his story in a continuous stream-of-consciousness flow as Doris sat patiently, listening to every word.

"Yeah, man, after the news starts, that reporter guy, Jorge Quiroga, comes on live and interrupts the news. He's doin' a live thing right from the scene of the murders. Talkin' 'bout a woman and two kids just got killed on Jacobs Street. That's when my mother tells me to go check on my girlfriend Donna and her two kids."

As he spoke, Gomes's eyes moved rapidly from side to side. The intensity of his voice increased.

"So I start running from my mother's house through a field and that's when I fell and cut my arm on a piece of glass," he added, pointing to the same area of his arm where he'd previously told police he had been stabbed by a black man with a large knife, then a white man in a racial incident, and then his girlfriend in an argument.

"When I got to my house, I look down the street and I could see the father of them kids on the porch screaming. He was on his knees yelling, 'They've murdered my family. My wife and kids are all dead.'"

Doris asked Gomes why he didn't go to help the father on the porch and where the reporters covering the story had gone, but he already knew the answers.

"I just went inside my house and called a cab to take me to BCH for the cut on my arm," Gomes told Doris blankly.

There was a pause as the punk with the sneer sat rocking back and forth in his chair across the table from the sergeant with two bad knees. He looked straight into the eyes of the homicide detective, waiting for a response to his story.

"I ain't buying it, kid, and I don't think a jury will, either," Doris said calmly as he stood from his chair and left the killer alone with his thoughts.

The next day, at just past six in the evening, Antonio Gomes took a cord from the lining of the mattress in his cell, fashioned it into a loop with a knot on one end, and placed the noose around his neck just beneath the hairline of his goatee. Gomes stared briefly at the narrow scar on his arm, lashed the cord to the cell wall, stepped off from his cot, and hung himself.

Gomes's feet dangled as the garrote slowly tightened, sucking the air from his lungs and brain. He was unconscious in a matter of seconds. A faint tint of blue colored his neck and face.

He would have been dead in less than three minutes.

Outside the cell, Officer Paul Bankowski was passing by when he discovered the unconscious prisoner suspended listlessly with a noose around his neck. Bankowski cut Gomes down from his self-imposed death sentence and resuscitated him.

The next day, the punk with the sneer was transferred to Charles Street Jail and held without bail.

38: Charles Street Jail

Robert L. "Bobby" Bond was a two-time loser.

More than a decade earlier, Bond was convicted of manslaughter, did his time, got paroled, and several months later was indicted for first-degree murder.

On a crisp autumn day in 1981, the body of Mary Foreman, a forty-two-year-old community activist, was discovered in the storage area of a building on Walnut Street, not far from the Beacon Street side of Boston Common. She had been shot twice in the head.

Three months later Bobby Bond was indicted for Foreman's murder and held without bail. Bond's trial for the murder of Mary Foreman was scheduled to begin in December 1982.

Charles Street Jail is located on the banks of its namesake river, half a mile from the Suffolk County Courthouse. Built in 1850, the jail was one of the oldest in the country. Constructed of large granite blocks and shaped like a crucifix, the jail's architecture was intended to reflect an enlightened change in attitude toward prisoners espoused by its designer, the Reverend Louis Dwight.

Inside, the tiers of crowded cells led into a central octagonal area that housed the jail's support facilities and guard rooms. Outside, a high, thick redbrick wall surgically separated the jail from nearby Massachusetts General Hospital, the original site of Harvard's Medical School. Also known as the Suffolk County Jail, "Charles Street" now housed more than 250 unhappy prisoners, double- and sometimes triple-bunked in four tiers of archaic bedlam.

A day before his trial was to begin, Bobby Bond was transferred to Charles Street from Walpole prison and eventually assigned to cell number 31. Five doors away, Lenny the Quahog sat, awaiting trial for the murder of Marie Iannuzzi.

Paradiso had met Bond seven years earlier at Walpole while doing time for the attempted rape of Connie Porter.

Darkly black, with a shaved head and a deep, low resonant voice, Bond was an intimidating specimen of physical strength who could dead-lift more than four hundred pounds. Paradiso admired Bond and frequently sought him out during their free time at the jail. He enjoyed bragging to Bond about his exploits with women and his plans to frame David Doyle for the murder of Marie Iannuzzi.

Theirs was a kinship of the damned, an uncommon bond forged from the unholy and unbridled acceptance of murder as ordinary.

On December 13, 1982, a jury on the eighth floor of the Suffolk County Courthouse convicted Bobby Bond for the second-degree murder of Mary Foreman.

When Bond was returned to his cell from court that day, the sympathetic large man with the potbelly, bad back, and poor grammar was there to greet him.

"Hey, Bobby, youse got fucked, man. That fuckin' jury never shoulda hooked ya. Was the jurors all white or what?"

Bond eyed the Fat Man and said nothing, simply nodding without expression there on the third tier of Charles Street Jail. Bond never spoke much and felt even less like talking today. Christmas was just twelve days away, and he knew he was going to spend the rest of his natural life in a prison.

"I got rid of my first lawyer. His name was Cipoletta. I got me two new lawyers now. Both of 'em used to be DAs. I had to give 'em my antique car, a '39 Oldsmobile, and one of my boats to get 'em ta represent me. I told 'em Doyle's the one that killed Iannuzzi. They both fuckin' bought it, hook, line, and sinker. My new lawyers told me they're gonna keep that rat fuck Doyle on the stand for six fuckin' days if they got to, just to make him look bad to the jurors. The fuckin' kid never even went to the bitch's funeral," the Fat Man said, gathering steam.

"Man, whatchu gonna put it on this Doyle dude fo'?" Bond reluctantly asked. "This ain't no parkin' ticket you talkin' 'bout."

There was a near-sexual frenzy to the Fat Man's words as he clenched and unclenched his hands into two large fists. "He's a fuckin' punk, man. He had a fight with the bitch at the wedding. He got scratches on his fuckin' hands and everythin'. Fuck him. He jus' fuckin' left her there."

As if he were a priest in a confessional, Bond simply nodded and listened as Paradiso continued in full voice.

"My girl give her a ride that night. She dropped da bitch off at this place in East Boston called the Cardinal's Nest. Later on, I took my girl to her place in Revere, and I cut me a beeline straight back to that fuckin' bar. You shoulda seen me runnin' all of dem fuckin' red lights to get back before some other fucker picked the bitch up."

"How you get her outta there wid you?" Bond said as he watched the Fat Man lick a small curl of saliva from the side of his mouth.

"I told the bitch I'd give her a ride ta Saugus ta 'pologize for the scene she made at the fuckin' reception. But I took her up ta this place where I used ta work outta instead. Bobby, you shoulda seen her. She had this like, ah, like red dress on. Sorta like a bodysuit. Nice tits, with a scarf around her neck." Lenny closed his eyes briefly, dragged a thick finger under the width of his nose, and murmured a long "hmm-mmm" before he spoke again.

"You shoulda seen her body jumpin' when I was chokin' the shit outta her. It was like she had the fuckin' hiccups. She passed out and I fucks her. All of a sudden she come to and started screamin'. So I killed the fuckin' whore and tossed her body. I torched the car I was driving that night. It was my girl's car. It had the bitch's blood in it. The cops never found the fuckin' car." He smiled at the black man with the shaved head.

"They got nobody who seen you?" Bond asked. The two men stood outside the cell hunched over a rail, their arms extended forward and hands clasped together as if in prayer.

"Naw, my girl's with me on this. I called her that night after I dumped the bitch on the rocks," the Fat Man replied. "She's gonna testify for me. The cops got someone seen the fuckin' whore leave with me. But my girl's gonna say she's in the car waiting outside for me when the bitch left the bar. She gonna say she saw her jus' walk down the fuckin' street. My girl's gonna say we left together and she was with me having fuckin' tea at my apartment. Bobby, can you fuckin' believe it?" Laughing, the Fat Man said, "That rat fuck Doyle's gonna take the whole rap."

"What's her name?" Bond asked as the two began to walk down the metal gangway toward the lunch room.

"You mean my girl or the whore?" Lenny responded. "My girl's name's Candy. The bitch's name is Iannuzzi, Marie Iannuzzi. But wait, Bobby, she ain't the only fuckin' one. I got me lots more to tell ya."

In a nearby cell, the sound of Elvis singing "Blue Christmas" on a tiny transistor radio filled a brief void of silence as the two men walked slowly past a lone prisoner seated inside on his bunk.

The large black man with the shaved head looked into the cell and unexpectedly turned back.

"That mothahfuckah did a mother and two little kids," Bond told his companion as he spat onto the cell's floor and glared at the inmate seated inside, daring him to respond.

"I hope he fucked her pussy good before he did her." The Fat Man rubbed his crotch with his right hand.

"You fuckin' sick, Lenny, you know that? Man, you jus' fuckin' sick. You got no code, man," Bond said with disgust just before he turned to the lone prisoner on the bunk and bellowed, "Yeah, mothahfuckah, I'm talkin' to you. You wanna piece of me?"

Inside the cell, Antonio Gomes sat alone on his bunk. He looked up at the large black man with the shaved head and shook his head.

On Christmas Eve, Bobby Bond called his wife collect from Charles Street Jail and wished her a merry Christmas. Then he returned to cell number 31 and began to write a nine-page letter to a prosecutor in the Homicide Unit.

It was a good letter.

Like the year before, Christmas Day 1982 wasn't very white in Boston. It was rainy and foggy at fifty-five degrees with thick banks of ominous gray clouds along the horizon. There was a spattering of fine sleet with some snow during the week, but as quickly as it came, it went.

Lenny stood on the crowded third tier of the jail where the two wings came together to form the shape of a crucifix. He looked out the barred windows toward the Charles River. He thought about the *Mala Femmena* and all the times he had spent moored off the Boston Esplanade watching the fireworks on the Fourth of July. This wasn't his first Christmas in jail, but Lenny seethed with anger knowing he might never be outside the walls again.

He wanted to kill the DA.

He sat on the metal bench and slowly pulled out a series of Lucky Strike matches from an oversized pack. With a flourish, he lit them one by one, holding them between his thick thumb and stubby, cigarette-yellowed forefingers. He enjoyed watching them burn down to a red-coaled ember, blistering the callused skin of the fingers on his right hand. Lenny loved the feel of the searing hot pain and the cold rushes it fed to his brain. Lenny wanted that DA to feel his pain.

Like a demented music box wound too tight, he played the same refrain over and over. "That mothahfuckin' Burke." He spat at the window and watched the thick saliva drain to the bottom of the pane.

The Quahog ambled slowly toward the family room and had a visit from Candy. He groused about how much his two new lawyers were costing him, ate the seafood and lobster stew she'd prepared for his Christmas dinner, returned to his cell, and took a three-hour nap. When he woke up, Lenny walked past cell 31 and wished Bobby Bond a merry Christmas.

Bobby couldn't talk. He was busy writing and seemed in a bad mood.

In Glen Ridge, New Jersey, Terry Webster placed Joan's favorite Christmas ornament on the Douglas fir closest to the angel at the top of the tree. She silently whispered a prayer and then carefully laid out a place setting at the table for her missing daughter.

The plain white envelope sat waiting on top of the radio between the tattered gray and the dark brown files.

It was addressed to the young prosecutor at the courthouse in Pemberton Square. It was written in angled block printing, with the unfamiliar name of Robert L. Bond on a return address in the upper left hand corner. A thin strip of cellophane tape sealed the flap, preventing the thick contents of the letter from spilling out.

January 5, 1983, was a Wednesday. It was an average winter day following a standard New Year's holiday weekend. As the lawyer began to read the letter, though, he felt his heart begin to race.

The author identified himself and provided graphic details about how Marie Iannuzzi's killer had lured her into his car and then strangled her in an obscure location on the Lynn Marsh Road. It was as if the author had been a passenger in the killer's car, a silent witness to a murder; an unrelenting human video camera recording the horror for all to see and know at a later date of his own choosing.

The letter was cold, clinical, and calculating in convincing detail.

The author knew much, much more about the Iannuzzi murder than either the prosecutor or the police. He knew the killer's alibi and the names and testimony of the defendant's witnesses, the strategy of the two new defense attorneys and their fee. He knew about the burning of a car to hide blood evidence, and about the killer's plan to frame another suspect, David Doyle.

The writer knew names, dates, times, places, and specifics that no person other than the killer could have told him. This was more than just the *who* and *how* of the murder. The letter tracked the core of the killer's mind-set: his emotions, his twisted sense of humor, his contempt for women. It was all there in angled block print.

It was breathtaking to read, to finally understand what was once only speculation and guesswork. The words bled from the pages as the lawyer read in horrifying detail of the last moments of a young woman's life, the discarding of her body on the rocks, and the conspiracy to shelter the killer from accountability.

"I gotta call Drew," the lawyer said to himself, reaching for the phone.

It seemed an eternity before the familiar voice answered.

The DA tried to sound calm as he began to speak, but it didn't work. "Drew,

I just got a letter from some guy at Charles Street Jail. Paradiso told him all about how he killed Marie. He says he's willing to testify."

"Wait, wait a minute. What'd you say?" Drew asked, sounding incredulous.

"Yeah, you heard me right. His name is Bobby Bond. He's an inmate. They knew each other when they were in Walpole. Paradiso told him everything about how he killed Marie. He says he's willing to testify," the lawyer repeated as he tried to slow the cadence of his voice.

"Holy shit," the ponytailed trooper said. "We gotta get this guy out of Charles Street before someone tries to kill him."

"We gotta have him take a polygraph to make sure he's on the money. Can you set that up?"

"Carmen'll get Jack Nasuti from the Polygraph Unit to test him. Jack's the best there is. If Bond's telling the truth we'll know it," the trooper said.

"Listen, Drew, there's something else that Bond talks about." The lawyer caught his breath as the words began to form in his mind. "It's all here in his letter. Can you and Carmen come over here? I want you to read the rest of it."

It took only fifteen minutes for the two troopers to walk into the tiny office on the sixth floor of the courthouse. It took more time for the pair to read the nine-page letter from Bobby Bond.

They were stunned.

"You were right. It wasn't just Marie. Paradiso killed Joan, too." Drew calmly put the last page of the letter down on the cluttered desk.

Bond's letter detailed information that wasn't publicly known about either woman's case. The letter described not only how Paradiso had killed Marie, but also how he'd murdered Joan Webster on November 28, 1981.

The three men dissected each line and each word from the letter and applied it to what they currently knew about Joan's disappearance.

"Bond says Paradiso told him she came in on a flight from New York," the lawyer began. "He could have confused the words *Newark* with *New York*."

"Okay, but how does he get her in the car with him?" Drew asked as he mentally ticked through a list of options.

"What about a cab? There's a ton of gypsy cabs at the airport. Anybody can rent them for a night."

"That's a perfect setup for him. He's a chicken hawker," Carmen added. "Driving a cab's easy cash money and he gets to play the airport with all the single women coming in. He looks harmless, but the airport's just like the bus terminal."

"Exactly. And there were a couple of people who saw a white cab stopped on the Lynn Marsh Road that same night. Right where Joan's wallet and handbag were found," the lawyer explained.

"You're right; she disappeared the same night as the Great Lynn Fire. They had all the roads blocked off goin' into Lynn from Revere," Drew said.

"There was a white ITOA taxi seen by two different witnesses at two different times on both sides of the road near Conley and Daggett's. The first time was around one and then just before three in the morning. That's more than a coincidence, don't you think?" the DA added.

The trio continued to evaluate the letter, taking turns reading sections and then comparing their thoughts as the radio played. Each section of the letter brought more questions than answers. At times the conversation seemed disturbingly dispassionate.

"Listen to this: Paradiso tells Bond he got Joan aboard the *Mala,* then raped her and beat her to death with one of the whiskey bottles he kept on the boat," Drew read from the letter. "Then Lenny says he took her body 'way out,' dumped it, and sank the *Mala* a coupla days later to hide the blood."

"Her flight landed just after ten thirty. It took maybe twenty minutes for her to get her bag and grab a cab. What is it, maybe ten more minutes in traffic to Pier 7?" Carmen said as both men nodded.

"That only gives Lenny two hours to get Joan on the boat and kill her. Take her body out in the harbor, sink it, and then make it up to the Lynn Marsh Road by one o'clock if he's driving the white cab the witnesses see there," Drew said.

"But what if 'way out' isn't in the harbor," the lawyer began. Both detectives stopped reading and raised their heads.

"There was a bad storm that night with forty-mile-an-hour gusts blowing. That's why the Lynn fire was so bad, because of the wind. Paradiso's boat's too small. He's not going out in the harbor in that kind of wind. If he's driving a cab, maybe he planned on taking Joan's body to the same place where he killed Iannuzzi. It's a clue to his identity. Maybe Paradiso's trying to leave a clue. That's why he tosses Joan's wallet there. He can't do anything with Joan's body because there's too many cars on the Lynn Marsh Road that night. The traffic's diverted because of the fire. He has to get rid of the body, and he's still got her small suitcase. He knows all about the Greyhound bus terminal and the storage lockers there. He stores her bag at the terminal after he gets rid of her body and plans on going back to get it later on. It's like a trophy thing for him, but things get too hot because of all the media. Maybe he thinks we found the suitcase and have the bus terminal staked out waiting for him. That's why the bag never gets claimed and winds up getting sent to the storage facility in New York City."

The lawyer wanted to continue, but there was awkward silence from the two troopers.

"What do you do, stay up all night thinking about this stuff?" Drew asked, turning to Carmen and spinning his right index finger in small circles around the right side of his temple.

"No, I just think I'm beginning to understand this guy's mind," the DA said defensively. "I think about him when I run. It all seems clearer then."

"Well, I think you've been running too far." Drew laughed, adding, "The first thing we gotta do is find his damn boat."

"And the second thing we gotta do is get a search warrant for Weyant's house," Carmen put in as he turned to another section of the letter.

"How come?" the DA and Ponytail said in unison.

"Because Bond says Paradiso hurt his hand during the struggle with Joan on the *Mala* that night. Lenny told Bond he's gonna claim a .50-caliber shell blew up in his hand to explain how he hurt his hand. Paradiso told Bond the .50-caliber shell is still in Weyant's house in Revere."

"That's a great idea," Drew said.

"How does this black guy from Roxbury know there's a .50-caliber shell sitting in Weyant's house in Revere unless Paradiso told him? That's great corroboration if we can find it there."

Their thoughts came in rapid succession, like dominoes falling one after the other.

"Maybe we should check out the hospitals and see if Lenny got any medical treatment around the time Joan disappeared," the DA offered.

"Hey, you've already got a list of every hospital in the Boston area," Drew reminded the lawyer.

"Exactly. We can do the same thing here as on the triple. I can send a request to all the hospitals and see if Paradiso was treated for an injury to his hand. If Bond's right that Paradiso hurt his hand the same day Joan disappeared, that's incredible. That's no coincidence."

"That's one more thing we can corroborate," Carmen concurred.

"Right, 365 days in the year and Paradiso just happens to hurt his hand the same day Webster disappears. What about the other alibis he told Bond about?" Ponytail asked.

Carmen began to read again from the letter.

"Paradiso says he's got two possible alibis for his whereabouts on the night of Joan's murder. He tells Bond that Weyant's family will swear he was at their home celebrating Thanksgiving dinner all day and all night. Or he can say he was up in Maine. He was supposedly working up there during Thanksgiving. He told Bond he rented a hotel room by the month up there."

Carmenooch turned to Drew. "When's the last time you went to Maine?"

"I can head up there anytime. I know Lenny used to go to Ellsworth to buy clams to sell at the Feasts. I'll take a ride up there and check it out," Drew replied. "Is there anything else Lenny says about his alibis?"

"Yeah, he says he's gonna use his girlfriend Candy and some other woman who visited him at Charles Street as part of his alibi in both cases. He wanted his attorneys to get a deathbed statement from the second woman; he told Bond she was recovering from a heart attack at Mass General."

"I'll have one of the other troopers check the visitors list for Paradiso at Charles Street and see if it matches anyone recently admitted to Mass General."

"When you find out, let me know. I'll send a subpoena to Mass General for her medical records. That'll be amazing if that pans out," the lawyer offered.

There was a pause as each of the three men considered the different directions the case could take.

"I'm gonna need to meet with Bond myself before we go any farther down this road," the lawyer said as he carefully placed the letter on the desk.

"Ya want company?" Drew asked.

"No, I should go alone. If Bond's gonna testify, I need to understand who he is."

41: The First Session

The First Session of the Suffolk County Criminal Court was the clearinghouse for every defendant indicted in the county. The "First" was the largest courtroom in the building. Two heavy double-hinged swinging doors granted access to a chaotic scene of clerks, lawyers, stenographers, probation officers, court officers, defendants, news reporters, and spectators all vying for the attention of the presiding judge. Located on the seventh floor of the courthouse in Boston's Pemberton Square, the First was where every serious felony case was sent for arraignments, bail appeals, status conferences, motion hearings, and trial assignments

Like a delirious, drunken moth drawn to a bright flame, every major criminal within a twenty-mile radius of Boston eventually found his or her way to the "Room of Doom." Each day was the same circus, just different clowns.

The prosecutor went to the First Session nearly every day. The "call" of the list of cases began promptly each morning at ten. If a case was scheduled for trial, it was called in the First and sent by the presiding judge to one of the courthouse's eight trial rooms.

It was the luck of the draw for lawyers seeking a favorable judge. Neither side had any control over which session their case was sent to. It was great theater to watch defense and prosecution lawyers alike perform their version of the Texas Two-Step to avoid being sent out to an unfavorable trial session.

On January 10, 1983, Antonio Gomes appeared with his attorney in the First Session to request the court to appoint a forensic expert to analyze the blood evidence found by police at the Jacobs Street murder scene.

The presiding judge that morning was James "Jumpin' Jimmy" Donoghue, a tough, crusty former prosecutor from Worcester County temporarily reassigned for the past three months to the Suffolk County First. Bald and bespectacled, with a booming voice, he was far from a shrinking violet. He had an unusual gift for resolving difficult cases through plea bargaining.

Realistic and pragmatic, with the credibility earned from years of prosecuting homicides, he was able to narrow the tremendous backlog of cases in Suffolk County every time he served a three-month stint there. If the parties couldn't agree on the plea, the judge would simply point upward to the jurors' waiting room overhead and say to both sides, "Bring down the citizens, we'll empanel for trial in one hour." It was amazing how many cases got resolved in his chambers.

Judge Donoghue allowed Gomes's motion for a blood expert.

As the prosecutor left the Room of Doom, a uniformed Boston police officer approached him.

"Hi, Mr. Burke?" the young cop asked.

"Yeah, how ya doin'?" the lawyer answered without knowing whom he was addressing.

"I'm Larry Fisher," the officer began. "You don't know me, but I was the first one to —"

"I know," the DA interrupted. "You were the first one on the scene that night."

The lawyer had read the cop's name far too many times to count in the police reports on the triple, but had never met him until that day.

"Yeah, I was the first one there. I just wanted to thank you for what you're doin'," the cop said. "It was the worst thing I've ever seen in my life."

It was an eerie meeting as the two stood outside the courtroom, connected by a common bond of shock and horror. The lawyer knew what was coming next. He wanted to stop the cop, but he couldn't speak.

"It's funny. It wasn't cold that night. It just kinda seemed cold. But the heat was on. The heat was on in the apartment. There was blood on the radiators. Just so much blood. Everywhere. And the kids' bodies were there. The kids were layin' there with their mother. Just layin' there. So still. Just so still. I could smell the blood on the radiators. I could smell the blood. The heat was on, ya know? I could smell it."

Fisher looked down to the marble floor and then back into the lawyer's eyes.

"The smell stayed with me for weeks. It seemed like forever. I'm not sure why I'm tellin' ya this, but I just wanted to let you know I appreciate what you're doin'." The cop abruptly turned away without waiting for a response.

— — —

That same morning, the prosecutor walked up one flight of stairs to meet with Bobby Bond for the first time at the prisoner's cellblock on the 7M floor of the courthouse. Standing by the narrow hallway leading to the cells was a friend of his — Jack Gillen, a huge court officer frequently assigned to guard the most difficult defendants. Big Jack made the formal introduction.

"Bobby, this is Mr. Burke. Are we gonna dance today or are you gonna behave?" Gillen asked as he eyeballed the large black man seated behind the heavy-mesh steel cell door.

"This be the man, huh?" Bond looked out at the young lawyer from behind the grated cell. "Naw, I'm cool, Jack. I been wantin' to meet Lenny's pal. Lenny done told me all 'bout chu," the man with the shaved head said, nodding at the DA.

As Bond began to talk from the darkness of his cell, a thick iron bar placed at eye level made it impossible to see his eyes. He stood in the farthest part of the small cell; the lawyer could see only the outline of his heavily muscled body, and could barely hear the man's low, resonating voice.

"You ain't gotta believe me, man, but he killed her. Lenny done both of 'em. I know, 'cause I know all about killings," Bond said without remorse or guilt.

"Why you doin' this?" the DA asked without accusation or emotion.

"You ain't gonna understand no matter what I say," the killer answered. "Maybe I jus' needs to make it right once."

"I appreciate what you're doin'," the lawyer responded. An uneasy calm settled between the two men standing alone in the darkness of 7M.

"When did you first meet Lenny Paradiso?" the lawyer began.

"I knew Lenny when we's both in Walpole in '75. He wanted me to help him lose weight. He sez he got him a bad back, but he wants to get strong like me. Then I seen him again this December, when we's both at Charles Street. Soon as I gets there, he starts talkin' to me 'bout his case. First thing Lenny sez to me is, 'They got me for a three-year-old murder.' I tell Lenny, 'I'm under the same thing.'"

There was no hesitation, no doubt in Bond's voice as he spoke to the DA in the darkness of the cellblock. To each question the prosecutor asked, he offered a vivid and sometimes graphic response — usually beginning with "Lenny sez" — that fleshed out the numerous conversations between Bond and Paradiso at Charles Street Jail.

"Lenny sez to me, 'I wish I had my grand jury minutes, I'd show you. They indicted me on a John Doe case. My girl's got the minutes. They don't even put my fuckin' name on it. They got some cunt named Christine who seen me leave with the bitch I killed.' Lenny sez, 'I know she seen me 'cause I read what she says in the grand jury stuff my girl's got.'"

"Where were you located at the jail? Like, what cell area were you in when you started talking to him?" the lawyer asked as he visualized Paradiso reading the grand jury testimony of Christine DeLisi.

"First I was in cell 68 on the third tier and then I got moved to cell 31. It was Lenny asked them to move me. And they done it, 'cause he had connections. He was like in cell 36. They made us jus' like fuckin' neighbors. So like every

day we get time outta the cells between nine thirty and ten thirty in the mornin'
and then for two hours till three thirty in the afternoon. Lenny used ta talk ta
me every day. Some days I tried ta duck him 'cause it's the same thing every
day. First he tells me 'bout Marie Iannuzzi, then he starts talkin' 'bout that
Webster girl. I sez to Lenny, man, you goin' off the deep end. They gonna be
taking you to the fuckin' state hospital in Bridgewater, 'cause he was indicted
for one murder and talkin' 'bout killin' some other girl."

"Okay, tell me from the beginning what Paradiso told you about killing
Marie Iannuzzi."

"Lenny sez to me, 'Bobby, I first noticed her at this place where they had
the reception. Lenny calls it the 'Ship' or somethin' like that. He sez, 'My
girlfriend's with me, I can't do nuthin'. When the wedding starts to thin out
she needs a ride 'cause her boyfriend ain't there. My girl took her to this bar in
East Boston and dropped her off. Then I takes my girl home to her place in
Revere. I was driving my girl's car, it's a '73 Buick.' He sez, 'Ya shoulda fuckin'
seen me, I was running all of the red lights so I could get back ta the bar before
she left.'"

The DA thought about asking more questions, but like a priest in a
confessional, he simply let the man with the shaved head talk. Bond's memory
was amazing.

"Lenny sez, 'When I get back to the bar, she was still there.' He sez to me,
'Bobby, she had on this red wraparound-like skirt. You could see her ass the
way she had her legs crossed and she had on these black panty hose. I was
making passes and rubbing her legs. We had a coupla drinks. I asked her to
take a ride with me back to the Milanos' s'posedly to pick up my girl. I sez to
her she gotta 'pologize for actin' up at the Milanos'. She sez okay. It was 'round
one in the mornin' when we leaves.'"

"Did he say where he took her?" the prosecutor asked, knowing full well
their destination.

"Lenny sez ta me, 'We left and drove up to the Lynn Marsh Road, on the
Saugus line, to a place I used ta work. We started kissing. I tried to pull her
panty hose down. She wouldn't let me and then she sez ta take her back to the
bar.' He sez, 'That's when I grabbed the fuckin' scarf she was wearing 'round
her neck. She was scratching me on my sides and stomach. She passed out and
I fucked her. She come to and started hollerin' 'Help, help.' I punched her in
the head and started chokin' her.' Lenny sez, 'Bobby, ya shoulda seen her body
jumpin' an' jerkin' like she had the hiccups.'"

The DA wanted to ask another question but was afraid to interrupt.

"Lenny sez to me, 'I was drunk, I was all fucked up. I pulled her outta the car and fuckin' fell down, 'cause it was fuckin' rainin' that night. I tried to throw her in the river and let the fuckin' crabs eat her. Two days later, the cops talked ta me and my girl.'"

"Did Paradiso say where he went after he took Marie's body out of the car?" the lawyer continued.

Bond nodded. "He sez he went back to his apartment and calls his girlfriend Candy. Lenny sez when he calls Candy, he tells her to wake her mother up so he could say hi so the mother could testify that she had talked to him on the phone that night. Then Candy takes a cab to East Boston, where they talk about his alibi."

"What does Paradsio tell Candy about Marie?"

"Lenny sez that he tells Candy he stopped at the bar on his way home and picked Marie up to give her a ride home. Lenny sez that on the way home they get into an argument about the scene that Marie made at the Milanos' and that he grabbed her scarf and didn't realize how hard he choked her and she was dead. Candy don't know he took her up there and had sex wid her and then killed her. Candy starts crying on the phone. Lenny sez whatever he tells the cops, his girl's gonna say the same thing."

"So Candy knows that Lenny killed Marie and she's gonna be his alibi," the attorney said. He was thinking about another crime: accessory after the fact of murder.

"Lenny sez to me the next day he went out to Candy's car to get his coat and Marie's black shoes and panty hose was still in the Buick. Lenny sez to me, 'Bobby, you shoulda seen me get rid of that stuff 'cause my girl was still in my apartment.'"

"Did Paradiso say what he did with the car?" the DA asked, knowing it had been reported stolen after Marie's murder.

"Lenny sez, 'A couple of weeks later, I burned my girl's car up. They ain't got nothin' on me, her boyfriend David Doyle tried to kill her before and he got scratch marks on his hands.'"

"Tell me what Paradiso said to you about killing Joan Webster," the DA said.

"Lenny sez he picked her up at the airport around ten thirty that night. He asked her where she was coming from and she says 'New York' and that she was going to school in Cambridge."

"Did he tell you how he was able to pick her up?"

"He don't say directly, but later he sez something 'bout drivin' a cab. Lenny sez he starts feeding her some bullshit about how he owns two fish companies and a boat. He tells her he's gotta get some papers outta his office first and then he would take her to Cambridge."

"Did he say where he was working or where he kept this boat?" the prosecutor began as he envisioned the *Mala Femmena*.

"Lenny sez to me, 'Bobby, I went to Pier 7 where I worked at. That's where I kept my boat. I got her on the boat and made a coupla drinks. I always kept a lot of booze on my boat. She didn't want nothin' to drink."

"Did he say how he got her to go on the boat, was it voluntary?" The DA was thinking about Florence White being directed at gunpoint to the house on Cottage Street.

"No, he don't tell me that. Lenny jus' sez ta me, 'I made a pass at her,' and then he sez ta me, 'This bitch said no right away. We started fightin' and I beat that bitch's ass all over my boat. She give up 'cause I hit her with a whiskey bottle. She had a hole in the back of her head from the bottle.'"

As he spoke, Bond raised his thick arm and pointed to the rear right side of his own head. "Lenny sez, 'After I hit her here, I fucked her. I had blood all over me and my boat.'"

The lawyer listened as the words flowed without emotion. The savagery of the rape and murder seemed so mundane, yet so ungodly and appallingly real as Bond continued without hesitation.

"Lenny sez, 'I took her body way out and dumped it. The next day I look at my boat and there's blood all over it. Two days later, I took my boat and sunk it. The boat was in my girl's name. If worse comes to worse, I'll tell the fuckin' cops where the boat is, but they ain't gonna find no body in it.'"

The imagery, the detail, the horror of the loss of a human life transfixed the attorney as he struggled to understand the flow of Joan's murder.

"Lenny sez, 'The salt water gonna get rid of the blood.' He sez, 'They don't got nothin' 'cause they gots to have a body before they can take you ta trial.'"

In an instant, the irony of the 1850 Webster case flashed through the lawyer's mind. He briefly wondered what Paradiso knew about the need for a body to prosecute a murder. "Did Paradiso say what he meant about taking her 'way out' and dumping her body?"

"No, he don't say where for sure, maybe the harbor. Then the last two days I'm at Charles Street, Lenny tells me somethin' diff'rent. He sez he don't take her out in the water. He sez he takes her up someplace and buries her body, so's nobody's gonna find it."

"Did he tell you what he did with his boat?"

"Lenny sez he reported the boat stolen in July '81 for the insurance. He sez, 'The cops don't even know I still got the fuckin' boat in November '81. No one knows where the boat is sunk but me, tha's my ace in the hole. The boat ain't burned up, it's all still intact.' He sez somethin' 'bout pulling the sea cock and sinking it, but he don't say where it's at."

"Is that all Paradiso told you?"

"No, Lenny sez he's pissed on account a he hurt his hand the night he killed her. Lenny tells Candy a .50-caliber shell goes off in his hand. It's bullshit, but that's what he's gonna say happened if you finds the records from the doctors. But it ain't no shell blew up. Lenny sez he hits his own hand when he's killin' her."

"Do you know what he's gonna use for an alibi?"

"First Lenny sez his girl Candy is with him that night, then he sez he got some uddah place he goes to up in Maine. Lenny sez maybe he can say he was up there the night she gets killed."

Before the lawyer could ask another question, the large man with the shaved head stepped out of the darkness and approached the cell door. For the first time Bond's eyes were visible as he spoke.

"There somethin' else, man. Lenny know all 'bout chu. He talk 'bout chu all the time. Fuckin' Burke this, mothahfuckin' Burke that. He say you a fuckin' crazy man. Like some fuckin' mad dog don't quit for nothin'."

There was a pause before Bond offered the rest.

"Lenny sez if he get the chance, he gonna do ya."

42: Route 2

After the meeting with the DA on 7M, Bobby Bond was moved from Charles Street Jail to a safer location. Four days later the man with the shaved head was formally interviewed by the state police. Bond volunteered to undergo a polygraph test about Paradiso's statements on both murders. The tests were scheduled for the middle of January and conducted by the head of the Massachusetts State Police's Polygraph Unit.

"Hey Jack, how are all the little Nasutis doin'?" the DA asked the father of ten as the two men stood outside the police barracks just off the Route 2 rotary in Concord.

"They're all doin' great, 'cept they're not all that little anymore. My oldest just told me he wants to apply to the state police academy."

"If you Italian guys keep it up you won't have any Irish troopers working there anymore."

"There's still a few of 'em here, but they have all of the easy jobs that don't require a whole lotta thought or effort. Ya see, the Irish got here first, but now we're trying to phase 'em out," the polygraph expert responded in kind.

Before Burke left, Nasuti said he'd call his office with the results of Bond's polygraph test.

He took forever to call.

The polygraph test administered to Robert Bond took more than four hours to complete. It was administered at the state police barracks located across from the Concord prison where Bond was being held. The questions were straightforward and designed to verify the truthfulness of selected portions of the information Bond had sent in his letter to the prosecutor. Bond's physiological responses — heart rate, blood pressure, breathing rate, and perspiration rate — were then compared with his answers to the control questions he was asked.

Finally the polygraph expert called the lawyer and gave him the results.

"First let me read ya some of the questions and the answers I got from Bond before I tell ya the rest," Nasuti said.

"Did Lenny Paradiso tell you he hit Joan Webster on the head with a whiskey bottle?"

Answer: "Yes."

"In December of 1982, did Lenny Paradiso tell you he choked Marie Iannuzzi with her scarf?"

Answer: "Yes."

"Did Lenny tell you that he had blood all over him and his boat from hitting Joan Webster with the bottle?"

Answer: "Yes."

"In December of 1982, did Lenny Paradiso describe to you the way Marie Iannuzzi reacted as he was choking her?"

Answer: "Yes."

"Did Lenny tell you that he took the boat out two days later and sank it?"

Answer: "Yes."

"Did you read any of the police reports about the Iannuzzi case?"

Answer: "No."

"Did you make this story up for your own personal gain?"

Answer: "No."

The lawyer waited impatiently as Nasuti cleared his throat. "Bond's telling you the truth. There's no doubt in my mind. There wasn't a blip on anything he's telling you guys."

"Thanks, Jack," the DA said as he let out a sigh of relief. "I just needed to know Bond wasn't making this stuff up. There's too much information for him to have concocted it all. It had to have come from Paradiso."

"I agree. Bond's got an incredible amount of detail about what Paradiso told him. He may have confused *New York* for *Newark* or even what Lenny meant when he said he took her body 'way out' and dumped it, but he's telling the truth. That part is very clear. Have you guys been able to corroborate any of the other stuff Bond told you about, like the injury to Lenny's hand or the motel records up in Maine?"

"Not yet. Drew's going up to Maine real soon," the prosecutor responded. "I'm drafting a search warrant right now for Weyant's house to look for the .50-caliber shell."

"You're friggin' nuts. You know that? But hey, if you can corroborate any of this stuff, it would go one hell of a long way to establishing Bond's credibility," Nasuti said — a note of encouragement as the men ended their call.

Shortly after the polygraph, information began to emerge in the Boston newspapers about the developments in the Webster case. On the front page of the *Globe,* a headline announced a new "Break in the Disappearance of the Harvard Graduate Student." The *Herald* ran a similar notice. Television stations picked up the story the same day. Later that night the picture of Lenny Paradiso appeared on all three major TV stations in the Boston metropolitan area. It was the lead story on all three stations.

Janet McCarthy sat watching the news with her mother as the fleeting image of the Quahog passed on the screen.

"Oh my gawd, that looks just like the guy that tried to kill me," the young woman said to her mother.

"Are you sure?" the older woman asked.

"Yeah, I am. It's him. I know it's him," McCarthy responded as her mother reached for the telephone.

"Who did they say to call? What was his name?"

"Palombo. Trooper Andrew Palombo."

— — —

The next morning the lawyer's office phone rang. It was Carol Ball, an assistant district attorney from Middlesex County and a classmate from law school.

"Hey, Tim, I've been reading about the Webster case in the newspapers for the past couple of days, sounds like this new witness is incredible. I got some more news for ya. I don't know how reliable it is yet, but we just got a call from another inmate who says he knew Paradiso in prison. Paradiso told him he killed Webster and the Iannuzzi girl. He's willing to testify," the former Philadelphia debutante related.

"Anybody check this guy out?" the prosecutor asked his friend.

"Yeah, we did. He's already done thirteen years on a murder case out of here. He's got about two years before he's eligible for parole. He says he's not interested in the reward the Websters offered, but he's probably looking to shorten his sentence to time served if he cooperates. He's worried about his family's safety. I guess he probably should be. I hear this Quahog guy's a real animal."

"He is. What's this guy's name?"

"His name's Pisa. They call him Death Row Tony," she responded.

"Nice name. What do you wanna do with him?"

"We're not gonna make any promises to him. That's for sure. We gotta check his story out. Polygraph him, corroborate what he says, that kind of stuff. I'll get him brought into the courthouse over here so you can talk to him. Who's doing this case with ya?"

"Andy Palombo and Carmen Tammaro. We can get Jack Nasuti to polygraph this Pisa guy," the DA told his counterpart.

"What the hell ever happened to all the Irish troopers?" she quipped.

"You're startin' to sound like me. Drew says they're phasing them out." The

DA smiled just as the large Italian trooper with the ponytail walked in the door.

"We got another victim. Wait till you hear who I just spoke to," Drew mouthed to the lawyer as he quickly ended the call with Carol Ball.

"Who is it?"

"Her name's Janet McCarthy. Lenny tried to rape her just off Winthrop Avenue back in 1980. She saw him on the tube last night when the stories broke about the Quahog being a suspect in Joan's disappearance."

"That's terrific. Let's get her in here right away." The DA paused.

"Drew, how many women do ya think there are out there who Lenny hurt?"

43: Saugus High School

Doreen Kennedy was late, just missing her ride home on the yellow Saugus High School bus that day in early January 1967. The sun lay hidden in a dark ocher sky; the temperature had been shivering below fifteen degrees for most of the week. Her coat was a cheap thin fabric, providing little comfort from the depth of the intense cold. As the seventeen-year-old began the solitary walk to her home, a darkened car behind her rolled to a gradual stop with a crunch of hardened rubber on the ice-covered pavement.

"Hmm-mmm, sweet young thang," the driver of the maroon station wagon said. He dragged a thick finger beneath the width of his nose as he slowed down to take a look at the forlorn figure trudging along Route 1.

"Hiya. Youse needs a ride?" the large smiling man in the white T-shirt inquired of the shivering teen through the partially open side window.

My father will kill me, she thought in that briefest of moments when decisions are made. Her toes and fingers had already become numb from the cold in the short time she had been walking. She had no gloves, and the wind whipped drifted snow from the banks into her face.

"Come on, I won't hurt youse," the driver encouraged as another blast of arctic cold seemingly directed her body toward the station wagon's passenger side door. She smiled an almost imperceptible smile in response beneath her thin red scarf as she opened the snow-caked door and quickly entered the warmth of the car's interior.

"Thanks, I was freezing," she stammered as the driver reached across her body to lock the door and deftly produced an eight-inch boning knife from beneath his large thigh. The smell of dead fish permeated her nostrils as she turned to see the smiling dark curly-haired driver bring the cutting edge of the blade upward to her throat.

"Youse gonna die today, bitch. I'm gonna cut off your tits and slice you up into six pieces and dump your fuckin' body in the woods behind the Saugus Iron Works where nobody's ever gonna find ya," the large man hissed. The girl began to vomit into her scarf.

The abandoned ironworks were less than a mile from Saugus High School and a shorter distance from the Saugus River, snaking its now frozen path to the Point of Pines. As the mismatched couple in the maroon car pulled from the side of Route 1, the girl turned her head back to see the faint outline of the high school receding in the distance.

— — —

Sixteen years later the female caller to state police headquarters tried to explain the horror of that day. She was confronting her past for the first time.

"I saw someone on the news last night. It was the same person that tried to kill me back in 1967. I never told anyone. He said he was gonna rape me and then cut my body up into pieces. It happened a long time ago, but I knew it was him as soon as I saw his face on the TV."

"Are you talking about the guy that's the suspect in the Webster case?"

"Yes, it's him. I was a senior at Saugus High. It was late in the afternoon, right after school got out. I missed my bus ride home. And I started to walk home. It was bitter cold out, and he offered me a ride."

"Yeah, okay, go on," the man's voice dsaid flatly.

"He was driving a maroon station wagon. I can still remember the license plate number. The inside of his car smelled like dead fish. There were papers everywhere. It looked like he lived out of his car. As soon as I got inside I knew it was a mistake. He was dressed in a white T-shirt even though it was so cold outside. He was so full of hate. He pulled a fish-boning knife that he had hidden under his leg. He told me he was gonna skin me alive while he was raping me."

"How long ago did this happen?"

"It was the winter of 1967. I was only seventeen. I never told anybody about what he did until now. I was so afraid to tell my father. I knew he would've beaten me for getting in a stranger's car. I feel so guilty now. I know if I'd told someone then, all these girls might still be alive today."

"How did you get away from this guy?" the cop asked skeptically.

"I jumped out of the car as he slowed down to make a turn and ran away in the other direction," Doreen tried to explain.

"Listen, lady, that was more than sixteen years ago. I don't know what the hell you think we're gonna do for ya now," the officer responded coldly.

There was a bluntness to his tone that placed her on edge. It was another rejection, another man who didn't understand.

"I, I, I guess I just wanted to tell the Websters how sorry I am," she stammered. "They must have loved their daughter very much. I hope maybe they can forgive me." The phone went dead.

44: Joe Tecce's

It was warm for Boston on February 1, 1983, if you consider forty-two degrees warm.

"Hey, I got some news for you," Carmenooch began as the DA stepped out from the First Session into the crowded corridor. "Ya know that girl I told ya about from the North End? The one Lenny pulled the gun on near Pier 7 about eleven or twelve years ago?"

"Yeah, Patti somethin', right?" the lawyer said.

"Well, I reached out to her, and she called me back. She's gonna testify about what happened to her. She's a great witness. She told me the whole story about what Lenny did to her at Pier 7."

"And she's willing to testify?"

"Yeah, she is. She told me she saw him New Year's Eve a couple of years ago at Joe Tecce's restaurant on North Washington Street." Carmen took a breath and started to smile as he spoke.

Tecce's was home to some of the best Italian food in the North End. Frequented by mobsters and cops alike, plastic grapes, gaudy tile murals and frescoes of gondolas plying the canals of Venice adorned the dark, grotto-styled dining rooms. The place was awash with enough pasta, Chianti, antipasto, and "Steak Mafia" to last two lifetimes.

"What happened?" the DA asked.

"This girl's got guts. She walks right up to Paradiso at the stroke of midnight, just as Guy Lombardo is singing 'Auld Lang Syne.' She says to Lenny, 'You sick bastard, I'll never forget what you did to me that night. I know you're the one that killed the Iannuzzi girl, too.'"

"You're kidding. She said that to him?" the lawyer asked.

Carmen's grin widened, and he nodded.

"What the hell did Paradiso do?"

"He didn't say a thing. Some of Fopiano's crew were there that night. They were just waiting for Lenny to do something stupid so they could thump him again."

"Wishful thinkin'," the lawyer responded coldly.

"Patti told me she called the Saugus PD a year ago when the news first came out about Joan disappearing. She wouldn't leave her name, but she told the dispatcher Lenny may have done it," Carmen said without expression.

"She was right."

"That makes three different women we can use to prove a behavioral pattern for Lenny at the Iannuzzi trial. If a judge lets all of these other women testify, I've got a good shot at convicting him. I have John Doris from Homicide trying to find the first one from the Combat Zone. She was only sixteen when Paradiso kidnapped and raped her. No one knows where the hell she is," the lawyer said.

"Is Doris going by himself? I didn't think those three guys ever went anywhere alone," Carmen said, laughing. "They're all Irish, aren't they?"

It might have been a coincidence, but as the two men spoke outside the First Session, one of Paradiso's new attorneys emerged from the bank of elevators and headed directly toward them. The duo had been on the case now for more than two months, flooding the DA with discovery motions.

As Lenny's new lawyer approached, the DA looked at the pair of alligator-skin cowboy boots he was wearing and knew Drew would have loved them. The only thing was, Drew would never tell defense lawyers he liked anything about them.

Carmen was different. He was nicer.

"Hi, Judd," Carmen offered warmly. "Nice boots."

A former state and federal prosecutor now specializing in criminal defense, Judd Carhart maintained an office across the street from the old courthouse and the Steaming Kettle at 15 Court Square. Confident and athletic, Carhart was a talented lawyer with great jury skills. Six feet tall with blue eyes and blond hair, he had a penchant for cowboy boots and unanticipated acquittals.

"Hey, Carmenooch," Carhart replied to the ever-affable detective sergeant. "Don't they have any Irish troopers left at the airport?"

"What the hell is it with you Irish guys? You guys are like locusts," Carmen joked. "We keep trying to get rid of 'em, but they keep coming back, swarms of 'em."

Carhart shook hands with the DA, then Carmen, and told the pair that Lenny's second lawyer would soon be joining him in the First Session. "You know Walter Prince, don't you, Tim? We used to work together in the US Attorney's office."

"Yeah, that's before the two of you went over to the dark side," the DA shot back, dreading the fact the pair would now be aligned in Paradiso's defense. They were both experienced trial lawyers with a flair for the dramatic. One white, one black. What one lawyer didn't think of, the other would.

The prospects for a conviction on the case had taken a turn for the worse.

After the exchange of social graces, Paradiso's lawyer turned to his adversary and got down to the purpose for his visit: "I don't suppose you'd wanna talk about the possibility of a manslaughter plea on his case, would ya?"

"Sorry, Judd, as a matter of fact your client's got some more bad news comin'," the DA said with a false sense of confidence. "Carmen just spoke with a woman from the North End your guy tried to kill about ten years ago."

"I'll be interested in seeing the police report on her. I'll file a motion," Carhart said, apparently unaffected by the news. He shook hands with Carmenooch, then the prosecutor, and headed toward the First.

"Ya know ya got a really tough case to prove with the two of them representing Lenny. They're both excellent lawyers," Carmen said as he watched the door to the First Session close behind the defense attorney.

"Yeah, I know," the DA said, anxiously shifting his weight from one foot to the other.

"They'll kill Doyle on cross. You know that, too, don't ya?"

"I know. That's why the evidence of a pattern of conduct is so important — to show how Paradiso operates. I just don't know if a judge would let these three women testify at trial."

"What happens if he won't?"

"If their testimony doesn't come in, I'm basically left with Bond's statement against Candy's alibi."

"You've done miracles before," Carmen said with his usual smile.

"Thanks, Carmen. I appreciate it. I gotta run upstairs to the Supreme Judicial Court for a hearing on the Gomes case."

"Really, what's goin' on up in the ivory towers of the Supreme Court?"

"Gomes's lawyer is trying to get him out on bail. There was only a drop of blood on the Christmas present. When the FBI tested it, they used the entire sample. Now Gomes's expert can't retest it. So the defense attorney says Gomes should be released on bail because we destroyed the blood evidence," the DA explained.

"Don't let that happen," Carmen said as he watched the DA head for the bank of elevators. Jimmy from Southie stood holding the brass doors open.

45: The Supreme Judicial Court
— —

The Supreme Judicial Court is the highest court in the Commonwealth of Massachusetts.

The bail hearing for Antonio Gomes lasted more than an hour. The Single Justice who heard the appeal "took the case under advisement," which is the polite legal way of saying *We'll get back to ya.*

The DA left the SJC courtroom and walked to the center elevator, where Jimmy from Southie stood waiting, holding the doors as the rest of the courthouse cursed the slowest lifts in the city. Jimmy turned down the volume of his transistor radio and smiled as the DA entered his claustrophobic domain.

Orphaned by a drunk driver at the age of five, Jimmy Callahan grew up with his auntie Rose and her six screaming kids in a hardscrabble five-room flat in the Old Colony projects of Irish South Boston. Freckled, with fair skin and red hair that seemed to go nowhere and everywhere at the same time, Jimmy from Southie spent his summers at Carson Beach and Fenway Park. In the winter, he spent his time dreaming of Carson Beach and Fenway Park.

The rest of the time Jimmy spent in his elevator at the courthouse.

Jimmy read the *Globe* and the *Herald* cover-to-cover every day, starting with the obits. He loved country music and his Red Sox. He hated the Yankees and Bucky Dent. Jimmy relished the drama of the law. It was amazing what he learned just standing in his elevator for eight and a half hours every day.

"How's it goin', Jimmy?" the lawyer asked as he glanced up at the worn Red Sox cap atop the shock of thick red hair. There was no Muzak on Jimmy's elevator, only Loretta Lynn singing "Coal Miner's Daughter" on his transistor.

"Hey, Mr. Burke, did ya see Mr. Carhart's new cowboy boots today? He sez yer gonna try to get all those women to testify against the Quahog."

"You shoulda been a reporter, Jimmy. You got more sources than the *New York Times*." The lawyer laughed as the elevator operator closed the polished brass doors behind him. Jimmy turned the brass handle south and slowly directed the elevator seven floors down to the DA's office.

"Hey, that's what Jeremiah Murphy says to me, too, but he says I shoulda been a reporter for the *Boston Globe*."

There was a gap of silence as Jimmy momentarily struggled with his thoughts and then blurted out, "Lenny's a very bad man isn't he, Mr. Burke?"

"Yeah, he is, Jimmy," the DA said quietly.

There was another brief pause in the flow of conversation as "America's Sweetheart" twanged her song.

"Ya wanna buy a used Chevy pickup?"

"Naw, I got a car already, Jimmy. How come you're sellin' it?"

"Someone stole it outta the projects. It was wrecked when the cops found it. I ain't got no 'surance. I gotta get rid of it," Jimmy explained. "I tried the *Bargain Hunter's Guide,* but nobody's called me."

"What's the *Bargain Hunter's Guide?*"

"It's like a advertisement thing. Everybody's using it now to sell all kinds of stuff. Ya know like cars and boats and —"

"Wait a minute. Does this thing go all over the city? Like somebody from Revere can sell something in Southie, that kinda thing?"

"Yeah, it does," Jimmy answered as the elevator gradually came to a stop on the sixth floor. Seven people grumbled about their wait as they came aboard.

"Thanks, Jimmy," the lawyer said as he waved good-bye, then walked quickly to his office and called Drew.

"Hey, Drew, ya know how Candy and Lenny had all of those insurance claims about their stolen cars and boats?"

"Yeah, what about it?"

"I wanna get all of the *Bargain Hunter's Guide*s for the past four or five years and go through them. Maybe the two of them tried to sell some of the cars or boats around the same time they claimed they were stolen," the lawyer explained.

"You're fuckin'nuts. You know that, don't you?"

"Yeah, I think you told me that once or twice before."

46: Middlesex County

Middlesex County was due west of Boston and the commonwealth's largest population center, with about one and a half million people. Home to Harvard University, MIT, and a slew of other colleges, the city of Cambridge was the academic and cultural hub of the county. The Middlesex County Courthouse was a short hike from Harvard Square, down riverbound Memorial Drive. The twenty-story concrete monolith was located near the banks of the Charles River, opposite the Charles Street Jail.

In 1969 a Middlesex County jury convicted Tony Pisa of first-degree murder and gave him the death penalty. Thirteen years later Death Row Tony contacted the same district attorney's office that prosecuted him and said he had some information on two murders. He told them the killer's name was Lenny Paradiso.

Pisa wanted to talk to the lawyer prosecuting the Quahog.

"Lenny could never do the hard time," Death Row Tony explained as the lawyer sat in the DA's office on the second floor of the Middlesex County Courthouse on a Friday in early March.

A waft of cigarette smoke curled around Pisa as he carefully chose the words he used to describe Paradiso.

"Lenny talked the talk, but he was a pussy at heart. He whined from the day he was inside the walls."

"Is this when you were both together at the auto school in Norfolk?"

"No, I seen him before that in the yard at Walpole, before we both got shipped over to Norfolk. Anyway, one day the Quahog shows up at the auto school and one of the other cons starts a fight with him. The guy's name was Dexter Hadley. He was another slug with more toes than teeth. So Dexter's got a crowbar and he's gonna make a crease in Lenny's squash. He took a swing at Lenny and hit him. I think he broke Lenny's hand."

Pisa pulled out another cigarette from inside his blue work shirt, took a long drag, released the smoke into the air above him, and started to speak once again.

"I separated the two of 'em and that's kinda how it all began. After that Lenny was like a puppy chewing on my leg every day. Just talkin' nonstop 'bout his case. Ya know? Talkin' how he couldn't do the time and how he was never comin' back here again. He wasn't gonna make the same mistake and leave any witnesses behind the next time."

"So much for rehabilitation," the lawyer said sarcastically.

"In some ways he was a fuckin' dope. You'd have to explain shit to him three or four times for it ta sink in. In other ways he was scary smart. He was always wantin' ta know about evidence and cases. That's why I told him about the old Webster case. Ya know, the one with the Harvard professor? The one where they never found the body. I'd explain it to him and then he'd say shit like, 'No witnesses, no case, no body, and no trial, right?' He didn't get it. I told him they hung the guy thirty days later. It didn't make any difference to him."

"Why was he so interested in that case?"

"He's just one sick fuck, man. You gotta understand where his head's at. He's not like what you're used to. He's a one-trick pony. That's all he knows, man. The Quahog likes what he does. He's a skinner. He likes rapin' and killin' women. He ain't gonna quit unless you stop him. It's just that simple."

"Are you willing to testify about what he's told you?" the DA asked as he looked at the man with the narrow face and dark eyes.

"Listen man, I got thirteen long hard years inside done already. I'm eligible for parole in two more years. I ain't gonna screw up and tell ya somethin' that didn't happen. Everything I told you is what Lenny told me. Put me on the box. Do whatever you gotta do ta show I'm telling ya the truth. But you gotta understand one thing. I got five kids. If I talk and he walks, and I'm still inside, he'll kill my kids," Pisa said matter-of-factly, waiting for the spark of understanding he needed from the DA.

There was a moment of silence as Pisa took another long draw on his cigarette, exhaled, and continued to stare into the lawyer's eyes. The con raised the hand that held his cigarette and pointed a long finger at the prosecutor's chest.

"The pressure's on you, man. You gotta win this case."

Leonard Paradiso and the *Mala Femmena* circa 1981.

Paradiso with shotgun outside the Summit Motel in Florida, Massachusetts, late fall 1974.

Paradiso in hunting garb and bandolier.

The bumper sticker on Paradiso's truck: EVERY GIRL NEEDS A BIG ITALIAN GUY.

Paradiso aboard the *Mala Femmena*.

The interior of the *Mala Femmena*. Robert Bond said Paradiso told him he used the half-gallon liquor bottles to kill Joan Webster.

Pier 7 and the Erie Barge in late May 1981. The *Mala Femmena* is tied up between the pier and the barge, just beneath the ramp.

4

SUMMARY OF CASE

EVIDENCE AND FACTS

Sometime between 1.30 a.m. and 2.00 a.m. on January 5,1970
when opposite the South Seas Rest. on Harrison Avenue,Boston,Mass. Florence
White was offered a ride home by an unknown man,whom she described as 27-
5-6-Looked Italian or Jewish with a pot belly.She got into the car and the
man pulled a gun on her and told her she was going with him.They went throug
the tunnel and the man used a ticket to pay the toll.He took a street not
on the ramp towards the airport.On a street off Meridian Street he took me
to the top floor of a house with a grey door,into a two room apartment.There
guns on the wall,he called a man on the phone.He then put a gun to her head
and made her undress and made made me suck him,at this time he showed me a
switch blade knife.He then made me take off her boots.At this time a second
man showed up and she was forced to suck him.The second man left and the
defendant raped her.The defendant took a $165.00 ladies diamond ring and
$90.00 in US Monies from the victim.The defendant also showed Miss White
bullets with pointed heads and other bullets with with round heads.On Sunnda
January 11,1970 Detectives Mahoney and Norton arrested one Leonard Paradiso
31 Cottage Street,East Boston,Mass. on Warrants issued by the E.B. District
Court after the victim had made positive identiiation of the defendant's
photograph.At the apartment at 31 Cottage Street,E.B. Detectives Mahoney and
Norton by virtue of a search warrant seized one 38 cal. Smith and Wesson
Revolver (fully loaded)with pointed bullets,8 round headed bullets,one Switc
blade knife.The Smith and Wesson Revolver had the serial number obliterated.

Report submitted by *Edward J. Mahony*

Detective..........................Division..Seven......

Division No.......................

TRIAL IN SUPERIOR COURT

Date of trial.......................................Name of Judge.........................

Name of Prosecuting District Attorney.................................

Disposition ....

Remarks ....

....

....

Report submitted by......................................

....

Court Supervising Sergeant
District Attorney's Office.

Boston police detective Edward Mahoney's report of the abduction and rape of
Florence White on January 5, 1970, from the Combat Zone.

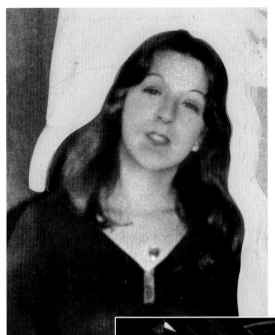

Marie Iannuzzi, 20, East
Boston, Massachusetts.

Joan Webster in
Ellsworth, Maine,
October, 1981.

The Commercial Lobster Company, where Paradiso worked and moored his boat, located at the entrance to Pier 7 on Northern Avenue, South Boston.

The *Mala Femmena* being raised by crane near the dry dock at Pier 7 on September 26, 1983. (*Boston Herald* photo)

The judge and jury at the scene of Marie Iannuzzi's murder behind Conley and Daggettt's on the Lynn Marsh Road. (*Lynne (MA) Item* photo)

Candy Weyant's residence at 212 Crescent Avenue in Revere. Also shown are a .50 caliber shell and Paradiso's book shelf, both taken from Weyant's home during the state police search.

Attorney Steven Rappaport and Leonard Paradiso in Courtroom 808. (*Boston Hearld* photo)

47: Courtroom 808

The Fourth Amendment to the US Constitution protects citizens against unreasonable searches.

A linchpin of the Bill of Rights, the Fourth Amendment came about as a result of random, warrantless searches of homes and seizures of property by British troops stationed in Boston before the Revolutionary War. The Founding Fathers' new Constitution required a neutral judge or magistrate to be presented with a written application before a house could be searched. The search warrant application requires an accompanying affidavit to establish the existence of probable cause that evidence of a crime can be found at the specified location.

"What judge is handling the hearing on our search warrant?" Drew asked as the prosecutor left the First Session.

"Don't ask," the lawyer replied simply as they trudged up the stairs to Courtroom 808. The pair announced their presence to the clerk seated in the vacant room and were quickly ushered into a side room.

"Let me get this straight. You want me to issue a search warrant to try to find a .50-caliber shell that some inmate convicted of murder in this very courtroom three months ago told you is located in this woman's house in Revere? Is that what you are asking me to do, Mr. Burke?" the man in the black robe asked.

The lawyer and the detective nodded to each other for reassurance and then to Hizzoner as they sat in the familiar chambers of the same judge who had issued the vampire warrant for a sample of Antonio Gomes's blood.

The judge's clerk that morning was Joe Rubino. He was a friendly sort, with curly blond hair and a permanent smile, weighing in at 140 pounds in a soaking rainstorm. The watchdog of the court's day-to-day business, Joltin' Joe stood five foot nine and would roll his eyes upward seemingly into the back of his head whenever he saw it coming.

He could clearly see this one coming.

"Yes, Your Honor, that's exactly what we're asking this court to do," the prosecutor responded as *wild goose chase* once again echoed through his mind. *Damn it, I knew I should've talked to Mr. Leary before I did this,* he thought.

Searching for moral support, the lawyer glanced at his friend with the ponytail. This time Drew seemed preoccupied, looking down as if to make sure his shoes were properly tied, even though he was wearing cowboy boots.

The DA anxiously turned his gaze to the clerk's face next and could see only white where Rubino's pupils used to be.

"And you, sir." The judge nodded toward Drew. "You are the affiant and are prepared to sign this affidavit, I presume?"

"Yes, Your Honor, Trooper Andrew Palombo," Drew said firmly as he quietly considered the option of leaving and taking a ride on his Harley.

"Well it sounds like a bit of a wild goose chase to me, but I will review this highly unusual request, Mr. Burke," the judge intoned as he carefully reached under his robe and removed gold-rimmed reading glasses from the breast pocket of his charcoal gray pin-striped suit coat.

The jurist then combed the remaining nine hairs in the center of his balding pate back into position and began to read. The application and affidavit were five pages long, with twenty-three pages of attachments and photographs. When the judge completed his first run, he began to read everything once again.

"Gawd, he's taking forever," the lawyer whispered to his large companion, who nodded in silent agreement.

It was half an hour before Hizzoner glanced up from the paperwork.

"Doesn't the state police have a dress code, Trooper?" The judge shifted his gaze from the warrant, straightening the Brooks Brothers tie that hung from the collar of his periwinkle-blue buttondown shirt. Before Ponytail could respond, Hizzoner removed the Mont Blanc pen from his starched shirt pocket and signed on the dotted line.

"We do, Your Honor, but it only applies to the Irish troopers. We're trying to phase them out," Drew said to the judge as Rubino's eyes rolled back to white.

It would be the second time in less than a year that Drew stood on the doorstep of 212 Crescent Avenue in Revere. This time Lenny wasn't there. He was still holed up at Charles Street Jail.

Drew placed the search warrant for Candy Weyant's parents' home inside the same pocket of his black leather coat that previously held Paradiso's arrest warrant. He smiled a rare smile. The sound of music came from inside the house as Drew walked up the stairs and knocked three times.

The bleached blonde answered the door and calmly sat where she was instructed while the eight troopers conducted the room-to-room search. In the kitchen, an ancient Philco played an oldies station, where a proud Tina Turner sang, "There's just one thing. We never, ever do nuthin' nice and easy. We always do it nice and rough."

"Yeah. Big wheel keep on turnin', Proud Mary keep on burnin'," Ponytail chorused as he headed for the basement.

Several hours later Drew held the phone tightly in his huge hand as he spoke to his friend.

"You won't believe what we found. We got the .50-caliber shell. It was sitting in the cellar just like Bond said it would be. It took us forever to search the house," the trooper said, unusual excitement in his voice.

"I guess the Quahog won't be using that shell for his alibi now. Bond was right," the lawyer retorted.

"There's more. It's kinda weird. Lenny's got his own little room in Weyant's house. He's got all kinds of books on a shelf here. He's got books on Big Foot, My Life in the Mafia, Patton, Deer Hunter's Bible, Killers of the Seas, poisonous snakes, ya know, dumb crap like that, but there's another book here that sticks out like a sore thumb," Pony Tail explained.

"What kind of a book is it?"

"It's a book on Mayan architecture and civilization."

"This guy drops outta school in the eighth grade and he's reading a book on Mayan civilization? What's wrong with that picture?"

"Maybe he's thinkin' of movin' to Mexico?" Drew said in jest.

"Wait a minute. Remember the project Joan was working on at Harvard? She was building a model of an ancient temple. Remember that?"

"Yeah, I do. There's more stuff here, too. Ya know how he says the *Mala* was supposedly stolen in July '81? Well, guess what else is here in the house?" Ponytail asked.

"I dunno. Tell me."

"We found the damn boat's depthfinder, the compass, and the ship-to-shore radio. They're all here. He stripped it before he reported it stolen to the insurance company. That boat was never stolen. The *Mala* was still above water in November. He was probably tryin' ta sell it and collect the insurance money at the same time. That explains why he never canceled the mooring fees at Pier 7."

"That's incredible. Was there anything else?"

"Yeah, you're gonna love this. Remember how Bond said Paradiso told him he always had booze on his boat? And that Lenny might have used a whiskey bottle to kill Joan with?"

"Yeah, I do. Paradiso told Bond he hit her in the head with it, why?"

"Well, because I found a picture of the inside of the cabin on the *Mala Femmena*. You can see the outline of three half-gallon whiskey bottles sittin' on a shelf right above the bed next to some windows in the cabin. It was those big bottles of Seagram's and VO, that kinda stuff. I think that may be what the bastard used to kill her. Just like Bond said." Drew's voice elevated with an air of certainty.

"Even more reason we need to find the *Mala*. Did you find anything else in Lenny's room?"

"Yeah, we did. There's a picture of a really pretty woman in here. It's obviously not Candy. We got no idea who she is. It's kinda strange, she looks a lot like Joan Webster," Drew said.

"Really?"

"Yeah, she does. The girl's got long dark hair just like Joan. There's a bunch of other pictures here, too, one of 'em shows Lenny buck naked steering the *Mala* and smiling at whoever it is taking his picture. What a lard-ass." Drew laughed.

"The judge will get a kick outta that one when we make the return on the search warrant to him."

"Lenny's also got a bunch of Polaroid pictures of himself deer hunting with some other guys out in the Berkshires. There's some handwriting on the back of one of the photos that says 'Lenny, Florida, Mass. 1974.' He's holdin' his huntin' rifle and standin' out in front of this place with a big sign on the roof. It's called the Summit Motel."

"Where the hell is Florida, Massachusetts?"

"It's out near North Adams, near the Vermont border. I knew some troopers who got stuck out there when they first got out of the academy," Drew responded quickly. "As the saying goes, it's a nice place to visit, but you sure the hell wouldn't wanna live there for more than two weeks."

"I wonder what the hell Lenny was doing out there?" the lawyer asked, unaware sixteen-year-old Kim Benoit had been found strangled in mid-November 1974. "We gotta check that out, Drew."

"Wait, there's another picture of him in the same place in Florida, but it looks like it's taken at an earlier time than the hunting pictures. He coulda gone out there before hunting season started. There isn't any snow on the ground in this picture and it doesn't say when it was taken. Get this, in this one he's wearing a purple leather coat. That's right. I said purple leather. This mope's right outta *Gentleman's Quarterly*. The slug's a disgrace to his Italian heritage." Drew cackled. "Hey, and one last thing."

"Yeah?"

"Make sure you tell that Irish judge we found the .50-caliber shell."

"Hi, we're George and Terry Webster," the distinguished-looking gentleman said as he extended his right hand to the young lawyer. He had piano-player fingers and a warm, strong grip. "This is my wife, Terry," he added, directing his smile to the attractive, diminutive woman at his side.

The couple had an aura about them, a certain undefinable grace and internal strength under the worst possible conditions. The DA liked them immediately.

He had seen their image on the news frequently during the past several months. Parents in obvious turmoil over the loss of their daughter. As they stood outside the entrance to his tiny office on the sixth floor of the courthouse, he thought of what he should share with them about the disappearance of their daughter.

"Sergeant Tammaro has told us all about you. We heard the good news. You're getting ready for another baby. It's so different now, with the fathers being there at the birth and all. Do you know if it's a boy or a girl yet?" Mrs. Webster asked.

Amazing that she could think of someone else's happiness in the midst of the loss of her youngest child.

"Our first was a boy. His name is Jordan. He's three. We decided to go with the *J* names. If it's a boy, it'll be Jared. If it's a little girl, it'll be Joan, after my older sister out in California," the lawyer said. The woman's sad eyes began to tear. The lawyer wished he hadn't mentioned Joan's name.

"Sergeant Tammaro also tells us you're running the Boston Marathon in two weeks," Mr. Webster added as the trio entered the office and sat near the desk with the dark brown and tattered gray files unceremoniously positioned at both ends. "I just want you to know how much we both appreciate what you're all doing to help find our daughter."

There was a momentary pause as the lawyer struggled to frame the words that he knew had to be said to Joan's parents. He remembered his own son's words — *her lost* — and then began to speak.

"I think Joan is lost to you."

It was as if an unexpected rush of wind had suddenly entered the room and lifted the weight of the unknown and the doubt from their collective minds. They both sank deeper into their chairs and reached to hold hands.

"Thank you for being honest with us. Sergeant Tammaro told us you all felt there was little hope. That Joan was murdered. You understand we had to hold out until someone could try to make sense out of it all. Will you just tell us what you know?" Mr. Webster quietly asked. "I think it would help us just to know what you know."

And so it began, in small bits and pieces. The letter from Bond. The polygraph. The *Mala Femmena*. The search of Weyant's house. The .50-caliber shell. The Mayan book. The statements to Pisa. The other victims. Florence White. Patti Bono. Connie Porter. Janet McCarthy. Conley and Daggett's. The Lynn Marsh Road and the murder of Marie Iannuzzi.

"The difficulty is we really can't prosecute Paradiso without Joan's body," the lawyer began as he explained the irony of the Webster case of 1850.

"Is there anything we can do to help in Marie's case?" Mrs. Webster asked selflessly. "It would help us just to be there during the trial and support her family. We share this horrible connection with them."

Murder, the DA realized suddenly, had become a common thread that coursed through the lives of these two very different families.

In that moment Marie's case became the Websters' case.

"I know the Iannuzzi family would like that," the DA told them.

50: Ellsworth, Maine

Located 260 miles northeast of Boston — four and a half hours by car — Ellsworth was a small tourist town of fewer than six thousand inhabitants. It was positioned at the gateway to Acadia National Park on the southeastern coast of Maine.

The park was a scenic hash of granite cliffs, green forests, pounding surf, and miles of coastline with some of the finest ocean views in the country. Acadia was a place of great beauty, capped by 1,530-foot-high Cadillac Mountain. The little town of Ellsworth was Hancock County's commercial center, home to dozens of fishermen, lobstermen, clamdiggers, and clamshuckers. A guy from Boston could buy seafood cheap in Ellsworth, ship it south, and make a good profit.

The Quahog loved Ellsworth.

On the same day the lawyer met with the Websters on the sixth floor of the courthouse, Drew headed north up Route 95 to Ellsworth. His lawyer friend wanted him to check Paradiso's claim that he'd stayed in Maine during Thanksgiving 1981. Ponytail, with his earrings, leather coat, and cowboy boots, contacted a crew-cut Maine trooper outfitted in traditional starched blues, and together they went door-to-door to every one of the hotels and motels in the area.

"Okay, I got some news for ya," Drew began late that afternoon as the lawyer listened on the phone back in his office.

"We got a lot of records up here for him. He was in Ellsworth all the time for three years right after he made parole. From June '78 through November '81, he was up here hustlin' his clams and seafood to ship to Boston. Lenny used to stay at a coupla different places up here. One was the Colonial and the other one was the Brookside. The Colonial's about three miles outside town on Route 3, 'bout fifteen miles from Acadia Park."

"How about the day Joan disappeared?" the DA asked anxiously.

"Lenny was close, but no cigar. He was at the Brookside the week *before* Thanksgiving," Drew said for emphasis. "Lenny came in on the tenth of November and left the Brookside on the seventeenth. He told the desk clerk up here he had ta go ta court the next week. Maybe it was for his bankruptcy case. When the hell was that?"

"Yeah, I think he was in bankruptcy court in Boston that week. It may have even been Friday, the day before Joan disappeared." The lawyer fumbled through the mound of papers on his desk.

"We also ran a computer check on him up here. They found one of the cars Lenny claimed was stolen in Revere in '79. It was torched up here in Machias, Maine, about an hour from Ellsworth. He probably drove it up here, lit it up, and then reported it stolen."

"The two of them had a real racket goin' with all the insurance claims they made. Surprised he filed for bankruptcy," the DA said as he finally retrieved the list of stolen cars. "Here it is. Lenny got three grand from Travelers Insurance on that claim. He told his parole officer he was goin' to Ellsworth the same weekend he was supposedly haulin' some clams back to Boston."

"Here's somethin' else. Paradiso was arrested up here for driving a stolen car with some other guy by the name of James Hornbraye. This guy Hornbraye gave an address of Cottage Street in East Boston. Wasn't there some other guy with Lenny when he raped Florence White on Cottage Street?" Drew asked.

"Yeah, there were two of them, but she couldn't identify the other guy."

"Anyway, there's more. I got ta talkin' with the trooper from Maine and he says a girl was strangled and left by the side of the road here six years ago. It was June '77. Her case has never been solved. Kinda interesting. Same fact patterns. She was climbing Cadillac Mountain with her dog that had a red bandanna tied around his neck. They found her body at the base of the mountain. Half naked, strangled."

"Wait a minute, did you say she was climbing Cadillac Mountain with a dog?" the lawyer said incredulously.

"Yeah, why?"

"Okay, you're not gonna believe this, but my wife and I were climbing Cadillac Mountain the same day this girl was killed. We had our dog with us, a big Airedale. We put a red bandanna around his neck so we could see him in the woods. The next day we heard on the news a girl with long dark hair was found dead. I called the police to tell 'em not to confuse any information they might get about us with the victim and the other dog with the red bandanna. I was working in the DA's office then and gave them my number to call if they needed any other information. I never heard anything about it till now."

"Where the hell was Lenny in June '77?" Drew asked. "You think he coulda been up there the same time you were there? How weird is that?"

"He was supposed to be at the Salem House of Correction then, wasn't he?" the lawyer asked uncertainly.

"Yeah, he was supposed to be. But he was out on furlough a lot of the time, too, wasn't he? You told me he was out for more than sixty hours at a stretch. That's more than two and a half days. We need to check it out," Drew said.

"Hey Drew, there's one other thing."

"Yeah?"

"I told the Irish judge you found the .50-caliber shell."

"Yeah, what'd he say?"

"He said you were a good cop, but you needed a haircut."

51: Tombstone, Arizona

The Amoco Oil Company couldn't have been more cooperative when the DA called to ask for a copy of Paradiso's credit record. The Quahog had accrued more than fifty-four hundred dollars in credit card charges over the past three years and had never paid any of them.

Tracing every stop for gas at a friendly Amoco station produced Paradiso's route across the country. Lenny had been to a lot of places. It wasn't just Ellsworth, Maine. The lawyer bought a large map of the United States and put a red flag in every city where Lenny had stopped for gas on his business trips.

"What are ya doin'? Taking a vacation?" Drew asked as he entered the DA's office and saw the map for the first time.

"Not exactly, but somebody else did. Did you know Lenny took off from Boston two days after you served him with the grand jury subpoena for Iannuzzi back in March '82? He was gone for six weeks and never got permission to leave the state. Lenny never even told his parole officer he was leaving town. He sent his PO a postcard from Tombstone, Arizona, and told him he left town for 'business reasons.' They were gonna revoke Lenny's parole, but good ol' Candy came through for him. She called Lenny's PO and smoothed things over."

"Are you kiddin' me?"

"No, I read the postcard Lenny sent from Tombstone. Every card and letter Paradiso writes begins with the same line, 'Dear So and So, I hope this letter finds you in the best of health.' He did the same thing with the postcard."

"How the hell did you find this out?" Drew hated it when the DA knew something he didn't.

"I went back and read all of his parole records again and then I got his credit card charges from Amoco after he declared bankruptcy. Lenny never paid them the five grand he charged for gas on his cross-country trip. So I took all the charge slips and marked all the places he stopped for gas on this map. I'm gonna send a letter to all these same locations to see if there are any unsolved rapes or murders during the different time periods Lenny was on his 'vacations.'"

"You're fuckin' nuts. You know that?"

"I also found out from the bankruptcy papers that Lenny and Candy have a safe-deposit box at the Haymarket Bank in Maverick Square, in East Boston," the DA told Ponytail. "I sent the bank a request for dates when either one of them went into the box."

"Good idea," Drew said. He approached the map with the tiny red flags positioned across its width and began repeating the names of some of the cities Paradiso had passed through.

"Let me see where the hell he went. Charlotte, New Orleans, and El Paso. San Diego, Seattle, and Billings, Montana. Chicago and Cleveland. He really was all over the country, wasn't he?"

"Yeah, and not a single business contact gets made for all the time he spent out there. D'ya think he really was out there looking for business, or just making himself unavailable to the grand jury for six weeks?" the lawyer asked rhetorically.

"You already know the answer to that one," Drew said as he turned from the map. "How do ya think it all fits in here?"

"Ya gotta get inside his mind. Joan disappears on November 28, right?"

"Yeah."

"They find her handbag near Conley and Daggett's on December 3, right?"

"Okay," Drew answered as he followed the time line.

"The story about the purse being found is all over the newspapers during this time period. Then just before Christmas Paradiso tells Pisa he killed Joan. Lenny knows he's made a mistake talkin' to Pisa. The pressure's starting to build on him. Now he's worried Pisa will talk."

Drew nodded. "I'm with ya so far."

"I checked the records. Right after Christmas '81 Lenny gets paid forty-five hundred bucks from Liberty Mutual for another one of his 'stolen' cars. Right after *that*, Lenny calls his parole officer and says he wants to take a trip 'out west.' His PO tells Lenny he's gotta give him an itinerary before he'll give permission to leave."

"So why doesn't he leave then if they'll approve the trip?"

"It's simple: He doesn't give them an itinerary because there is no 'business trip' planned."

"So what do you think he's doin'? Just setting it up so he can leave the state quick with 'permission,' but without telling his PO where he's goin'?"

"Yeah, a month later we find Webster's suitcase in the Greyhound storage place in New York City. The story's all over the newspapers again. Now Lenny knows we got her suitcase, but he doesn't know if we got his fingerprints."

"Okay, so when Lenny gets the subpoena on Iannuzzi in March, he panics, is that it?" Drew asked, filling in the blanks.

"Exactly. Lenny was subpoenaed to the grand jury on the fifth of March. He doesn't know what the hell he's gonna get asked if he has to testify. That's why he suddenly takes off on this 'business trip' without telling his PO."

"So the longer Lenny can put the grand jury off, the better it is for him. Maybe he thinks we'll indict David Doyle," Drew suggested.

"Maybe, but at the same time, Paradiso knows if he doesn't respond to the subpoena, we'll try to revoke his parole. That's why he takes the Fifth when he finally does go to the grand jury in June," the lawyer added.

"Do me a favor, will ya?" Drew asked.

"Sure, what is it?"

"If I ever screw up?"

"Yeah."

"Don't get assigned to my case," Ponytail said with a smile.

"I won't. I promise. But wait, Drew, there's more. Guess what happened to the car Lenny was driving on his 'business' trip in the spring of '82?" the lawyer asked.

"It was stolen," the trooper said with feigned surprise.

"Yup, a week after Lenny gets back, the silver Cutlass he was driving is mysteriously stolen from right out in front of 212 Crescent Avenue. It's the same thing that happened to the Chevy Caprice he was driving cross-country in the spring of '79."

"That street address has to be the stolen-car capital of the United States," Drew mocked.

"Yeah, you're right. The Cutlass is recovered from Boston Harbor, near Jeffrey's Point in East Boston by QB's tow company," the lawyer explained. "I found out that a coupla days after Joan disappeared, Paradiso was there, at QB's. One of his 'stolen' cars was towed there after they pulled it outta Boston Harbor. Lenny got into a beef over the storage fee and wound up beatin' the owner's dog with a lead pipe. The dog was chained to a barbed-wire fence. Too bad, the dog woulda had a better chance if it wasn't tied up. The owner called Boston PD, but the case never went anywhere."

"Well," Drew replied, "I got some more info for ya on that person you asked me to interview." He pulled a typewritten sheet from his black leather coat pocket.

"Which one? There were about thirty names on the list."

"Lenny's ex-mother-in-law. I found her. She lives in a third-floor apartment on West Wyoming Avenue in Melrose."

"Great, I'm sure she has some interesting thoughts about her former son-in-law."

"Does she ever. She told me Lenny first met her daughter Dorothy on a blind date. She said she knew Lenny was no good right from the start. Lenny used to hit her daughter all the time and tried to strangle her twice after they were married. He beat her daughter up really bad one time in their bathroom. He would fly into theses blind rages. It got so bad he threatened to kill everyone in the family. Lenny told everyone he was gonna get help, but he never did."

"Anything else?"

"Yeah, Lenny used ta take a pellet gun, put it to his wife's head, and pull the trigger. Dorothy had marks on her forehead all the time. Even when she was pregnant. She said Lenny never worked, and that one time she and her daughter were goin' to visit her sister in Saugus. They were outside in the car when Lenny came outta the house with a gun screamin' 'Don't move or I'll fuckin' shoot both of ya.'"

"This guy is whacked."

"There's more. Lenny's daughter, Angela, was with them. She was only eight or nine at the time. Someone had given her a kitten. Lenny hated the cat and strangled the poor thing right in front of his wife. Can you imagine that?" Drew slowly shook his head.

"Yeah, I can imagine that," the lawyer said, glancing up at the map of the United States, red flags crisscrossing its width.

Van Morrison was singing about a brown-eyed girl and making love in the green grass when the call came into the lawyer's office from the Lynn Hospital. It was just after nine in the morning on Tax Day.

A brick-faced community hospital, with more than one hundred beds, the "Lynn" was located in the center of the namesake city, about four miles from Paradiso's former apartment on Lynn Shore Drive. The Lynn was one of more than thirty hospitals in the Boston area that received subpoenas requesting treatment records for the Quahog.

"Good mohning. Is this Mistah Burke?" a nurse asked.

"Yes, this is Tim Burke."

"Hi, I'm Colleen Wentworth from Lynn Hospital. I have those medical records heah you were looking fah on Leonard Paradiso."

"Really," the lawyer answered, holding his breath, just as the caller placed him on hold to take another call.

"Sorry 'bout that," Nurse Wentworth said when she returned. She explained that she was filling in for a hospital administrator out on maternity leave.

"Yes, our records show Mr. Paradiso was treated on the thirtieth of Novembah 1981. He came into the emergency room around midnight, complaining about an injury to his left index finger. He told the ER people the injury happened two days earlier, on the twenty-eighth," the nurse related.

As she spoke, the import of her news settled into the lawyer's mind.

"Bond was right. Paradiso hurt his hand the night he killed Joan," the lawyer blurted to the unsuspecting woman on the other end of the phone.

"Excuse me?" the nurse responded.

"Sorry, I was just talkin' to myself."

"It's really kinda strange. Mr. Paradiso told the doctor a 'cherry bomb' went off while he was holding it. He said it left some kind of metal fragment in his hand. I didn't think cherry bombs had metal in them, do they?" the nurse asked cautiously.

"No, they don't," the lawyer responded.

"Well, it says heah the doc took two of the three pieces out, but theah's another one still in his finger. It was in too deep to remove without anesthesia," the nurse explained. "The patient was scheduled to come back and have it removed, but he never did."

"So he still has a piece of metal in his left finger?" the lawyer wanted to know.

"Yes, it appears he does. Mr. Paradiso returned heah to radiology on Decembah 22 for an X-ray. You can see it on the X-ray, but that doesn't necessarily mean it's metal. It could be thick glass. Whatevah it is, it's still in his fingah."

"Good," the DA said to the nurse without explaining why.

53: The Boston Marathon

It felt good to run. Things always seemed clearer when he ran.

The Boston Marathon is the world's oldest and most famous annual road race. It's run each year on Patriots' Day, the third Monday in April. The starting line is located in the quaint village square of Hopkinton, Massachusetts, a rustic community due west of Boston. At the stroke of noon more than ten thousand qualifiers take off to run 26.2 miles toward the finish line at Copley Square in the heart of America's Greatest City.

Every year, the Boston Red Sox play a home game on Patriots' Day. After the ninth, the crowd empties from Fenway Park just in time to see the race leaders pass through nearby Kenmore Square. From the rural communities of Hopkinton and Ashland through the towns of Framingham, Wellesley, and Newton, to the city streets of Brookline and Boston, more than a million spectators jam the roadways to cheer the runners homeward.

The Boston Marathon is high camp and great theater.

What makes it such a difficult race are the geography and the weather. Temperatures can range from twenty-nine to ninety-two degrees. It's almost always either rainy or windy, sometimes both. After running nearly twenty miles, the runners must then travail a series of four seemingly endless hills up Commonwealth Avenue until they reach the longest and steepest of the bunch. Located just before Boston College, it's aptly called Heartbreak Hill. Many a runner has seen months and even years of training come to a screeching halt on this slope. A Red Cross tent strategically located at the crest welcomes the unfortunates who are unable to continue.

"Can you just tell me one thing?" Drew said to his friend as he drove the silver Jag with the three bullet holes in the driver's-side door out Route 135 toward the starting line.

"Sure. Ask away."

"Why the hell would anyone with any brains inflict this kinda pain on their body?"

"I dunno. Just crazy maybe." The lawyer turned the question around. "Can you just tell me one thing?"

"Sure. Ask away." Drew smiled.

"Why the hell would anyone with any brains ride a motorcycle?"

"I dunno. Just crazy maybe."

There was a fleeting instant of premonition for the lawyer that passed as quickly as it came. He dismissed the thought from his mind as Ponytail pulled the Jag over to the side of the road, not far from the village green in Hopkinton.

"Thanks, Drew, I really appreciate the ride."

"Hey, no problem. I'll see ya at the top of Heartbreak Hill. You better not quit," the trooper said, watching the vast sea of runners slowly making their way to the starting line.

"Don't worry, I won't," the lawyer promised. He closed the door and walked away.

For the briefest of moments, the DA envisioned his friend riding his Harley and turned back to speak, but it was too late. He squinted into the morning sun, only to see Drew disappear from sight.

The two men shook hands as they met beneath the huge golden teakettle spewing a cloud of vaporous steam from its spout into the misty air on Court Street.

"Betcha I can guess exactly how much water this kettle can hold." The DA pointed upward.

Drew hated it when the lawyer knew something he didn't.

"How much?"

"How much money or how much water?"

"Water," Drew said, choosing the cheaper alternative.

"It can hold 227 gallons, two quarts, one pint and three gills of water," the DA said with an air of confidence.

"What the hell is a *gill?*"

"It's like a 'nip,' about a quarter of a pint." The lawyer smiled.

"How the hell do you know that?"

"I looked it up, and besides it's written on the side of the teakettle right up there," he said, pointing to the small fine print on the side of the kettle.

"Sometimes you really piss me off, you know that?" Drew laughed as he turned to head inside the Steaming Kettle.

The tall, broad windows of the Kettle had just the hint of mist from an early-morning patch of fog. Outside, the haze had yet to burn off from a sun hidden in the midst of a thick bank of dark, gray clouds. The tiny restaurant was a great place to people-watch in the early afternoon as the crush of cars and foot traffic battled for dominance outside on busy Court Street.

"I got a couple of ideas on the Webster case," the lawyer offered as the two sat spooning their chowder.

"I'm listening."

"How 'bout we give Candy immunity from prosecution if she testifies about Paradiso and the *Mala Femmena?*"

Drew swallowed hard and paused. "We gotta find the boat first, don't we?"

"No, I don't think so. Maybe Candy knows where Paradiso sank it. Weyant had the stuff from the *Mala* in her house when you searched it. Maybe she was at the pier with Paradiso when he stripped it," the lawyer speculated.

"Yeah, but the boat doesn't get sunk until late November. That doesn't mean Weyant was there with him when Lenny sank it, does it?"

"Gawd, you should represent her, Drew." The lawyer laughed as his friend cringed.

"What's involved in giving her immunity?" Drew said, quickly coming back to the prosecution camp.

"Well, we'd have to put her into the grand jury again. Get her to take the Fifth, which you know she'll do, and then go to the Supreme Judicial Court for them to grant her immunity from prosecution in exchange for her truthful testimony. That's the only court that can give her immunity," the lawyer explained as much to himself as to his friend.

"What happens if she refuses to testify?"

"Well, once she's given immunity, she has to. If she doesn't, she can be held in contempt of the SJC's order to talk and then held in jail until she does testify. The feds do it all the time."

"But she can still lie even if she's given immunity, right?" Drew asked.

"Of course, but it's still an opportunity to find out more information about what Paradiso did and where he was the night Joan disappeared. If nothing else, it's a way of finding out what his alibi is going to be. Right now we're just trying to exhaust as many sources of information as we can. At a minimum, she has to explain how the compass and the ship-to-shore radio from the boat found their way into her house."

"Make sure you ask Candy what Lenny knows about Mayan civilization when she's in the grand jury," Drew said as he went down the list of items seized from Weyant's house.

"I got another idea, too. Ya know how I got the search warrant and had the doctor from BCH take a sample of Gomes's blood?"

"Yeah, you mean the vampire warrant on the triple?"

"Okay, so we got the call from Lynn Hospital, right? And they said Lenny's still got something in his left index finger, right?"

As the lawyer spoke, Drew turned to face him and slowly exhaled. "Yeah, right. Why?"

"Well, how 'bout we petition the court to have the piece of whatever it is inside his finger surgically removed and then have the crime lab tell us what it is?" the lawyer said, quite pleased with himself.

"You are fuckin' nuts. Ya know that. Anybody ever done that before?" Drew asked as the sound of a siren ebbed and flowed outside on Court Street, then gradually wound its way up Tremont.

"Well, not exactly. There's a US Supreme Court case that says you can't pump out some guy's stomach to see what's inside, but this is a little different. I wanna try it anyway and see what a judge will do."

"Let me guess. You dreamed this stuff up when you're runnin', right?" Drew said as he drained the remainder of his soup.

"Yeah, actually, I was thinkin' 'bout it when I was runnin' up Heartbreak Hill last week. I didn't tell ya then, but I appreciate you being there that day," the lawyer told his large friend.

He acknowledged this with a nod. "Yeah, it's a good thing ya didn't quit, I was gonna jump in and run the last couple of miles with ya if ya stopped."

"That's what I was afraid of. That's why I didn't stop."

"So how do ya think Lenny got this thing in his finger?" Ponytail asked.

"This is the way Bond described it to me," the lawyer said. "Paradiso said he grabbed Joan by the hair when he hit her in the head. He's right-hand-dominant. If he grabs her hair with his left hand and clenches it into a fist, it's the outside part of his left index finger that's gonna get hit at the same time he's hitting her with whatever's in his right hand."

"Okay, I see what you mean," Drew said as he clenched his left hand into a fist.

"So that's why he winds up with something stuck in the outside part of his left index finger."

"Yeah, well, ya know what I think?" Ponytail asked without waiting for a response. "I think we outta offer a reward for finding the *Mala Femmena*."

"That's a great idea," the DA said as they walked out of the Kettle and into the gray.

55: 40 Avalon Street

A little over a month after the powwow with Drew at the Steaming Kettle, Lenny's girlfriend was required by subpoena to make an appearance with her rotund attorney before the Suffolk County Grand Jury. Candace Weyant was the first person called as a witness in the investigation concerning the disappearance of Joan Webster.

The prosecutor expected Weyant to walk defiantly into the mahogany-paneled room, glare at the group of twenty-three jurors, and take the Fifth.

She did just that.

Candy was dressed in the same dark stretch pants and matching black-and-white floral print blouse she had worn a year earlier when she and Lenny sat across from David Doyle. This year the bleached blonde had a new companion seated on the heavy wooden bench opposite her. The new witness's name was Bobby Bond.

After her appearance, Weyant was one step closer to being immunized as a witness against the Quahog. The marble-floored lobby was essentially empty as Candy left the grand jury room with her attorney and mouthed the words "fuck you" to the DA. She headed for Jimmy from Southie's elevator and turned back just as Bond was being brought inside to testify.

When the lawyer returned to his office on the sixth floor, the phone was ringing.

"Hey, I got some news for ya. I'm out here in the friggin' boondocks," Drew said. "This is the only pay phone in Florida, Massachusetts."

"I got some news for you, too," the lawyer began.

"Whatta ya got?" Drew asked.

"Remember how Paradiso wanted his two new lawyers to get a statement from some woman being treated for a heart issue at Mass General?"

"Yeah, the mystery woman who was gonna be one of Lenny's alibi witnesses for the night Webster disappeared, right?"

"Exactly. Bond didn't know the mystery woman's name, but Paradiso told him both Candy and this other woman were gonna be alibi witnesses on Iannuzzi, too. Anyway, Carmen just called. They got some records at Charles Street that an Elaine 'Bunny' Covino visited Paradiso a bunch of times between July and November '82."

"That name sounds familiar, who the hell is she?" Drew asked.

"Covino's from the North End. She was dating Lenny when he claimed the

Mala Femmena was stolen from Pier 7. Covino's name is listed on the police report as a witness to the theft," the lawyer explained.

"You know that's bullshit," Drew said, his voice reflecting his increased agitation. "If it was stolen, how did all the stuff from the boat wind up in Candy's house? We know Paradiso stripped the boat before he claimed it was stolen for the insurance money."

"I know, but wait, Drew, there's more. Guess what the medical records I subpoenaed from Mass General tell us about the same Elaine 'Bunny' Covino?"

"Okay, I give up. What do the hospital records say about Elaine 'Bunny' Covino?"

"I am so glad you asked that question. Covino's the mystery woman who was treated at Mass General for a heart condition in November '82. She's the woman the Quahog told his lawyers to get the 'deathbed statement' from. How the hell is that for corroboration of Bond?"

"That's amazing. Did anybody interview her yet?"

"Yeah, Carmen just sent one of the troopers in your unit over to Covino's house to talk to her. She lives at 40 Avalon Street in Revere," the lawyer answered.

"I wonder how far Covino's house is from Weyant's place?"

"I dunno, but guess what? We found out Bunny Covino does Candy's hair for her. How weird is that?"

"This guy is unbelievable."

"And guess who just happens to show up to say hello when the trooper is there interviewing Bunny? You guessed it. Lenny's girl Candy. Covino's in the same boat as Candy. She'll say or do anything for Paradiso. Bond was right about her. Covino was gonna be a part of Lenny's alibi in both Iannuzzi and Webster. Bond just didn't know Covino's name when he wrote me the letter."

"Did you find out anything else?" Drew asked.

"Yeah, just about a month before you arrested Paradiso for the Iannuzzi murder, Covino bought a car from him for short money."

"This plot just keeps gettin' thicker," Drew said.

"That's what I got here on my end. Tell me what you found out about the girl murdered in Florida."

"Her name was Kim Benoit. It was deer-hunting season when they found her body. She was sixteen, just a kid. Probably hitchhikin'. Once he has her in his car it's all over. Just like the rest of 'em. They found her in the woods, down a gully, a couple of miles from the Summit Motel. Not far from where the fat

bastard had his picture taken. She was strangled," Drew explained, his voice
growing intense with anger.

"You think it's just another one of these coincidences?"

"No, I think it was him. It's just one of those feelings I got. Ya know what I
mean? It's instinctive. This isn't a coincidence, him being out here 'round the
same time she's killed. Are you ever gonna be able to prove it? No, but you
know it and I know it. He did it. I feel it in my bones and my head and my
soul."

56: The Six O'Clock News

It was a Thursday as the Three Amigos and the DA sat in his office playing tapes from the three TV stations' six o'clock news that had aired nearly three and a half years earlier.

"We need ta be able to prove Gomes is lyin' about seeing a live newscast from the scene of the murders on Jacobs Street at six o'clock," the lawyer told the three compadres.

"Where do ya wanna start?" Cashman asked.

The DA paused the tape and turned to the three detectives. "The medical examiner says time of death was between 5:30 and 6:30 PM. Gomes's alibi is based on him being at his mother's house when the murders take place. The victims' father gets home at just before six thirty, and Larry Fisher is the first cop on the scene at six thirty-six."

"Gomes told me he actually sees the news live on the TV at his mother's house at six o'clock. He was certain it was the Channel 5 reporter Jorge Quiroga doing the live shot from the murder scene. He says that's when he runs home, falls, and gets the cut on his arm. When he gets to his house, Gomes said he sees the father on the porch screamin' 'bout his family being murdered. Gomes don't help him. He just calls a cab to BCH and says at the same time Channel 5 is doin' the live shot out in front of the house. What a crock of shit," the normally taciturn Doris said to the gathering.

"There's no way there was any live broadcast that early," Cashman said as the first tape began to roll. "I got there just after the first call came in ta headquarters and there were only two or three uniformed guys at the scene when I arrived. The TV trucks didn't show up till the eleven o'clock news. He is full of shit."

After the run through of three hours of news and commercials, it was clear that Cashman was right.

Channel 4 had no mention of a mother and two children being murdered in Boston during their six o'clock news. Channel 5 never sent Jorge Quiroga to 12 Jacobs Street that night, nor did they even mention the story on their *News at Six*. They carried the story live on the eleven o'clock news. Ron Sanders from Channel 7 was the first reporter from any channel at the scene that night. He arrived at 9 PM and never did a live broadcast.

"Hey, Mark," the lawyer said to one of the Amigos, "would you mind going back to the part of the tape from Channel 5 that mentions the new invention by that professor from MIT?"

"You mean the one with the sonar thing?"

"Exactly. We've been sending divers all over Boston Harbor trying to find Paradiso's boat, but it's like trying to find the proverbial needle in a haystack. We can't search every foot of the harbor with divers. It's just too big. There's too much area to cover. Maybe this professor's sonar invention can help," the DA said as the tape rolled again.

And there it was on the eleven o'clock news for December 5, 1979, the night of the triple homicide, an interview with the famous MIT professor about his invention of a side-scanning sonar system. The invention could "see" objects over a wide area on the bottom of the ocean floor.

"I'm gonna call this guy tomorrow and see if he's willing to help us find the *Mala Femmena*."

"You're friggin' nuts, you know that?" Doris smiled.

"Yeah, I think I've heard that before."

57: Point of Pines
_____

The Massachusetts Institute of Technology is the college world's Brains ' R' Us.

Harold E. "Doc" Edgerton was a professor at MIT and possessed one of the biggest brains on campus. Early in his career Doc had worked with a stroboscope to invent ultra-high-speed and stop-action photography. He moved on to underwater photography with his friend Jacques Cousteau. The first detailed photographs of the sunken *Titanic* were taken from a camera Doc designed.

"I'd be personally delighted to assist you, young man," the professor told the lawyer on the telephone. "There's one caveat, however. I'd like to accompany the divers when I have a free moment in the next few weeks. In the meantime, I will instruct them on how to use the sonar system. They can begin the search for this fellow's boat immediately."

"That would be terrific, Dr. Edgerton," the DA enthused warmly.

"What did you call his boat — the 'Evil Woman'?"

"Yes, it's actually the *Mala Femmena,* and I know the divers would enjoy having you out with them, too," the DA said as he checked the monthly calendar on his desk. "I had them search the area around Pier 7 first. They're going to search the Pines River near Saugus in a couple of weeks. Are you available to go out with them then?"

"Why, yes, I am," Doc replied.

The scheduled search date in late May was a windy Wednesday. The MIT professor boarded the Boston police harbor patrol boat and said hello to the three wet suits with black fins and goggles as they set out for the Pines River.

In the lawyer's office on the same windy day, two men thumbed through the four tall stacks of *Bargain Hunter's Guides*. The stacks were neatly positioned beneath the red-flagged map of Paradiso's cross-country travels from a year earlier. The tiny room smelled of rough wood-pulp paper and cheap print ink. The pair sat on the floor cross-legged scanning the past four years of want ads for everything from used refrigerators to curling irons to bowling balls.

"Hey, Drew, I found something here. It's for the week of July 28, 1981. Take a look. Lenny listed the *Mala Femmena* for sale two days after he says it was stolen. Look, the ad says 'For Sale, 1972, 26-foot Chris-Craft in excellent condition.' They listed Candy's phone number," the DA explained.

Drew took the ad, read it twice, and said, "The two of them been living on the edge for a long time. Ya know what, Weyant's the real reason Lenny hasn't gotten grabbed yet. She's always been there to cover for him. You gotta wonder what she knows. She's a part of everything he does. All the stolen cars and boats, even the murders. I can't wait till she's given immunity and has ta testify."

"She may still lie for him, but you're right: She holds the key to everything he's done," the DA said.

"Speaking of cars, guess who registered an antique 1939 Oldsmobile that just happened to be previously owned by one Leonard J. Paradiso?" Drew smirked.

The DA hated it when Ponytail knew something he didn't.

"Let me guess. Is he a lawyer and does he wear cowboy boots?"

"You got it. One of Lenny's new lawyers registered the Olds right after they took over the case from Cipoletta," Drew advised.

"So Bond was right about what Lenny paid his new lawyers, wasn't he?"

"Yeah, he was." Drew shifted gears. "I wonder how Doc and the divers are doin' out there today?"

Just off the Point of Pines near the narrow inlet to the Pines River, Doc and his gang of three made haste slowly as the sonar beeped, the seagulls cawed, and the rocks on the shoreline behind Conley and Daggett's loomed eerily ahead. They would search for the remainder of the day and find nothing.

"Ya know, I was going through Joan's sketchbook before you got here today," the DA said as they finished the last of the *Bargain Hunter's Guide*s. "Her mother gave it to me when they were here. I found an entry Joan made for a fine arts course she was plannin' to take in the fall of '81. It wasn't a regular architecture course. That's why we couldn't find the Mayan book listed as part of the regular curriculum at Harvard. Guess what the name of the course was?"

Before the trooper could guess, the lawyer told him: "Ancient Architecture, 2200 BC Through AD 1500."

"Ya think it might have something to do with the Mayan book we found?" Drew asked.

"Yeah, I think there's a connection, but I just don't know how to prove it yet. The course tracks the same time period as the Mayan civilization. Joan was into architecture and temple building. That's what the project she was working on was about when she disappeared. I can't link it for certain, but I do know it doesn't make sense for the Quahog to have that book."

"Well, you had Boston fingerprint the book, and they couldn't find any prints, right?" Drew asked.

"Right. They said it looked like it had been wiped clean, just a couple of smudges. I wanna have it sent to the FBI and see if they can do anything with laser printing. Do you know anybody over at the Bureau?" the DA asked his friend.

"Are you kidding? I wouldn't tell the FBI if their fuckin' coat was on fire," Drew responded without smiling.

58: Egg Rock Light

It was another day looking for the *Mala*.

For nearly three months the dive team had searched the huge harbor and beyond, scanning the murky waters with Doc's invention, with nothing to show for it. The divers were just off the craggy edge of Egg Rock, a small island north of Boston Harbor, halfway between the shoreline of the city of Lynn and the Nahant Peninsula.

Egg Rock itself was a seventy-five-foot-high, three-acre stone outcropping shaped in the form of a stationary beluga whale, plunked more than a mile off the coast in the gray Atlantic. The lonely rock was due east from Point of Pines and the Saugus River.

For more than a hundred years, until it permanently went dark in 1922, Egg Rock Light was home to a red-tinted, beaconed lighthouse that guarded the safe passage of clipper ships, small dories, fishing boats, and cruise liners alike.

The dive team wasn't far away.

The sun shone brightly in the cloudless sky as the black fins and masks came out of the police boat's locker. The yellow air tanks on deck gently clanked together to the rhythm of the ocean's waves as the men prepared to dive again.

"What the hell are we doing lookin' so far out here?" Nick Saggesse, one of the divers, wanted to know.

His friend and fellow diver Richie Famalare was quick to respond. "Didn't you hear? Some woman Paradiso used to date told Burke that Lenny told her he used to dump his victims' bodies out near Egg Rock. Andy Palombo called yesterday and said the DA wanted us to check it out. So here we are, lookin' for 'em."

Saggesse was Boston PD and a dead ringer for Andy Palombo. Two inches shorter and twenty pounds lighter, Saggesse loved to tell the story of walking into an East Boston bar late one night and having some drunken slug mistakenly tell the Boston cop an interesting confession.

"I haven't hit my wife since you arrested me, Trooper Palombo. You taught me a good lesson, man. Now I know what it feels like to get hit that hard. Just don't beat the shit outta me again. I promise, I'll never fuckin' hit her again," the drunk told Saggesse, who smiled as he repeated the story once again for the crew.

"I wouldn't want that fuckin' guy on my case if I ever whacked anyone," Palombo's look-alike mentioned as the sonar beeped, signaling a dark shadow on the ocean floor beneath them.

"Hey, what the hell is that?" Famalare pointed to the sonar screen and looked back at his friend.

"It's a fuckin' boat. Look, you can see the silhouette," Saggesse yelled as he reached for his tank and fins. "Get Burke on the ship-to-shore. Tell him we found a boat. He's gonna go nuts if it's the *Mala*."

The call was patched through to the DA's office as he sat reading a motion he was scheduled to argue at two o'clock in Courtroom 808. On the radio, Journey sang "Don't Stop Believing." It was just after 1:50 PM when the lawyer answered the call. The sound of Famalare's voice was surprisingly clear — almost as if the diver was sitting in the next room with his wet suit on.

"Timmy, this is Richie. You're not gonna believe this, but we're out near Egg Rock and we just got a hit on Doc's sonar. It looks like a boat. Nicky's diving down there right now. It could be the *Mala*. It looks like it's about the right size," the cop diver said excitedly just as the ship-to-shore connection went dead.

It was late spring.

The Celtics had been swept 4–0 in the Eastern Conference semifinals, and the Red Sox were off to another slow start in what was to be Yaz's eighteenth and final year with the team. It was the end of an era as the "Ole Towne Team" struggled just to play .500 baseball.

The lawyer and the trooper made it from his office at the courthouse to the statue of Sam Adams in front of Faneuil Hall in less than the standard eight minutes of walking.

Built in 1742 by French merchant Peter Faneuil, the four-story brick structure would later become known as America's "Cradle of Liberty." For more than twenty years the building served as the site of Boston's town meetings, providing a forum for fiery speeches by patriot Sam Adams in protest of British rule. Surrounded on four sides by a cobblestone garden, and separated from Boston Harbor by Quincy Marketplace, Faneuil Hall was a hotbed of historical clues to the nation's past.

"Did you know Sam Adams was the first cousin of John Adams, the second president of the United States?" the lawyer asked his friend as they passed beneath the larger-than-life statue.

"Yeah, I think I knew that," Drew responded, wondering where the conversation was headed.

"Yeah, but did you know John Adams was a lawyer?"

"Yeah, I think I knew that, too," Drew nodded.

"Okay, but did you know John Adams represented one of the British soldiers tried for murder in the Boston Massacre?" the lawyer continued.

"Are you sure it was John Adams, the president?"

"Yeah, he defended a captain by the name of Thomas Preston, who was in charge of the British troops that fired into a crowd of civilians throwing sticks and snowballs at the soldiers. The British troops shot and killed five people that day. One of them was Crispus Attucks, the first black man to die in the cause of the Revolution," the lawyer said.

"Wait a minute. John Adams is defending this British captain after his troops shot and killed some of our guys here in Boston?" Drew said in amazement.

"Yeah, turns out the captain told his troops 'Don't fire' as the crowd was goin' wild, taunting 'em and daring 'em to shoot. Preston's troops thought he gave them the go-ahead to shoot. So they started firing at the crowd," the lawyer explained as they walked toward the North Market building for lunch.

"What'd the jury do?" Drew asked.

"They found the captain not guilty."

The larger man briefly paused and then walked on in silence.

The DA could tell Drew was thinking. They were inside the restaurant before they began to speak again. The lawyer decided it was a good time to change the subject.

"The Department of Corrections sent over the rest of their file on Paradiso today. I went through it all and found this letter Candy sent to Norfolk prison when Lenny was serving time for the Connie Porter case. Let me read some of this to ya," the lawyer said as he and Drew sat on the second floor of Durgin Park restaurant surveying a lunch menu they could recite from memory.

"She wrote it in October '76. It really shows you where her head was at." The DA held up Candy's stationery with a picture of a Labrador retriever imprinted for his friend to see.

"I think I already know where her head is at," Drew said quickly. "I think I'm gonna order the Yankee pot roast today."

"That sounds good, but I'm sticking with the Poor Man's Roast Beef." The DA began to read from Candy's letter, addressed "To Whom It May Concern" at Norfolk prison.

I am writing this letter on behalf of my boyfriend, Leonard J. Paradiso.
I was disappointed to hear about his recent furlough denial.

"I didn't know Lenny ever got denied a furlough. It must have been the only one," Drew said as he placed the elbows of his large arms on the red-and-white-checked tablecloth.

"Listen to this part," the lawyer said:

I have been dating Lenny for 5 years now, since I was 18 years old.
This November begins our 6th year together. Since then neither
one of us had any interest in seeing anyone else. I am not putting
words in his mouth, he has stated this to me on several occasions
over the years. There are no secrets kept from each other. We had
planned to be married, but he was hesitant with the legal matter
hanging over him.

"Did she actually say Lenny wasn't 'interested in seeing anyone else'?" Drew said in mock amazement. "What about all the other women he's picked up and tried to rape? She thinks Lenny has no secrets?"

"She's probably never had another boyfriend in her life. That's why she'll do anything for him," the lawyer said as their lunch arrived at the table.

"You think she's that desperate to have someone, anyone, love her? Even someone like Lenny?"

"What the letter shows is how blinded she is to whatever he does and just how needy she is trying to hang on to him. It's either that or she's scared to death of him. Afraid of what he might do to her. She's gotta know what he's capable of. Listen to this part."

> I definitely don't believe Lenny is guilty of attempted rape. If I had the slightest doubt in my mind, I would not be writing this letter or have anything more to do with him. He always conducts himself as a gentleman. If a few guys are visiting and someone accidentally swears, Lenny has them apologize out of respect for me.

"Always the perfect gentleman." Drew slowly shook his large head from side to side.

"Wait. There's more."

> Since Lenny has been incarcerated, he has done everything the authorities asked of him. Tonight, while I was out, Lenny called my house to inform me he had an accident while working in the garage today. Lenny told my mother and father he was taking a pin out of a truck and, accidentally, the instructor hit his hand with a 16-pound sledge hammer. Now his hand is in a cast. Accidents do happen, but why to Lenny?

"Lenny's a victim? Yeah, that's a good one." Drew smiled a thin smile. "Didn't Pisa tell us Paradiso started a fight with an inmate and the other con broke Lenny's hand before Pisa broke it up?"

"Yeah, the con's name was Dexter something. I think it happened around the same date she writes this letter. That must be the 'accident' she's talkin' about."

"So what was she writing to Norfolk for?" Drew asked.

"She was trying to convince them to grant him a furlough from prison. Maybe she was offering to be his sponsor or something. Listen to this part."

When his furlough has finally been approved, there is no way he would not go back. Why should he do something to hurt his record for something he didn't do to begin with? I realize you only carry out what the courts decide, but hopefully things will be changing. Soon the real truth will be heard and things will be different. Thank you for reading this as I am deeply concerned about his welfare.

Very truly yours, Candace Weyant, Revere, 02151

Drew was having a difficult time containing himself. "Is she in denial or what? Candy testifies as Lenny's alibi on the Porter case, so she's gotta know what the evidence against him is. Her 'boyfriend of six years' has semen all over the front of his pants and the victim's blood on his jacket. The girl's face looks like hamburger and Candy wants to get him a furlough?"

Ponytail clearly wasn't done talking. He leaned forward in his chair, closer to the lawyer.

"The cops find him on top of Porter, trying to strangle her. He's zipping up his pants when they arrest him. He's got a .38 with the serial number obliterated hidden under the front seat of his car. There's a blackjack in the front and a machete in the trunk. And somehow Candy doesn't think he's a sick bastard? Is this woman so blind to everything Lenny's done she can ignore the truth like that? I ain't buying it. I don't think she's afraid of him at all."

The DA sat looking at his friend and decided not to respond.

"Let me ask you something, Tim. You don't think our jury's gonna let Lenny go free, do ya?" The DA could tell that thoughts of Captain Preston and John Adams were passing through his friend's mind.

The fine art of fund-raising is a necessary talent for every successful political candidate in the city of Boston. The district attorney of Suffolk County was no different.

Charismatically Irish Catholic and prematurely gray at thirty-five, Newman Flanagan was enormously popular with large voter blocks in both the Italian and Irish wards of the city.

Stocky at five foot ten, with a collection of the most god-awful flamboyant ties known to humankind, Flanagan was one hell of a lawyer in front of a jury. He understood and genuinely liked people. In return, people liked his charm, his wit, and his ability to relate to their lives. When he spoke, juries believed him.

In 1978 Flanagan ran for DA against his aging predecessor and won in a landslide over the thirty-year incumbent. Four years later he won again handily. Each succeeding year brought another fund-raising "time" for the next upcoming election. This year's event was held on a warm summer evening in late June '83, at the Pier 4 Restaurant in South Boston. Everybody was going.

Anthony Athanas was Albanian American. He was small in stature, shrewd by nature, and the owner of Pier 4, one of the highest-grossing restaurants in the country. He was a good friend of Newman Flanagan and knew countless other celebrities, politicians, and athletes. By the early '80s, Anthony's Pier 4 had become the gathering place of those who had arrived in life, those who had merely bought their tickets, and the rest of the lot standing on shore, waving good-bye.

You could tell just by looking at the pictures on the walls of his place. Anthony Athanas knew some people. It was "eyes right" when you walked past the wall of fame and saw the photographic likenesses of JFK and Jackie O, Jimmy Carter, Tricky Dick, Gerald Ford, Ol' Blue Eyes, Deano, Liz and Liza, Judy Garland and Bob Hope, Arnie, Jack Nicklaus, Jack Nicholson, the "Yankee Clipper," Joltin' Joe DiMaggio, and Boston sports greats Bobby Orr, Carl Yastrzemski, Bob Cousey, Bill Russell, and Larry Bird.

They were all there, the great and the near great, shaking the diminutive owner's hand or planting a buss on his cheek. It was great PR, and Anthony still made them all pay for dinner. The freshly baked popovers and strawberry baked Alaska were alone worth the price of admission.

Located on the waterfront that paralleled Northern Avenue, Anthony's

Pier 4 provided diners with a panoramic view of Boston Harbor and the skyline. The two-story, brick-faced building featured an antique train engine cemented, sans tracks, near its canopied entrance. The restaurant itself was situated across the harbor from Logan Airport and a short distance from Pier 7 and Commercial Lobster, where Paradiso moored his boat and delivered shellfish from Ellsworth, Maine.

The young lawyer walked through the double-door entrance and past the huge lobster tank, where bug-eyed two- and three-pounders were mixed in with the rare blue, and even rarer albino, crustaceans, motionlessly awaiting their boiled fate. He inched toward the receiving line where the district attorney and "Mr. Leary" stood at the helm beneath a bare-breasted wooden maiden, taken from the bow of an ancient whaling ship.

Overhead, the sounds of Harold Melvin and the Blue Notes blared "The Love I Lost" to the crowded backdrop of mingling lawyers, judges, politicians, clerks, cops, and assorted hangers-on. Everybody was there. Drew wore his best boots. Carmen wore his new camel-colored Armani; the Three Amigos had donned freshly pressed and starched short-sleeved buttondown blue oxfords with nearly identical blue-and-red-striped ties. The lawyer wondered aloud if the three had gone to the same parochial school.

"How are ya, boss?" the lawyer said to the smiling DA as he clasped his right hand, smiled back, and caught a faint whiff of Old Spice.

"I hear you ran the marathon this year. Proud of ya, kid, but you shoulda wore a FLANAGAN FOR DA T-shirt runnin' up Heartbreak Hill. There's a million potential votes out there," Flanagan joked.

"This kid could swing an election your way just by getting his family to vote for ya, Newman," Mr. Leary said with a smile. "He's the youngest of twelve. Too bad they're all still back on the farm in upstate New York."

"You got enough cases to keep you occupied?" Flanagan asked.

"I do, sir," the lawyer said as he thought of the tattered brown and gray files sitting on his desk and the other twenty-odd murder cases he owned.

"He's been busy with that cold case. Remember that triple outta Dorchester. And then there's his 'friend,' Lenny the Quahog, Newman," Mr. Leary added as he placed his hand on the young lawyer's back, making a small triangle of conversation for the three men.

"That's one sick bastard, kid. He's probably a serial killer. No luck finding his boat yet, huh?" the district attorney said as he glanced back over his shoulder toward the wide expanse of the inner harbor.

"Not yet. We thought we had it — found a boat sunk off Egg Rock Light we were sure was it. Turned out to be something called the *Lucky Penny*," the lawyer replied. "So we're still looking. I'll find it. I don't care what it takes. I'll find it, and I'll convict him."

There was a momentary pause as the two older men searched the expression on the younger man's face, sensing for the first time the driven intensity about him. It was undefined, unspoken, but necessary to match the malevolence that he was confronting. The two older men understood the allure and obsession of good versus evil, the certain versus the unknown. They understood there would be no options.

"You gotta win these two cases, kid," the DA told him. "Everything happens for a reason. Ya know, in some way maybe it's your destiny. That's why you've been put here."

The lawyer heard the words, but didn't truly understand their meaning. He smiled at the two older men, shook their hands, and walked into the large second-floor function room with a carved wooden sign whose gold-leaf letters read BOSTON. He took a seat at a white-linen-covered table with the Three Amigos, Drew, and Carmen. Behind them, the DJ played "Every Breath You Take."

"Did ya get a raise?" Drew wanted to know.

"Yeah, that was quite an audience you had with His Eminence," one of the Amigos said, laughing. "I was timing it. You lasted longer than the mayor."

After the speeches, jokes, guffaws, and campaign rhetoric, the assembled retired to their cigars, their Tanqueray and tonics, and the warm night air breezing over the sundecks overlooking the harbor. A week past the summer solstice, the evening still held the remnants of sunlight slowly drifting into the purple-hazed twilight separating day from night. The water rippled with reflected light, momentarily capturing the city skyline.

It was a gorgeous night.

"Ya wanna take a ride over to Pier 7?" the lawyer said to Drew as they headed past the lobster tank and into the night. A thin hint of fog unexpectedly gathered along the water's edge as the big trooper looked up quizzically.

"We've been there twenty times already."

"I know, but we never went there at night. I wanna see what it looks like in the dark."

61: The Lancaster Street Garage

The law enforcement community in Massachusetts was separated into jurisdictional camps of bitter rivalry and mistrust.

Not unlike the ancient cities of Sparta and Athens, the Massachusetts State Police and the Federal Bureau of Investigation were a house divided against itself. With separate missions and resources, each agency eyed the other as an unwanted stepchild in the world of cops and robbers. Neither could function without the other, and neither would admit its need for the other. Hidden beneath a public veneer of cooperation and solidarity, the two agencies secretly warred for years over informants, jurisdiction, headlines, and high-profile cases. All was well in plain view, but behind closed doors the two hated each other.

Much of the mistrust between the MSP and the FBI arose from an investigation of the Irish mob in South Boston conducted by the state police and the Suffolk County DA's office in the early 1980s. The state police's Major Crime Unit secretly targeted a career mobster out of Southie who had led a charmed life of violent crime for more than twenty years. James "Whitey" Bulger was a stone-cold killer and the head of the Irish mob. Whitey's brother Billy just happened to be the president of the Massachusetts Senate.

Like the biblical Cain and Abel, each man wielded incredible power within his personal sphere of influence.

At the same time the state police began their covert investigation of Bulger in South Boston, the Feds were setting up a wiretap on the Anguilo crime family in the North End. What the state police didn't know at the time was the fact that Whitey Bulger was a protected informant for the FBI.

Every attempt by the state police to wiretap Bulger's haunts, his car, or his phone was met with frustration for the MSP and avoidance by Whitey. It was as if Bulger knew in advance where the next listening device was being placed. Once the bug was installed in a particular location, Bulger stopped going there.

For more than a year, the young prosecutor drafted affidavit after affidavit for the right to have the MSP wiretap Bulger's conversations. For weeks on end, troopers watched from their observation post on the third floor of the cockroach-infested flophouses across the street from the Lancaster Street Garage, where Bulger met with his underlings and members of the Anguilo crime family. Each day the troopers reported their observations at the "Garage" back to the DA. Never once in that year did they observe a car's oil being changed.

Located only a couple of long jump shots from Boston Garden, the Lancaster Street Garage was the mob's equivalent of Anthony's Pier 4.

Everybody who was anybody in organized crime went to Lancaster Street. All the dons, capos, button men, loan sharks, hit men, leg breakers, drug dealers, enforcers, and long-ball hitters were there. It was truly a Who's Who of OC thugs and slugs, including the local head of La Cosa Nostra, Jerry Anguilo, and his two brothers. Not to mention local mobsters Larry Zannino, Nicky Femia, Michael Caruana, George Kaufman, Phil Waggonheim, Stevie "the Rifleman" Flemmi, Kevin Weeks, and of course Whitey.

They were all there. And just like Pier 4, the MSP had the eight-and-a-half-by-eleven-inch glossy photos of the organized crime celebrities to prove it. Unfortunately, the troopers never got a chance to hear any of the conversations among the assembled mobsters.

Drew seldom swore. He lost his temper less often, but he was really angry at his friend that early-summer day in 1983.

"Are you outta your fuckin' mind?" Drew screamed at the lawyer in his office. "You're gonna call the fuckin' FBI in on Paradiso's case?"

"It's a federal crime, Drew. We don't have any jurisdiction to prosecute Paradiso for bankruptcy fraud. The feds can give him ten years on it if he's convicted," the DA tried to explain.

"So just fuckin' convict him on Iannuzzi," Drew shot back.

"We don't know what a jury will do on the Iannuzzi trial. We got a case that's built on the testimony of two convicted murderers. We don't even know if Pisa and Bond will still testify three months from now, let alone in another year. We can't find Joan's body. We can't find the *Mala*. Janet McCarthy's case is a one-person identification from more than two years ago. Paradiso can walk on all this in less than a year. You really want that psychotic killer back out on the street again?" the DA asked, trying to sound convincing.

"Are you really askin' me?" Drew paused and quickly added, "No, I don't fuckin' want him back on the street. But I gotta tell ya, Tim, after what happened on Whitey's wiretap, I don't think many of our guys are gonna be really happy about you calling the feebs into Paradiso's case. Everybody knows goddamn well Bulger got tipped off about what you were doin' with our guys down at Lancaster Street. And everybody thinks it was the feds because Bulger's one of their rat informants."

"I know Bulger was tipped, Drew, and we may never be able to prove it, but I still can't ignore this bankruptcy fraud," the lawyer said as he picked up the phone and began to dial the FBI.

62: The JFK Building

"FBI, can I help you?" the woman's voice asked.

"Yes, you can. I'm trying to reach your white-collar crime section," the lawyer responded. The operator redirected the call.

"This is Agent John Clattenoff. How can I help you?"

"Hi, my name's Tim Burke. I'm an assistant DA in the Homicide Unit here in Boston, and I wanted to talk to someone about a murder case I've been working on. It involves a possible bankruptcy fraud," the lawyer explained.

"Okay, well the agent that usually handles those kinda cases isn't in the office right now. Let me take your number, and I'll have him contact you when he returns from lunch, or I can just have him stop over at the courthouse. We're right across the street from you guys in the JFK Building on Cambridge Street," the agent offered.

"That would be great. If he wants to come over here I can fill him in on the background and show him what I've got. I'm on the sixth floor of the courthouse. Just have him ask for me. I'll be here for the rest of the afternoon."

The agent said he would pass the message on. "His name is Steve Broce. I'll have him get in touch as soon as he comes back."

The DA didn't have long to wait.

"Hi, I'm Agent Steve Broce," the man said with a smile as Burke waved him inside his office while talking on the phone.

The two shook hands without speaking until the lawyer could end the call. The man from the FBI took a seat and surveyed his surroundings. He was a quick study. You could tell just by looking at him. Agent Steve Broce could have recited every detail and facet of the interior of the lawyer's office and completed a two-page incident report to his supervisor before the conversation even began.

Broce was athletic, about five foot ten, with a mustache and dark hair. He dressed the way you'd expect a white-collar-crime guy to dress: conservative brown suit, conservative tie, conservative white buttondown shirt, with conservative brown lace-up shoes and socks to match the suit. He said the words *car, bar, far,* and *park* with an *r* and not an *h* so you knew right away he wasn't from Boston. Somehow there was a California blend to him that made you think of Wine Country and surfboards.

Turned out Steve Broce was from Sacramento.

"Hi, I'm Tim Burke. Thanks for coming over. I've got a case with a guy by the name of Lenny Paradiso that we've been working —"

"The Quahog?" Broce interrupted.

"Yeah, Lenny the Quahog."

"I know who you're talking about. I've followed everything that's been in the newspapers about him. He's a sick bastard. I'll do whatever I can to help you."

There was no hesitation in the agent's voice. No reluctance to become involved. No limitation placed on the effort he was willing to expend. Broce was direct and sincere.

It was just the kind of response the DA was hoping for. The lawyer liked Broce immediately and knew Drew would eventually do the same. The two men spent the next four hours going over each fact and detail of the entire case, from Florence White to Candy Weyant, from Tony Pisa to Bobby Bond, from Marie Iannuzzi to Joan Webster.

63: Harvard Yard

Despite the phrase's frequent use to describe a Boston accent phonetically, no one is actually allowed to "Park your car in Harvard Yard."

If you're lucky, you'll just get a parking ticket. More likely, your cah will be towed to one of the many nearby lots surrounded by a high barbed-wire fence and signs telling you how much you owe. The tow lots are located in another world, just across the Charles River, in a place called Brighton. The kind of lots with a nasty dog that sits chained out front, panting and snarling. Just waiting to say hi when you come to get your cah back.

Parking your car at Harvard University is harder than getting a degree there. Named after its original benefactor, Puritan minister John Harvard, the oldest college in the country was established in 1636 by the Great and General Court of Massachusetts.

Surrounded and defined by its seven-foot-high black wrought-iron fences, the twenty-plus-acre site lies adjacent to Harvard Square in the center of Cambridge. A world onto itself, Harvard Yard is home to numerous unique, ivy-covered redbrick student dormitories and academic buildings. Most come with a view of the nearby Charles River.

You have to be very smaht to hang out there.

The campus police weren't located in Harvard Yard, but they should have been. They were situated off campus, at 29 Garden Street, not far from Radcliffe College. The cop from Harvard University was personally involved in Joan's case and committed to solving her disappearance.

It was another warm summer day as Lieutenant Larry Murphy sat in the lawyer's office with his neatly arranged file and began to sift through what he had talked about every day for the past eighteen months. As expected, Larry brought along the mandatory dozen doughnuts from "Dunks," with two large black coffees for himself and two Diet Cokes for the DA. It was going to be a long session. It was hot outside, and hotter inside. The fan wasn't working, and there wasn't a view of the Charles.

"You asked me to check the Harvard bookstore on the Mayan book, Tim, but there doesn't seem to be a connection between the book and any of Joan's classes as a required reading," Murphy began. "She had a book bag with her that was never found. So the Mayan book is still kinda up in the air, ya know what I mean? It's just weird that a guy like Paradiso would have something in his personal library on Mayan civilization."

"Yeah, I know. We're having the book fingerprinted by the FBI," the DA mentioned, wondering if he could have been wrong about the book's connection to Joan.

Murphy shrugged and continued, "We also ran a check on all of the phone calls made from Joan's dorm room. They all check out, nothing significant. Her sister Anne used the phone after Joan was reported missing, but we verified all of those calls. There were a lot of notes left tacked up outside Joan's door over the weekend by her friends. So we're certain she didn't return to her room at Perkins Hall."

The lawyer gestured in agreement. "I spoke to Anne. She said Joan wore gray shoes to see *The Pirates of Penzance* the night before she came back to Boston. Her shoes were packed in the suitcase with some pictures from a vacation in Nantucket. That jives with what Bond told me about Paradiso findin' some photographs in Joan's suitcase. Paradiso told Bond they were stuck inside a pair of gray shoes to keep from getting bent."

"How the hell could Bond have known about the shoes and pictures if Paradiso didn't tell him?"

"Yeah, we had everything in the Lark suitcase they found in the Greyhound storage facility in New York City dusted for fingerprints, but there were no prints on the photographs," the lawyer said with a sense of frustration.

"Paradiso's a con. He's not that stupid. Lenny's not gonna leave any prints and make your job easy. Dollars to doughnuts you don't find any prints on the Mayan book, either," Murphy predicted.

The lawyer nodded.

"Anne said she talked to Joan on the way to Newark Airport about how much it cost to take a cab from Logan to Cambridge. Anne said Joan didn't have a great sense of direction. Joan wouldn't have known if she was going the wrong way when they left the airport. She only knew Boston from the subway system. They actually talked about cabbies going to Revere and over the bridge instead of through the tunnel. That may have made her more comfortable if Paradiso had gone a different direction."

"Joan was bright, but she's no match for him. He coulda bullshit her about where he was takin' her and she would have believed it," Murphy said with the knowledge that comes from understanding a child taught to trust.

"Tell me what you think, Larry," the DA asked. "What's Joan's mind-set when she lands at the airport?"

"Well, we know she was mugged two times when she lived in New York City. So that may have affected her willingness to take the MBTA from the airport back to her dorm. We checked all of the T stops up to Wonderland in Revere looking for her luggage. We didn't find anything. No one sees her on the shuttle from the airport over to the T station, either. That's why we don't think she took the T that night."

"I know you guys spent a lot of time interviewing people on the flights that came in that night. Is there something else we're missing here?"

"I don't think so. She didn't have a car, but we checked the parking lots anyway and found nothing there. There was no metered parking near the terminal she landed at, so it's not likely someone drove to the airport to pick her up."

"How about bars in the area?"

"We went to all of the bars at the airport and checked them out, too. No one saw her there. She wasn't much of a drinker, but we checked just to be sure."

"Does Harvard have one of those Share a Ride things for students coming back on the holidays?"

"Yeah, we do, but her name wasn't listed," Murphy told the DA. "We checked with all the employees around the baggage carousel that night. None of them remembered anything about her. Her plane landed right around 10:35 PM. There were two flights that landed from Newark at almost the same time. So the carousel area was crowded, but the baggage handlers told us there were plenty of cabs."

"You know we have a couple of witnesses who said they saw Paradiso driving a white ITOA cab, right?" the DA asked.

"Yeah, I heard that. We checked the taxi pool, too. One cabbie took a fare from the airport over to Harvard Square, but it wasn't Perkins Hall where Joan lived. We spoke to everyone on the plane that night. One woman remembers a girl changing cabs, but that's all she could give us," Murphy said with a shrug.

"You have a sense for what Joan was like, Larry. Do you see her getting in a strange car with someone she doesn't know and taking a ride? Or is she gonna take a cab?"

"No way, not gonna happen. She's not getting in a stranger's car. It just doesn't fit who she is. He's weeds and she's roses. She may not have been street-smart, but she was sophisticated. She's twenty-five years old. She's not gonna be hitchhiking from Logan Airport alone at night. And she's not gonna take the T," Murphy replied without hesitation.

The DA nodded. "I agree. I think she took a cab, too. It's late at night. Like you said, nobody hitchhikes outta the airport. She's not gonna just stick out her thumb, especially carrying luggage. Besides, we know her father gave her twenty bucks to get a cab when they were back in New Jersey."

"Ya know, a gypsy cab driver dropping someone off coulda avoided the cabbie pool, especially when it's busy. You had a lot of people coming out of the terminal at the same time lookin' for taxi rides," Murphy suggested.

The lawyer paused, considering.

"One of the investigators from my office interviewed the tollbooth collectors at the entrance to the tunnel in East Boston. He showed him a picture of Paradiso. The toll taker told him he saw Lenny driving a white ITOA cab through the tunnels toward the airport a few times right around the time Joan disappeared."

"That's great information. Is there anything else that ties the white cab theory in?" Murphy asked.

"Yeah, there is. There was a witness who saw a white ITOA cab stopped on the side of the Lynn Marsh Road near Conley and Daggett's the night Joan disappeared. It was right around 1 AM on the southbound side going toward Boston," the lawyer explained to the cop.

"I don't believe in coincidences, do you?"

The lawyer shook his head from side to side. "There's a Chelsea cop I spoke to who lives near Paradiso's girlfriend in Revere. He says he's seen Lenny driving a white taxi before, too."

"You know Joan disappeared the night of the Great Lynn Fire, don't you?" Murphy asked the DA, already certain of his answer.

"Yeah, we did some checking on the roadblocks they put up that night. They were set up north of Conley and Daggett's, closer to Lynn. There were a lot of blue lights and police activity on the Lynn Marsh Road when the fire was burning."

"So if Paradiso sees the blue lights at the roadblocks and turns around, it would explain why Joan's wallet was found on the other side of the road across from the lobster pound," the lieutenant said as he visualized the scene.

"Right."

"That could be when the witness saw the white cab parked on the southbound side of the road without headlights," Murphy quickly added.

"Exactly."

"But doesn't Bond say Paradiso took her body 'way out' in the harbor to get rid of it? Why is Lenny up on the Lynn Marsh Road?" Murphy asked.

"There's two possible scenarios here. One, Paradiso killed Joan on the boat and took her body out somewhere in the harbor and dumped it. That's why we keep searching for his boat. The other possibility is he killed her and took her body somewhere else to get rid of it."

"That means her body was probably in the trunk of the cab when he's on the Lynn Marsh Road," the cop surmised.

"That's one of the choices."

"What do you think? Which one is it?" Murphy asked simply.

"I think the weather was too bad to go out on the *Mala* that night. If Paradiso did go out in the harbor, why wouldn't he have gotten rid of her pocketbook or the suitcase and the rest of her stuff at the same time? I think he killed her on the *Mala* and took her somewhere else to bury the body. I think Paradiso was headed to Lynn where he lived when he runs into one of the roadblocks they set up because of the fire. Lenny gets spooked when he sees the blue lights and turns around. Now he's headed back toward Boston, that's when he pulls over and throws her wallet and handbag on the side of the road across from Conley and Daggett's."

There was a pause in the conversation as the men sat quietly mulling the variations on the theory behind Joan's disappearance.

"I think Lenny originally planned on leaving Joan's body near where he killed Iannuzzi. Most people had forgotten about Marie by then. It's more than two years later when he kills Joan in November '81. Lenny thinks he's home free on Iannuzzi. Besides, there's no known connection between Lenny and Joan at that point. It becomes this mystery that only Lenny will know the answer to."

"Maybe he thinks he's gonna try to throw the cops off by putting her body in the marshes," Murphy offered.

"That's a possibility, too. I thought about that, Larry. The problem is, with all these police in the area that night Lenny can't risk taking the body outta the trunk of the cab. He wants to show how smart he is, and at the same time he's leavin' a clue to who killed her. Lenny doesn't even know it, but I think he wants to get caught."

"What's Paradiso's mind-set at this time?"

"We know Paradiso was up in Ellsworth until the middle of November and came back to Boston the week before Thanksgiving. He had a hearing on his bankruptcy the day before Joan disappeared," the lawyer explained.

"How d'ya think the bankruptcy fits in here?"

"Lenny needs money, but he doesn't want to show any income. That's why he's driving a cab. What better way to make some cash, not declare it. and play the airport at the same time? Once Paradiso has someone in his cab, he owns her. It's the same pattern — he has control once he gets them in his car."

"It's all beginning to make sense. This guy's under a lot of financial pressure.

His world's falling apart. This is one way for him to get control over a part of his life."

"There's more: A couple days after he kills Joan he beats a tow lot guard dog with a lead pipe."

"Are you kidding?" The cop from Harvard Yard shook his head in disbelief. "This guy's a goddamn animal."

He was a likable sort, this defense lawyer with the reptile-skin cowboy boots.

Drew would be upset to hear his friend say he liked Paradiso's attorney, but he did. The two lawyers sat in the DA's office talking about their mutual case and the upcoming trial as the Drifters sang "Under the Boardwalk" in the background on the radio.

Outside, the sun beat down and burned the tar up on the courthouse roof.

It was late July and eighty-nine degrees out on Tremont Street. It was ninety-three degrees, without air-conditioning, inside the prosecutor's office. The fan didn't work, either.

"Every time I come in here, you got music playing," Carhart said as he tapped the alligator toe of his boot to the bass of the song and joined in a chorus of "you can almost taste the hot dogs and french fries they sell."

"There's nothing in life that transports us quite like music," the DA explained.

"You're gonna need some really soothing music to calm that 'savage beast' when I kick your ass at the Quahog's trial."

"It's 'savage breast,' not beast," the DA said with a smile.

Carhart never blinked.

It was clear to the casual observer the two men respected each other despite the tactical jockeying for dominance in their conversation. Nevertheless, as the case wore on, the psychological chess game continued to play itself out between the two egos.

"So tell me how you're gonna explain to the jury that one of your star witnesses just got arrested again this past weekend," Carhart smirked.

The prosecutor shrugged, as if David Doyle's recent drug arrest was no big deal. It was a very big deal. Doyle's arrest hurt the case. The DA knew it. He also knew what Carhart would say next.

"No matter what happens to Doyle's case, it's good for us and bad for you. If Doyle gets convicted, we can use it at trial to impeach his credibility. If he gets off, we can say you guys gave him a break to testify against Paradiso. Either way you got another problem to explain to the jury. Add that loser to the list of convicted killers you plan on calling. This is gonna be one hell of a trial, Timmy Boy."

"You seem to forget the motion I'm gonna file to allow all the women he's raped and tried to kill to testify at his trial. That jury's gonna be very interested in hearing what your client's been doing for the past fifteen years," the prosecutor retorted.

"Good luck with that. There's no way in hell any judge is gonna let that other stuff in at trial. It's just gonna be your two killer cons and Doyle leading the parade of mopes from the Cardinal's Nest. Your winning streak is gonna end real soon." Clearly Carhart thought he was beginning to get to his adversary, especially with the part about the thought of losing.

There was a momentary pause in the flow of the conversation as the DA pondered what Lenny's newest lawyer said. He knew Carhart was right on both counts. There was little likelihood a judge would allow the other women to testify at Paradiso's trial, and — more importantly — he couldn't bear the thought of losing this case.

"With all the problems you've got, I'm surprised you haven't tried to convince me to talk plea," Carhart said, testing the waters, trying to catch a reaction from the younger lawyer.

Theirs was a game of high-stakes bluff. You never really said exactly what you thought.

"We're not gonna offer Lenny a chance to plead to manslaughter on Iannuzzi," the prosecutor began after considering his options.

"So what'd you call me over here for?"

"Actually, I asked you to come over here because I wanted to tell you we may be indicting your client on another case," the DA responded, hoping to surprise his adversary.

"Are you crazy? You're gonna indict him on the Webster case? You can't prove he killed her without finding her body first," Carhart said. Both men simultaneously thought of the 1850 Webster murder case.

"No, I know that. There's something you need to know. Paradiso tried to rape and murder another girl in July 1980. She saw him on the news a few months ago. I'm holding off on doin' a photo identification so you can't say the news influenced her if she picks him out," the DA shot back.

"Who is she?"

"Her name is Janet McCarthy. It's the same MO with him. He picked her up hitchhiking in the North End and took her to Revere near Candy's house and tried to strangle her. She fought her way out of the car and got away. It's all starting to catch up with your guy," the DA said as he carefully watched the expression on Carhart's face.

It didn't take the defense attorney long to respond. What he said wasn't what the prosecutor expected. "Well, I got some bad news for you too, Timmy

Boy. Maybe it's not bad news, but I don't think Walter Prince and I are gonna be representing Mr. Paradiso much longer. Seems as though some people think I'm too friendly with you. Lenny wants another lawyer. We planned on filing our motion to withdraw next week. I wasn't gonna tell ya till then," Carhart said. He'd managed to upstage the news about the hitchhiker from the North End.

"You can't do that, Judd. The Iannuzzi case is scheduled for trial in two months. How can you guys just dump him now? Another lawyer coming into the case this late in the day is gonna postpone the trial for another six months, maybe a year. I've gotta oppose your motion to withdraw." Was Paradiso firing his lawyers intentionally to delay the trial?

"You know there isn't a judge that's gonna make us try the case if Paradiso doesn't want Prince and me to represent him anymore. We're out of the case next week. Sorry, Tim, it's just the way it is." The defense lawyer extended his right hand.

He knew Carhart was right. And with the assignment of a new lawyer, Paradiso's trial was now a long way away.

"Besides, you need a vacation," Carhart suggested to his opponent. "I heard you were going down to the beach for a couple of weeks."

"Who told you that, Jimmy from Southie? Yeah, we're going to Marsh Vegas. You know, the Irish Riviera," he replied, referring to the small beach community of Marshfield on Boston's South Shore.

"Good place to go," Carhart agreed as he reached for the door and began to sing. "Down by the sea, on a blanket with my baby . . . is where I'll be."

"Hey, Judd," the prosecutor began with a smile.

"Yeah?"

"Does Lenny want ya ta give him back the '39 Olds?"

65: The Fairview Inn

The Fairview Inn in Marshfield, Massachusetts, was a grand old weather-beaten, gray-shingled structure on the raw Atlantic coast.

A brothel in the 1930s, the inn was located in the seaside Brant Rock section of town on Ocean Street, just off Route 139. The Ol' Dame was fronted by a narrow dirt parking lot that overlooked a rock-strewn, horseshoe-shaped inlet twenty-five feet below.

Straight ahead, three thousand miles due east, lay the west coast of Portugal.

Home to pup seals on the rocks in the winter, and offering a scenic view of tramp steamers passing by throughout the year, the Fairview was a great place to down a couple of jars as the seabirds played touch and go overhead.

A large Aztec sun painted on the roadway beneath the carved wooden FAIRVIEW INN sign pointed the direction, and the distance in miles, to exotic places and faraway ports of call that the seabirds, seals, passing ships, and patrons sometimes migrated to: Rio de Janeiro 4,291, San Francisco 3,136, Puerto Rico 2,278, Key Largo 1,591.

For those who never left port, an afternoon delight or a moonlit night spent on the Fairview patio was a very pleasant alternative.

It was a Saturday, the first day of vacation. One of those days you dreamed of in the dead of winter. No snow, no ice, no work, no phones. No clouds, no humidity, just plenty of sunshine with a warm breeze, a blue, blue sky, and the sapphire Atlantic Ocean.

The lawyer and the FBI agent sat outside talking on the patio deck.

"You want the good news or the bad news?" Steve Broce, dressed in his conservative brown suit, tie, and shoes, asked the lawyer in shorts, sandals, and a Jimmy Buffett T-shirt.

"I like good news," the DA said as he smiled from behind his sunglasses.

"You know the picture of the woman Andy found when he did the search warrant at Weyant's house? The one we couldn't figure out who she was or how Paradiso knew her?" Broce began.

"Yeah, she looked a lot like Joan, right? Her picture was mixed in with the photographs of Lenny out in Florida near the Summit Motel?" The lawyer tried to recall what she looked like. "She was a kind of a pretty woman, wasn't she?"

"She was. We wondered what she saw in Lenny. Well, I found out who she is and interviewed her. I tried to call ya late, but you'd already left, so I brought the report down for you to read. Her name's Charlene Bullerwell. I spoke to her for about an hour yesterday. She used to date Paradiso off and on for over a year from the summer of '80 through '81. She lives in Revere now, on Crescent Avenue, not far from Candy Weyant. Do you believe that?"

"How the hell does this guy do it?"

"I don't know. She said she first met Lenny at Bill Ash's. It's a bar on Revere Beach. She says he was always acting like a clown, wisecracking with her. Lenny told her he worked at some lobster company on the Lynn Marsh Road. They went out a couple of times and then one day Lenny invites her to take a ride on his boat."

"Tell me she didn't go with him."

"No, it's not what you think. She goes out on the boat with him. They're naked, making out on the bed in the cabin, and all of a sudden Lenny pushes her against the wall and starts screaming at her, 'Shut up, shut up and I mean right now.'"

"Really?"

"Yeah, really. She says it was the weirdest thing. He's got this crazy look on his face. She was kissing him at the time. She wasn't even talkin' when he started screamin' to shut up. She moves away from him and falls asleep at the kitchen table. The next morning, she woke up and the boat was crashing against a buoy out in the harbor. Paradiso never says a word to her about what happened the night before."

"You're kidding. That's weird. What d'ya think, maybe Lenny couldn't perform with her? It sounds like what happened with Patti Bono, doesn't it?"

"That's just the beginning. She says he's got a really violent temper. She went on his boat another time right after Labor Day in 1980. This time she has her son with her. They go fishing. Nothing happens till they pull back into Pier 7. Some other car is blocking Lenny's Cutlass. He goes nuts and starts ramming the other car until he pushes it out of the way."

"Hey, I know parking's tough in Boston, but this is three miles from downtown," the lawyer said, seizing the opportunity.

"She told me it's right around the same time that Lenny starts telling her he's gonna sink the *Mala* and collect the insurance on it," the agent continued. "Lenny told her he wants to buy a bigger boat. He said he might try to sink it near Pier 7."

"We already checked the Pier 7 area. That's one of the first places I had the divers look. It was almost impossible for them to see because there was so much silt in the water from all the boats coming in and outta there. The other problem was a bunch of broken pilings that prevented the boat from getting close enough to have the sonar do the whole area. Maybe I should send them back?"

The agent nodded. "Funny you would say that, because Lenny told Bullerwell, 'There's so many boats in and out of Pier 7, no one would ever suspect the *Mala Femmena* was sunk there.'"

"I guess you know the first place we'll start looking again when I get back from vacation. It's kinda funny, right after Bond sent me the letter, I called every aerial photographer in the area and asked them to send me copies of any pictures they took of Boston Harbor around Pier 7 between June and December 1981," the lawyer began as the first cloud of the day temporarily hid the sun.

"What were you lookin' for — pictures of Lenny's boat?" Broce guessed.

"Exactly. Lenny claimed it was 'stolen' in July '81. So I was trying to see if there were any aerial photographs taken of the *Mala* at Pier 7 after he says it was missing. I even sent a letter to the CIA and asked them to check. They have these spy satellites now, y'know, that can take incredible pictures from a hundred miles above us. They never responded," the lawyer explained.

"Did anyone else respond?"

"Yeah, there were two of them. One aerial photo was taken in late May '81. It's incredible, you can actually see the *Mala* tied at the pier. There's another one taken on November 30 and the boat's gone. That was the same day Lenny told Bond he sank the *Mala,* two days after he killed Joan." The lawyer's voice trailed off into thought.

"Lenny's girlfriend Charlene had a lot more to say, Tim," Broce said.

"Really?"

"Yeah, the other agent and I were just talking with her, just askin' some background questions about where Lenny worked, things like that. All of a sudden she starts crying hysterically and blurts out 'Lenny told me he was a hit man for the mob.'" He was clearly trying hard not to be dramatic.

"That's what she said to you?"

"Yeah, she did. She was scared. Real scared. Lenny told her if she ever told anyone what he said he would kill her. He was adamant. He said he'd kill her if she talked. No matter how long it took him to find her."

"Is that all she would tell you about him?"

"No, Lenny told her he had killed a number of people. Lenny said he liked 'doin' women.' Women were easy to kill because they were small and weak.

He bragged about taking them out and tying on cinder blocks and tossin' 'em in the ocean. He said how much they weighed would determine how many cinder blocks he would use to sink their bodies. He told her he would tie one to the arms, legs, neck, and waist, and just toss them overboard."

"Ya believe her, Steve?"

"Yeah, I do. She knew him pretty well. We know he's violent. You've seen and heard what he's done with other women. It's clear he has a hatred of women. She was scared to death of him. She's seen his violence firsthand. He used to get rough with her and say things like 'I'd like to rip you apart' and 'I'd love to cut your chest off,'" Broce repeated, his face hard.

"Past conduct is the best indicator of future conduct, I guess."

"Yeah, there was some jewelry he gave her, too. A gold seahorse, an ivory elephant, a purple ring, and some shark's teeth. At some point in the summer of '81 she tells Lenny she doesn't want to see him anymore and he comes into a sub shop where she's working and pulls a nutty. He tells her to give him the stuff he gave her back." The lone cloud of the day cleared the sun.

"Bullerwell is a wealth of information on the Quahog. Did she give the stuff back?"

"Yeah she did. She didn't want it anyway. She also told me what Lenny said about his wife and the name for his boat," the agent said as his expression softened.

"Really?"

"Yeah, Lenny told her he named his boat because of his ex-wife. Bullerwell said Lenny really hated his ex. He said she had done a number on his head and was his 'ruination.' Lenny told Bullerwell he hated women because they were backstabbers who just used men," Broce explained.

"We should find his wife and try to interview her," the lawyer said, wondering what Mrs. Paradiso looked like.

"There's more. Lenny told Bullerwell he hated his daughter because she went 'punk' and got a job as a stripper. She told me they were at a wedding for one of Paradiso's nephews when his daughter approached her and started to talk to her. Paradiso came over and told his daughter to 'get the fuck away' because she wasn't 'good enough' to talk to Bullerwell."

"Man. This guy really is nuts."

"Once she started talkin' about Lenny she wouldn't stop. Bullerwell said when she first heard that Joan Webster was missing and her pocketbook was found on the Lynn Marsh Road, she immediately thought of Lenny Paradiso because of what he had told her and because she knew he was connected with some lobster company up there. She said on the night of the Great Lynn Fire, she drove down the Lynn Marsh Road and there were all kinds of cruisers and a helicopter flying around." Broce took a long slow breath.

"Okay," the lawyer replied at last. "You told me the good news, what's the bad?"

"The US Attorney's office doesn't think there's enough evidence to indict Candy on the bankruptcy or insurance fraud. They're gonna indict Lenny later this month, but they're not sure about Candy," Steve said.

"Hey, ya know what? If I get Candy immunized by the SJC, we may be able to get more information about Lenny. Let's just make sure we convict him."

Established in 1826, when the Boston shoreline was at the edge of Quincy Marketplace, Durgin Park was one of those institutions that defined "Bean Town."

The second-floor walk-up restaurant cooked and served up more than fifty pounds of molasses-soaked Boston baked beans in dark ceramic crocks every day, and that wasn't all. Poor Man's Roast Beef with real mashed potatoes and gravy for $2.95, Yankee pot roast for a dollar more, and a dozen oysters for a dime made the place a feeding ground beyond comparison.

Each meal was served with warm homemade corn bread and enough attitude from the waitresses to provide patrons with perspective on their personal significance in the world. The place was an eight-minute walk from the courthouse, and the lawyer and the trooper were regulars.

The first-floor entrance of Durgin Park featured a larger-than-life-sized photograph — it took up an entire wall — of some of the toughest-talkin', hardest-workin', foulest-mouthed waitresses in the city. It was as if the owner wanted to give you fair warning of what awaited you upstairs while you waited to get the call for your table.

Many of the fainthearted turned back.

The second floor was bedlam, the clang of heavy porcelain dishes and shouts between waitresses and cooks echoing off the foot-square sections of pounded-tin ceiling. But boy, the food was good.

Durgin Park was the great equalizer.

There was no distinction made by social status, religion, or party affiliation. There was no special seating and no reservations. Everybody ate together at the same tables, long ones (seating twenty each) covered with red-and-white-checked tablecloths in three separate rooms. When two people left, two more came up from downstairs to fill the empties. The lines were out the door at lunch as hungry Bostonians and tourists alike waited to be seated and — in the Durgin Park tradition — verbally abused by the likes of Dottie Lamb and Gina Schertzer.

Gina loved to whistle. She had the teeth for it. They were pretty, straight little white Chiclets, with just the smallest gap between the two front ones that allowed her to hit all the notes in a song. She loved to dance when she whistled.

If you weren't snotty or a pain in the ass, Gina called you "Sparky."

"Oh look, Dottie," Gina said to her friend. "It's the lawyah and the troopah with the ponytail.

"Hi, Sparky," she called to the lawyer as she began to whistle "Singin' in the Rain."

Not unlike Debbie Reynolds, Gina grabbed the large man with the cowboy boots around the waist and began to dance with him between the tables filled with openmouthed jealous suitors. Drew hated it. The lawyer loved it.

Red-faced, Drew sat down, ordered a cup of chowder, took a spoonful, and wished he had gotten a bowl. Gina took the rest of the order for lunch and yelled it across three tables to the head chef, Tommy Ryan.

"Hey, Tommy, kill me a coupla steers for my favorite dancin' pahtnah, Gene Kelly, and his big-shot lawyah ovah heah."

The place roared as the lawyer grinned and Drew simply dropped his head and shook it slowly.

"I just got off the phone with Mrs. Webster before we walked down here. Guess where Joan was about six weeks before she disappeared?" the lawyer asked his friend as they sat at the end of the table.

"Okay, where was she?" Drew asked, by now well accustomed to the game of Twenty Questions.

"In Ellsworth, Maine. She went up there with a guy she was dating for the weekend in early October. I spoke to him this morning, right after I heard she was up there. He said they went hiking in a quarry and then went to a couple of markets while they were in Ellsworth. They ate at the Trenton Bridge Lobster Pound twice over the weekend."

"D'ya think there's a connection?" Drew asked, trying to place the restaurant in his mind. "Like they might have run into Paradiso somehow?"

"It seems really remote. I asked him that. The two of them were together the whole time they were up there. He said nothing like that happened. There was no opportunity to encounter Lenny. The two of them spent a lot of the time hiking and shopping and going out to dinner. Ya know the picture Mrs. Webster sent of Joan sittin' on the rusted steam engine in the quarry with the hiking boots on? That's when it was taken. Around October 9," the lawyer explained.

"You know Paradiso was renting a room up there until the middle of November, right?"

"I know, Drew, we gotta consider everything, but I think it's just one of those coincidences. I sent her boyfriend a picture of Paradiso and asked him to let me know if he remembers seeing him anywhere up there."

"That's weird, though, that they both may have been in Ellsworth at the same time," Drew wondered aloud.

"Anyway, I also called the parking ticket division over at Logan Airport and asked them to run a list of all of the tickets you guys handed out the night Joan disappeared. That's how they got the Son of Sam killer, remember?" the lawyer said as Gina smiled at her dancing partner, took the empty chowder cup, and brought the Poor Man's Roast Beef to them both.

"Yeah, David Berkowitz, right?" Drew offered a rare smile as he made short work of the beef and spuds.

"Right."

"Anything else happenin'?"

"Carhart was in the office a couple of days ago," the lawyer said between bites. "He and Prince are out of the case next week. They filed a motion to withdraw. I'm not sure who's gonna be representing Lenny next."

"Damn it. That means the trial's off, right?"

"Probably, unless the judge denies the motion."

"Ya think Lenny's just tryin' to stall, switching lawyers?"

"Maybe. I think Paradiso hopes something will happen to Bond or Pisa to make 'em change their mind about testifying. The longer it goes, the better Lenny's chances are. Delays almost always work in the defendant's favor," the lawyer said amid the din.

"You mean like David Doyle getting arrested again last month?"

"Exactly," the lawyer said.

"When's Lenny scheduled to come back to court?"

"The next pretrial conference date is the first week in August. Before he fired Carhart and Prince we were gonna try the Iannuzzi case this September."

"You know the trial's not gonna happen now. Not with another lawyer coming in," Ponytail speculated.

"You're right, it's gonna be at least another six months. It does give us some more time to focus on Joan's investigation," the lawyer said, trying to find the bright side.

"Listen, Tim, I'm not a lawyer, but you can't indict Lenny on the Webster case unless you find her body. I know why you wanna find the *Mala* so bad. It's 'cause you think there's gonna be some blood evidence on the boat that you can use to prosecute him even if we don't find her body. If he sank the boat, the salt water's gonna destroy any blood that's left there. Lenny's not stupid enough to leave her body on the boat. You can't build a circumstantial case like that without Joan's body or without blood. The only way you're gonna put him away for good is by convicting him on Iannuzzi. Face it, man, you gotta get him on Iannuzzi."

The lawyer hated it, but he knew Drew was right. "Okay, but I still wanna do a search warrant for his finger."

"You really think you can convince a judge to let a surgeon remove whatever he's got in there?"

"Actually I do," the lawyer said without hesitation.

"What happened with the petition for immunity for Candy?" Drew said, changing the subject.

"I applied to get immunity for her and Bunny Covino at the same time. I went up to the SJC yesterday. Candy and Bunny were both there. Candy just sat there the whole time staring at me. Get this, Drew: Bunny, she's all dressed in purple: Purple dress, purple shoes, purple bag, purple nails, and matching purple lipstick."

"Only you would notice that." Drew smiled.

"I'm a trained observer, just like you, Drew. Anyway, the good news is the judge allowed the immunity petition and actually said he was impressed with the affidavit by the commonwealth," the lawyer said proudly.

"He musta been Italian."

"No, he's Greek. It was Liacos," the lawyer responded.

"You've been busy. Anything else goin' on?" the trooper asked as Gina cleared the empty plates.

"I talked to Steve Broce this morning. He's getting a search warrant for Candy and Lenny's safe-deposit box at the Haymarket Bank in East Boston. The US attorney told him she plans on indicting Paradiso later this month for the bankruptcy and insurance fraud," the lawyer said. Then he quickly added, with an air of expectation, "Who knows what they kept in the safe-deposit box?"

The big trooper smiled. "I didn't like it when you brought the feds in, but I gotta tell ya Broce is one hell of a good cop. He did a great job interviewing Charlene Bullerwell."

"Yeah, he did. He said the FBI lab tried the fingerprinting of the Mayan book and couldn't come up with anything. It was basically the same result as the Boston PD. There were just some smudges and partials. I told Steve that Mrs. Webster was gonna send me a sample of Joan's hair and her dental records so we can use it for comparison if we ever find the *Mala* or her body."

"That's a good idea, but it's not *if*, it's *when* we find them. We'll find 'em both." Drew nodded to his friend just as Gina pulled him out onto the tiled dance floor a second time.

What'd they find in Lenny's safe-deposit box? Drew wanted to know as the two men sat at Dandelions café. Located closer than a sand-wedge shot from the front door of the courthouse, Dandy's offered sandwiches piled high with a broad choice of cold cuts to tempt the occupants of the nearby nineteen-story building. Many a deliberating jury next door debated the issues of proof beyond a reasonable doubt while noshing on a sour dill pickle and a Reuben from Dandelions, courtesy of the commonwealth.

"I spoke to Steve after he got the locksmith to open it up. It seems Candy might have beaten us to it. The bank records show she was there two days before we got the search warrant," the DA explained.

"Was there anything left?"

"Yeah, it's kinda strange, though. All he found was the jewelry we think Lenny had given Bullerwell, some Susan B. Anthony coins, and a coupla business cards. One was for an upholsterer in Revere, and the other was for a plastic surgeon that specializes in hands. I had Steve interview both of them, but the surgeon said he didn't know who Paradiso was."

"Maybe Lenny was gonna have him remove the sliver from his finger?"

"That makes sense, doesn't it? Why else would Paradiso have his business card?"

"What about the other card, the upholsterer?" Ponytail asked.

"He did some work for Lenny on his '39 Oldsmobile and on the canopy for the *Mala* just before it was 'stolen.'"

"Is that the same antique Olds Lenny gave Judd Carhart to represent him?"

"Yeah, it is. Steve did a report on his interview with the guy. His name is Joe Gulla. He owns the All Nu Upholstery place on Revere Beach Parkway and apparently didn't like the Quahog too much. Seems Lenny wanted the interior redone and left the Olds there one night. He came back during the day and complained about a scratch on one of the fenders. He tried to tell Gulla they had to paint the whole car for free. Gulla told Paradiso he thought he did the scratch himself. It turned into a scene and Lenny backed down."

"Yeah, Lenny's really tough with women. He ain't so tough when a guy challenges him."

"So Lenny tries to make amends with Gulla. He offers him some frozen crabmeat, but Gulla doesn't want it and gives it to one of his employees."

"Wait, let me guess," Drew said before the lawyer could finish. "The guy gets really sick from eating Lenny's frozen crabmeat, right?"

"Yeah, how the hell did ya know that? D'ya talk to Broce already?"

Drew smiled in self-satisfaction. "I just know what this animal is like."

"You're right, the guy had to be rushed to the hospital with food poisoning."

"How you making out on the reward posters for the *Mala*?" the lawyer asked.

"We distributed more than three hundred all over the city, down along the waterfront, and to every one of the TV stations and newspapers in the area this past week. Carmen got a call yesterday from a woman in New London, Connecticut. She wanted the reward. She was sure she found the *Mala Femmena*. She told Carmen, 'It's sitting in the harbor down here. It's right next to my boat.' So we drove down there and checked it out. It was the *Mala* all right. Unfortunately, it was Paradiso's first version of the *Mala*, a 1964 Owens. Lenny sold it back in 1974 to pay for his lawyer to represent him on the Connie Porter case." Drew laughed.

"Another case of mistaken boat identification. Sounds like the one the divers found sunk off Egg Island. What was the name of that one, the *Lucky Penny*?"

Drew nodded. "Those guys still out there lookin'?"

"Yeah, they are. Channel 7 just did another feature story on Doc Edgerton and his sonar invention. It had Doc on the Boston PD boat out in the harbor looking for the *Mala* with your twin brother Nick Saggesse and the rest of the divers."

"I saw that, but he doesn't look anything like me."

"Who, Doc Edgerton?" the DA said with a wry smile.

"No, Saggesse. And if you see Nick, tell him I said to stop telling everybody I whacked the shit outta that wife beater in East Boston."

- -

Earlier that summer, the Webster family had offered a ten-thousand-dollar reward for information leading to the discovery of the *Mala Femmena*. Pictures of the missing boat had been seized during the search of Weyant's house, printed in color, and then distributed to more than three hundred locations in and around Boston.

A month later three hundred more reward posters went out.

For five months Boston and state police divers searched the inner harbor and beyond with Doc's sonar system . . . and found nothing. Piers, boathouses, dealers, yacht clubs, and mooring spots were checked and rechecked. When the investigators were done, the DA sent them back to check again.

"Ya got any other ideas?" Drew asked his friend on a Friday in late September.

His friend answered with another question. "Ya know how Bond said Paradiso told him that if the cops find the *Mala*, there won't be anything there except a lot of mud?"

Drew noded. "I think the exact quote was, 'The boat's still intact. All the numbers are still on it. All they'll find is a lot of mud in the boat.'"

"I think Paradiso's mentioning 'the mud' may say something about the bottom of the harbor where the boat is sunk. I was looking at these geodesic charts, and they can tell you what the surface is like in different areas of the harbor. Some are rocky, some are straight ledge, and others are just mud. The area around Pier 7 is very muddy. That's why the divers had such a hard time seeing down there. All the silt and mud gets stirred up because there's so many boats coming in and out."

"Okay, but you already had the divers look there right after you got the letter from Bond," Drew said. "The guys at headquarters for Boston PD and my job aren't gonna be happy about going back and doin' the same area twice."

"I know, but Charlene Bullerwell told Steve Broce that Lenny talked about sinking his boat at Pier 7. If he went out any farther than that, he'd need another boat to get back into shore," the lawyer said, looking at a chart of the harbor.

"Listen, you know the divers will do anything you ask 'em to. It's the bosses you gotta convince," Drew said.

"Don't worry about that," the lawyer said confidently.

— — —

The following Monday twelve divers gathered on Pier 7, preparing to conduct a second search of the area. It was the third week in September and seventy-one degrees — a short-sleeve-shirt kind of day. The lawyer, Ponytail, and the Three Amigos stood high and dry on the lonely wharf, watching.

"Do I wanna know how you managed to get all of these divers down here?" Drew asked his friend.

"I called Boston and told them the MSP were sending a couple of divers over to Pier 7. Then I called the MSP and told them that Boston PD was sending four divers over. Then I called Boston back and told them I had it wrong, the MSP and the metro police were both sending four divers, and here you are," the lawyer said with a grin.

"I hope you're right about this mud thing, because all of a sudden we got a lot of company." Drew waved a hand at the caravan of trucks, vans, and cars heading down Northern Avenue, each vehicle marked with a different numerical logo.

"What did ya do, send a press release to every TV and radio station in the state?"

The camera crews set up wherever there was space, jostling for the best view. A big-haired blonde from Channel 5 bought the Amigos coffee and asked for details they didn't have. She had a warm smile, an inquiring mind, and the ability to woo even the most hardened career skeptic.

Drew stepped beyond the official yellow POLICE LINE tape and was immediately engulfed in a frenzy of microphones, cameras, and inquiries.

The imposing trooper had the same answer for each question he was asked.

"You'll have to ask attorney Burke that question," Ponytail said politely as the cameras whirred, the reporters preened, and the seagulls squawked.

Next door, on Pier 5, the sudden activity brought curious eyes to the windows that stretched along the entire length of the Fish Pier. Early risers and fishermen eating at the "No Name" restaurant across the expanse of water from Pier 7 requested a second and then a third cup of joe as they lingered to watch the scene play out. Lobster boats and small pleasure craft intent on taking advantage of the Indian summer weather paused in the smooth waters at the pier to drop anchor in close company with the nearby MSP and Boston police harbor boats.

Overhead, the gulls and terns yelled to their friends and neighbors to come and join the spectators. Soon there were more than a hundred of them, diving, swooping down and around the piers and pilings, waiting and watching.

"I got a guy here says he wants to talk to ya," Drew told his friend as they stood in the epicenter of the search. "He operates the dry dock here. He says it won't go all the way down to the bottom of the harbor anymore. It worked fine when they first installed it back in the summer of '81, and then later that fall it started to jam. What d'ya think?"

"I think we oughta get the divers up and start looking near the dry dock," the lawyer said.

Drew raised the walkie-talkie to his ear and called the two police boats anchored nearby. "Yeah, Lieutenant, this is Andy, the DA wants the guys to start working the area around the dry dock..." When the trooper's conversation was over, he turned to his friend and smiled.

"What'd the guy say?"

"He said you'd better be right, because if you're not, you're buying lunch for everybody."

It took Sergeant Eric Hahn and Nick Saggesse three minutes to dive down to the harbor floor forty feet beneath the dry dock at Pier 7. Two patterns of bubbles brought their expended breath back to the surface as they slowly maneuvered through the dimly lit water.

The divers were the only participants who weren't holding their breath as the crowd of spectators, reporters, cops, boaters, birds, and fishermen watched and waited. And waited and watched.

Then suddenly came a surreal sight: A blue door held above the surface of the water. "It's the *Mala*. We found it. We found his boat," Eric Hahn hollered as he tread water and lifted the mud-covered cabin door aloft for all to see.

The cheering started slowly then, as the significance of the moment sank in, swelled to a crescendo of yells and applause matched by the screeching of the seabirds.

- -

Early the next morning a twenty-five-ton crane and a flatbed truck wheeled off Northern Avenue and slowly inched toward the far end of Pier 7. Escorted by three state police cruisers, four TV trucks, and a smattering of smaller news vehicles, the scene took on the feel of controlled chaos. The weather was unusually warm, the breeze off the harbor was mild, and excitement filled the air as the DA and the trooper took a spot aboard the police boat to watch the raising of the *Mala Femmena*.

"Listen, you know Joan's body's not gonna be in the boat, don't you? Lenny's not that stupid," Drew said in an attempt to lower his friend's expectations. "And the salt water's destroyed any blood evidence. It's been almost two years."

"I know, but just finding the *Mala* confirms what Bond told us. I know we're going to find something that will help us put this guy away," the DA enthused as the crane lowered two enormous canvas straps into the water near the black dry dock at the end of the pier.

The divers widened the slings, gradually directing them toward the boat waiting forty feet below. There the straps were slowly moved into place, fore and aft, around and under Lenny's boat. Then, moving at the pace of a Canadian glacier, the crane operator revved his engine and gradually raised the cabin cruiser from the murk and muck of Boston Harbor.

Minutes ticked by as the boom of the crane lifted and strained under the weight of the water-shrouded boat. Finally the crowd of spectators shuffled forward to the farthest edge of the docks for their first glimpse of the apparition.

The shadowy frame of the *Mala* slowly crested the surface of the water, draped with seaweed and brackish streaks of mud and slime. The seagulls went silent and the spectators tilted their necks skyward as the mighty crane's engine ground to a halt. Like a casket suspended 20 feet above the ocean's surface, the *Mala* hung in midair, swaying in the ocean breeze.

Seawater poured noisily from the barnacle-encrusted boat into the harbor as the DA wondered aloud what secrets the Evil Woman would tell.

Pier 7 was the bastard child of the South Boston waterfront.

A distant cousin to the high-end style of Pier 4, and the bustling activity of its Pier 5 neighbor, the seedy wharf was an afterthought of broken pilings and empty promise.

Located just east of Jimmy's Harborside Restaurant, the lonely 7 sat neglected and mired in saltwater decay until the early 1980s. Spurred by a $2.1 million federal grant and a loan from the city of Boston, developer John O'Connell planned to rehabilitate the pier. He wanted to add a floating dry dock, build an ice plant, and provide maintenance for local fishermen who usually traveled to the ports of Gloucester and New Bedford for boat repairs.

O'Connell was an interesting guy. A graduate of Brown University, with a master's degree in management from Boston College, he owned four fishing boats and had high hopes for the rekindling of a dormant fishing industry in the city of Boston.

In the middle of October 1982, John O'Connell was arrested by the FBI and charged with falsifying the federal grant application he had submitted for the new dry dock at Pier 7. Less than a year later O'Connell sat in the federal courthouse in downtown Boston with two US marshals, telling the DA everything he knew about Pier 7 and Lenny Paradiso.

"This O'Connell guy's been charged with perjury. Who the hell is gonna believe what he says now?" Drew started in. "What are ya gonna do, put him on the witness stand and tell the jury to forget it? I can hear ya now. 'Excuse me, folks, I just wanted to tell ya, even though my witness is currently doin' time for lying under oath, you can still believe him.' Can you tell me how the hell you ever manage to win all those other cases?"

For once music wasn't playing in the lawyer's office. He tried to remain calm. "Listen, O'Connell told two FBI agents the same thing he just told me. He was at Pier 7 every day when Paradiso moored his boat there. He knows an awful lot about what went on down there," the DA quietly began.

"So now for witnesses in Iannuzzi we got two convicted killers and the victim's boyfriend, who, do I need to remind you, just got arrested again. And for our next act, in ring number two, we bring you the former owner of Pier 7, currently resident in a federal penitentiary for lying in front of a grand jury."

"Listen, Drew, O'Connell leased space on Pier 7 to Commercial Lobster. The Zanti brothers owned Commercial. That's where Paradiso worked.

O'Connell told me that's how Paradiso got to keep the *Mala Femmena* there. When O'Connell leased the space to the Zanti brothers, he told them they could keep two lobster boats there. Paradiso's boat wasn't a lobster boat. So when O'Connell asked the Zantis about it, they told him the *Mala* was their boat, but he checked the boat's registration and found out it belonged to Paradiso. That's why he made Lenny pay a hundred bucks a month to keep it there."

"Okay, I know what O'Connell says makes sense. You still can't use him as a witness."

"Maybe not, but what he says is important. He told me the *Mala* was definitely moored there after Paradiso says it was 'stolen' in July '81. Lenny never complained to O'Connell about his boat being stolen, and Lenny never stopped paying the hundred bucks every month for the mooring fees. O'Connell told me Lenny's boat disappeared at around the same time Joan was reported missing," the lawyer said.

Drew sat motionless, listening. "Anything else?"

"Yeah, O'Connell also said he remembers seeing a white cab parked at Commercial Lobster Company all the time and the driver wasn't there to buy lobsters," the lawyer said. "And I never mentioned anything to him about Lenny driving a cab. O'Connell just brought it up."

"What else did he tell ya?" Drew asked, his curiosity piqued.

"He said there was no guard on duty at night at Pier 7 between July and November '81. Lenny had a key to the padlock. Sometimes O'Connell used to work late and he would see Lenny on his boat at night. O'Connell said there was a lot of smugglin' goin' on with some of the boats coming in and out the pier. They'd smuggle grass and put the load into one of the big Dumpsters near Commercial Lobster Company, and the next day it'd get hauled away."

"Now we know why Lenny always had grass." Drew smiled.

"There's something else."

The trooper raised his eyebrows.

"Ya know how we always wondered how Lenny got Joan to go on the *Mala* with him?"

"Yeah, I don't think it was voluntary. I think he forced her on the boat somehow," Drew replied with the certainty that came from interviewing Joan's family and friends.

"O'Connell told me one of the guys that worked at Pier 7 was a skin diver. He said the guy was diving in the spring of '82 and found a gun right beneath where Paradiso kept his boat moored. He found it submerged between the

Erie Barge and the pier. The diver brought the gun into O'Connell's office to show him and O'Connell had him go back outside and point out where he found the gun in the water."

"Holy shit. Where's the gun now?"

"Glad you asked that question. O'Connell said they threw the gun back in the exact spot where the diver found it," the DA responded.

"Does he remember where?"

"Better than that, O'Connell drew a diagram of the entire area and showed me. I called our divers and they're gonna meet us over there tomorrow so I can show them where to look." The lawyer sat back, crossed his arms, and smiled at his big friend.

"Okay, okay, find the gun tomorrow and maybe I'll change my mind about calling O'Connell as a witness."

71: The Erie Barge

The weather was clear and cool for the Boston Harbor version of *Sea Hunt* that Friday in late October.

The lawyer met his trooper friend at Pier 7 early that morning and showed him the map drawn by John O'Connell. A large X marked the spot where the gun had been found in spring '82, more than a year earlier.

The divers were just pulling on their wet suits aboard the Boston PD boat named after the thirty-fifth president. The *JFK* was situated in a narrow channel of water between Pier 7 and the old Erie Barge. The hundred-foot-long barge was anchored twenty feet from the pier, providing additional mooring space for the four lobster boats tied to each side of its rusting hulk.

"It should be right in this area here," the lawyer said to Ponytail, pointing to the X. "Look. This is the same area where Paradiso used to moor his boat. O'Connell said his diver found the gun right below it. I showed the divers where to look before you got here."

"Who's with the dive team today?" Drew asked as he waved to the three indistinguishable men in black masks and wet suits aboard the *JFK*.

"Your twin brother, Nick Saggesse, Richie Famalare, and Eric Hahn," the DA said with a smile. "Nicky told me that story again this morning about the guy in the bar in East Boston mistaking him for you. The one who says you punched him out for whacking his wife."

Ponytail just grinned. "Who called the TV news crews?" he added. Out on Northern Avenue two trucks sat with their cameras pointed at the divers about to enter the cold, murky water.

"The divers told me the TV trucks have been down here almost every day since we found the *Mala*," the lawyer said as Sergeant Eric Hahn did a back roll off the back of the boat into the water, quickly disappearing from sight.

"It's gonna be awful hard to find something that small with all the mud and silt in this part of the harbor." Drew watched Saggesse and Famalare enter the water. "You really think O'Connell's telling you the truth?"

"Yeah, I do."

"Well, I guess we'll find out real soon," Drew said as he watched the air bubbles rise from beneath the surface.

He didn't have long to wait.

It was fifty degrees with a northeast wind gusting at twenty-five miles an hour. The air smelled of stale salt water mixed with a heavy dose of diesel fuel from the water traffic passing by. The scurry of activity and the presence of human life hinted at the possibility of a free meal to the dozens of seagulls floating overhead and perched on the broken pilings jutting up from the bottom of the harbor. They squawked, argued, and jockeyed for position on the seats closest to the action. The birds collectively took flight as the black glove broke the water's pane gripping a silver-and-rust-colored object.

"I found it. I found the gun," Hahn yelled to his audience as he raised his right hand high above his head and held the black mask in his left.

The gulls screeched with excitement as if to congratulate the diver and then dove toward the object held aloft in the hope it was food.

Located in the Finger Lakes region of New York State, sixty-two miles south of Rochester, the village of Cohocton was a forgotten footnote to Route 390, the four-lane highway that had passed the town by twenty years earlier. Iroquois for "log in the river," and occasionally referred to as the "Buckwheat Capital of the World," tiny Cohocton was a bucolic mix of farmers and quiet conversations about the weather, the crops, and the cows.

Each October the self-proclaimed "Friendly Community in a Scenic Valley" held a Fall Foliage Festival featuring a "tree-sitting contest" once heralded in an ancient edition of *National Geographic* and the subject of a Trivial Pursuit question.

Other than the infrequent drought or early frost, life was pretty tame and predictable in the land that time forgot.

The center of town's lone blinking traffic light signaled to the nonexistent traffic. It kept pace with a blinking orange neon arrow angled above the only bar within ten miles of the intersection. A second neon sign outside the saloon traced the outline of a bowler-style hat, providing the occasional passerby an indication of the establishment's moniker.

"Derby's" bar and grill was a turquoise-colored, time-battered three-story saloon with a horseshoe-shaped bar and a big bass jukebox offering tunes from Frank's "Fly Me to the Moon" to Hank's "Your Cheating Heart" to Chubby Checker's "Peppermint Twist."

Genesee beer and watered-down shots were the order of the day for Ervin "Derby" Smith, the owner and chief bartender of the tired taproom. Derby occupied the second floor with his pretty but unhappy wife, Leola.

The couple shared their uneasy existence one flight above the smoke-filled, dingy bar. Derby was a pleasant enough fella, frail and balding, with dark-rimmed glassses and a patient smile. He blindly adored the woman who betrayed him. On the night of the cuckold's discovery, Derby took his wayward wife's bone-colored, three-inch high-heeled shoe and in a rage of jealousy placed a three-inch hole in her golden-haired cranium.

It was a rainy windy Sunday morning in April 1961 when Derby Smith drove to the county sheriff's office to say he had just killed the woman he loved.

"So how the hell did you ever get involved in murder cases?" the big trooper with the ponytail wanted to know as they sat at the Steaming Kettle discussing the results of the FBI's search of the *Mala*.

"I grew up in this really small town in upstate New York. There were a lot more cows there than people," the lawyer began between spoonfuls of chowder.

"What's the name of the place?" Drew asked as he floated the tiny oyster crackers into the plastic bowl.

"It's called Cohocton now. It used to be Liberty before they changed it around 1890. Only about eight hundred people live there, half of them my relatives. If you ever found the place, it means you're lost. It's so small that people who live five miles away never heard of it."

"Sounds like a great place to grow up," Drew said, a hint of envy in his voice.

"Yeah. It was like this sleepy little version of *Green Acres*. They even used to have a contest to see who could sit in a tree the longest every fall. There was only one —"

Drew cut him off midsentence. "They did *what?*"

"Yeah, you heard me. They had a tree-sitting contest. There was only one bar in town. There wasn't even a police department. They didn't need one, there wasn't any crime," the lawyer said, his eyes adrift.

"Sounds like a long way from Easta Bost and the Cardinal's Nest."

"It was a very long way from the Nest," the DA answered. The city street outside the restaurant roared with midday traffic. "Anyway, I remember this one day the guy who owned the bar caught his wife cheating on him, and he went nuts and killed her with her high-heeled shoe. He turned himself in the same day and wound up getting sentenced for manslaughter, but never spent any time in jail. You can imagine, it was a real big deal in town. Nothing like that ever happened before. Big scandal, people talked about it for years. I guess not much went on back then. I was only a kid, but I remember it like it happened yesterday. I was intrigued by the whole scene, the arrest, the investigation, the courts, and what finally happened to the guy."

Drew sat silently looking at his friend. Sometimes Drew just let him talk.

"Ever since then, I knew this is what I wanted to do," the lawyer finished.

Drew nodded. "Maybe it was one of those destiny kinda things, ya know what I mean?" He finished off the chowder before asking his next question. "What do ya wanna do now? We found the *Mala,* you got Candy to testify before the grand jury, and we got the hearing to search Lenny's finger coming up."

The lawyer thought before he answered. "If the FBI was able to say the blood traces they found on the *Mala* were human, we'd have a chance to indict

Lenny on Joan's case. But I think you've been right all along to concentrate on winning the Iannuzzi trial. Without blood evidence we can't prove Lenny killed Joan, and we can't be sure Bond or Pisa will testify in another year, either."

"At least the broken glass from the whiskey bottle the FBI found on the *Mala* confirms what Bond said about how Lenny killed Joan. She must have put up a hell of a fight," Drew said, envisioning the blow to the back of the young woman's skull. "Tell me again what Candy said when you made her testify last week."

"Well, it took me three times to finally get her in before the grand jury. Even though she was immunized, she kept taking the Fifth and refusing to talk until the judge told her she was going to jail if she didn't. The transcript should be ready soon, but basically Candy said she met Lenny in the fall of '69 when she was seventeen or eighteen and that she was in love with him," the lawyer began.

"How 'bout the *Mala?*"

"Candy told me she was at Pier 7 with Lenny over thirty times and admitted stripping the boat with Lenny. Ya know the stuff you found in her house, the compass, depthfinder, and his ship-to-shore radio? She said Lenny told her to help him do it. They put the stuff in her car, took it back to her house, and stored it there until you found it," the DA told Ponytail.

"She say when they stripped the boat?"

"Yeah, Candy told the grand jury it was the same day Paradiso reported it stolen, in July '81. I asked her flat-out whether or not the boat was stolen and she said no. It was still above water that day in July."

Drew simply nodded, as if to say *I told ya so.*

"And we now know Paradiso couldn't have taken the boat out in the harbor that night with a broken rudder. We had an expert examine the *Mala*, and he said the rudder was missing — Lenny wouldn't have been able to steer. So he musta taken Joan's body somewhere else to get rid of it," the DA explained.

"Ya think he took it someplace and buried it? That's what Bond told you, isn't it?"

"Yeah. And I think that's what Lenny was planning on doing when the two witnesses saw the white cab near Conley and Daggett's that night. It's just a matter of finding out where he would have gone after he left there."

"Probably somewhere up on the North Shore. That's the most logical direction given where he was headed," Drew mused.

1010 Commonwealth Avenue was a squat four-story building with a single elevator that never worked, a parking lot without enough parking spaces, and small, cramped rooms with paper-thin walls, doors that didn't shut, and windows that didn't open. Cold in the winter and hot in the summer, the brown, dimple-patterned edifice sat adjacent to the trolley tracks on "Comm. Ave" like a bunkered fortress on Normandy Beach.

Home to and general headquarters for the Massachusetts State Police, "ten-ten" — as it was affectionately known — was the central beehive of activity for the thousand troopers assigned throughout the commonwealth.

Drew hated to go to ten-ten. Some crew-cut major with nothing else to do was always telling Ponytail he needed to cut his hair.

"Ooh-rah, mister," the former Jarhead with the gold bars on his shoulders would proclaim. "You are in serious need of a barber."

"Sir, yes sir," Drew would say, until he was out of earshot and then added "asshole."

Whenever the lawyer and trooper were supposed to meet at ten-ten, Drew chose a hole-in-the-wall across the street called T. Anthony's Pub. T's had great Buffalo wings and, unlike MSP headquarters, it had heat in the winter and air-conditioning in the summer. Not many officers above the rank of sergeant were welcomed inside.

"I just got the results of the test on the gun we found at Pier 7 the other day," the lawyer said to Ponytail as they sat with a large order of wings. "It was actually a pellet gun. A replica of a real gun. The guys at the lab across the street said you wouldn't know the difference looking at it. It looks and weighs the same as a real gun. They said it coulda fooled Clint Eastwood."

"Hey — remember what Lenny's ex-mother-in-law told me? About how he used to put a gun up to his wife's head and pull the trigger? It's probably the same gun," Drew exclaimed.

"I bet you're right. I hear a lot of the wise guys are doin' now because of the gun law in Massachusetts. Ya know, if you get caught with a gun without a license you automatically serve a minimum of one year in jail? So they're carrying these replicas to scare the hell outta somebody. If they get caught, it's not a real gun, so the automatic one-year sentence doesn't apply. Smart, Lenny, very smart."

"Ya think that's what he used to get Joan on the *Mala*?" Drew asked, reaching for a tall glass of ice water to cool his mouth from the spicy wings.

"Before the gun law changed, Lenny always carried a .38 in his car. He had a gun when he grabbed both Connie Porter and Florence White. Now he's on parole for the six-to-fifteen he got on Porter's case. If he gets nabbed with a real gun, he's gonna get his parole revoked and wind up doin' the rest of the sentence. This is the best of both worlds for him. He can use the replica and not worry about the automatic jail term." The lawyer polished off the last of the wings.

"Joan would never have voluntarily gone on that boat with Lenny. He must have forced her. She probably thought the gun was real. Lenny threatened her just like he did Florence White," Ponytail said.

"Exactly."

"The guys at the lab said the metal on these replicas isn't hardened steel like a real gun. The barrel doesn't have to be as hard because there's no bullet fired through it. So the metal they use to make 'em is a lot cheaper. I asked them if they thought that might be what Lenny has stuck in his left index finger."

"What'd they say?" Drew asked, signaling for his friend to wait as he sauntered to the nearby jukebox, pulled out a roll of quarters, and pushed the buttons for every Neil Diamond song the old Wurlitzer listed.

When Ponytail returned, the lawyer picked up where they'd left off. "They said it was certainly possible. It depends on how hard he hit her with it. There were a coupla areas near the cylinder and barrel of the replica with small chunks missing. If we can get the piece out of his finger, whether it's glass or metal, the guys at ten-ten can test it against the metal from the replica gun or the broken whiskey bottle glass we found inside the cabin of the *Mala*."

"So what are ya gonna do about it?" Drew asked impatiently.

"I drafted the search warrant for the court's permission to surgically remove whatever it is from Lenny's finger. I'm filing it and requesting a hearing. We need to have an X-ray taken first to make sure it's still in there and ask the judge for the right to use physical force if he doesn't cooperate."

"I think I might want to be there for that part of the operation," Drew said with a smile as Neil began to sing about a sweet girl by the name of Caroline.

"Yeah, but I'm afraid if the court doesn't order the X-ray right away, Lenny will cut it out of his finger himself before we get the chance."

"There's a hundred guys at Walpole who'd be glad to do it for him," Drew answered. "We've gotta beat him to the punch somehow."

The hearing over whether to order a surgical search of the Quahog's finger was a first in the commonwealth. Paradiso refused to leave his cell that morning; he had to be physically removed by the prison staff and forcibly brought to court. Once inside the courtroom, Lenny had his obligatory greeting for the DA seated nearby at the prosecution table with Drew.

"Fuck youse, ya lousy mothahfuckah. Youse ain't gonna fuck wid my finger," Lenny muttered, clenching his powerful hands as the court officer directed the angry defendant to his seat at the defense table behind the trooper and DA.

The judge assigned to hear the commonwealth's motion was a quiet, soft-spoken gray-haired gentleman from the southeastern Massachusetts fishing port of Fall River. A senior jurist with more than forty years of trial experience, James P. McGuire's cases were seldom overturned. A navy lieutenant and veteran of World War II, McGuire had previously presided over several cases with unique issues of law, including the murder case in which an X-ray identification of the victim's body was first allowed into evidence.

A graduate of Catholic University, McGuire was a man of substance and character. He loved the law and lectured at the law schools of Boston University, Suffolk University, and Boston College.

McGuire was the same judge who had revoked Paradiso's parole status at his arraignment for the murder of Marie Iannuzzi.

"All rise," court officer Jack Gillen pronounced loudly as the judge left his chambers and took his seat above the assembled gathering, whose collective eyes were fixed on him.

"Hear ye, hear ye, hear ye, now give your attendance and you shall be heard before this honorable court, Justice James McGuire presiding. God save the Commonwealth of Massachusetts," Gillen proclaimed as the Quahog slowly rose to his feet.

"All right, Mr. Burke, this is your motion. I'll hear you," Hizzoner said as Jack Gillen lingered near the defendant's table.

As the DA began to speak, there was a rush of noise behind the prosecutor's back.

The Quahog had forcefully pushed back his chair and his windbreaker rustled as he rose abruptly from his seat. Drew matched Lenny's move, rising and standing between his friend and the defendant.

"He's fuckin' crazy, Judge. He's obsessed. He keeps making all these wild accusations," Lenny began in an almost plaintive cry, pointing to the lawyer seated in front of him. "I wanna file a motion to have Burke psychiatrically evaluated."

As big Jack Gillen placed his hand on the Quahog's shoulder, Drew turned to his friend and whispered, "I never thought I'd agree with Lenny, but there have been one hell of a lot of times that I wanted ta file the same motion."

"Thanks a lot, Drew," was the best the prosecutor could summon.

"That motion is denied, Mr. Paradiso," Judge McGuire said calmly. "I suggest you listen to your attorney the next time he tells you not to talk."

There was a titter of faint laughter from the gallery as the reporters and spectators in attendance exchanged glances and small smiles. In the front row, the doe-eyed, dark-haired, and very pregnant reporter from the *Boston Herald* scribbled feverishly to accurately capture Lenny's quotes for the next day's edition.

"That's probably youse fuckin' kid, too, ain't it Burke? You mothahfuckah," Lenny said in a hoarse whisper, just loud enough for everyone but the judge to hear, gesturing to a startled Bev Ford, the reporter.

"He certainly has a way with women, doesn't he, Drew?" the DA said as he shrugged an apology to the mother-to-be.

"Yeah, he's real smooth. I overheard him talkin' to a reporter from the *Lynn Item* this morning, too. Lenny was telling him this surgical search is a violation of his civil rights. He said he didn't eat anything this morning, because he was afraid we might give him general anesthesia today. Lenny says he's got a lung condition and was worried he might have a bad reaction. Gawd, do you believe this mutt?" Drew returned as the DA called the commonwealth's expert witness to the stand.

The hearing didn't last long. Dr. Harry Bush from Mass General explained to Judge McGuire there was little, if any, risk to the patient during the surgical procedure. At the end of his testimony the judge thanked the doctor and turned his attention to the parties.

"Let me just conclude this hearing by saying this is a complex matter legally. There are any number of constitutional issues involved here. I want briefs from both sides. The order preventing you from removing any object from your finger remains in effect, Mr. Paradiso." Lenny smirked in response before being led to the waiting van for the trip back to his cell.

"How long will it take for the judge to make a decision?" the pregnant *Herald* reporter asked the prosecutor. "Aren't you afraid Lenny will just cut the thing out before you get a chance to find out what it is?"

"Yeah, we hoped we could get a decision from the judge today. It's a real concern Paradiso will remove it before we can examine his finger," the lawyer said as he and the reporter headed to Jimmy from Southie's elevator.

— — —

It took Judge McGuire nearly two months to research and write his sixteen-page decision, which ordered the Quahog to submit to an X-ray of his left index finger. The court said force could be used by prison guards to compel Lenny to cooperate.

Lenny wasn't in a cooperative mood that day. It took six guards to get his hand x-rayed.

"Hey, Timmy, what the hell happened to Lenny yesterday?" the conservative FBI agent wanted to know the day after the procedure.

"Why, what did you hear?"

"Lenny was in federal court this morning on his bankruptcy case. He comes in all banged up, limping and whining to the judge about how some three-hundred-pound guard they call the 'Whale' sat on him last night and made him take an X-ray of his finger."

"He wouldn't cooperate with the court's order, so the guards in Walpole forced him to have his hand x-rayed. The radiologist hasn't had a chance to look at the charts yet, but the guards told Drew there was a red mark on his left index finger."

"Ya think he took it out himself?"

"I dunno. It's been a coupla months since the hearing, so he's had plenty of time to do it. Anyway, he's appealing Judge McGuire's order to a Single Justice of the Supreme Judicial Court."

"Who's the Single Justice sitting right now?" Broce asked.

"It's Ruth Abrams."

"Wasn't she the trial judge on the Connie Porter case?"

"Yeah, she was," the DA responded flatly.

You could tell Judge John Irwin's emotional temperature by the hue of his complexion.

A tall, thin, angular man with a shock of thick bright white hair, the former prosecutor's face was alternating between a dark scarlet and a deep crimson as he read the Motion to Withdraw filed by Carhart and Prince.

The First Session went silent as the two lawyers for Paradiso and the prosecutor stood at the podium waiting for the jurist's response. In the prisoner's dock, a handcuffed Quahog smirked and smiled at his adversary and mouthed the now familiar, obligatory "fuck youse" while the judge's head was lowered. Joltin' Joe Rubino was the clerk in the First that morning. He could definitely see this one coming, and his eyes rolled to white.

"This is the third lawyer you will have had on this case, Mr. Paradiso," the judge said sternly as Lenny quickly turned to face Hizzoner. "This case was scheduled to go to trial in September, and here it is November. Now you're requesting this court to appoint attorney Steven Rappaport to represent you instead of attorneys Carhart and Prince. Why should I do that, Mr. Paradiso?"

"I got no more money to pay dem two," Lenny began to whine as he gestured to his two lawyers standing at the podium. "I already give 'em my boat and a antique car. I'm broke."

"Is attorney Rappaport in the courtroom?" the judge inquired, his face one shade darker.

"I am, Your Honor," the Great Schmoozer said warmly as he rose from his seat in the middle of the lawyers' gallery to the right of the podium.

All eyes turned to inspect Lenny's soon-to-be new lawyer as he made his way to the microphone. Steve Rappaport was an excellent defense attorney. The first murder case he ever tried was a not-guilty. So was the second.

"Good morning, Mr. Rappaport," the judge intoned as his eyes moved from the Quahog to the gallery and then to the podium. "Are you willing to accept this appointment to represent Mr. Paradiso?"

"I am, Your Honor," Rappaport repeated, smiling broadly at the judge and then at his happy new client.

"This is it, Mr. Paradiso. Do not, let me say that again, do not come back here again and ask for another attorney to be appointed to represent you. Do we understand each other?" The jurist's face had ripened to the color of beets.

"Yes sir, Your Honor, oh yes sir," a contented Lenny said as he turned his eyes from the judge to the prosecutor, who mouthed "fuck you" back at him. The DA left the podium and shook hands with the departing Carhart and Prince, wondering aloud what they knew about Lenny's new attorney.

"He's a good guy. He's honest," the cowboy-booted Carhart said as he and Prince took their leave and headed toward the elevators where Jimmy from Southie stood waiting.

In a strange way the DA was sorry to see them go.

The meeting with Lenny's new lawyer outside the First Session was brief. Like it or not, you had to deal with the person on the other side of a case. It was always easier if you could believe what he told you.

"Judd says you're an honest guy," the young prosecutor said to the young defense attorney.

"Absolutely," a smiling Rappaport said, "I tell the truth 95 percent of the time."

"What about the other 5 percent of the time?"

"Hey, I'm an honest man," Lenny's third new lawyer replied.

Steve Rappaport was six feet tall and married with two kids. He had a pleasant, easygoing style and could talk forever. If you allowed yourself to listen to him long enough, he could convince you of anything. The Great Schmoozer could tell you "that tomato sitting over there is really a red potato" and you'd have to take a second and then a third look to make sure your eyes hadn't failed you.

A full beard, thick curly brown hair, and lightly tinted glasses gave him the appearance of a rebel in search of a cause. You knew just by looking at him that back in the 1960s the lawyer-in-training had manned the barricades at some sit-in protest. He'd probably smoked some weed, too.

Schmoozer had an innate inclination toward civil disobedience. By the time he was sixteen and started to drive, he placed a bumper sticker that read QUESTION AUTHORITY on the back of his 1964 blue T-bird. Every car he'd owned since had sported the same message.

Rappaport was doing prison defense work when he met a killer named "Lefty" Gilday doing a life stretch at Walpole prison. When Paradiso was shipped from Charles Street Jail to Walpole, Lefty had told him that the Great Schmoozer was the only lawyer for the job. Rappaport was in. Carhart and Prince were out. Sometimes it was just that simple.

The two adversaries shook hands that day outside the First and went their separate ways.

Shortly afterward, the two young lawyers would meet again outside the First Session on another case involving the rape and attempted murder of a young woman by two men in the now familiar angry streets of East Boston.

Michael Quarto and David Giacalone were friends and neighbors. Around midnight in early December the duo happened upon a young woman searching for her car parked near Faneuil Hall. When the three located the missing car, the two men asked for a ride home in exchange for their assistance.

Reluctantly, the woman drove through the Callahan Tunnel to East Boston with the two men in the front seat. She made several turns as directed and stopped at a dead-end street where Giacalone put a knife to her throat and grabbed her keys.

For the next four hours the men took turns raping the hysterical young woman in the backseat of her car. When one was done, the other would step in, taking turns driving around the streets of East Boston in a ride from hell.

During the ride, Quarto cut a clump of the young woman's hair and began to slash her arms and legs with the knife. As she screamed in pain, he stabbed her in the thigh and held it there, slowly twisting the four-inch blade from side to side as she begged him to stop.

They eventually drove the victim to a pier not far from Maverick Square, where she was dragged from her car naked and knocked to the ground. Quarto then kicked the young woman in the face until she was unconscious. They threw her body off the pier, twenty-five feet down into the freezing water below.

The two men laughed as they drove off and later set the victim's car on fire to destroy any evidence. Then they went on with their lives as though it were just another Saturday night.

But Ginnie Freeman — left for dead — was a water baby. She'd learned to swim by the time she was eighteen months old. It saved her life that cold windy night in December. Naked and unconscious from the last kick to her face, she came to from the shock when she hit the water. Instinctively she began to swim toward the shore. Six minutes later Ginnie waded, then stumbled and crawled to a security guard shack just outside the Boston Shipyard Company.

Unrecognizable, with blood openly seeping from the knife wounds, she was rushed to Mass General Hospital, where her body core temperature was registered at eighty-six degrees.

Ten days later Ginnie went through five hundred mug shots at District 7 and without hesitation picked out the two sadists from East Boston as her assailants. When she was asked if they had any other identifying characteristics, she told the cops Giacalone was circumcised and Quarto wasn't.

She was right.

Later indicted, the two friends and neighbors from East Boston were brought into the First Session for arraignment. The Great Schmoozer was assigned to represent David Giacalone and waited outside the Room of Doom for the prosecutor assigned to the case to arrive.

"So what did ya do, Timmy, tell them to appoint me to Giacalone's case just so I can't spend all my time getting ready for Lenny's trial?" Schmoozer began.

"No," the prosecutor responded evenly, thinking about *the other 5 percent of the time* the defense attorney said he didn't tell the truth. "Hey, I've already got twenty murders and fifteen other cases like this one to deal with. You can keep one more plate spinning on a stick, too."

"That's right, you've got the trial on that triple homicide coming up soon, don't you?" Lenny's lawyer said, perhaps thinking of his own two children.

"It's scheduled to go to trial two months after Paradiso's case."

"I don't think I've ever said this to a DA before, but you'd better win that fuckin' case."

"I will," the prosecutor said resolutely, trying to hide his fear.

"I hope you do, man. I really hope you do. Hey, we've got the hearing coming up on that crazy motion of yours to have all those women testify against the Quahog. If you win it and the judge lets them all testify, there's no way Iannuzzi's a tryable case. We're gonna have ta talk after that motion gets decided," Schmoozer said. They shook hands and headed to the elevator.

It was the day before Christmas 1919.

"Shoeless" Joe Jackson and the Chicago White Sox had just rigged the World Series, Babe Ruth would be traded from the Red Sox to the Yankees in ten days, World War I had ended the year before, and a patriotic nation was terrified by the "Red Scare" of communism. Mother Russia had turned to the teachings of a revolutionary by the name of Lenin. In America, the Department of Justice was deporting socialists, communists, and anarchists by the hundreds.

At seven in the morning on December 24, 1919, two robbers armed with a shotgun and a revolver attempted to hijack a White Shoe Company payroll truck in the small college town of Bridgewater, Massachusetts. The unsuccessful robbers were described as "dark and foreign" and escaped the area with two other accomplices in a large Buick or Hudson Overland. The local chief of police believed the group was linked to "radicals" attempting to finance their activities through the robbery.

Four months later the paymaster and a guard from the Morrill Shoe factory in South Braintree were murdered by three gunmen, who escaped the scene in a large Buick with more than fifteen thousand dollars.

On May 5, 1920, two Italian immigrant anarchists, Nicola Sacco and Bartolomeo Vanzetti, were arrested for the murders, tried before a jury, and eventually executed seven years later.

Vanzetti, a fish peddler, and Sacco, a factory worker, were committed to the cause of social reform through anarchy. Both had left the United States for Mexico when World War I began, and they stayed for the duration. Neither would support a war they believed was begun by and beneficial only to capitalists.

To the population at large, the two defendants were Italian foreigners, radicals, anarchists, "Reds" whose guilt was an assumption, if not a foregone conclusion. In the historical aftermath, their trial was a classic example of two men prosecuted more for who they were and what they believed than for what they did.

Just before Christmas sixty-four years later, the DA and Ponytail walked into the bustle of the Steaming Kettle.

"I checked with the Department of Corrections last week about Lenny. He's been hanging out with some of the lifers ever since he got transferred to Walpole from Charles Street a coupla months ago," the lawyer began.

"I wonder how's he making the transition back into prison society?" Drew responded. He found a pair of stools by the window on the Court Street side of the restaurant.

"Not too well, I think. They told me he's gotten a coupla disciplinary reports since he's been out there. I just read one of them. He spent a day or two in isolation for assaulting another inmate with feces."

"Charming," Drew responded.

"I had sent them a subpoena for all Lenny's visitor records and his correspondence. They sent me a copy of a letter he wrote to some friend of his named Sammy. Wait till you hear some of the stuff Lenny has to say." The lawyer smiled.

"Do we have any idea who Sammy is?" Drew asked.

"I got no idea, but Lenny wrote to his parole officer, too. He told his PO he's worried Marie's stepbrother, Dennis Day, is gonna kill him for murdering Marie. He wants to know where Day is incarcerated so he can protect himself," the lawyer told his friend as they both ordered the same thing, chowder.

"You mean the Dennis Day from East Boston — the guy that's doin' life for murder?"

"Yeah, that's the one. Lenny thinks he's Marie's stepbrother because she's related to some Day family from East Boston, but it's the wrong family. Lenny's just a little paranoid, I think," the lawyer added with a hint of pleasure in his tone.

"No, ya know why he's worried about Dennis Day? Marie's keys had the last name DAY written on 'em the night she was killed. It was on the keyring she had with her in the Nest when Lenny was sitting at the bar talkin' to her. I betcha that's why he's worried about gettin' whacked. Too bad. If it really was her stepbrother, Lenny'd be toast by now."

"Let me read ya Lenny's letter to his friend Sammy. He wrote it on March 30, right after the press found out about Bond's letter to me and did the story about Lenny being a suspect in the two murders." the lawyer cleared his throat and began to read over the din.

> Hi Sammy, I hope this letter finds you and the family in the best of
> health, myself I am okay.

"He always says the same thing about 'finding you in good health' when he writes a letter," Drew remarked.

"Yeah he does. It's weird. Take a look at how he capitalizes a lot of different words in this letter too. Probably for emphasis," the DA suggested:

Sam enclose is a copy of the original Police Report, Read it and tell me the Law is not trying to give me a Screwing. Check the Dates of the Report, it was made 2 years after the girl got killed and 1 year before I got Arrested. So who shitting who. The kids family got money and Pull with the Politicians. He's a Junkie and a thief. Because I got a Record and am in Walpole they want to Pin it on me, it makes me sick, he out there free, and I am behind Bars.

"Man, this clown is delusional. Lenny thinks Doyle's got money and that's why he's in jail," Drew said, his voice rising.

"Wait, there's more, he's got a real persecution complex. Listen to this."

Sammy, I may not be perfect, but the only thing I ever kill was a Quahog. I don't understand. I help everyone and give the Shirt off my Back and I get the Shit end of the Stick, Story of my life.

"I'm sure all the women you beat the shit outta and raped and killed might have a different opinion, Lenny. I think they got the shit end of the stick," Drew said, as if the author of the letter were seated next to him.

"He talks about Bond, too. Let me read this part to ya." Drew turned to read over his friend's shoulder.

Also Enclose is a newspaper clipping of the guy who said I confess to him. He's a Big Nigger, looking to get out of Jail. He's done it before, the Bastard, kill two of his girls before. Now after all the Shit the Law put in the news, they checked the Records and found my boat was gone long before Webster disappear, everyone said I should sew them, what will I get, nothing.

The lawyer paused long enough for Drew to respond once again to the author. "You want to sue us now that we found your boat, Lenny, and can prove it was never stolen when you said it was?"

"He obviously wrote the letter before he got indicted for bankruptcy fraud," the DA offered.

The cops can't change the police report or the facts. Everytime I Read it I can't Believe it what they are doing to me, let's face it. Somebody

wants me off the Streets for good. I feel like they want to do to me like
what they done to Sacco and Vanzetti.

"Ya know what's weird? I went to Syracuse University. They had this mural
on the wall memorializing Sacco and Vanzetti. I walked past it every day for
four years, and never realized who they were until I went to law school," the
embarrassed lawyer confessed to his friend.

"Let me see that letter, will ya? Lenny's actually comparing himself to Sacco
and Vanzetti? He really thinks he's some kind of political prisoner. He's a
disgrace to every Italian man for hurtin' all of those women," Drew said as he
slowly began to read the last paragraph out loud.

I just hope I make it when my trial comes up. Sammy if I get convicted
it won't be because of Proof or Evidence, it will be Because of Bad
Publicity and nothing else. Read about Bob Bond the Nigger who
Said I Confess. Well Pal, take it easy drop me a line if you get a
chance, say hi to everyone for me. Your Pal, Lenny.

"Listen, Tim, I know we're not supposed to get personally involved in a case,
but this guy is pure evil and a racist to boot. Lenny's lied to himself for so long
he's startin' to believe what he says. He's brainwashed Candy, too. Just win the
case, will ya, and keep this scum off the streets?"

The big trooper left the Kettle without finishing his chowder. It was one
of those moments when you just kinda let him talk. There was no need to
respond. The lawyer quietly folded Lenny's letter to Sammy and followed his
friend.

The correspondence from the Quahog to the DA didn't have Lenny's usual "I hope this letter finds you in the best of health" greeting. It was only two paragraphs long and typed on plain white stationery with print small enough to make the reader squint. It was signed by the author in black ink, "Respectfully, Leonard Paradiso, Box 100, Walpole, Ma. 02071."

It arrived one year after Bobby Bond had sent his own letter to the DA from Charles Street Jail.

"Listen to this, he calls me 'Mr. Burke,'" the lawyer said to Ponytail as they sat in Room 603.

"That's an improvement on the usual 'fuck youse.' What else does he say?"

"Let me read the whole thing to ya. I think he's trying to set me up to talk to him so he can get me removed from the case. Some jailhouse lawyer at Walpole probably told Lenny if I talk to him I become a witness and can't prosecute him." The lawyer began to read Paradiso's letter aloud:

> Dear Mr. Burke, I'm informing you that some very important information has been brought to my attention, concerning the death of Marie Iannuzzi. Witnesses have been located who not only saw David Doyle (boyfriend of the deceased) outside the Cardinals Nest around 2:05 AM on August 12, 1979, but also saw David Doyle in the presence of Marie Iannuzzi.

"Drew, he actually puts 'boyfriend of the deceased' in parentheses."

"This guy is dumber than dirt. As if we don't know who Doyle is." Drew laughed.

"He didn't write this letter, someone else did. That's obvious."

Ponytail leaned forward as the lawyer continued to read aloud.

> These witnesses said there was a confrontation between them at the time. Their statement will show that David Doyle was not at home, and in fact was the last person to be seen with Marie Iannuzzi.

Drew was beside himself. "This clown has to be on drugs to think we're gonna just accept what he says. How come he doesn't tell you what the names of the witnesses are in the letter? It's because he knows we'll go out and interview them."

The lawyer nodded.

> Whatever other information develops from this, I assure you, I will notify you. I will talk to you on this, because I am acting Pro Se. Once I obtain counsel, I cannot.

"What the hell is he talking about 'I am acting Pro Se'?" The trooper roared as he reached for Lenny's letter. "He's already got Schmoozer representing him. Rappaport's gotta have no clue his client's gone off the reservation. Are ya gonna show him Paradiso's letter?"

"Yeah, of course. Lenny hopes I don't mention it so he can claim I withheld exculpatory evidence and use it to get a new trial if he's convicted. I wanna send someone with ya to talk to him. I don't want you to go alone. See if Carmen or one of the other guys from Homicide will do it," the lawyer said.

Drew picked up the phone. "Carmenooch," he explained to his boss, "Timmy wants you to go to Walpole because you knew Lenny. We know he's not gonna talk, but we don't want him saying at his trial that we didn't follow up on his offer."

"I'd love to have a chance to talk to Lenny again," Carmen answered enthusiastically. "I just bought a new Armani. Hey, ask your lawyer friend if he's running the Boston Marathon again this year."

"Yeah, he is. He roped me into driving him out to the starting line in Hopkinton again," Drew said, ending the call.

"Good morning, gentlemen," the DA said to the two smiling gray-haired men seated in the rear of the crowded courtroom.

"Good morning, Mr. DA," the elderly Isaac Shulman and Isaac Sullivan responded warmly in unison as the prosecutor and the big trooper entered Courtroom 808.

"So if you win this motion, we'll be able to call Patti Bono, Connie Porter, and Janet McCarthy as witnesses during the trial and have them tell the jury what Lenny did to them, right? Sorta like if he did it to those three women, he's likely to have killed Marie?" Drew asked his friend as the made their way to the prosecutor's table.

"No, actually, the case law says the previous crimes have to be very similar in the way they are committed or the location that's used. You can't use the previous crimes to show a propensity to have committed the crime he's on trial for. The previous crimes can't be too remote in time, either, so that's a problem for us, too," the prosecutor said.

"That really changes the whole strength of the case if you convince the judge to let these women testify," Drew offered.

"Yeah, Schmoozer will probably try to persuade me to let Lenny plead to second-degree murder if he knows they'll testify. Even if they don't, we've still got Bond and Pisa." The DA was hoping to project a positive outlook.

"Big difference between a case with two convicted killers testifying against Lenny and one with these innocent women talkin' 'bout him raping and beating the shit out of 'em," Drew said as he carefully placed the heavy file box on the table next to the clerk's desk.

Ponytail always had a way of getting to the heart of the matter.

"I know, keep your fingers crossed," the DA said just as the court officers were escorting Lenny from behind the heavy oak door leading to the prisoner's dock. The Quahog was *GQ*'ed up for the cameras on the first day of the hearing.

Outfitted in a dark, double-breasted suit and a bright white dress shirt with French cuffs and imitation-gold cufflinks, Lenny could have been a pallbearer or a wedding usher. A matching black, gray, and white striped tie nattily fixed beneath the folds of his thick neck brought a blush of red to the cheekbones below his deep-set dark eyes.

"Fuck youse, Burke," Lenny said to the DA as he took his seat and glanced at the gaggle of reporters standing behind him waiting for the judge to take the bench.

The press was out in full force on that cold, windy day. Diane from the *Globe* was there, Bev from the *Herald,* Victoria from WHDH, Ron from Channel 7, Sue, the big-haired blonde from Channel 5, and even the dean of the reporting circuit, Charlie Austin from Channel 4. There were a bunch of other reporters the prosecutor didn't recognize, but he waved to them all.

Members of the same fraternity, drawn together by the public's need to know, they clustered together chatting amiably and comparing notes on who would testify that morning. Outside the courtroom three women whose lives were entwined by a serial killer waited for their names to be called.

"All rise," the white-shirted court officer announced to the gathering as the man in the black robe left his chambers and strode briskly up the three steps to the large leather chair positioned behind the bench.

"Good morning, everyone," the judge said. "All right, let's get this show on the road. Call your first witness, Mr. Burke."

"The commonwealth calls Constance Porter," the DA said loudly as he turned to the Quahog, who offered a verbal pleasantry.

She'd been less than a minute away from passing over to the other side when the Andover police found her lying on the ground on a deserted dirt road with Lenny standing over her. Eleven years later, a pregnant Connie Porter looked about a minute away from going into labor with her first child as she took the witness stand.

"I wasn't pregnant when I told Paradiso I was that night, but I sure am now," Connie had said to Drew and the DA earlier that morning as they stood outside the courtroom talking with the other two victims.

The courtroom listened now without a sound as she described her brush with death and the killer's attempts to rape and strangle her on that lonely dirt road.

When the mother-to-be was finished, the DA called the commonwealth's second witness, Patti Bono.

The "girl from the North End" walked toward the witness stand and exchanged an anxious smile with Connie Porter, who slowly traced her steps to the back of the courtroom. One of the gray-haired gentlemen politely held the door open for the pregnant woman.

Like the first, the second witness explained in graphic detail how Lenny had convinced her to drive him from the Jib to an area near Pier 7, where he'd tried to rape her after pulling a gun and punching her in the face. Patti seemed to take particular pleasure in telling the judge that Lenny couldn't perform sexually after she told him he turned her on.

"Patti Bono is gonna make a great witness at trial if we win this motion. She hates Lenny worse than we do," Drew said as the girl from the North End left the witness stand, still glaring at the Quahog, who looked away.

"I know, but there may be too much of a time gap between when Lenny attacked her at Pier 7 and when he killed Marie," the prosecutor said as the two elderly Isaacs held the heavy oak doors open for Patti.

It was cathartic for the victims to face the man who'd tried to end their lives. Each of them described in excruciating and tearful detail the time she'd spent with the defendant. As they testified, Lenny brought his left hand up to his broad forehead and shielded his eyes.

"Who's next, Mr. Burke?" the judge asked as Lenny lifted his head for air.

"Janet McCarthy, Your Honor." He turned to watch Lenny once again raise his left hand to protect his eyes as if from the glare of the sun.

Janet McCarthy exchanged seats with Patti Bono and told the court every detail about her ride with the Quahog. From Salem Street in the North End to an isolated marsh near Crescent Avenue, McCarthy's experience seemed all too similar to those of the other women.

"I had my hand over my eyes, and I was screaming to the driver that somebody tried to rape and kill me. When I took my hand away from my eyes it was him," McCarthy said as she pointed her finger at the large man hiding his face behind his hand.

"Do you have anyone else, Mr. Burke?"

"Yes, I do, Your Honor. The commonwealth calls Charlene Bullerwell."

Bullerwell wasn't a victim, but she testified about a number of statements Paradiso had made to her about how easy it was to kill women and how much he enjoyed "doing" them because they were small and weak. The witness's testimony paralleled the statement she'd made to Agent Steve Broce months earlier. She anxiously told the judge that Paradiso had repeatedly bragged to her about being a "hit man for the mob," and that he'd threatened to murder her if she ever revealed his confession. Bullerwell wrung her hands and refused to look toward the defendant as she described Paradiso's claim of taking his victims' bodies out to Boston Harbor, where he would discard them after weighing them down with cinder blocks. The next day the newspapers would lead with Bullerwell's revelations on the front page: "My Lover Boasted of Murders at Sea."

At the conclusion of the hearing, the judge told the lawyers he would rule on the commonwealth's motion by the middle of March. The judge always kept his word.

— — —

Two weeks later, Ponytail sat in Room 603 as the DA anxiously held the court's decision in his hand. The prosecutor began to read out loud as Drew pulled his chair closer, reaching to turn down the volume of the radio.

"'The Commonwealth seeks to offer evidence at the trial of this case, of the defendant's involvement in other crimes for the purpose of showing a common scheme, course of conduct, *modus operandi* or motive. A protracted hearing was held and evidence was presented by a number of witnesses,'" the DA read.

"Why don't you just go to the end and tell me the decision?" Drew asked.

His friend shook him off and kept reading. "'There was testimony from three witnesses who claimed to have been sexually assaulted by the defendant in 1972, 1973 and 1980. The victim in this case, Marie Iannuzzi, met her death on August 12, 1979, and, as a result of said homicide, the defendant is charged with first degree murder and rape.'"

"I like this judge," Drew said with an expectation of where the ruling was headed.

The DA nodded and went on. "'There are certain limited similarities in the circumstances surrounding the death of Marie Iannuzzi and the assaults in 1972, 1973 and 1980. For example, the assaults took place in isolated places, the same excuse was given by the defendant for going to the isolated areas, similarities of age and hair length of the victims, the victims were assaulted near the ocean or water areas and the defendant was familiar with the areas where the assaults took place.'"

"Lenny, you can kiss your fat ass good-bye," Drew said, chortling.

"'However, there is a time problem involved in regards to the occurrence of each assault. There is the 1972 assault at the end of Pier 7, there is a 1973 assault in a wooded area in Andover and there is a 1980 assault in an isolated place near the ocean in Revere. There also are dissimilarities in the types of assault, the circumstances of each assault, and the end result of each assault. There is no close time sequence, similar sexual act or the same locus for each of these assaults. It is a close, factual question in some respects.'"

As he read from the last page of the judge's decision, the DA's words slowed and the volume of his voice dropped noticeably.

"'I find and rule that the government has not sustained the burden of proving a common scheme, common motive or intent, or similar course of conduct by the defendant. Accordingly, the Commonwealth's motion to admit the testimony of the 1972, 1973 and 1980 assaults is denied.'" The prosecutor slumped in his chair and tossed the decision onto his desk.

"You gotta be kiddin' me. What the hell does he mean? We can't have the three women testify? Is that what he said?"

"Yeah, that's what he said," the DA said without emotion. "The judge set the trial date for July 9, because of all the publicity."

"This case just got a whole lot tougher," Drew said as he answered the ringing phone for his friend. After listening, he held out the phone: "It's Bev Ford from the *Boston Herald*. She wants ta know your reaction to the judge's decision."

It was a short conversation.

Then she called Schmoozer. "No, I haven't seen the judge's decision yet," Rappaport said in response to the reporter's question. "What did Timmy say about it?"

"He was devastated. He couldn't believe it," the *Herald* reporter said, echoing the DA's response.

"Well, if he's devastated, then it's a great decision. I'm ecstatic. It's a great ruling by the court. My client and I look forward to trying this case," Lenny's lawyer enthused as he ended the call and went looking for the decision from the court in the day's mail.

78: Feeding Ground

"Ever since we found out about the girl in Florida being strangled, I've been going back and pullin' all the unsolved homicides in Boston over the last ten years," the DA said to his friend as the two men sat in the familiar Steaming Kettle with their usual order positioned in front of them.

"And?"

"I found out there were three girls missing from the Combat Zone in a ten-month time period between late '74 and the summer of '75. They were all strangled and left alongside the road in the same general area where Connie Porter was attacked in 1973. All three of 'em were just like Florence White, young street hookers workin' outta the Zone. Two of them hooked outta the same place on Washington Street. None of their murders were ever solved."

"Okay, so what's that prove?"

"I think you have to take everything we know about Lenny and put it together before it makes any sense."

"I'm listening," Drew said, turning from the bowl of chowder to face his friend.

"Okay, start with his first known victim, Florence White in 1970. Lenny picks her up outta the Zone. He pulls a gun once she's in his car. He gets away with it because she won't testify against him. Now he's emboldened. Lenny thinks he's invincible. Even though he was lookin' at a ton of time on White's case, Lenny doesn't stop what he's doing. He can't. He's driven by this internal sexual force he's got no control over. It's like it's ingrained in his mind," the DA offered.

"Then he gets away with attacking Lawson and Bono, right?" Drew chimed in.

"Exactly, even though Lawson and Bono aren't hookers. With each victim he learns something else. He gets smarter, and at the same time he's still following a pattern of behavior. Later on, the three other young women from the Combat Zone become just like Florence White to Paradiso. It's become an acquired response for him. Lenny needs the thrill of the kill for sexual gratification."

There was a rush in his voice as the DA continued.

"Lenny couldn't stop even if he wanted to. He likes flirting with disaster, trying to fool the cops. He wants recognition for what he's done, and despite everything else I think he wants to get caught. That's why he goes back to the same places. He's following a pattern and leaving clues," the lawyer said.

Drew pulled closer. "Okay, tell me more."

"It isn't all about the sex, either. Lenny's lookin' for emotional relief from all the built-up rage he's got kickin' around inside his mind."

"So what's the connection to Andover and Connie Porter?" Ponytail wanted to know.

"I think psychologically, the two most exciting and traumatic events in Lenny's life were his arrests for White and Porter," the DA answered.

"Okay, so what?

"In his mind these new victims are a combination of his arrests for White and Porter. He's repeating his history with these new girls from the Zone. It's become the same experience for him. He's trying to duplicate the experience when he picked up Connie Porter hitchhiking and took her up Route 93 to Andover and tried to rape and strangle her."

"You mean he's like reliving what happened to him before?"

"Yeah, Drew, the shrinks call it 'repetition compulsion.' The Combat Zone is like a feeding ground for him. Once he's got them in his car, Lenny knows he owns them. Every time he gets another woman in his car, he gets the chance to relive his sexual experiences with White and Porter all over again. He took these hookers from the Zone and brought them up Route 93 to the Andover area to kill them, just like he tried to do with Porter."

"It's like being fixated with the same sexual experience, isn't it?" Drew said, trying to think like the killer.

"Yeah, it's all about the excitement, the possibility of him getting caught. It's a game. He likes living on the edge. Showing he's smarter than the cops. I think that's why one of the girl's bodies was dumped near the state police barracks in Andover."

Ponytail sat motionless, listening, thinking.

"You really think he killed these other girls too, don't ya?" he asked finally, knowing the answer before it was given.

"Yeah, I do. Look at the timing of these other three murders. They start right after he gets convicted on Porter's case, and they stop just before he gets sent to Walpole in July. The last one is more violent than the others. That's because he knows he's goin' to jail in three days. She's stabbed over twenty times. I'm sure in his mind, he blames these women for what happened to him. Maybe it's a mother thing for Lenny," the lawyer said, thinking of the North End apartment on Prince Street where Paradiso grew up.

"What's he think he is, another Albert DeSalvo?" the trooper asked, referring to the infamous Boston Strangler.

"That's probably a whole hell of a lot closer than Lenny thinking he's like Sacco and Vanzetti." Both men laughed.

"What's the modus operandi for these other girls?"

"It's the same basic MO. All of them were reported missing from the Zone and all three of 'em were taken north on Route 93 to locations between Andover and Salem, New Hampshire. Their bodies are found within five to ten miles from where Porter was attacked. All three were beaten and strangled, and they all used taxis to get to and from work."

"You thinking what I am about Lenny and the taxi connection?"

"Yeah, I am."

"So you think it's like a clue — the reason Lenny's taking them up to the Andover area to kill 'em?"

"Yeah, it's a message, just like him leaving Joan's ID near Conley and Daggett's. I don't think it's a coincidence Lenny left Joan's wallet near where he killed Iannuzzi. He's trying to leave a clue to his identity. Maybe he wants credit for what he's done. Who knows, maybe you're right and Lenny thinks he's another DeSalvo. What I do know is there's a pattern to what serial killers do. He may not even be aware of what he's doing or why he's doin' it," the DA said as the flow of pedestrian traffic during the noon hour once again filled Court Street.

Drew pushed his empty bowl of chowder away and leaned toward his friend. "This guy's capable of killing anyone. He likes it. If you don't get him on Iannuzzi, he'll just keep doing it over and over again. These three girls from the Combat Zone had to be easy pickings."

"Yeah, remember Connie Porter's statement to the Andover police? Lenny told her he used to go down to the Combat Zone all the time."

"Okay, so how does Lenny get these other three girls in his car?"

"That's the easy part. It's one of two ways. Either he picks them up like any straight john situation and pulls a gun like he did with Florence White, or else he's driving a cab. Like I said, none of these girls owned cars. I read the old Boston police reports, too. All three girls depended on cabs to get back and forth to work."

"What about other suspects?" Ponytail asked, playing the role of devil's advocate.

"Early on, the cops thought the girls' pimps might have done it," the DA said.

Drew scratched his head. "But these three girls didn't all have the same pimp, did they?"

"No, they didn't."

"So why would a pimp wanna kill someone making money for him? And why the hell would he take her all the way up Route 93 to Andover to get rid of the body?"

"It doesn't make any sense, Drew. That's why the cases never went anywhere. The murders had some notoriety for a coupla months, and then public interest died out. There was the issue of jurisdiction, too. The women were missing from Suffolk County and two of the bodies were found in Essex County. The third body was discovered just over the border in New Hampshire."

"Sounds like the same thing with Webster and Iannuzzi. The women are last seen in Suffolk County, and evidence in their case is discovered in Essex County." The big trooper paused before he asked, "Ya think Lenny's that smart?"

"I dunno, Drew. I just don't believe coincidences happen that often. The more you know about Lenny, the more you understand what he's capable of."

The conversation lapsed for a moment as the two men sat silently staring out the floor-to-ceiling windows at the world passing by.

"There's something else I found out," the lawyer mentioned, breaking the silence.

"Okay, what is it?" Ponytail inquired patiently.

"There was another girl who worked out of the Combat Zone. They discovered her body on June 27, 1974. She was strangled. They never solved her murder, either. Her name was Lois Centafante," the DA explained.

"Where'd they find her body?"

"Near the Governor Edwards Bridge in Revere, not far from the Point of Pines," the lawyer said, remembering the sounds of seagulls passing overhead.

"Are you kidding me? That's only a coupla miles from Candy's house on Crescent Avenue."

"I know, Drew. It's not far from Conley and Daggett's, either."

"We were sorry to hear the judge didn't allow the motion to have the other women testify at Marie's trial," Terry Webster said to the DA as she sat with her husband in Room 603.

"We still have a good case," the prosecutor fudged.

"Is everything else set to go for the trial?" George asked.

"Yes, I've spoken to all of our witnesses several times. They're all ready to testify."

"How do you go about getting ready for a trial like this?"

"I usually write out my closing argument first. Then I draft the opening statement and the areas of my cross-examination for all his witnesses," the DA said without mentioning the defendant by name.

"Interesting that you would start from the end of the case and work backward like that. Do we know for sure when it will begin?" Terry asked.

"As far as I can tell, it should start next week," the lawyer said anxiously. He couldn't dismiss the chance of another postponement.

"Well, we're happy to be here to help in any way we can. We have all the confidence in the world in you, don't we, George?"

"Yes, we do. We know nothing is guaranteed, but this is the best chance we have of getting this character put away." Apparently George wouldn't speak the defendant's name, either.

"Don't worry about us," Terry put in. "We'll just be there in the courtroom with you and the Iannuzzis. By the way, we got the drawing your son Jordan sent us. It's on the refrigerator. And how's your other little baby boy doing? He must be just over a year old now, isn't he?"

"Both of them are doing fine, thank you."

There was a motherly kindness to the diminutive woman who'd lost her youngest child and had yet to experience the closure of a funeral service.

Over the past two years there had been dozens of phone calls among the lawyer, Drew, Carmen, and the Websters. Joan's parents knew every aspect of the Ianuzzi case as well as their own, and they'd developed a close connection to the men trying to solve the mystery of Joan's disappearance.

"What do we do if the worst happens?" Terry asked, and then immediately raised her hand to cover her mouth, as if even asking the question was a mistake.

"We still have the other case to try, the one with the young woman he tried to rape near Weyant's house in 1980. And Paradiso still has the bankruptcy indictment pending in federal court."

The DA wanted to add Joan Webster's name to the list of cases to be tried. But he knew it would be difficult, if not impossible, to prove her death without a body or blood evidence, and with just the testimony of Bond and Pisa.

"I am certain the grand jury would indict him for Joan's death," he began, still omitting Paradiso's name. "But there's a huge difference between probable cause and proof beyond a reasonable doubt at a trial. Will you ever be able to accept the jury's verdict if they acquit him?"

There was a long pause as the two parents looked at each other, and then turned to their friend and silently shook their heads no.

"Please win this case, Tim," Terry Webster said as she took his hand.

"I promise you. I'll convict him on Marie's case. I'll put him away for the rest of his life," the lawyer said quickly, then just as quickly regretted saying it.

- -

July 9, 1984, was a bright, sunny day in Boston. It was a Monday and the case of *Commonwealth v. Leonard J. Paradiso* was finally going to trial, two years after his arrest at Candy's place on Crescent Avenue.

Picking a jury in a murder case is part voodoo, part instinct, part luck, and some science, but not much. The 120 jurors chosen at random from voter registration lists in Suffolk County filed their way into the empty courtroom and stared at the lawyers, the defendant, and the judge as the white-shirted court officers quietly ushered them to the hard wooden benches.

Big Jack Gillen was the courtroom maître d' that morning, directing the citizens to their seats with a smile that made them momentarily believe they were getting a window seat at the Ritz overlooking the Swan Boats in the Boston Public Garden.

The prospective jurors carried their *Globe*s and *Herald*s, their brown bags for lunch, and their umbrellas, just in case. Some clutched books, hardback and paperback, partially read, to while away the time. Both those in front of the wooden bar separating the jurors from the lawyers and those behind it were curious. The jurors wanted to know about the case; the lawyers needed to know whom they were selecting to sit in judgment.

Each lawyer would have less than a minute to read the printed sheet containing the juror's name, address, marital status, employment history, and prior jury service. As each name was called, the juror answered "present" and walked from the courtroom gallery up to the side of the judge's bench near the witness stand. There Judge Roger Donahue asked the prospective jurors the same list of standard questions about their impartiality. The Quahog and Drew remained at the defense and prosecution tables as Schmoozer and the prosecutor stood next to Hizzoner.

As the questioning continued, the lawyers turned to look at each anxious candidate, reading his or her body language, and then listening to the answers given to the judge's questions. If the judge declared a candidate impartial, he or she was seated in the jury box. Once there were sixteen jurors initially seated, the defense and prosecution would have the opportunity to use their challenges to remove up to sixteen jurors from the panel.

A challenged juror was removed from the panel; another juror would be interviewed, declared impartial by the judge, and seated. If both sides were satisfied with the replacement juror, the process would continue until each side was content — or ran out of challenges. It was a tedious, time-consuming task.

"Take a look at the names of any of the newspapers or books the jurors are reading as they come up to the side of the bar," the DA whispered to Drew as he made his way to the front of the courtroom with Schmoozer.

When the first sixteen jurors were seated, the prosecutor returned to the table where Ponytail waited with the list of reading materials.

"You got two Sidney Sheldons, one Robert Parker, one *New York Times*, five *Boston Herald*s, two *Boston Globe*s, and one crossword puzzle. The other four aren't reading anything," Drew said. His friend immediately challenged the four nonreaders.

By the end of the day there were nine jurors seated, seven of them women.

"I hope you know what you're doing," Drew said with an air of skepticism as the lawyer gathered the paperwork from their table and the pair headed down the stairway to the sixth floor.

"We want women on this jury, and the better-educated they are, the easier it will be for them to figure this out," the DA said to Drew back in his office, the radio providing background noise. "These women aren't gonna identify with Lenny. They'll see him for what he is. They'll understand the control he has over Candy, too."

"I'm just afraid what'll happen if you pack the jury with women. Lenny's always been able to fool the women he's hurt. He's got this *I wouldn't do that* puppy-dog kinda look. Ya know what I mean? He can be very disarming. Joan was smart, too," Drew countered.

"I agree, but Lenny had all of them in his car under his control. This is different," the prosecutor said.

"Do ya think Lenny challenged the black guy on the jury because he thinks the guy'll believe Bond's testimony?" Drew asked as he reviewed the printed list of jurors.

"Yeah, I do. You could tell Schmoozer didn't want to challenge him. It was Lenny's decision. Lenny's a racist at heart. You read the letter he wrote to his friend Sammy. Maybe he's afraid we'll introduce the letter."

"Ya know the shorter woman in the business suit and the ascot scarf? The one with the *New York Times*? What did ya think 'bout her? She looks like she's got a clue, don't ya think?"

"I saw Judge Donahue reading her profile on the jurors' questionnaire. She's got a master's. I betcha he makes her the forelady," the DA answered quickly.

"What about the tall blonde? She looked like she might be pregnant," Drew asked, referring to the second juror selected. She was nearly six feet, with a Lady Di haircut and a blue calico dress that hid her belly.

"I liked her. When the judge asked her if there was anything that would prevent her from sitting on a murder case, she looked right over to Lenny and said no. She never hesitated."

"Yeah, I saw that. I just hope you get some alpha males on the jury who aren't Italians from East Boston or the North End," Ponytail said as he headed for the door.

"Spoken like a true alpha male from Easta Bost. I'll see ya tomorrow, Drew," the lawyer responded.

It took less time the following morning to fill the remaining empty seats in the jury box. Both sides had used most of their challenges the day before.

"Okay, that short chubby guy with the Mr. Peepers glasses ain't exactly what I would call an alpha male," Drew squawked to his friend as the second day of jury selection began in Judge Roger Donahue's trial session.

Roger Donahue was the son of Judge "Daisy" Donahue, a stern taskmaster who had occupied the same courtroom years earlier. A cigar-smoking scholar with straight salt-and-pepper hair, Roger was a warm, engaging man who loved to quote Shakespeare and grow vegetables in his two gardens.

"Is the commonwealth content with this juror, Mr. Burke?" Hizzoner asked patiently as Mr. Peepers smiled at the judge, then dropped his chin and peered anxiously over his horn-rims at the DA.

"We don't have many challenges left, Drew," the prosecutor told his friend as he turned to the judge and smiled uncomfortably, nodding faintly.

"Yes, Your Honor. The commonwealth is content with this juror," the DA fibbed.

It took Schmoozer all of three seconds to reply.

"The defendant is also content with this juror," Lenny's lawyer waxed enthusiastically as Mr. Peepers pushed his glasses back over the break in his nose and took his seat in the jury box, smiling warmly at Rappaport.

"Shit, I told ya I didn't like him," Drew said under his breath loud enough for Schmoozer to hear. The man's smile widened.

All but one brown leather chair had been filled when Jack Gillen pulled the switch that triggered the two noisy air conditioners protruding from the elongated windows on either side of the jurors' box. It was close to noon. The defense had no more challenges; the prosecution had one.

"This must be the day for tall women," Drew said as the thin black woman with large round glasses and Jheri curls approached. Younger looking than her stated age, she was pretty, smiled often during the judge's questioning, and made eye contact with each lawyer.

"The commonwealth is content with this juror," the prosecutor said as he looked behind him to see Lenny shaking his head in the direction of Schmoozer.

"It appears you're out of challenges, Mr. Rappaport," Judge Donahue advised.

"Nevertheless, I'm also content with this juror," Lenny's lawyer said as he smiled at number sixteen.

They had a jury. Eight men and eight women.

"I am going to ask juror in seat number seven to serve as forelady in this case," the judge said as the two lawyers took their seats at counsel tables.

"I told ya so," the DA said to Ponytail as the woman in the business suit with the *New York Times* nodded politely at Hizzoner and took the front-row seat closest to the witness stand.

The sixteen jurors had no idea they would be taking a bus ride that morning. Mr. Shulman and Mr. Sullivan couldn't go. It wasn't that kind of bus ride.

"Ladies and gentlemen of the jury, the district attorney has made a request for what we call a view. What that means is we will be transporting you to several different locations this morning to familiarize you with the places whose names may be mentioned during the course of the trial. Give me those names again, will you, Mr. Burke?" the judge asked as he removed a silver pen from beneath his robe and poised his hand to write.

"Yes, Your Honor. The first location is the Cardinal's Nest bar in East Boston, the next is 212 Crescent Avenue in Revere, then the Ship Restaurant in Saugus, and the last is Conley and Daggett's on the Lynn Marsh Road," the prosecutor rattled off quickly, as Drew nodded and the jurors wondered.

"All right then, let me give you jurors a preliminary instruction about a view," the judge began after he jotted the final name down on his yellow legal pad. "You will not be able to ask questions of either party while we are on the view. Some of you may be old enough to recall those signs you used to see at railroad track intersections. The ones that said STOP, LOOK AND LISTEN. Well, that's what you are required to do, simply go to these places and stop, look, and listen. When we return, we will have the opening statements of counsel and begin the taking of testimony."

"All rise," the court officer announced as Hizzoner left the bench and headed for his chambers. "Jurors, right this way," the court officer directed as the judge closed the door and removed his robe for the trip. Once the jurors left the courtroom, the two large court officers placed handcuffs on Paradiso, who quickly turned to the DA and provided the obligatory "Fuck youse, ya mothahfuckin' piece of shit."

"Yeah, Lenny, we'll be sure to tell Candy you said hello," Drew responded as the Quahog was led back to the detention area on 7M. He had for some reason elected not to take the ride.

Twenty minutes later the group gathered outside the rear entrance to the courthouse and boarded a chartered bus headed to East Boston. The judge sat behind the driver, braced by four white-shirted court officers. The prosecutor sat in the next row with Drew angled across from Lenny's defense attorney. Several rows back, the jurors sat and chatted amiably as the large Greyhound wound its way precariously through traffic with a state police cruiser fore and aft; three television news crews trailed behind.

"Where's your client?" the DA asked in an effort to bait his opposition as the Greyhound passed through the Callahan Tunnel toward East Boston.

"He had something else to do this morning," Rappaport retorted.

"Like what, cleaning out his sock drawer?" Drew chimed in.

"Naw, he did that yesterday. Today's laundry day. He's back at Charles Street sortin' out the darks from the whites."

Drew just smiled in appreciation of the defense lawyer's sense of humor.

The bus eventually found its way to the Nest and the occupants descended to the front sidewalk like anxious tourists on a balmy cruise to nowhere special.

The DA began to speak as he pointed to the area where Candy said she'd parked her car and waited for Lenny while he took half an hour to return Marie's keys.

"Ladies and gentleman, I direct your attention to the area outside the bar where those cars are parked and ask you to fix that location in your mind as you look at the front door."

As the prosecutor spoke, two winos with two months' growth and two tin cups seized upon the opportunity to ask for loose change from the assembled group. The duo quickly beat feet down Maverick Street when Drew loomed large and directed them onward with the merest glance. Ponytail was always good to have around.

The three news stations recorded the jurors' entry to and departure from the Nest's parking lot as the bus churned its smoky exhaust into the crowded street and headed off toward Crescent Avenue. Candy's quiet, narrow street received the entourage well as the bus parked directly behind Lenny's brown Chevy Blazer. Neatly positioned next to the license plate was Lenny's bumper sticker: EVERY GIRL NEEDS A BIG ITALIAN GUY.

On the front porch, a Labrador retriever barked cheerfully as he greeted the visitors to his domain. The bleached blonde next to the Lab wasn't as happy. Candy scowled at the passengers who would soon decide her lover's fate.

"Ladies and gentlemen, this is 212 Crescent Avenue in Revere. I ask that you simply note the vehicle parked here in front of the house and the amount of time it took for us to travel from the Cardinal's Nest to this location," the DA said. He gave the jurors the opportunity to examine the rear of the Quahog's Blazer and the blond woman tugging at the dog's collar.

"That was a nice move, pointing out Lenny's bumper sticker," Drew said as the Greyhound pulled away. "Ya think any of the jurors picked up on it?"

"I dunno. It's something for them to think about. One more piece of information, that's all," the lawyer said as he turned back to see an angry Candy yank the dog back into the gray house.

The Ship Restaurant should have been the subject of a Fitz Hugh Lane painting anchored in the middle of Boston Harbor in 1849, when Dr. Parkman disappeared. Instead the triple-masted boat was inappropriately situated on a busy stretch of highway just off Route 1 in Saugus. The landlocked replica of the USS *Constitution* was a ninety-foot-long, three-story icon amid an infamous strip of tacky restaurants. Seemingly run aground not far from a fifty-foot sequoia cactus and a herd of plastic cows grazing motionlessly in front of the Hilltop Steak House, the Ship had hosted Marie's first encounter with her killer.

"Ladies and gentlemen, you will be hearing more about the Ship Restaurant during the trial. I would ask that you look around and note its proximity to the other locations you have been taken to earlier this morning," the lawyer said as traffic whizzed by on busy Route 1. It was a brief stop.

"They seem interested, ya know what I mean?" Drew said to his friend as the group boarded the Greyhound one more time.

"You're right. It's like this big Rubik's Cube for them to piece together. The more information they have, the better they'll be able to sort things out. Let's see what their reaction is when we take them to Conley and Daggett's." The lawyer settled into his seat and quietly began to rehearse his opening statement with Ponytail. It didn't take long for the caravan to reach the location where Marie's body had been found.

Maybe it was him, but the place struck the lawyer as having the smell of death to it, so close to the city and yet so distant from reality. Isolated, desolate, and strangely forlorn, the murder itself played out in his mind's eye like a clip from an Alfred Hitchcock movie.

There was a discernible change in the jurors' demeanor as they silently walked in twos and threes down the dirt road behind the ramshackle seafood plant toward the river's edge, needing no directions to the kill site. As the seagulls screeched above, the DA wished her murderer were with them to share the moment.

"This, ladies and gentlemen, is where Marie Iannuzzi's body was discovered." He raised his hand and pointed. "I would like you to first look toward the rocks near the river's edge and then turn back toward the highway and see how isolated this location is from the Lynn Marsh Road."

The DA wanted to tell the jurors, *It's a perfect place for a murder,* but he sensed they knew it already.

82: Opening Statements

Opening statements were like the first night of a Broadway show.

Two nervous actors delivered their lines to the small intimate audience of twelve jurors and four alternates. It was the first chance for both sides to tell their story to the jury. Each scripted word was measured to bring the uncertain listeners to accept the speaker's theory of the case. Before the openings began, Judge Donahue carefully instructed the jurors not to consider what was said by the attorneys as evidence. "An opening is a blueprint, a road map, an expectation of what the witnesses are going to say under oath, nothing more."

The prosecution opened first.

"May it please the court? Ladies and gentlemen of the jury, by way of introduction, my name is Tim Burke and this is Trooper Andrew Palombo seated over at the prosecution table. Let me begin by telling you that this isn't just an ordinary case. This is a murder case. It's an interesting case because it presents a side of life that very few of you have ever been exposed to." The DA slowly turned his eyes from the jury and looked at the defendant.

And so it began, the slow, methodical promise to the jurors of what the prosecution's evidence in the case would be. As he spoke, the anxiety left his mind; the words flowed as if he were telling a familiar story to a close friend. The courtroom became a stage, and he was master of ceremonies. He introduced the forthcoming witnesses by name, explaining who they were and what they were going to tell the jury.

From Christine DeLisi to David Doyle to Bobby Bond, the prosecutor wove a tale of lust, deceit, and death. He used the places the jury had seen on the view just a few hours before to set the stage for each upcoming witness's testimony. Between the words of explanation, he exchanged glances with the Iannuzzis and the Websters huddled together in the gallery of the crowded courtroom not far from the two Isaacs. The jurors' eyes followed his own as the DA at times spoke to the group without looking at them.

"You will hear from Christine DeLisi that Marie turned to her just as she was about to leave the Cardinal's Nest with the defendant and said, 'Wait right here for me. I'll be back in a half an hour.' Marie walked to the door, the large man following behind her. The door closed. And Marie was never seen alive again," the prosecutor said in a hushed tone, leaving the jurors to visualize the ceiling fan stirring the smoky air, the steps taken on the sticky linoleum floor, and the heavy dark door slowly shutting behind the stranger and the lady in red.

After pausing to take a breath and glance at the Quahog, the DA verbally led the jurors to the scene by the Pines River. "The police found Marie the next day behind Conley and Daggett's, where Mr. Paradiso once worked. Her body was discovered partially submerged in the tidewaters of the marsh. She had been beaten and raped. Her scarf was braided tightly around her neck, suffocating her."

"You will also hear from two inmates how Mr. Paradiso bragged to them about strangling Marie. They will tell you how Paradiso told them he would never be prosecuted because there were no witnesses to the murder. Paradiso told them how he torched the car he was driving that night to destroy the evidence of the victim's bloodstains and later reported the car stolen to the police."

At the end of his opening, the DA pointed at the defendant, then turned to the jury and said, "I will prove this man murdered Marie Iannuzzi."

When the prosecution finished, the defense began its counterattack. The Great Schmoozer was ready to go. He jabbed, ducked, bobbed, and weaved like a prizefighter in the ring, quickly capitalizing on an easy target as he announced that Marie's drug-dealing boyfriend should be the one seated in his unfortunate client's place.

Schmoozer told the jurors he agreed with the prosecutor about several things that had taken place prior to Marie's arrival at the Cardinal's Nest. He even agreed that his client and Marie had left the bar simultaneously, but not together. It was at this juncture that the two lawyers' stories diverged dramatically as Rappaport told the jurors what to expect from Candy. "She was waiting outside for Lenny while he delivered the keys to Marie in the bar. When Marie came out, they offered her a ride home and she refused."

Lenny's lawyer smoothly shifted legal gears in an attempt to provide the jury with a substitute suspect to the murder.

"Somebody else had the motive to commit this crime, had the opportunity, the intent. Somebody else was at least as likely, if not more likely to commit this crime than Mr. Paradiso. Who is that person? That person is David Doyle," Schmoozer said as he raised his hand and pointed to an invisible alternative killer. He was just getting warmed up.

"It was a stormy relationship," Rappaport continued. "There was a very, very violent argument between Marie and Doyle at the wedding. It wasn't an isolated incident. They had argued before, often violently. The next day Doyle was seen with deep gouge marks on his hand and scratches on his face. You'll hear witnesses tell you the same David Doyle tried to hide the scratches during Marie's wake."

Lenny's lawyer was on a roll.

"When Marie left the bar, she would cross paths with Doyle once again that fateful night," Schmoozer said, reminding the jurors that the couple lived at Jeffrey's Point, a short distance from the bar.

"That's the direction Candy Weyant saw her walking toward when Marie refused a ride home." Lenny's lawyer nodded in the direction of his client. "Doyle was still angry about the fight they had after the wedding. He was mad Marie tried to go skinny-dippin' at the Milanos' pool." This was a new twist that the prosecution hadn't mentioned.

"But wait, there's more. Her own boyfriend, David Doyle, didn't even go to Marie's funeral. He was arrested three days later in New Jersey for using a false name right after Marie was found dead," Schmoozer told the jurors as he shook his head incredulously.

"Finally, there is the issue of the credibility of the two inmates — a very key issue in this case. You will have to make a determination as to whether you believe what these two individuals say. Their credibility, their character is at issue in this case. If you apply your God-given common sense in assessing their credibility, you will not be convinced that Leonard Paradiso committed these offenses. You will return the only verdict which is in keeping with your common sense and that is, Leonard Paradiso is not guilty of these crimes. Thank you."

By the time Schmoozer was done the jury didn't have a clue who or what to believe.

Did he say it was a tomato or a red potato?

The TV news crews in the courtroom recorded the drama for all but the sixteen seated jurors to see later that evening. The gang of sixteen was sequestered by order of the court in a remote hotel, immune from the sway of public opinion, television news, radio talk shows, and newspaper articles. Each day the jury would be given the *Herald* and the *Globe* with the previous day's events carefully clipped out. The significance of the previous day's witness testimony could be measured by how much of the next day's newspaper was censored.

To present its case the commonwealth followed chronological order, using different witnesses to explain to the jury the flow of events leading up to Marie's murder. Father Aidan Walsh had officiated at the wedding of Maureen Trotto and Michael Milano.

He was the government's first witness. As the priest walked to the stand, the prosecutor thought of the Schmoozer's powers of persuasion and wondered if he would try to convince the jury that Walsh was a rabbi.

The priest solemnly raised his right hand, took the oath, and quietly told the jury he had attended the wedding reception at the Ship Restaurant, where he first met the Quahog and a "young lady" by the name of Candy. Between questions Walsh explained that he'd later talked briefly with the defendant at the Milano house party in Saugus; there he'd also met the victim, who clearly had been drinking. The Milanos "seemed embarrassed by her behavior." Their younger son, Freddy Milano, appeared interested in Marie, to his parents' dismay. As a result, the priest offered Marie a ride to her home in East Boston.

She refused.

On cross-examination, Schmoozer used the priest's observations to show that Marie was noticeably more intoxicated than the other people at the reception. Schmoozer suggested that his client was unfailingly polite; that he seemed attentive to his girlfriend, Candy; and that one of the Milano sons was hoping to leave with Marie that night. Father Aidan Walsh was a quick witness.

The two Isaacs and the Websters nodded in sequence as the priest solemnly passed by their seats and then reached to gently touch the shoulder of Marie's oldest sister.

"Do you have another witness, Mr. Burke?" Judge Donahue inquired as he removed his glasses. "We have about fifteen minutes left in the day."

"Yes, I do, Your Honor. The commonwealth calls Ruth Scully."

Ruth Scully was a mapmaker. She'd been working in the trial assignment session of the prosecutor's office when she had casually mentioned her love of maps and charts to the young DA. At the time, the lawyer had explained his obsession with the unsolved triple homicide and asked her to diagram the scene of the murders at Jacobs Street. It was a gruesome task. What she produced was a macabre masterpiece of detail and content. Scully became a fast friend of the DA's and had since his request begun a new career meticulously preparing each chart, map, or diagram used in every major felony case throughout the district attorney's office.

Lenny pulled out a yellow legal pad and Bic pen as the witness was sworn and provided her name to the jury.

"What do you have for us today?" the prosecutor asked after the witness settled into her seat loaded with rolled charts, maps, and blueprints.

"I have a diagram that represents the Cardinal's Nest. It's drawn to scale. It's based on the original floor plans of the building and on-site measurements that I made," the witness explained to the eager jurors leaning forward in their seats.

Schmoozer knew better than to object as Scully went through the schematic, explaining the layout of the bar's interior. It took all of three minutes. The Nest looked and smelled much better on paper.

"What's the second chart you have?"

"This is from the Massachusetts Department of Public Works highway charts. It depicts the area of Suffolk and Essex Counties. The different-colored pins represent different locations of interest in the case."

"Can you explain to the jury what they represent?"

"Sure. The blue pin is Crescent Avenue, in Revere. The red one is the Milanos' home on Gilway Road in Saugus. The orange pin is 134 Princeton Street, East Boston. Green is Jeffrey's Point in East Boston, and the yellow one is 202 Maverick Street in East Boston, where the Cardinal's Nest is located." Scully pointed with enthusiasm as the jurors smiled.

"Now, do you know where the border of Suffolk County is located in relation to Conley and Daggett's, what is now the Atlantic Lobster Company?"

"Yes, the Suffolk County border is in the middle of the Pines River," the mapmaker explained to the jury.

"Did you make certain measurements there?"

"Yes I did. We needed to make sure the case was within the jurisdiction of Suffolk County."

"How did you do that?"

"I went to the middle of the bridge crossing the Pines River and measured from there to the far corner of the Atlantic Lobster Company. I included the building in the measurement. Then I measured at a right angle to the corner of the back of the building and then basically the hypotenuse of the triangle back to the bridge for the distance," the witness explained with Lenny nodding in agreement, clearly not knowing why.

"What was the distance you came up with?"

"It's 1,578.5 feet from the bridge to the far corner of Conley and Daggett's and 195 feet to the back of the building. Basically, it's A squared plus B squared equals C squared, and C squared is the hypotenuse, which came out to be 1,590 feet," Scully told the jurors.

"Do you know what a rod is?" the DA asked as he briefly thought of his same question to Marie's sister three years earlier, which had led him to this place and time.

The cartographer didn't hesitate.

"Yes, a rod is an ancient measurement of distance. A rod is sixteen and a half feet long. One hundred rods is 1,650 feet. So the distance from the border on the middle of the bridge over the Pines River to the back of Conley and Daggett's is sixty feet within the jurisdiction of Suffolk County."

The DA thanked the witness for her testimony and turned to watch Lenny with paper and pen desperately doing the math. He stood by the prosecution table, watching until the defendant completed his task. The jurors followed a silent suit until the Quahog raised his head and turned to Schmoozer.

"She's fuckin' right," Paradiso whispered to his lawyer.

Two witnesses down. Twenty-seven to go.

"You may call your next witness, Mr. Burke," Judge Donahue said the following morning as Jack Gillen fired up the two large air conditioners flanking the jury box.

It was going to be a warm day.

"Yes, Your Honor. The Commonwealth calls Christine DeLisi." The DA turned to look at Drew, who in turn watched to see if Lenny would try the *you're next* eyes of death routine on DeLisi.

After the petite dark-haired woman took the stand, the prosecutor positioned his body to prevent the defendant from being able to see the witness as she testified.

"Can you tell the jury your name please," he asked.

There was another pause as everyone in the courtroom could see the witness's mouth move, but no sound appeared to come out.

"It's Christine, Christine DeLisi. D-e-L-i-s-i," Marie's friend said hesitantly as she searched the courtroom for a friendly face and briefly settled her eyes on two familiar women seated in the first row of the spectators' gallery.

Christine took a deep breath and turned her attention to the jury, making eye contact with the reassuring woman forelady seated closest to her. She then closed her eyes and began to cry. The judge handed the clerk a box of tissues, who gave it to the court reporter, who in turn handed it to the witness. Behind him the DA could hear Lenny's chair move to the right as the Quahog tried to see what the commotion was all about. The commonwealth's lawyer moved in the same direction.

Christine apologized to the judge and the jury for her tears and said unconvincingly "I'm fine" as the gallery watched her hands tremble.

Christine told the jury she had arrived at the Nest just before midnight. Michael Kamer was still inside, and Marie was at the bar talking with a stranger. The stranger was a large white man, about forty years old. DeLisi described Marie's clothes to the forward-leaning jurors, explaining that she looked "gorgeous." Some jurors nodded, as if they had been in attendance the night of the murder.

The witness hesitantly told the jury that when Marie was leaving with the stranger, she'd turned and asked DeLisi to wait at the bar until she returned.

"I won't be long," the victim told her friend. While the two women spoke, the same heavyset man stood waiting for Marie, patiently holding the door open.

There was a pause without a question as the witness closed her eyes tightly and spoke softly, but loud enough for everyone in the courtroom to hear.

"The door closed behind Marie and I never saw her again," DeLisi said as she reached for the box of tissues.

The prosecutor held the moment as long as he could while the jurors' eyes raced from the witness stand to the defense table.

"I ask you to look around the courtroom, Ms. DeLisi, and tell this jury if you see the man who left the Cardinal's Nest with Marie Iannuzzi the night she was murdered?"

As he spoke the words, the DA for the first time moved out of the line of sight separating the defendant from the witness.

DeLisi's left hand moved to her mouth as the right extended forward. "It's him." She pointed to Lenny for a full ten seconds.

"Where is he?"

"Right there," the witness told the jurors as the Quahog sat silently.

"When is the next time you saw Marie Iannuzzi?" the DA asked, setting the stage.

"At her wake," the witness recalled, raising a tissue to her face.

"Your witness," the government's lawyer smiled to Lenny's attorney. The Quahog's face had turned the color of ripened tomatoes.

"You were best friends with Marie, weren't you?" Schmoozer began slowly.

"Yes I was."

"She spent four or five days with you in May, about two months before she was killed, didn't she?"

"Yes, she did," DeLisi readily agreed as Lenny's large head began an involuntary up-and-down motion.

"Would you tell the jurors what you observed about her neck when she came to stay with you?"

"She had scratches on her neck."

"Is that all?"

"I think so," DeLisi hesitated, creating an opportunity for Lenny's lawyer to do some damage.

"Didn't you tell the grand jury that you saw strangulation marks around her neck when she came to stay with you?"

"I don't remember saying that."

"Well, let me refresh your memory, if I may," Schmoozer obliged. He began to read from the transcript of DeLisi's grand jury testimony.

There was a sense of dread for the DA and the trooper as they listened to Rappaport seize the microphone and shine a negative spotlight on one of their crucial witnesses.

"Didn't you tell the grand jury that 'Marie came running up to the house carrying a bag of clothes. She was screaming and crying. She had strangulation marks on her neck, fairly red marks and handprints around her neck'?"

Christine made no response. She didn't need to.

"When Ms. Iannuzzi came to your house that time, do you know where she was coming from with the bag of clothes?"

"From David's house."

"David Doyle, right?"

"Yes."

"Marie had very long fingernails, didn't she?" Schmoozer asked, quickly setting the stage for his future questions about the lack of fingernail scrapings.

"Yes, she did," DeLisi agreed, unsure of where Lenny's defense attorney was headed.

"And when Marie came to live with you for those four or five days, did David Doyle call your house at any time?"

"I don't remember," she replied, heading to safer ground.

"No further questions," Lenny's lawyer said as he smiled at the DA, knowing he had knocked the ball out of the park.

The jurors must have been wondering what the prosecutor could do to make them understand. He turned to the universal truth of love.

"You knew Marie and David, didn't you?"

"Yes, I did."

"Did David love Marie?"

"Yes, he did."

"And Marie loved David, didn't she?"

"Yes, she did."

"And after the fight they had, when she came to stay with you, did she go back and live with David?"

"Yes, she did. She loved him and he loved her."

"I have no further questions," the DA announced as he looked apprehensively to the jury for affirmation.

There was none, as he dejectedly returned to his seat.

— — —

Michael Kamer really didn't want to be in the crowded courtroom testifying about the large stranger he'd seen Marie sitting with at the Cardinal's Nest the night she was murdered. Kamer knew Lenny had connections, but he came to court anyway. He owed Marie that much.

Kamer was of average height, weight, intellect, and memory, but was very clear about what he knew. Kamer told the jury he'd arrived at the Nest around 11 PM and briefly spoken with Marie. He saw her talking and drinking at the bar for thirty to forty-five minutes with another man.

"Do you know who that person was?"

"The gentleman over there," Kamer said, bracing himself as he pointed to the Quahog.

"Did you see any notebook or papers with Marie?" the DA asked, attempting to undermine Paradiso's reason for returning to the bar.

"No sir, I didn't see any papers or notebooks with Marie that night," Kamer replied, adding that he'd left the bar shortly after midnight.

"Your witness," the DA said as Lenny shook his large head for some unknown reason.

"You arrived at the bar at what time?" Schmoozer asked.

"Eleven o'clock."

"And Christine DeLisi arrived at what time?"

"I don't know whether she was there before me or after me."

"Do you remember telling one of the investigators in this case that they were there for twenty minutes?"

"No, I don't remember that," Kamer said flatly as Lenny smiled and nodded with his thick lips pursed forward.

"Well, do you remember whether Christine was in the bar a long time or a short time?"

"What do you mean a long time, short time?" Kamer asked, sensing that no matter what he answered, it would be wrong. "She was there about an hour, maybe an hour and a half."

"Do you know what time the Cardinal's Nest closes on a Saturday night?"

"I don't know. Maybe around one thirty, two o'clock. I don't really know," Kamer estimated and then looked to the DA for approval.

When the examination was completed, Kamer left the stand and glanced at the defense table. Lenny smirked as his eyes turned to follow the witness's path, glaring at the back of Kamer's head as he quietly left the courtroom.

Rick Fraelick had been the first trooper to arrive at the scene behind Conley and Daggett's where Marie's body was found. Assigned to the Major Crime Unit, Fraelick was a ten-year veteran of the MSP, working undercover for the past four years. He'd previously spent a considerable amount of time holed up on the third floor of a flophouse on Lancaster Street, taking the eight-and-a-half-by-eleven glossies of Whitey Bulger and friends as the mobsters visited the garage across the street.

Each day Fraelick would call the prosecutor and tell him what he was seeing from his perch overlooking the Lancaster Street Garage. What Fraelick saw provided the probable cause to bug the garage. The DA used the information to draft a hundred-page affidavit that convinced a judge to give investigators a "black bag" search warrant, enabling them to secretly break into the garage and install the listening devices.

Too bad we never got to listen, the lawyer for the commonwealth reminded himself as the curly-haired trooper took the stand.

Fraelick told the jury that he'd arrived at the scene shortly after 4 PM and walked through an open gate toward the Pines River, where he saw the body of a young woman in a red dress with spaghetti straps lying facedown on the rocks. Her legs were in the water midway up her calves. She wasn't wearing shoes or stockings. The tide was going out, and she had a black scarf tightly knotted around her neck. When the body was turned over, her arms remained in the same position as when she was lying facedown. He told the jury Marie's fingers were clenched, and rigor mortis was clearly present. Fraelick's observations about the onset of rigor mortis had helped the medical examiner calculate Marie's time of death.

The trooper then explained to the jury that the victim and the scene were photographed before the body was moved. Drew and the DA used the same photographs to visualize the scene on their first trip to Conley and Daggett's. Now the DA presented the commonwealth's witness with ten of the same photographs and asked him the standard question before their introduction as exhibits.

"I show you these photographs, Trooper Fraelick, and ask you whether or not they are fair and accurate representations of the scene and of the victim as they appeared on the day the body was discovered."

"Yes sir, they are," Fraelick responded quickly as the DA retrieved the photographs, had them marked as exhibits, and asked the court's permission to circulate them to the jury.

Judge Donahue allowed it, and the jury anxiously compared the photographs with their memory of the scene three days earlier. When the jurors concluded their review, the DA attempted to place the scene into perspective.

"Trooper, have you had a chance to determine what passersby would be able to see driving a car past Conley and Daggett's at night?"

The question was a shorthand way of telling the jury that the area behind Conley and Daggett's was a perfect place for a murder. Fraelick knew exactly where the DA was going.

"A person coming from Revere toward Lynn would have a very, very brief view of that area if it was daylight. They would have to take their eyes from the road and they would only have a split second to observe the area. That's in daylight. At night, they wouldn't be able to see into the area behind Conley and Daggett's at all."

On cross, Schmoozer couldn't touch the first trooper on the scene.

— — —

George Katsas was the medical examiner. He was a quiet, self-effacing, round-faced man who had fled his native Hungary shortly after the Russian occupation. Short and stocky, with wire-rimmed glasses and a mild accent, Katsas always pronounced the DA's first name *Teem*. Meticulous in every detail, the ME had performed Marie Iannuzzi's autopsy the day after her body was discovered in mid-August 1979.

Six months later, the ME would do an autopsy on the prosecutor's thirty-five-year-old brother. As Katsas walked past him toward the witness stand, the DA briefly thought about the words the doctor had used to explain the cause of his older brother's sudden death.

"'Teem, your brother vas born with an undersized heart. It vas just a matter of time.'"

"Good afternoon, sir, would you please state your name for the jury," the prosecutor asked the smiling witness moments after he was sworn in.

"Yes, good afternoon, ladies and gentlemen, my name is George Katsas. I am a forensic pathologist and the county medical examiner."

Dr. Katsas had a personal presence that jurors liked instinctively. You felt you could trust what he told you. He explained the autopsy procedure in dry, easily understood medical terms and then recited his findings from a four-page report as he periodically made eye contact with the jury. They hung on his every word.

"Did you perform an examination of Ms. Iannuzzi's body?"

"Yes sir, I did."

"Can you tell the jury what your findings were?"

The doctor told the jury that the scarf around Marie's neck was tied so tightly that it left scratches, abrasions, and bruising of the skin encircling her entire neck. There were other scratches above her right eyebrow, on her neck, and on the lower side of her abdomen. There was a three-inch bruise on her right thigh, another on her right toe, and three more on the back of her right hand and on her left arm. Intact sperm were found in her vagina, but there were no signs of injury to her genitalia. Her blood contained .11 percent alcohol at the time of her death, just over the legal limit to operate a car.

When he had elicited the remainder of the medical examiner's autopsy findings, the prosecutor turned to look at the defendant as he spoke. The Quahog offered a baleful look as he listened.

"And sir, based upon your examination of the deceased and your medical experience, do you have an opinion, based upon a reasonable degree of medical certainty, what the cause of Marie Iannuzzi's death was?"

"Yes sir, I do have such an opinion," the doctor answered without hesitating.

"Would you tell the jury what was the cause of Marie's Iannuzzi's death?" the DA asked without an objection from the defense.

"The cause of death was asphyxia due to strangulation by ligature. In other words, she was strangled with her own scarf," the doctor responded evenly as the jury's collective eyes turned from the witness to the prosecutor and then to the defendant, who maintained his hate-filled glare.

"And sir, based upon the onset of rigor mortis could you estimate the approximate time of death for the victim?" the DA asked the witness as the jurors prepared to do the math.

"Yes, the victim had been dead for approximately twelve hours before her body was found," Katsas offered.

"You said that you had found intact spermatozoa in her vagina?"

"Yes sir. I did. That is consistent with the deceased having had sexual intercourse at some point between as few as three hours and as many as eighteen hours before her death."

"Could Marie Iannuzzi have had sexual intercourse within five minutes before her death?"

"That's possible."

"Or three minutes after her death?"

"That's also possible."

"You said the victim died of strangulation. I show you this photograph and ask you if it fairly and accurately represents the injuries to Marie's throat as you saw them at the time of the autopsy," the DA asked, handing the image of the purple shroud encircling the neck of the lifeless woman.

"Yes sir. It does."

"May I circulate this photograph to the jury, Your Honor?"

"Yes, you may," Hizzoner responded as the picture was passed slowly from one juror to the next.

"Your witness," the attorney for the commonwealth said.

Lenny's lawyer rose from his seat, heading toward the podium armed with three medical textbooks and two legal pads filled with questions for the state's medical expert.

Schmoozer momentarily looked toward the witness stand and the waiting Dr. Katsas as he attempted to place the pile of books and materials on the lawyer's lectern. The collection easily weighed fifteen pounds.

He missed by about three inches.

It was a great introduction to Rappaport's cross-examination as the judge knocked over his water glass and the jurors all left their seats at the sound of the crash amid the flutter of yellow papers slowly drifting to the tiled floor.

Drew had a hard time containing himself as Lenny brought both hands to the sides of his head and ran his fingers through the curly dark hair, his head moving slowly from side to side.

And as if he spent the previous night rehearsing the scene, Schmoozer calmly turned toward the startled jurors. "Am I smooth or what?" he said.

In those three seconds Lenny's lawyer lost and regained the jury's acceptance. The group issued a collective smile of approval for his humility.

Schmoozer discarded his original lengthy list of questions for the ME. His cross was brief, designed to highlight the commonwealth's failure to perform a critical test.

"Sir, do you know whether or not any test was performed in this case to determine the blood type of the person who had deposited the seminal fluid in Miss Iannuzzi's vagina?"

"I have no report that the test was done."

"Certainly, that type of identification process can be used to exclude somebody as having been the one to deposit the seminal fluid in the victim's vagina, correct?" Schmoozer asked quizzically, raising both hands palms up.

"Yes, it can be used to do that. It is used more and more as the methods become more refined," the medical examiner related to the jurors, who listened impassively and then turned to the DA as if to say, *How come no one did the test?*

"What are you always talkin' to those two old gray-haired coots in the back of the courtroom for?" Drew wanted to know as the two packed the day's paperwork and headed downstairs to the DA's office.

The lawyer didn't respond as he struggled with the huge brown file.

"And how come they're always comin' around to all your cases? What, ya got relatives up here I don't know about?"

"No, they're just a couple of court-watchers. They're both retired. They come to court every day. It's cheap entertainment for 'em, I guess. Maybe they always wanted to be lawyers. Anyway, I like finding out what they think about how a witness testifies or what they think the jury is doin' or how they think the cross is going. It's sorta like a day-to-day opinion poll."

"You're nuts. You know that?" his friend advised.

"Both of them are very smart. I think it makes them feel good when I ask them what they think. They helped me out in my first murder trial," the DA said.

"Yeah, but they can screw you up, too. You can't rely on what they say," Drew said skeptically. "They don't know the case like we do. What if they tell ya somethin' that's dead wrong?"

The lawyer didn't respond. He knew Ponytail was probably right. There was too much at stake to rely on the opinion of two strangers he didn't know well enough to call by their first names; it was always Mr. Shulman and Mr. Sullivan.

Isaac Shulman was a Holocaust survivor, a tailor by trade who grew up in the Jewish quarter of Warsaw. A thin man with short gray hair, he'd worn a bow tie and a long-sleeved shirt every day of his adult life. He wore bow ties because he liked them and thought them fashionable. He wore long-sleeved shirts because they covered the numbers tattooed on his left wrist.

Each day, Mr. Shulman would go to the deli in Coolidge Corner, order pastrami on dark rye, and take the Green Line trolley from Brookline into Government Center. The seventy-three-year-old would slowly walk up the flight of stairs to the plaza near the Steaming Kettle, buy his *Boston Globe*, and order a large coffee with one cream and two sugars. When he finished consuming the coffee and the *Globe*, Mr. Shulman would cross Tremont Street and head for the courthouse to meet his best friend.

Isaac Sullivan didn't read the *Globe*. He preferred the *Boston Herald*. The oldest of seven children born to a Jewish mother and a Catholic father, he had endured a lifetime of taunts growing up in the cloistered Irish community of South Boston. Mr. Sullivan was a rarity who could speak both Gaelic and Hebrew. A paratrooper in World War II, he received a Purple Heart after a German grenade took most of his ear and all of the hearing from the left side of his head.

Mr. Shulman always sat on Mr. Sullivan's right in court.

Each day, Mr. Sullivan would go to the corner package store on Broadway Street in Southie and order a roast beef on light rye, a Sprite, a small bag of Doritos, and a *Herald*. At eight fourteen each morning he would take the D line into downtown Boston. Mr. Sullivan didn't drink coffee. He preferred tea, which he would buy at the Kettle, and then head for the courtroom of choice to wait for his best friend to arrive.

Each afternoon recess, the two widowers would take their sandwiches, one dark rye, the other light rye, and head outside, weather permitting, where they would dissect the trial of the day and their one remaining true love, the Boston Red Sox.

"Oy vey, Mister DA, vat a good day you had today," Mr. Shulman said to the prosecutor as he left the courtroom with Drew shortly after four that afternoon.

"Thank you, Mr. Shulman," the DA responded. Drew looked on skeptically.

"Yeah, but I don't like that juror sitting in the front row with the funny glasses. He keeps smiling at the Quahog's lawyer, like he knows something we don't," Mr. Sullivan said loudly to his friend and anyone else within earshot.

"He's talking about Mr. Peepers, isn't he? I told you I didn't like that guy," Drew suddenly agreed.

"I know," the lawyer responded with a smile, as the second Isaac began his analysis.

"That Lenny is meshuga. He's crazy — crazy like the fox. Did you see the vay he looks at you, Mr. DA?" Mr. Shulman asked as Marie's sisters nodded.

"His lawyer couldn't do anything with Dr. Katsas on cross-examination. Did you see that?" Mr. Sullivan said louder than he needed to. "And that forelady is very smart. She's just taking it all in. I don't think she likes Lenny."

"Vat's there to like, Isaac?" Mr. Shulman added quickly.

The prosecutor and Ponytail thanked the two gray-haired men and said they looked forward to seeing them tomorrow.

-- -- -- -- -- -- -- -- -- -- -- -- -- -- -- -- --

Victor Anchukitis was an important witness for the commonwealth. A nondescript man with a ruddy complexion and monotone voice, he happily told the jury that he'd recently retired after serving as a parole officer for more than twenty years. He'd supervised the Quahog for the last two.

"Sir, I direct your attention to the second week in August of 1979. Did you have occasion to speak with the defendant?" the prosecutor formally asked as he stood at the far end of the jury box behind defense counsel's table.

"Yes I did. It was on August 13, around nine thirty in the morning, I got a phone call from Lenny. He told me he needed to talk to me. Lenny was being transferred to another parole officer and he hadn't heard from him yet," the PO said as he raised a hand to his balding pate.

For some reason the witness squinted and rubbed the top of his forehead after each question, wincing as if in pain.

"Did you see Mr. Paradiso that day?"

"Yes sir, I did. Lenny came to my office in Somerville around noonish the same day. It was a Monday, that's the day I'm usually in my office. He brought some young lady friend with him whose last name sounded like *Wynette.*"

"Can you tell the jury what they said when they came to your office that day?" the DA, fleetingly thinking of Tammy's "Stand By Your Man."

"Lenny told me he and his girlfriend, 'Wynette,' were at a wedding that weekend. They went to the reception and the groom's house party. A young woman became unruly there and Candy gave her a ride to a bar in East Boston. Candy returned to the house party. Later, she and Lenny left. On the way home they find the girl's keys and papers in the car. They drive to the bar where the girl was drinking. She comes out of the bar and they give her the keys and papers back. Candy asked her if she wanted a ride home and the girl told her 'No way' and kept walking down Maverick Street," Anchukitis related as he squinted and raised a hand to his forehead.

"Mr. Paradiso never mentioned anything to you about being inside the Cardinal's Nest for twenty-five minutes, did he?"

"No sir, he didn't," Anchukitis agreed.

"They told you that Ms. Iannuzzi came outside of the bar to their car and Candy gave Marie her keys, didn't they?"

"Uh, yes they did," the PO reluctantly agreed.

"Paradiso calls you around nine thirty in the morning and says he needs to talk to you?"

"That's right."

"Did Paradiso say anything to you about a body being found?"

"I'm vague on that, sir. I just can't recall anything else," the witness hedged.

"Do you know what time Marie Iannuzzi's body was actually identified by her next of kin?" the prosecutor asked, knowing it wasn't until later that Monday morning when investigators brought Marie's father and David Doyle to view her body.

Sometimes the DA asked a witness a question just to make the jury think about the topic. It didn't matter what the current witness knew, or said. The question was a setup for a future witness to answer. When the jury heard the answer from the subsequent witness, they would feel they were solving the puzzle of the case piece by piece.

"No sir, I do not." Anchukitis said as he slowly shook his head, squinted, and raised his hand to rub his brow even harder.

Once the jurors heard the time-lapse testimony, there was a pause as each of them had a chance to wonder why Lenny would need to tell his PO his whereabouts after the reception if no one knew Marie was dead yet.

"Let me show you your office records. Did you ever have occasion to be at a place called the Atlantic Lobster Company?" The prosecutor handed the PO a folder of his written summary of interaction with the parolee.

"Yes sir, I went there sometime in early April of 1980," Anchukitis said, referring to his notes for the exact date. "It was the second of April, I believe."

"And how did you have occasion to go there?" the DA asked as he unconsciously raised his hand to rub his own forehead.

"I was on my way home when I ran into Lenny. I stopped and we had a cup of coffee and a doughnut. He asked me if I wanted to see where he worked out of. We stopped off at the Atlantic Lobster Company on the Lynn Marsh Road," Anchukitis explained as the forelady squinted and then placed her left hand up to her brow, moving it slowly from side to side.

"And do you know the name of the place before it became Atlantic Lobster Company?"

"I think it used to be an Irish name, something like Conley and Daggett. Lenny introduced me to the owner and told me he did business with the people for years. He showed me how the tanks operated when they bring the lobsters in and how they ship them out fresh. He gave me a tour of the whole place," Anchukitis said, moving his right hand around in a circular motion in front of him and then up to his forehead again.

"During the period of time he was under your supervision, did Mr. Paradiso explain what kind of a business he was in?"

"Yeah, he was hauling fish, bringing fish down from somewhere up in Maine, taking trips to make connections in his own business. Lenny said he was working for the Commercial Lobster Company over on the waterfront, too," the PO said. By now his forehead had taken on the color of a baked stuffed crustacean.

"No further questions," the DA concluded, envisioning the *Mala Femmena* moored at Pier 7.

Schmoozer took the podium and brought his left hand to his forehead in sync with the witness, asking his first question with the assurance of a positive response.

"Did my client ever give you any problems while he was on parole?"

"No sir, none whatsoever," Anchukitis enthusiastically told the jurors, smiling in the direction of the Quahog, who responded with a crooked smile in kind.

"Did he cooperate with you in every way?"

"Very much, sir."

Drew looked at his friend seated next to him and said nothing as the lines on Ponytail's face instinctively hardened. And so the PO's love fest with Lenny went. The Quahog was a model parolee. A hardworking, misunderstood con who had lost his way and, despite his minor transgressions, somehow found redemption with the bleached-blond cheerleader.

"Do you know what the telephone call was about that Mr. Paradiso made to you on the morning of the thirteenth?"

"Yes sir. It was about a change in his parole supervision. He was getting a new supervisor. Lenny hadn't heard from him yet."

"There was nothing in your written records that says Mr. Paradiso was coming in to talk about a problem that morning, is there?"

"No sir, there isn't," the willing participant agreed.

"And my client never tried to hide the fact from you that he was familiar with Conley and Daggett's, did he?"

"No sir." The PO smiled warmly.

"In fact, he brought you over there to show you around, didn't he?"

"Yes sir. He did." The witness nodded and massaged his forehead for the final time. Lenny's lawyer took a moment to check in with the jury to see if they got the point: The PO supported his parolee. As Anchukitis stepped down from the stand, Judge Donahue caught the fever, joined the choir, and rubbed his brow from side to side.

Schmoozer had turned a negative into a positive. That's what he did best. You hated the son of a bitch, but you knew he was good. The DA momentarily wavered before he called his next witness to the stand. For the first time he felt defensive and worried about what Lenny's lawyer could do to twist the jurors' minds against his case. It was irrational. He knew that, but what was so clear had suddenly become so muddied, so subjective. He looked to Drew, who understood his friend's hesitation about calling the next person on the witness list.

"You may call your next witness, Mr. Burke," Hizzoner said with the first note of impatience.

"Judge, may I see you at the sidebar, please?"

"Certainly," Donahue responded. Schmoozer must have sensed a problem.

"Life never goes the way you expect it to. My next witness, Charlene Bullerwell, is outside and she says, 'I'm not going to testify. I'm not even coming in the courtroom.' She wants to talk to you, Judge," the DA explained.

"She does?" the jurist responded, without elaborating.

"I'm in a bit of a quandary. First of all, I don't know how I'm going to get her into the courtroom, and second, I don't how much of her statement about Paradiso you'll let me get into."

Schmoozer loved it. "I'm interested in that answer."

"The only thing I am trying to get out of her is the statement she testified to at the motion hearing. The one Paradiso made to her about 'I've done girls before. Girls are fun and easy to do,'" the prosecutor explained.

"Let me think about it. I'll make a decision between now and two o'clock," Hizzoner announced while the jurors tilted an ear to the conference in a vain attempt to hear the exchange.

"That's provided I can get her in the door. It's the cameras. People don't want to testify if they know they're going to be on TV."

"We'll be in recess till then," the judge said, then stepped down from the bench and headed toward his chambers to a chorus of "All rise" from the four court officers.

— — —

The cramped judge's chambers set off from Courtroom 808 were painted a light powder blue with one narrow nine-paned window. The Spartan furnishings consisted of one metal desk and chair, two brown vinyl couches, and three oak bookcases filled with a collection of tan numbered books that held the written decisions from the court of appeals. One of the oldest books contained the case *Commonwealth v. John Webster.*

"I had you come in here because you have some reluctance about testifying. Why don't you tell me about it?" the judge said softly to the pretty woman with long dark hair.

"Since I was here the last time, I've had several seizures because of all this. I've had brain surgery. I don't remember anything. I don't have any testimony. I don't remember anything," Charlene began, as tears welled and her hands shook.

"I realize there's a lot of stress and strain coming to court. I can have the cameras turned down so they don't show your face," Hizzoner offered.

The pretty woman would have none of it.

"I don't remember anything anyway. I don't even remember what I said the last time I was here. They told me my name wasn't going to get out. The next day it was plastered all over the television, all over the front page of the papers."

There was a risk that a jury would misinterpret Bullerwell's fear or that she would deny her previous statements and weaken the case. The prosecutor couldn't take that chance.

"Is there anything else that I need to cover, gentlemen?" Hizzoner said as he looked up to see the DA slowly shake his head.

"Well, it appears that we won't be able to reach you today," the judge told the reluctant witness.

She turned to Schmoozer as if to give Lenny a message. "I don't remember anything," she told him.

In the courtroom, the air conditioners on both sides of the jury box struggled to combat the heat of the midday sun. It was futile. Some of the jurors were using their hands as fans to stir a small breeze around their flushed faces as the lawyers left the judge's chambers.

"The commonwealth calls Carl Sjoberg," the DA said woodenly as he searched the gallery for a friendly face and saw only Schmoozer and Lenny staring up at him from defense table with the same smile of satisfaction.

Trooper Carl Sjoberg was assigned to the Essex County DA's office. Stocky and blond, he had conducted the follow-up interviews after the discovery of the unidentified woman's body on Sunday, August 12.

"Sir, I direct your attention to the date in question and ask you to tell the jury when the young woman's body was formally identified," the DA said, trying to regain a sense of momentum.

"Yes sir, the unidentified woman's body was taken to the morgue on Sunday afternoon and wasn't formally identified by her family until the following day. It was sometime Monday, late morning," Sjoberg said in a clear voice as the jury nodded, fanning themselves in unison.

"So at nine thirty Monday morning on the thirteenth, Marie's body hadn't been identified, had it?" the DA exclaimed loudly as he suddenly found an avenue to explore.

"No sir, she had not been identified at that time."

"Do you know what time the defendant called his parole officer that Monday morning, the thirteenth?" the prosecutor asked, looking to the jury for some sign that they had made the connection.

"No sir, I'm sorry, I don't know that," Sjoberg said, puzzled by the DA's question.

"Who went with you to identify the body?" the prosecutor asked, bringing the witness back to familiar territory. It was an opportunity to offset some of the damage he knew Schmoozer would do when Doyle took the stand.

"It was the victim's father, her brother-in-law, and David Doyle. They went with us to the morgue to identify the body. Doyle was crying. His eyes were red. They were all very upset. Doyle answered all of my questions. He was emotionally disturbed over the fact his girlfriend had been murdered," Sjoberg said as Lenny smirked, shook his head, and wiped the sweat forming along the ridge of his hairline.

"Did you speak to anyone else that day?" the DA asked as he watched Schmoozer admonish his client.

"Yes, I did. I talked to the Milanos. 'Red' Milano told me a man by the name of Lenny and his girlfriend had given Marie a ride home. He said he didn't know Lenny's last name, but had his number. He gave him a call and arranged an interview. As soon as I left the Milanos, I went directly to his apartment at 134 Princeton Street and talked to Mr. Paradiso," Sjoberg said as the jurors turned to look at the defendant.

"How would you describe his appearance when you arrived there?"

"He appeared to be very, very nervous," Sjoberg said pantomiming Lenny's hand motions. "He was chain-smoking. At one point, he lit two cigarettes at once and was pacing around his apartment." Sjoberg brought two imaginary cigarettes up to his mouth. "They were Camels or Lucky Strikes," he added as an afterthought.

"Did you notice anything else about his person?" the DA asked, sensing that the jurors wanted to know more about Lenny's response.

"Yes sir, I did. When I shook hands with him, I noticed his hands were sweaty and they appeared to be shaking."

"Did he say anything about his interaction with the victim that evening?"

"He told me how Candy had given Marie a ride to the Cardinal's Nest and how he went inside to give Marie some keys he said they found in Ms. Weyant's car."

"Did he tell you how long he was inside the bar?" the prosecutor asked, knowing Kamer and DeLisi had testified that the defendant was inside talking to Marie for more than half an hour.

"Mr. Paradiso told me he was inside the Cardinal's Nest for about five or six minutes," the trooper said matter-of-factly.

"So Mr. Paradiso told you he was only in the Cardinal's Nest for five or six minutes, gave Marie the keys, and then left?" the DA asked with a measure of doubt as he repeated the witness's answer and turned to face the jury.

"Yes sir, that's what he told me," Sjoberg said, calmly confirming the time period.

"How would you describe Candy Weyant?"

"She would be in her late twenties, early thirties, five foot six, five foot four, very stout."

"Very stout?"

"Yes sir."

"And Mr. Paradiso told you Candy was patiently waiting outside in her car for him while Lenny was inside the Cardinal's Nest talking to Marie?"

"That's what he said. Yes sir."

"Did you ever see any pictures of Marie?"

"Yes sir. I did."

"Tell the jury, how would you describe her?"

"Stunning."

"Nice figure?"

"Excellent," the witness explained as Mr. Peepers in the front row of the jury box frowned at the Quahog for the first time.

"Did he say what happened next?"

"Yes sir. Mr. Paradiso said Marie followed him out the door, turned the corner, walked down Maverick Street, and he never saw her again. Mr. Paradiso told me his girlfriend, Candy Weyant, was waiting in her car outside the bar the whole time he was inside," the trooper said with a straight face as the DA crinkled his nose and mouth in obvious disbelief.

"What did you do after your interview with the defendant?"

"After I spoke to Mr. Paradiso, I went directly to Northeast Petroleum in Chelsea where his girlfriend worked. I spoke with her that same day outside the plant," Sjoberg explained, helping the jurors make a mental note of the time line.

"Can you describe Ms. Weyant's appearance as you spoke with her?"

"She was visibly shaken. During the interview, she got cotton-mouthed and kept trying to wet her lips so she could speak. She told me the same story Mr. Paradiso did, almost word for word. It appeared as if it had been rehearsed," the trooper said as he looked anxiously at Schmoozer.

"Do you recall what kind of car she was driving that day?"

"Yes sir, she was driving a yellow, two-door 1973 Buick LeSabre. Ms. Weyant told me she and Mr. Paradiso were driving it the night the victim was killed. I later learned the same Buick was reported stolen approximately three weeks after Marie's murder. The car was never recovered," Sjoberg volunteered.

"Did you ever have any further contact with Ms. Weyant after that interview?" the DA asked, leading the witness to Lenny's meeting with Tony Pisa at attorney John Cavicchi's home.

"Yes sir, we did. Just before Christmas of 1979, I went to Northeast Petroleum again and told Ms. Weyant we had a break in the case and that we were going to the grand jury," Sjoberg said.

"Did you ever go to the grand jury?"

"No sir, we didn't. I was hoping Candy would talk if she knew how serious the case was."

"Did she ever talk to you that day?"

"No sir. She told me she had nothing more to say," Sjoberg responded as he mimicked the previous witness and brought his right hand slowly up to rub his forehead.

"And this conversation with Ms. Weyant took place shortly before Christmas, right?" the DA asked, attempting to set the stage for the next witness, Death Row Tony Pisa.

"Yes sir, I talked to her on December 12, in 1979," the trooper obliged as the DA turned the witness over to Schmoozer for cross-examination.

"May I see counsel over at sidebar?" the judge requested before Lenny's lawyer could begin.

"I'm pretty tired at this point. Do you mind if we adjourn for the day?" Hizzoner asked the pair of lawyers.

"Fine with me. I've got about an hour of cross," Schmoozer advised.

"It's fine with me, too. It's awfully hot in here. The jury's falling asleep," the DA agreed.

"It's not the heat. It's your direct examination. You're boring the hell outta them," Schmoozer said out of Hizzoner's earshot as the pair returned to their seats. The jurors were excused from the sweltering courtroom with the court's daily instruction not to discuss the case, happy to board an air-conditioned Greyhound to their undisclosed motel. They would be back early the next morning to a cooled courtroom.

Lenny's lawyer took advantage of the extra half day to prepare for his cross-examination.

"Trooper, you seemed surprised yesterday that two people would tell you the same story about what they had seen," the defense attorney said as he began to repair the damage. "Is it your experience that two people who see the same series of events tell you something different occurred?"

"I guess I would expect they would say the same thing if they were telling the truth," Sjoberg hesitantly agreed.

"Of course Weyant's story's gonna be the same as Lenny's. Wouldn't you expect them to be? They saw the same thing," Schmoozer declared loudly as the witness reluctantly agreed and the DA ground his teeth on the side of his mouth the jury couldn't see. God, he hated the son of a bitch.

"Now, when you saw Ms. Weyant next on December 12, you told her she was gonna be charged as an accessory, didn't you? You threatened her, didn't you?" Lenny's lawyer said, moving closer to the witness stand.

"No sir. I did not threaten her. I suggested she needed to tell the truth."

"You don't consider that a threat?" the lawyer bellowed as he turned to gauge the jury's reaction.

"No sir. I don't."

Lenny was enjoying the show, nodding with encouragement to his advocate at each point raised.

"You never saw Mr. Doyle actually crying when Marie's body was identified, did you?"

Before Sjoberg could answer, Paradiso was already shaking his head.

"No, I didn't. His eyes were red, as if he had been crying."

"Did Mr. Doyle attend Marie's funeral?"

"Not to my knowledge, no."

"You know where Doyle was five days after Marie's death, don't you?"

"Yes I do, he was arrested in New Jersey," the witness announced, his voice trailing off.

"You know that some people saw scratches on Mr. Doyle's hands after the murder, don't you?"

"I didn't see any, but other people reported they did around the time of the wake."

"Marie had long fingernails, didn't she?"

"Yes sir. She did."

"You didn't see any scratches on Mr. Paradiso the day after the murder, did you?"

"No sir. I didn't."

"You were looking for scratches on my client, weren't you?"

"Yes sir. I was."

"Now, when you went to Mr. Paradiso's apartment, you said he seemed nervous, right?"

"Yes sir."

"Did you know he was on parole when you spoke to him?"

"No sir. I did not."

"There's nothing unusual about a man in that position being nervous, is there?"

"I don't find it unusual," the witness retreated.

"In fact, it'd be unusual if he wasn't nervous at all, don't you think?"

There was a pause long enough for Schmoozer to ask another question before Sjoberg could answer the previous one.

"Are you nervous today, Trooper? Testifying here in a murder case before a group of strangers?" Lenny's lawyer asked as he pointed toward the jurors' box.

"Of course I am. Anybody would be," the trooper agreed.

"Maybe your hands are sweaty, too," Schmoozer asked, and then again put another question to him before he could respond or the DA could object.

"It's no secret Mr. Paradiso was on parole then. He was being questioned by the police about the murder of a girl he had been with fifteen hours earlier. Of course he was nervous. You'd be nervous, too, wouldn't you, Trooper?" Schmoozer bellowed as Lenny nodded indignantly.

There was a pause from the witness stand. The longer the silence continued, the clearer the answer became. Schmoozer didn't wait for the witness to respond. He simply turned to the jurors and said, "No further questions."

The DA looked at Drew, then at Schmoozer, and grimaced. God, how he hated the son of a bitch.

-- -- -- -- -- -- -- -- -- -- -- -- -- -- -- -- -- --

Pisa and Bond would offer two different slices of the same pie, an insight into the demented and twisted reality of a serial killer. The two cons who had been there, done that, were about to tell sixteen average citizens how the mind of a murderer worked.

"I met Lenny when we were both doin' time in Norfolk Prison," Pisa began as he pushed his conservative blue-striped tie tighter around his neck. The witness had jet-black hair slicked back off his forehead, as well as an onyx pinkie ring. He talked about the defendant with a familiarity that came from months of day-to-day contact.

"It was the fall of '76 when I met him at the auto school. Lenny didn't adapt too well to prison. He was involved in a fight with another inmate and I broke it up. After that he used to talk with me all the time," Pisa explained, growing more comfortable with his role of witness.

With each statement Lenny bristled, grimaced, smirked, and shook his head in silent disbelief.

"Do you have any background in the law?"

"Yes sir. I do. There was a law library at Norfolk that I helped to establish. I began by just reading law books. Sorta trial and error."

"Did you ever give other inmates legal advice? Including Mr. Paradiso?"

"Yes, I did. Lenny used to talk to me about his case all the time," Pisa said, referring to the conviction for the attempted rape of Connie Porter.

"Do you remember what you used to talk about?"

"He used to ask me about circumstantial evidence. Lenny would say things like if somebody did something and the victim wasn't around to testify, there wouldn't be any case, right?" Pisa told the jurors, who alternately watched the witness and eyeballed the defendant.

"What did you tell him?" the DA asked.

"I told Lenny that wasn't necessarily true. I explained the John Webster case of 1850 to him. In that case, Webster killed Dr. Parkman and burned his body up. The police only found a piece of Parkman's jawbone and the jury still convicted Webster. They hung him thirty days later," Pisa added with a sense of finality, reaching for his tie a second time.

"I show you this document. Did you actually file some motions for Mr. Paradiso on his appeal?"

"Yes sir, I did. That document is a motion I filed for Lenny to get a copy of the transcript of his trial at the commonwealth's expense."

"Did you have occasion to see Mr. Paradiso after he was released from Norfolk?"

"Yeah, I did. It was Christmas Eve in 1979. I was on furlough. I went to East Boston to visit an attorney friend of mine by the name of John Cavicchi," Pisa said. The judge leaned forward and wrote something in his trial notebook.

"Who did you go there with?"

"My wife and my son," Pisa offered.

"Are they here today?"

"Yes, they are. They're seated back there." The witness gestured, and the jury turned a collective eye toward the rear of the courtroom. Lenny pursed his lips to curse.

"Tell the jury what happened at Cavicchi's home."

"I was there for about a half an hour when Lenny showed up with a bucket of lobsters."

"Did you talk to the defendant?" The DA knew that such an open-ended question would lead the witness to Lenny's confession.

There was a pause from Pisa, who cleared his throat and adjusted the onyx, then the striped tie.

"Yeah, at one point we walked to the door. Lenny said he wanted to show me his truck. When we were outside, he told me he was getting hassled by the cops. Lenny said he was gonna be indicted for Marie Iannuzzi's murder," Pisa told the jurors, quickly glancing to the back of the courtroom.

"This was Christmas Eve?"

"Yes."

The DA turned to the jury, wondering if they would make the connection with the police visiting Candy on December 12 to tell her they planned to go to the grand jury.

"Did Mr. Paradiso say anything else?"

"Yes, Lenny wanted Cavicchi to represent him. He was worried about how much it was gonna cost him because he had short money. He said it was a relatively easy case."

"What did you say?"

"I joked with him. I said you'd have to peddle a lot of fish, sell a lot of fish in order to get a good attorney," Pisa recounted. Lenny shook his head and ran his thick left index finger beneath his nose.

"Did Mr. Paradiso respond to that comment?"

"Yeah, he said, 'This is no joke. I killed the Iannuzzi broad and I'm in serious trouble. I need representation. It's an easy case. There's no witnesses. It should be simple to handle,'" Pisa said almost woodenly, as though the admission of murder were a common occurrence.

"Was that the last time you spoke to the defendant?"

"No, it wasn't. Right after that, Lenny called me at the Bay State Correctional Center and told me to keep my mouth shut in regard to the Iannuzzi case. He reminded me I had a family outside the walls and I was still incarcerated." As he spoke about his family Pisa turned from the jury, looked at the defendant, and tapped the front of the witness stand for emphasis.

"Why didn't you go to the police then?"

"I only had nine years in on a life sentence. I still had a family out there."

"When was the next time you heard from Mr. Paradiso?"

"The next time I heard from him was in December of 1981. I was still at Bay State."

The next logical question would be about the telephone call Paradiso made to Pisa one month after Joan Webster disappeared. Both lawyers knew it, and both knew it would put the DA on thin ice. Any conviction in this case could be overturned on appeal if he made a mistake here.

Schmoozer took the bait.

"Judge, can we see you at sidebar?" defense counsel asked.

When the two lawyers arrived, Hizzoner asked, "Is this about the statements made by the defendant regarding the Webster case?"

"Yes, Judge. Paradiso calls Pisa at Bay State and begins to ask him questions about the old 1850 Webster case. Pisa tells him that case doesn't apply, 'They found the body in your case' — meaning Iannuzzi. Then Paradiso says, 'They didn't find her body' — meaning Joan Webster. 'All they found was her pocketbook.' It's an admission," the DA offered.

Defense counsel quoted from two cases to the contrary.

The judge understood the moment and the significance of Paradiso's statement to the trial. The possibility of a reversal loomed in the minds of all three men as they huddled outside the hearing of the jury. "I'd like some time to think about this issue, gentlemen. If Mr. Burke wants to put Pisa back on at a later time, do you have any objection, Mr. Rappaport?"

"As long as I can call Pisa back as a witness, then I won't go into it now," the DA agreed.

"I have absolutely no objection to that." Schmoozer's sigh was filled with relief.

"I don't think the jurors are falling asleep today, do you, Steve?" the DA whispered to his counterpart as the two lawyers returned to their seats. "Your witness," he added at full voice, turning to look at Drew, who was watching the Quahog stare at Pisa.

Maybe it was the prison defense work Schmoozer did; maybe he just didn't like inmates testifying against other inmates. Whatever the reason, there was a clear edginess to his questions as he began his cross-examination of Pisa.

"You were convicted of first-degree murder and sentenced to die, weren't you?"

"That's correct."

"The jury in your case had a choice not to give you the death penalty, didn't they?"

"That's correct."

"But the jury decided you should die, didn't they?"

"That's right."

"You spent some time on death row, didn't you?"

"Yes sir. I did."

"After your conviction, while you were in prison, you filed an appeal and eight motions for new trials, didn't you?"

"That's probably right."

"Then the US Supreme Court vacated your death sentence. After that, your first-degree murder conviction was reduced to second-degree murder, wasn't it?"

"Yes sir."

"And the difference between a conviction for first- and second-degree murder is basically on a second degree you're eligible for parole after you've served fifteen years, right?"

"That's right."

"Now, you told us on direct that Mr. Paradiso didn't adapt well in prison?"

"That's correct," Pisa replied.

"Did you adapt well in prison?"

"At first I didn't, no. No, not at all."

"At what point did you begin to adapt well in prison?"

"Actually, it was after I read Shakespeare's *Hamlet*."

That wasn't an answer Schmoozer had expected.

"After you read *Hamlet*?"

"Yes sir."

"When was that, sir?"

"When I was on death row, in 1970."

"So you began to adapt well then? Why is that?"

"Well, I'd always heard the cliché, 'To be or not to be, that's the question.' Then I read what Shakespeare said about 'whether it's nobler in mind to suffer the slings and arrows of outrageous fortune or to take arms against the sea of trouble.' When I read that, I understood it for the first time, and I decided to take arms against the sea of trouble, meaning my conviction," Pisa explained with an intensity that surprised Schmoozer.

"So you say you took arms against a sea of outrageous fortune?"

"Sea of trouble," the man in the black robe, who read Shakespeare, corrected. "It's 'arms against the sea of trouble.'"

"Sea of trouble. Thank you, Your Honor," a momentarily deflated Schmoozer repeated.

"Yes I did. I tried to reeducate myself the best I could under the circumstances," Pisa offered.

"But you felt you were suffering the 'slings and arrows of outrageous fortune,' didn't you?"

"I felt I was."

"Okay. Did you commit the crime that you were sentenced to death row for?"

There was an awkward pause as the witness thought about his answer.

"No, I didn't."

"The jury made a mistake in that case?"

"No, the jury didn't make a mistake. If I was a juror, I would have convicted myself, too. I had an attorney that never completed law school. He offered no defense. Trials are funny. I was uneducated. I was ignorant of the law then and what happens in a courtroom. I had a defense, but my lawyer just rested after my wife and I testified. I'd have found myself guilty, too."

"So over all the years in jail, all eight of your motions for new trial were denied, including a motion to be released on bail, right?"

"Yes sir."

"Then three months ago, the day after you testified on a motion in this case, you were granted bail, weren't you?"

"Yes, I was."

"The district attorney's office did that for you, didn't they?"

"They recommended that to the judge." Pisa nodded, turning to the prosecution table for confirmation.

"You said, listen, I've got this information and I want to come forward, but I'd like some favorable consideration as a result?"

"No, I said I'd like to come forward, but it's tough to come forward when you're still incarcerated. I couldn't come forward in a murder case and return to prison and live to tell about it."

"Wasn't part of your motivation in coming forward to help get Tony Pisa out of jail?"

"I certainly hoped the commonwealth would take it into consideration."

"Can you tell the jury why you waited for more than three years to come forward with this information about my client?"

Pisa hesitated before he answered. "There are people serving time behind the wall, and maybe I'm doing them a favor, too. They have wives and they have loved ones out there. If this man isn't stopped and put behind bars where he belongs —"

Lenny's lawyer didn't wait for the end of Pisa's sentence. "You want this jury to believe that's why you're here?"

"I'm here to protect anybody I can," Pisa said.

"You're not here to help Tony Pisa?" Schmoozer demanded loudly as he moved closer to the witness stand, pointing at the man who was pointing at the defense attorney.

"To help Tony Pisa?" the witness stammered, "Yeah, I always wanna help Tony Pisa."

"And you'd do anything you could to help Tony Pisa, wouldn't you?" Schmoozer bellowed.

Lenny's lawyer had reached Pisa, and Pisa knew it. So did the DA.

"I certainly would," Pisa responded at the same decibel level as Schmoozer nodded in obvious agreement.

"Including lying about Lenny Paradiso, wouldn't you," Lenny's lawyer asked as a statement of fact, not a question.

"I wouldn't perjure myself in a capital case for anybody —" Pisa declared loudly, drilling three fingers into the witness stand for emphasis.

Schmoozer smirked and turned his back before Pisa could finish his answer. No response was needed; the jury was already wondering what Pisa's motive was for testifying.

The seed of doubt had been not only planted, but well watered.

"Do you have any redirect for the witness?" Hizzoner asked as the DA slowly rose.

"Yes, Judge. I do." The prosecutor asked the next series of questions facing the jury.

"Mr. Pisa, how much time have you spent in jail?"

"Fourteen years, two days."

"Do you know what the penalty is for perjury in a murder case?"

"Yes, it's life in prison."

"You want to go back there?"

"No sir, I don't," Pisa answered, straightening his tie for the last time.

"Are you willing to risk the rest of your life in prison to perjure yourself in this case?"

"No, I am not."

"Is what you told these people the truth?" the DA asked, pointing at the group of eight women and eight men.

"Yes, it is," Pisa said, as his dark eyes searched the crowded courtroom for his wife and son.

At the conclusion of each day of the trial, George and Terry Webster quietly retreated to the DA's office. Sometimes the pair would initiate the conversation, but most times they didn't, preferring to wait for their friend to ask his standard question.

"So, what'd you think?" the lawyer asked at the end of the day following Tony Pisa's testimony, reaching for the volume dial on the ever-present radio.

There was a pause as the couple exchanged glances. George nodded his approval for Terry to express their thoughts.

In the background, Joni Mitchell softly sang "Both Sides Now."

"We know what you're trying to do, Tim," Terry said.

"You do?"

"Yes, we know you may never be able to try Paradiso for Joan's murder. We think you want to give us some peace of mind by introducing his statements about killing Joan in this case." It was the first time Terry had spoken the name of her daughter's murderer.

"Okay, I hear what you're saying."

"That's what the sidebar with Judge Donahue was about today, wasn't it?"

"Yes, it was. The judge said he needed more time to think about whether or not he'll let me ask Pisa about his conversation with Paradiso."

"It's just that we don't want you to risk having this case overturned because you want to prove he murdered our daughter," Joan's mother said.

"I understand how the two of you feel, but this is going to be our only chance to —" the DA started.

George cut off the younger man before he could finish. "It's too dangerous. We just can't stand the thought of him getting back out if you are able to convict him. So if you're doing this for us, we don't need to hear it here. Convicting him is more important than the two of us."

"And we don't want to influence you in some way that could affect your chance to convict him in this case," Terry seconded.

There was another pause as the woman cleared her voice.

"We've decided to return to New Jersey after you've completed your case and wait for the verdict there. Will you promise to call us as soon as the jury comes back? No matter what happens, we will always know you did everything you could to help us," Joan's mother said as she momentarily touched his hand.

It was exactly what he had come to expect from the couple.

After the Websters said their good-byes and left his office, the DA silently walked to the door and locked it. He turned up the radio as he stared at the gray and brown files on his desk.

He closed his eyes and began to cry for the first time in years.

Drew had become a familiar figure to the jurors as he sat quietly taking notes at the prosecution table during the first week of trial. You knew the case was important to Ponytail. He cut his hair, took out his earring, and wore a different suit and matching tie each day. He even switched his cowboy boots for laced-up Florsheims on the first day of trial. The rebel overcame him after day one, as he switched back to his familiar boots. The stacked heels made him two inches taller as he stood in anticipation by his chair.

"The commonwealth calls Trooper Andrew Palombo."

The eight women in the jury box smiled approvingly as the trooper turned to face them and raised his right hand. Some of the men did the same, with the exception of Mr. Peepers, who frowned at the alpha male, wrinkled his nose, and briefly glanced toward the Quahog.

As Drew took the oath, a thin bead of perspiration emerged around the rim of Lenny's hairline. The sweat slowly trickled down until it was met by two dark strips of crimson flesh tracing upward from a vein in Paradiso's neck, over his thick jowls to the top of his broad forehead.

Lenny hated the next witness almost as much as he did the DA.

They stood between him and freedom.

Drew would be a quick witness sandwiched between Pisa and Bond. He could explain Paradiso's arrest and detention at Charles Street Jail. Drew would also set the stage for Bond's upcoming testimony by telling the jury the police work he'd done to corroborate Paradiso's statements to his fellow inmate.

Drew settled into the straight-backed chair, nodded to the judge with the Irish surname, introduced himself, and smiled broadly at the forelady seated closest to the witness's enclosure. She warmly returned the favor. The DA went through the usual line of questions about the witness's background before directing the big trooper to his role in the case.

"Did you have occasion to go to Crescent Avenue in Revere on July 6, 1982?"

"Yes sir, I did."

"And what was the reason you went there?"

"I had an arrest warrant to serve on the defendant for the murder of Marie Iannuzzi," Drew advised as his eyes shifted to the Fat Man seated at the defense table.

Unlike the case with most witnesses, the DA knew exactly what Drew's responses would be. The countless hours the two men had spent together over the past three years made for an easy exchange. It was as if the prosecutor were testifying through his friend.

"Can you tell the jury what happened that day?"

"I went to Crescent Avenue with some other officers and saw Mr. Paradiso's new boat parked out in front attached to a Chevy Blazer. It was a nineteen-foot speedboat. He had obviously just been using it. It was still dripping water onto the street," Drew explained.

The jurors listened attentively as the trooper described the arrest, the reading of Paradiso's Miranda rights, and Lenny's statements as he was led handcuffed to the waiting cruiser.

"When I said to the defendant he didn't seem too surprised to see me, Mr. Paradiso told me that he had been waiting for this for three years."

Schmoozer tried hard not to react, but he knew the remark hurt his client's case. It was a subtle form of admission. The defense attorney would have to undermine its import on cross-examination and offer the jury another reason why his client had made the statement.

The DA sensed he had made his point with the jury and directed the trooper from Paradiso's arrest to Bond's letter.

"Do you know who Robert Bond is?"

As if the prosecutor were leading a dance partner, Drew nodded. "He's an inmate. He was awaiting trial for murder at Charles Street Jail in December of 1982 when he had a number of conversations with Mr. Paradiso."

"Sir, can you tell me, just yes or no, did you have a conversation with Robert Bond about what Mr. Paradiso told him in Charles Street Jail?" the DA asked.

"Yes sir, I did."

"And would you tell the jurors what you did as a result of your conversation with Mr. Bond?"

"I made attempts to corroborate some of the information Bond told me," Drew responded, knowing full well where his waltz partner was leading him.

"For example, did you make any efforts to determine what fees were paid to Mr. Paradiso's previous attorneys Carhart and Prince?"

"Yes, I got the registration off of the brown speedboat. It was MS 9 LP. It was the same boat I just mentioned I saw parked in front of Crescent Avenue when I arrested the defendant. Bond told me Paradiso subsequently gave the boat to attorney Walter Prince as part of the fee to represent him. Bond also said Paradiso told him he gave attorney Judd Carhart a 1939 antique Oldsmobile as part of his fee."

"Were you able to corroborate what Bond told you?"

"Yes, I was." Without moving his head, Drew turned his entire body to stare at Lenny.

"I show you this photograph and ask you if you can identify it for the jurors."

"Yes, it's a photograph of the same boat I saw at Crescent Avenue the day I arrested the defendant. However, this photograph is taken of the boat several months later in the driveway of attorney Prince's home," Drew responded as the duo box-stepped in unison.

"What about the antique Olds?"

"I went to the Registry of Motor Vehicles and found out that the car was originally registered to Candace Weyant, then later transferred to attorney Judd Carhart," the trooper answered as he took the paperwork from the DA, glanced at it briefly, and then handed it back to his friend.

"I ask that the photograph of the boat and the application for the registration of the '39 Oldsmobile be admitted as commonwealth's exhibits."

"No objection," Schmoozer groaned. The court reporter placed a small sticker to identify each of the exhibits.

"Your witness," the DA said. Ponytail changed dance partners.

"Sir, you were aware of the autopsy report in this case, weren't you?" Lenny's lawyer asked, shifting the direction of questions.

"Yes sir, I was."

"As the chief investigating officer you learned that there were intact spermatozoa in the victim's vagina, didn't you?"

"That's true," Drew said. His new dance mate was swaying to a different tune.

"Was there ever an analysis done of the seminal fluid found in Miss Iannuzzi's vagina?"

"I'm not aware that any analysis was done," Drew responded as he glanced toward the jury box for a reaction.

"And you know that at the time Miss Iannuzzi's body was found, she had long manicured fingernails?"

"Yes."

"Well, can you tell the jury whether or not any scrapings were ever performed to see whether there was any evidence under her fingernails?"

"I'm not aware of any."

"We all know it had been raining the night Miss Iannuzzi was killed. Were there any plaster molds made to preserve the tire marks left where the body was found?"

"That was never done," Drew responded slowly as Schmoozer was gaining momentum.

"Do you know whether or not there was any attempt to fingerprint any of Miss Iannuzzi's clothing?"

"I don't know if that was ever done."

Drew was forced to admit all of the shortcomings of the case that he inherited two years after the murder. The DA wanted to cut in, but Drew's dance card was full.

"Now, you said you were bringing my client to the cruiser and you said to Mr. Paradiso, 'You don't seem too surprised to see me'?"

"Right."

"Well you know he had been inquired of by law enforcement officials right after the murder, didn't you?"

"Yes sir."

"And you knew that his girlfriend was told by Trooper Sjoberg that she better come clean or she'd be charged with being an accessory to murder, right."

"I'm aware of it now, yes."

"So for three years prior to the time you arrested him, Mr. Paradiso was a suspect in this case?"

"That's correct."

"And when you arrested him, he merely said, 'I've been waiting for this for three years.' Is that correct?"

"He said that, yes."

Schmoozer looked to the jury to see if they got it. It was clear that they did. Rappaport had successfully neutralized Lenny's statement, but he wasn't done.

"You were also aware that Mr. Doyle was a suspect in this case as well?"

"Yes, he was."

"You've spoken to him twenty to thirty times?"

"Yes sir."

"Do you remember the sum and substance of each of your conversations with Mr. Doyle?"

"No, I don't."

"But you certainly remembered what Mr. Paradiso told you, didn't you?" Schmoozer said, challenging the chief investigator's impartiality.

"No further questions," Lenny's lawyer added over Drew's belated response.

The DA smoothed some of the edges to Schmoozer's cross-examination on redirect, but the damage had been done. The jury had been given another healthy dose of reasonable doubt. Lenny smiled at the prosecutor and cautiously extended the middle finger of his right hand out of the jurors' sight as Drew left the stand.

It was ten minutes to four when the DA asked to see Judge Donahue at the sidebar.

"Do you have another witness?" Hizzoner intoned, glancing at his watch.

"That's all the entertainment I can provide for today, Your Honor. Robert Bond is our next witness. I expect he will take most of tomorrow morning," the DA announced as Schmoozer's head wagged in agreement.

"Then we'll conclude for the day." Hizzoner excused the jury with the expected admonition not to discuss the case.

_ _

Pisa's testimony — a glimpse into the mind-set of a killer — was an appetizer. Bond provided a full meal, featuring lust, deception, and intrigue.

"The commonwealth calls Robert Bond as its next witness," the prosecutor said loudly as he looked toward the gallery and made eye contact with George and Terry Webster, seated next to Carmen, Mr. Leary, and Steve Broce. The courtroom went electric. Like a high-tension wire sparking and flashing, the room momentarily buzzed with anticipation and then just as quickly went silent.

The news crews from the three stations adjusted their camera lenses. Television and print reporters leaned forward, pens and notebooks in hand, to capture the words of the prosecution's principal witness.

It was showtime.

Like a thunderhead rolling over the prairie on a warm summer day, Bond strode out from behind the prisoner's dock door, slowly advancing to the witness stand. He was enormous. His walk took no more than twenty seconds, but in that moment his presence created a sense of expectation that brought all the people in the courtroom to the edge of their seats. The DA positioned himself at the end of the jury box and exchanged glances with Bond, and then a subtle nod, as the clerk administered the oath.

"Good morning sir, would you tell the ladies and gentlemen of the jury your name," the prosecutor began. There were no dress rehearsals for this part of the case.

"My name is Robert Bond, B-o-n-d," the witness said in a low, compelling voice that echoed through the courtroom.

Lenny suddenly stopped smirking and pushed his large frame away from the defense table, crossing his thick arms as the witness began to testify.

It was a warm, sticky summer day. Bond was dressed in a short-sleeved red polo shirt that, despite being an extra-large, was still one or maybe two sizes too small. He had a smooth shaved head and Popeye the Sailor arms that stretched the thin fabric of his shirt to the point of exhaustion. He spoke with a street twang, yet you could sense that Bond was smart, very smart.

"Lenny told me he murdered Marie Iannuzzi," Bond announced to Judge Donahue as Hizzoner removed his eyeglasses and placed his right hand up to his face, covering his now open mouth.

"When did you first meet Mr. Paradiso?" the prosecutor interrupted, trying to slow the runaway freight train.

"I met Lenny at Walpole in '75," Bond said.

"Can you describe how that happened?"

"He asked me about weight lifting. Lenny had a big ol' stomach on him then," Bond said as the Quahog uncrossed his arms, unconsciously pulled his suit jacket together, and buttoned it snugly over his potbelly. "I didn't see him again till December of '82."

"Where was that?"

"Charles Street Jail," Bond said quickly.

"Why were you at Charles Street?" The DA ventured uneasily into the topic of Bond's background.

"I was waiting trial on a murder case," the witness responded without emotion as the jurors craned forward in their seats.

"And how long were you at Charles Street?"

"From December 8 ta December 29," Bond recalled without benefit of a calendar.

"And during that time period did you ever have occasion to speak with the defendant?" the DA asked, reverting to the formality of speech meant for an appeals court hearing.

"Jesus Christ, we used ta talk four, five times a day. At first Lenny sez the polize tried to frame him. Later on Lenny tells me he killed Marie," Bond said, moving his eyes from the jury to the defendant.

As long as we're here, we might as well keep going, the prosecutor thought. "What did he tell you?"

Bond was almost childlike as he spoke. "Lenny told me how he murdered Marie, and he sez all the evidence points toward David Doyle, her boyfriend."

"Did he say how he met Marie?"

"Lenny sez he met her at a weddin' party at the Milanos' house. He noticed her first at the reception at the Ship. At the house, Marie made a scene. She liked Freddy Milano. Lenny tells Marie to behave becuz David Doyle was Freddy's cousin, she was high and didn't pay him any attention."

"What else did Mr. Paradiso tell you about Marie?"

"Marie needed a ride from the party and Lenny asks Candy to offer her a ride and they give her a ride in Candy's '73 yellow Buick to the Cardinal's Nest. Lenny sez he felt he could make out with Marie so he wanted to hurry up and get his girlfriend home ta Revere."

He's like a videotape of the murder, the DA thought. "What did the defendant tell you happened next?"

"Lenny sez, 'You shoulda seen me runnin' the red lights to get back there.' Lenny sez he got ta the Cardinal's Nest around eleven. He bought him and Marie a drink and they started talkin' 'bout the wedding. He starts making passes at Marie. She had her legs crossed and you could see the upper part of her thigh. Lenny tells her he wants her to go back to the Milanos to 'pologize and he would bring her back to the bar."

"What happened next?"

"Marie says somethin' to her girlfriend Christine when they leave. Lenny sez he's 'fraid Christine's gonna testify at this trial." Bond paused and looked directly at the defendant, who refused to lift his head from the imaginary notes he was writing on a yellow legal pad.

"Did he tell you where they went?" the DA asked as he joined Bond's gaze toward the defendant.

"Yeah, he sez they go up the Lynn Marsh Road near the Lynn–Saugus line."

"Where did you grow up, Mr. Bond?"

"Me? Roxbury," the witness said with a sense of pride.

"Ever been to Lynn before?"

"No, never."

"Did the defendant tell you what happened next?"

"Yeah, Lenny sez he started makin' passes at her. He kissed her, but every time he tried to get her panty hose down, she would either hold his hand or she would push his hand away." Bond animated for the jury with his own hand.

In the gallery there was a small sound of movement as Mr. Webster placed a protective arm around the shoulder of his wife. He knew what was coming next; so did Schmoozer. So did Lenny.

"Would you please tell the jury what Mr. Paradiso told you he did after Marie pushed his hand away?"

"Lenny sez he grabbed her neck and started chokin' her. She passed out. He sez he had sex wid her. Marie come to and she started hollerin'. Like she was startled. Lenny sez he slapped at her. He grabbed her scarf and choked her. He sez her body was jumpin' like she had the hiccups." As he spoke Bond brought his hand to his upturned neck and made a twisting motion, tightening an imaginary garrote.

The prosecutor paused long enough to allow the vision of Marie's last moments to engulf the jurors' minds.

"Did he say what happened next?"

"Lenny told me it was rainin' that night. He sez he slipped and fell takin' her body outta the car. He puts her body near the edge of the river behind Conley and Daggett's. He sez it was closed and now they call it Atlantic Lobster."

"Did he tell you where he went after he killed Marie?"

"Yeah, Lenny sez he drove to his apartment and call his girl, Candy. Lenny told her he went back to the bar. Marie was still there and he offers her a ride home. On the way home, Lenny tells Candy him and Marie argues over the scene Marie made at the Milanos. Lenny sez ta Candy he started chokin' Marie and he killed her. Candy starts to cry and Lenny sez he wants ta talk ta Candy's mother ta use as part of his alibi. Lenny told me Candy took a taxi to his apartment so they can get their stories together ta tell the polize."

The details of Bond's testimony came so fast, it was hard to absorb them all at once. At the end of each answer the prosecutor paused to allow the jurors to visualize the actions described by the witness and to anticipate the next question.

"Had Mr. Paradiso been driving Ms. Weyant's Buick that night?"

"Yeah, the nex' mornin' Lenny goes to the car and sees Marie's black shoes and her panty hose. Lenny sez, 'You shoulda seen me gettin' rid of that stuff, 'cause my girl is still in my place. There was some blood on the door and between the seats. 'Bout ten days later Lenny burns the car and Candy reports it stolen."

"Do you know who David Doyle is, Mr. Bond?"

"I don't knows him, but Lenny told me how all the evidence points to Marie's boyfriend, David Doyle." Bond again glanced at the Quahog and then back to the jury.

"What 'evidence' did the defendant tell you pointed to David Doyle?"

"Lenny sez Marie and Doyle had a fight the day she was murdered. Doyle tried to strangle Marie two months before her murder. Doyle found out she was dating some other guy, Eddie Fisher. Doyle pack her things the night she was killed and had scratch marks on his hands and don't go to the funeral. Doyle know all 'bout the area where her body was found, 'cause he works for some trash company that uses the Lynn Marsh Road." Bond ticked off the items like a grocery list.

"Is that all Mr. Paradiso told you about Doyle?"

"No, Lenny sez Doyle sold drugs, and maybe they can say Marie coulda got killed over a bad drug deal. He told me Doyle passed a lie detector."

"Did Mr. Paradiso explain to you what one of his possible alibis was going to be in this case?" the prosecutor asked, offering the jury an insight into the world of criminal defense and Lenny's logic.

"Lenny sez he wants to use Candy for his alibi. She gonna say she was with him outside the bar when he leave the place."

"Did Mr. Paradiso tell you anything about the two attorneys representing him at that time?"

"Yeah, Lenny sez they both former prosecutors, and they gonna focus the case on David Doyle. Lenny give them his boat and an ol' antique car to represent him. Lenny told me your name, too, that's how I know who to write to."

"Do you recognize these papers?"

"Yeah, that's my handwriting. I wrote you that letter from Charles Street Jail in December," the witness responded. The DA requested that the document be marked for identification.

"Have there been any promises made to you for your testimony here today?"

"Yeah, you said I would be moved to another prison outta state after I testify. I asked to get attorney Norman Zalkind to represent me on my appeal."

"And was Mr. Zalkind appointed to represent you on your appeal?"

"Yeah, he was, and my case got overturned by the appeals court," Bond said with a note of vindication.

"And you are currently awaiting retrial on your case?"

"Yeah, I am," Bond said as he turned to Schmoozer, who was rising for his cross-examination. Before Lenny's lawyer could begin, Judge Donahue broke in.

"We'll take the morning recess at this point," Hizzoner told the eight men and eight women.

After the jurors' departure from the courtroom, Paradiso was cuffed and led to the prisoners' holding area. He never looked back at the witness.

"He's intimidated by Bond. You can see it in his body," Drew said. The black man with the shaved head was also being handcuffed and led to another holding cell.

"I wonder what Schmoozer is gonna do with Bond on cross?" the DA asked as they waited for the jury to return from their daily coffee and doughnuts.

– – –

It didn't take long to find out. Lenny's lawyer produced a certified record of conviction from the stack of papers on his table.

"Sir, are you the same Robert Bond, also known as Richard Bond, who was indicted for the murder of Barbara Mitchell?"

"Yes, I am," the witness responded evenly.

"And you pleaded guilty to manslaughter in that case and received a sentence of fifteen to twenty years in prison, didn't you?" Schmoozer announced. He offered the record for the jury to read.

"Yes, I did," Bond answered without flinching.

"And eventually you were paroled?"

"June the fifteenth, 1981."

"And then you were arrested again, weren't you?" Schmoozer raised his voice as he faced the jury, waiting for Bond's response.

"Yes, I was."

"When was that?"

"November the twentieth, 1981."

"So a few months after you had been released on parole, you were charged with the murder of another woman, correct?"

There was an almost imperceptible stir among the jurors as they collectively stared at the witness, listening to the drama unfolding before them.

"Yes, Mary Foreman, a lady who I knew, or a lady who I was dating at the time," Bond offered without further explanation.

"Both women were good friends of yours, weren't they?"

"Yes, they were."

"So if you're convicted on this second murder charge of Ms. Foreman, you'll have to serve at least thirteen years before you'll be eligible for parole, won't you?"

"Yes."

"You'd be about sixty-five then, wouldn't you?" Schmoozer explained, offering a possible motive to the jury for Bond's testimony.

"Yeah, that'd be about right. But I could be out in September after my next trial, too," Bond countered.

Lenny's lawyer paused to let the jury evaluate the witness's motives before he moved to another topic.

"Well, sir, isn't there a unit in Walpole Prison which is more restrictive than the other units there?"

"You're talking about Ten Block?"

"Yeah, Ten Block. That's the segregation unit for prisoners who aren't doing well in prison, isn't it?"

"Yes."

"And you were in Ten Block, before you were sent to Charles Street to stand trial in December, weren't you?"

"Sure."

"It's more restrictive than the other units. You're locked up twenty-three hours a day there, aren't you?"

"Somethin' like that. Twenty-two or twenty-three."

"And you have no weights to lift. No library. No place to walk but back and forth in a little kennel-like area, right?"

"Right," the witness agreed.

"You didn't enjoy being housed there, did you?"

"No. Would you like to know how I came to get there?" Bond fought back.

It was one of those moments when as a lawyer you have to decide whether to take the bait. Schmoozer let the witness go.

"Sure, if you want to," he said.

Bond didn't hesitate.

"The soda machine wouldn't work for this inmate. He put a quarter in it. My wife and my daughter was visitin' me and he kicked the soda machine and was cursing around them. I asked him to chill out. He didn't pay me any attention. The next time I saw him, me and him had a fistfight and they put me in Ten Block. A fistfight, no weapons, just a fistfight," Bond explained. Mr. Peepers nodded in sympathy.

"Okay." Lenny's lawyer agreed without realizing it.

"That was about respect. That's all. If I never had the fight, I would never have gone to Ten Block."

It was the briefest of moments yet — for the crowded courtroom — a turning point. Each person had become a spectator, a voyeur, staring safely from the outside into another world. A world with different rules and values. The jurors despised Bond for his crimes, but he had given them an honest insight into his world. It was a savage place. The kind of place where Lenny could find acceptance and a willing audience to the horrors of his past.

The jurors sensed Bond still had a code.

"It's not in the back of your mind that the same district attorney's office that you're helping now is going to be prosecuting you later on?"

"Yeah, I know that."

"You want them to help you, don't you?"

"I understand what you're saying, but Mr. Burke don't have my case. Mr.

Flanagan's office has all of the cases, and, Jesus Christ, if they're gonna to do anything for me, I wish they'd let me know," Bond responded. Three of the jurors smiled for the first time.

"Isn't it fair to say the reason you came forward is to hurt Lenny?"

"No, no, no. I'm not doin' it to hurt Lenny. Lenny talked about puttin' David Doyle in jail like it was a traffic ticket. This ain't no traffic ticket." The witness made a circular motion with his finger around the courtroom.

"You don't want to see someone go to jail —"

Bond cut in, "— for something they didn't do."

"Just like you, right?" Lenny's lawyer mocked.

"Just like me," Bond responded evenly as two of the jurors nodded in agreement.

"No further questions," Schmoozer told the judge.

Hizzoner gestured the lawyers to a sidebar. "Do you have any more witnesses for us today, Mr. Burke?"

"No, Your Honor, I don't. I think that's going to do it for the commonwealth's case in chief. I'm not going to call David Doyle. I will let Mr. Rappaport do that," the DA said. Schmoozer smiled widely.

"Ladies and gentlemen of the jury, Mr. Burke informs me that the commonwealth has rested their case," Judge Donahue explained. Jurors exchanged looks ranging from relief to mild surprise. "I am going to have you take the luncheon recess before Mr. Rappaport calls his first witness."

"All rise," the court officers recited in unison.

The first witness called on behalf of the defendant was Marie's boyfriend, David Doyle.

The DA had, of course, not called Doyle. If the man had appeared as a witness in the Commonwealth's case, Schmoozer would have been allowed to cross-examine him as an adverse witness. Because Doyle appeared as the defendant's witness, Rappaport could only ask him "direct" questions; the DA would be able to cross-examine.

Doyle appeared calm as he approached the witness stand. The jurors' eyes sought him out as soon as his name was announced, following his every movement from the rear of the courtroom, past Marie's family, and into the enclosure. Doyle didn't shrink from the stare offered by the defendant as he took the oath. Just the opposite: He held eye contact with Paradiso for a full five seconds before he answered Schmoozer's first question.

"My name is David Doyle, and I live at 52 Jeffrey Street, in East Boston," Paradiso's first witness announced.

"And sir, did you know Marie Iannuzzi?"

"Yes, I did. She was my girlfriend. She lived with me on the third floor of my parents' house."

And so it went. The defense was limited to a straight Q-and-A with the first witness. The questions and answers were a slow, deliberate recital of the events leading up to Marie's murder.

"Did you two attend a wedding on August 11?" Lenny's lawyer asked, setting the stage.

"Yes, we did. It was me, Marie, my mother and father, my sister, and another couple. The wedding was at the Ship Restaurant on Route 1."

"Were you drinking that day?"

"We both were."

"Did you and Marie have an argument at the Ship?"

"Yes, I ripped my pants at the end of the reception. She wanted to go to the house party after the reception and I didn't. It turned into a yelling match. She said I never wanted to go places where there were parties."

"Were there any physical blows?"

"No sir. I never touched her."

"Well, didn't your mother have to pull you away?" Schmoozer asked, reading from a typed police report in hand.

"She grabbed me by the arm and said, 'Let's go home,'" Doyle clarified as Drew squirmed in his chair and Lenny smirked his approval.

"And what time did you leave the reception?"

"It was about six thirty."

"By the way, did Marie say who she was going to go to the party with?" Schmoozer asked, apparently not knowing what the witness's response would be.

It was one of those answers that neither attorney was prepared for.

"She told me she was going to get a ride with Lenny and his girlfriend, Candy," Doyle said without hesitation. The defendant's smirk evaporated.

No one had ever asked how Marie got to the Milanos' house before that moment. The reaction from the jury was palpable. Schmoozer never flinched, instead sidestepping the topic.

"Now, how long did you two go out?"

"For about three years."

"Do you know whether Marie was also seeing another man by the name of Eddie Fisher while you were dating?"

"I believe she did." Doyle grimaced as he answered softly.

"Did you and Marie have any physical confrontations?"

"Some of them were."

"Do you recall Marie moving in with a friend, Christine DeLisi, for four or five days in June of 1979, after a fight you had with her?"

"Yes."

"Tell the jury about that fight."

"I don't know what the fight was about, but it was physical and I did hold her back from me."

"Did you strangle her?"

"I didn't strangle her. I used one hand to hold her back. But I didn't choke her."

"Did you notice any finger marks on her neck?"

"I didn't notice any, but there could have been."

"Were you using drugs when the two of you were having those fights?"

"Not the day of the wedding, but yes, I was using Valium, grass, and angel dust during that time period."

"Where did you go after the reception?"

"I went home with my parents and stayed there until Marie called me later on that night. It was around eight thirty. She asked me whether she should spend the night someplace else. I told her it would be a good idea if she didn't come home because I was still upset about the scene she caused at the reception."

"What did you do the next day?"

"It was Sunday; I woke up, went downstairs around nine, and had coffee with my mother. Then I took the dogs out."

"Now, did you become concerned about Marie's whereabouts at some point?"

"I wasn't generally concerned because she had done this before. Gone out and stayed at a friend's house. Later on I made a call and spoke to Marie's sister Jeannie." Doyle gestured to the gallery where Marie's sisters were seated.

"Did Jeannie know anything?"

"No, she didn't. Later on Marie's mother called me. I told them if they didn't hear from Marie, they should call the police."

"Did something happen on Monday morning?"

"Marie's mother and sister came running up to the bedroom of my apartment and woke me up. It was around seven thirty in the morning."

"What happened?"

"Jeannie woke me up and said 'Where's Marie?' Her mother was on the verge of hysteria, saying she just heard an announcement on the radio about a woman's body they found. It sounded like the way Marie was dressed. They asked me what she was wearing and I told them. Then I got dressed and went with them to Marie's house on White Street."

"Did the police come there to the house and bring you to the morgue?"

"Yes, they did. Marie's brother-in-law and father and I went to the morgue."

"What happened there?"

"A guy wheeled her body out and I looked at Marie. I just threw the sheet back over her body," Doyle said, visibly fighting tears.

"Sir, I notice that you're teary-eyed right now."

"Are you asking me a question?" the witness shot back as he raised his hand to his eyes.

"Did you cry when you saw Marie's body at the morgue?" Schmoozer asked.

"No, I didn't. I was in shock. I didn't believe what happened."

Lenny's lawyer paused to consider Doyle's response before he moved on.

"Do you remember when the wakes were, Mr. Doyle?"

"Tuesday, Wednesday, and Thursday."

"Do you remember having any marks on your body at the time of the wakes?"

As he asked the question, Schmoozer curled the fingers of his right hand into the shape of a cat's claw.

"I don't remember any, no."

"Do you remember whether you had any scratches on your face?"

"I don't recall any scratches on my face."

"Do you remember having any scratches on your hands?"

Doyle hesitated. "I might have."

"Do you remember approaching the coffin at some point during the wakes and putting something in the coffin?"

"Yes, it was a letter to Marie from me."

"Do you remember being asked by Mr. Burke in the grand jury whether you put anything in Marie's casket at the wake?"

"I told him no. It wasn't a lie. I just didn't recall it when he asked me back then."

"Did you attend the funeral?"

"No sir, I didn't. I went to the airport. I was depressed. I wanted to get away. I took the first flight on the departure board at Eastern, and that happened to be New Jersey. I bought a round-trip ticket. It was Thursday. I was going to be back Friday for the funeral,"

"The reason you never made it back was because you got arrested in New Jersey by the airport police, didn't you?" Lenny's lawyer bellowed. His client smirked at the witness.

"Yes."

"We'll take the morning recess," Hizzoner instructed the packed courtroom at the conclusion of Schmoozer's direct examination.

The morning recess lasted twenty minutes, long enough to gulp a cup of coffee and a doughnut, bagel, or cream-filled cruller delivered fresh each day from Dandelions. The jury had been sequestered from their families in a nondescript motel for eight days. They were growing impatient.

"All right, Mr. Burke, you may proceed with your cross-examination," Judge Donahue intoned once the jurors were seated again.

"How did you feel about Marie?" The DA started slowly, trying to build a sense of the connection between the couple.

"I loved her very much. We even talked about getting married," Doyle said in a barely audible voice.

"Do you know how she felt about you?"

"She told me she loved me," he said quickly, searching for a gesture of approval from Marie's sisters in the gallery.

"During this whole investigation, did you ever tell the police, either here or in New Jersey, that you didn't want to talk to them?"

"I answered all of their questions, sir," the witness readily said.

"Did you tell them that you and Marie had fights?"

"Yes, I did."

"Did you try to hide the fact that you and Marie had an argument that night at the Ship?"

"No sir. I answered all of their questions."

"Was there some reason you told Marie not to come home when she called you at eight thirty that night?"

"I was very upset about what had happened. Everybody saw the fight. I embarrassed the family," Doyle explained as the jury listened impassively.

"Tell the jury, what were you thinking at this time, when you went to the morgue?"

"I'm thinking it's not true. I don't want to believe it. I still didn't believe it when I saw her. Her father didn't want to identify her body. He didn't want to see her. He asked me to do it."

"Did you want to see Marie's body?"

"No. I grabbed the sheet and pulled it down to make sure I was looking at her. I just threw the sheet back over her, because she was dead, she was gone," Doyle explained with a sweep of his hand over the front of the witness stand.

"You've been asked a lot of questions about scratches on your hands. Tell the jury what happened at the wake," the DA said as he moved from his usual spot by the far end of the jury box toward the witness.

"I was there with this other guy that was mentioned, Eddie Fisher," the witness began, his voiced cracking.

"He was the guy that cared about Marie, too, didn't he?"

"Yes, we talked about Marie. It's the first time I ever formally met him and he says, 'Why don't me and you go for a drink and talk about things? We have a lot in common; we both loved the same woman.'"

"What happened?"

"I felt upset, very upset about it, you know. Here he's telling me now that he's been with her. All I heard before was just, ya know, stuff on the street."

"Did you go for a drink with him?"

"Yeah, I did. The wake was at Langone's Funeral Home in the North End. The two of us went to some bar across the street and ordered a drink and talked about Marie," the witness explained.

"There was a guy next to us at the corner of the bar. He was laughing, enjoying himself, and having a good time. I asked him if he could keep it down a little, and he swore at me."

"Did you do something then?"

"Yeah, I knocked some of the stuff on the bar off and I picked up a bar stool and it turned into a fight." Doyle turned his eyes toward the jury.

"Did you learn that the police were told that people saw some scratches on your hands right after that fight?"

"Yes, I did."

"Did you feel that people were pointing the finger at you for Marie's death?"

"I know Marie's family was mad at me because I told her not to come home that night."

"They blamed you, didn't they?"

"They did. I was kinda isolated and alone. I needed to get away, that's why I went to the airport and just took the first flight out of Eastern. I bought a round-trip ticket from New Jersey back to Boston the next morning at eight. I just went crazy. I was taking Seconal and drinking on the way down there and when I was in the airport, too."

"Did you give the police in New Jersey a statement and tell them what you knew about Marie's murder?"

"Yes, I did. It's right there."

"I offer this statement, Your Honor, as the next exhibit," the DA said as Schmoozer rose to object.

"May I see it please?" Hizzoner asked, directing the lawyers to the sidebar. "What do you say, Mr. Rappaport?" he asked upon their arrival.

"It's a self-serving statement, Judge. It's hearsay," Schmoozer said.

"He's your witness," the DA countered.

"If Mr. Burke had put this witness on the witness stand, it would be a self-serving statement and he couldn't introduce it. But he didn't put the witness on the witness stand, so that law does not apply."

"Well, Judge, this trial is like a game of chess. I may have put him on the witness stand . . ."

"It doesn't make any difference to me how the chess game is played. I'm just saying that this is your witness. You told the jury it's just as likely that David Doyle did it as Paradiso, perhaps more likely. So what the commonwealth is doing is attempting to show that Doyle's statement never differed from day one when he was first interrogated. That's my ruling," Judge Donahue advised both attorneys, dispatching them to their previous positions.

"When was the last time you saw Marie Iannuzzi alive?" the DA said as he moved directly in front of the witness.

"That day at the reception."

"Did you see Marie after that?"

"Yes, at the morgue."

"Between the last time you saw her alive at the Ship and the morgue, did you ever have any further physical contact with Marie?"

"No."

"Did you hurt Marie that night?"

"No sir, I didn't."

"Did you do this to Marie?" the DA challenged Doyle in a loud voice, displaying the autopsy photograph of the lace scarf embedded around the young victim's throat.

It was a defining moment. A cruel, but necessary confrontation the jury needed to witness.

"No sir, I didn't do that to her. No, I didn't," Lenny's first witness tearfully replied, pulling back from the photograph placed before him.

"No further questions," the prosecutor said as he returned to his seat.

There was no turning back for either attorney. The DA needed certainty; Schmoozer needed doubt. He stood quickly to begin his second round of examination.

This time it would be different.

"When you were arrested in New Jersey, what name did you give the police?" Lenny's lawyer demanded, momentarily jolting the witness.

"Edward Day," Doyle told the jurors, and like spectators at a tennis match, their eyes shifted from the witness to the lawyer and back again.

"That's not your name, is it?" the antagonist shot back.

"No, it's not."

"You didn't give the police your Jeffrey Street address when they asked you where you lived either, did you?"

"No sir, I didn't."

"You ran away to New Jersey for a reason, didn't you?" Schmoozer exhaled ten decibels louder.

"I didn't run away." Doyle countered, scanning the courtroom for a friendly face.

"People were pointing the finger at you, weren't they? Everyone thought you killed Marie, didn't they?"

Rappaport was on a roll. The DA knew he should object. It was no longer direct examination. All of the defense attorney's questions were confrontational. It was cross-examination in its purest form. At the same time, the prosecutor sensed that the jury wanted to hear Doyle's answers. If he objected, the jury would think he was hiding something from them. As the DA began to rise, Drew placed a large hand on his friend's right arm.

"It's okay. Let him ask the questions. This jury's smart. They get it," the big trooper told the DA, nodding to Schmoozer.

"So you just happened to get on a plane the day before Marie's funeral and went down to New Jersey to clear your mind, right?" Lenny's lawyer continued.

"Yes, I did," Doyle said as he straightened himself in the stiff chair.

"You ran away because you felt guilty, didn't you?" Schmoozer countered.

"No, I didn't."

"You felt guilty about murdering Marie, didn't you?"

"I didn't murder Marie," Doyle calmly answered.

"She had done you wrong, running around with other men, didn't she?"

"She did."

"You felt you were losing her, didn't you?"

"Yes, I did."

"And she had embarrassed you in front of your family, hadn't she?" the lawyer asked as he pointed at the witness.

"Yes."

"Marie had long fingernails, didn't she?"

"Yes."

"And you say you don't remember having scratches on your hands at the time of the wake?"

"I may have," Doyle waffled.

"A couple of months earlier you two had been in a fight and she used her fingernails on you, didn't she?" Lenny's lawyer asked, building to a crescendo.

"Yes."

"Sir, when you ran away to New Jersey, you ran away because you didn't want to be arrested for —" Schmoozer was in full voice as the DA stood.

"Objection, Your Honor."

"— the murder of Marie Iannuzzi," Rappaport roared over his adversary.

"Objection sustained," Hizzoner ruled belatedly.

"No further questions," Schmoozer said.

Sometimes the DA wished he didn't trust his friend so much. He stood and slowly walked back to his familiar location at the far end of the jury box, momentarily pausing before he put his final question.

He needed to bring the jury back.

"You testified earlier you placed a letter in Marie's coffin?"

"Yes, I did."

"What did you say in that letter, David?"

"I told Marie I loved her. I told her I would see her again soon. I said to say hello to my friends up there," Doyle explained as he pointed to heaven.

"Nothing further, Your Honor."

"You may step down," Hizzoner announced to the first witness for the defense.

The attorney in the new Armani suit and cowboy boots strode confidently to the witness stand, nodding to both lawyers en route. He took the oath and smiled to Hizzoner, who warmly returned the greeting.

After the intro to the jury, Schmoozer cut to the chase.

"Did you and attorney Walter Prince previously represent Mr. Paradiso in regard to the murder of Marie Iannuzzi?"

"Yes sir. We did," Carhart responded from the unfamiliar role of answering, instead of asking, questions.

The attorney–client privilege protects all of the confidential communications a client has with his or her lawyer. A lawyer can never reveal what a client says in confidence unless the client permits it by waiving the privilege. The attorney's fees aren't included as part of that privilege.

"What was the fee?" Lenny's current lawyer asked the former.

"The fee for both of us was thirty thousand dollars. Mr. Paradiso made a partial payment with a speedboat and an antique car. Attorney Prince got the boat and my firm got the car," the witness explained with a glance toward the defendant.

"What was the value of the car?" Schmoozer continued.

A lawyer's words are his tools. Carhart chose his very carefully.

"It was represented to be about ten thousand dollars, but that's not so. It was worth less than that. It had a cracked engine block," the attorney calmly explained.

"I wonder if he just used the words *worth less* to suggest Paradiso's car was worthless," the DA whispered to Drew, thinking of All Nu Upholstery, Joe Gulla, the foul frozen crabmeat, and the trip to the emergency room.

"Did you visit Mr. Paradiso very often at Charles Street Jail?"

"Yes, I did. He was very familiar with his case. He had the grand jury transcripts, so he knew the case very well," Lenny's former lawyer offered in an effort to explain Bond's familiarity with the evidence in Paradiso's case.

"Was there another suspect in the case?"

The jury knew the obvious answer before the witness could speak.

"Yes, there was. His name was David Doyle. He was certainly worth exploring as far as the defense would go," Carhart offered without elaboration.

For the first time in the trial the DA felt the tension leave his body as he rose to question the witness. Carhart's testimony did little to affect the jury's ultimate impression of the case. He wondered why Schmoozer had even called Carhart as a witness. Suddenly the tension returned as he feared there was a trap being laid for him. In any event, it was good to see his former adversary again.

"Good afternoon, Mr. Carhart," he began with a note of familiar formality.

"Good afternoon, Mr. Burke," Mr. Carhart responded in kind.

"You and I have talked on numerous occasions, haven't we?" the DA asked, thinking about their last meeting in his overheated office a year earlier without the benefit of a fan.

Today was no different. It was eighty-three degrees outside, and it felt like ninety-five inside the crowded courtroom as the sun beat down and burned the tar up on the roof.

"Yes sir. We certainly have." The witness smiled, quietly tapping his alligator-toed boot to the unheard beat of the Drifter's "Under the Boardwalk."

"You were a former assistant district attorney and then an assistant US attorney before you went into private practice, weren't you?"

The DA was hoping to show the jury that Bond's knowledge about Paradiso's former lawyers could have come from only one source: the defendant himself.

"Yes sir. I was," the compliant witness agreed.

"Certainly you never told Mr. Bond that, did you?"

Carhart went one better. "I've never spoken to Mr. Bond in my life."

"But you did tell Mr. Paradiso that, didn't you?"

"Yes sir. I did."

"And you certainly never told Mr. Bond what your fee was?"

"No sir, I have never spoken to Mr. Bond," Carhart repeated, eliminating any other possible source of information.

"Now, you said your firm received a 1939 Oldsmobile from Mr. Paradiso, that he represented to you was valued at ten thousand dollars?"

"Yes sir."

"It wasn't worth anywhere near ten thousand dollars, was it?" the DA asked.

"I don't believe so. No sir, it wasn't."

"Of course, that wasn't an attempt on Mr. Paradiso's part to deceive you, his attorney, was it?" the DA mocked as he turned to the flushed defendant. Out of the corner of his eye, he could see Drew nodding vigorously.

The witness allowed a brief interlude to pass before he responded. "It's not the first time a client has told me something like that. No, I don't think it's an exception."

"And Mr. Paradiso knew all about the things the police had found out about David Doyle, didn't he?" the DA asked, without listing Doyle's scratches, the fights between the couple, his arrest in New Jersey, or his lack of emotion at the morgue.

"He did. I know he knew about David Doyle," Carhart agreed, inadvertently explaining how Bond could have learned about Lenny's plans to frame Marie's boyfriend.

"When you spoke to Mr. Paradiso, who was the person you were going to call as an alibi witness?"

"I don't think we discussed an alibi defense in the legal sense, except the name Candace Weyant came up."

"And did you have conversations with Candy Weyant?"

"Yes, I have."

"She's an important witness for Mr. Paradiso, isn't she?" the prosecutor asked, setting the stage for the defendant's alibi.

"Yes."

"That's all the questions I have, Your Honor. Thank you, Mr. Carhart."

The judge looked at Schmoozer, who nodded in rapid agreement, clearly anxious to have his predecessor depart the witness stand.

Schmoozer had his list of witnesses ready, willing, and able to be called on Lenny's behalf.

In some ways, the story line the defense planned to present paralleled the prosecution's case. Where the DA had Bond and Pisa, Lenny had his own witness who would claim that David Doyle had confessed to killing Marie.

David Dellaria was a razor-thin Easta Bost junkie whom the DA was currently prosecuting for the robbery of a White Hen Pantry convenience store in Maverick Square. Distinguished by a pair of narrow, beady eyes and an incessant twitch on the side of his face, Dellaria communicated using both hands for emphasis.

"Where are you living at this time?" Schmoozer asked, beginning with a negative in order to dispense with it.

"In a halfway house on Huntington Avenue, I just got out of Concord prison," Dellaria explained after giving the court reporter the correct spelling of his name.

Then Schmoozer quickly turned to the heart of the matter. "Did you ever have any conversations with David Doyle about Marie's death?"

"I'm not sure when, but it was at his house. We were getting high. Smokin' a little grass and drinkin'," the witness said, setting the stage.

"What did you hear Mr. Doyle say?"

"Doyle told me 'I did what I had to do,'" Dellaria explained as the cheerleader in the undertaker's suit at the defense table nodded in agreement.

At the prosecution table, Drew winced as if someone had stuck a red-hot needle into the back of his neck.

"And what did you think when Mr. Doyle said that to you?"

Before the DA could stand to object, Dellaria blurted out his response. "After Doyle told me that, I knew he had killed Marie." His eyes flashed from Lenny to the DA and back again.

The jurors clearly didn't expect to hear that Doyle had admitted to killing Marie. They collectively jerked their heads to the left to make sure they had heard the witness correctly. Lenny's lawyer asked the witness to repeat his answer to make sure they had all gotten the message. Schmoozer held the moment for the jury to absorb the new information and smiled at the flushed DA.

"Would you tell the jurors how you know David Doyle?"

"We all live on the same block in East Boston."

The DA and Drew knew what was coming next. Both of them knew they weren't going to like it. Schmoozer was on a roll.

"Did you have a conversation with some detectives from East Boston about what Mr. Doyle had told you?"

"Yes I did. I told Detective Charlie Gleason, 'Charlie, I believe he killed her.'"

"Did you happen to see Mr. Doyle at some time over the next couple of months?"

"Yes sir, I did. And Mr. Doyle attacked me twice." Dellaria flinched as if in pain.

"Do you know why Mr. Doyle did that to you?"

"He was pissed because I told the cops about him telling me he killed Marie."

"Why don't you describe the entire incident in your own words as best you can," Schmoozer oozed.

"When he found out I went to the police, Doyle tried to kill me for ratting him out. I was sitting all alone at Waterfront Park where I live. A car pulls up and I got whacked on the back of the head with a rubber pipe. He threw me in the trunk of his car and drove me somewhere in Lynn. He told me he was gonna kill me and leave me there."

"What happened then?"

"Alls I know is, they dragged me outta the trunk. It was on some sand dunes. There was a cinder-block building there. He tried beating me to death with the hose. There was another person who was there with him that stopped him. He's no longer with us. He passed on. He overdosed. Otherwise, he coulda confirmed it. Doyle started beating me about the head, the legs, like my face, my nose, and —"

For some reason Schmoozer stopped the beating midstream to ask another question. "When was the next time you saw Mr. Doyle?"

"I think it was two years ago. I was coming home one night and he sicced two gigantic German shepherds on me. He had the dogs attack me and pin me to the ground. And then he took out a knife from his waistband and stuck me in the neck and said, 'I'm gonna cut your throat, you rat,'" the coker nervously told the jury.

"Did the police tell you what you should do after Mr. Doyle tried to kill you?" Schmoozer asked, enjoying the moment.

"Yeah, the cops told me to file a complaint for attempted murder against Mr. Doyle in East Boston District Court," the model citizen informed the jury.

"Did you do that?"

"Yes sir, I sure did," Dellaria exclaimed. He and Lenny moved their heads up and down to the same rhythm.

"Let me show you this document. Is this a statement you gave to Mr. Paradiso's previous lawyers about what Mr. Doyle told you about Marie Iannuzzi?"

"Yes, it is."

For the DA, it was a low point in the trial. The ebb and flow of testimony had shifted against the prosecution. Dellaria offered the jury an alternative explanation for Marie's murder, together with enough reasonable doubt and unanswered questions to acquit Paradiso. Schmoozer had one more question for his latest witness.

"Do you know whether or not David Doyle has a temper?" the defense lawyer asked, knowing full well what to expect.

"That David Doyle is one crazy bastard, excuse my language," the suddenly repentant junkie offered.

"Your witness," Schmoozer said. He strode mightily back to his seat, where he was greeted with a pat on the back from his client.

Drew looked up at his friend as the prosecutor rose from the table to undo the damage.

"You've been doing drugs since you were eleven years old, haven't you?" the DA asked the witness with the familiar name and face.

"That's correct," Dellaria responded, glancing to Lenny for approval.

"What grade were you in when you were eleven years old?"

"The tenth grade I think," the witness said as he looked down toward the fingers on his hands and began to count loud enough for the jurors to hear.

"You were in the tenth grade when you were eleven years old?" the DA asked as he mimicked the witness counting his fingers.

"I don't remember. I don't remember," Dellaria rattled. His hands began an involuntary tremor.

"Tell the jury what kind of drugs you use."

"Reefer, amphetamines."

"A lot of amphetamines?"

"Yeah, a lot," Dellaria readily agreed. Two of the jurors placed neatly folded arms across their chests.

"Angel dust?"

"I smoked a lot of dust, sure."

"Cocaine?"

"I snorted a lot of cocaine, too."

"What kind of uppers?"

"Biphetamine twenty is what they call a 'black beauty,' which is an upper, sir."

"Any downers?"

"Seconal sodium powder, which is a Seconal barbiturate, yes sir."

The kid sounded like he had a degree in pharmacology. The DA wanted to ask that question, but Drew read his friend and shook his head.

"How about Valium?"

"Yes sir, a lot of Valium."

"How about heroin?"

"I never shot smack in my life," the junkie responded indignantly.

"But you used all the rest of those drugs since you were eleven years old?"

"Yes, I did. I don't go around copping all them drugs all at one time. Honestly, you'd be dead."

"When you say 'copping' drugs, tell the jury what you mean."

"Copping drugs means you go out and buy them."

"How did you support yourself during all of these years?"

"I had a family who supported my habit by giving me money so I wouldn't have to go out and do mad things, like stickups. You know what I mean?"

"Yeah, I know what you mean." The DA smiled and pulled a pair of documents from the thick brown file. "Are you the same David Dellaria that pled guilty and received a five-year sentence in 1983 for the crime of armed robbery?"

"That's me."

"Is that what you meant when you said something about not 'doing mad things'?"

"That's correct."

"Have you ever sold drugs to support your habit?"

"I never sold any narcotics."

"Mr. Dellaria . . ."

"Yes sir . . ."

"You've been taking drugs since you've been eleven years old and you never sold drugs?"

"I never sold any narcotics," the witness repeated unconvincingly, making the distinction once again between *drugs* and *narcotics*. "What I sold was myself. I don't mean prostitution-wise. I mean clothes, boots, stuff that I stole from my home."

"Has the constant use of drugs for the past seventeen years had any effect on your memory?"

"A little bit."

"A little bit?" the DA asked incredulously.

"That's correct. Not a total loss."

"Well, for instance, can you tell us what day Marie was murdered or the day you spoke to Mr. Doyle?"

"Nope."

"How about the year?"

"Obviously, it was the year she got murdered."

"What year was that?"

"It was 1981, right?"

The DA didn't correct him and say it was 1979.

"Do you recall what month it was you spoke to Mr. Doyle?"

"I don't recall."

"Summer, spring, winter, fall?"

"I think it was the summertime."

"What kind of drugs were you copping then?"

"Some reefer, could have been some gold —"

The DA didn't wait for the witness to finish his answer. "Incidentally, are you the same David Dellaria that assaulted a sixty-five-year-old woman whose name was Sally Lemire and robbed her of nine dollars from her handbag?"

There was no response from the witness, who searched the jury enclosure for a friendly face.

There weren't any. Two of the older jurors crossed their arms and turned to look away.

"Did you commit that crime and plead guilty to what I just read into the record, Mr. Dellaria?"

"Yes sir," Dellaria said. The side of his face began to twitch.

"Now, you said that you were smoking some reefer the day you spoke to Mr. Doyle. Were you doing anything else?"

"Percodan, I believe."

"You didn't have a prescription for Percodan, did you?"

"No sir."

"How many were you taking?"

"Four or five a day."

"Do you know the strength of these Percodans?"

"They were strong."

"How strong?"

"Very strong."

"You'd take them every day of the week, wouldn't you."

"Yes I did. Sometimes twice a day," Dellaria volunteered.

"Where did you get the money for the drugs?"

"Sometimes I would con my father and mother for money, my sisters."

"You'd lie to them wouldn't you?"

"I lied," the witness admitted.

"You said you had a conversation with David Doyle in the summer of 1981?"

"Yeah, initially we were down at the Waterfront Park, where I usually sit in the morning. I had my dose and Doyle had his dose."

"We're just talking about what *you* did for now. What did you have?"

"Okay. Maybe I had three Percs for openers and smoked around three joints. Yeah."

"All right, so you're mildly tuned. You've had your three Percs and three joints, right?"

"Yeah."

"Anything else?"

"When I got upstairs, I started smokin' some more and drinkin' a little bit."

"What were you drinking?"

"Three, four Heinekens."

"Okay, so let me make sure I've got the menu right. You had three Percs, three Heinekens, three smokes for openers, and then when you got upstairs you started smokin' again?"

"Yeah, after we walked upstairs."

"Did you walk up or fly up?" The DA smiled as Drew covered his mouth and Hizzoner turned his face away from the jurors to cough.

"No, I walked up and then we started smoking some more. It was just street-level commercial Colombian grade. Not more than an ounce."

"How was your state of mind at this time?"

"I was just starting to get off."

"Just starting to get off?" the prosecutor exclaimed in mock surprise.

"Right. Can I address something to the people of the jury?" the coker requested.

"No. Just answer the questions," the judge stated flatly as Dellaria looked to Lenny for direction.

"Were you ever held at Charles Street Jail?"

"That's correct."

"That's when you gave this statement to Mr. Paradiso's other attorney, wasn't it?"

"That's correct."

"Was it voluntary?"

"Well, it wasn't really voluntary. I feared for my life."

"From whom?"

"From ah Lenny," Dellaria explained as he placed a portion of his right hand over his mouth.

"You feared for your life from Lenny Paradiso?"

"Right. He called me a snitch. In the can strange things can happen. So I openly obliged to see his lawyer."

"As a matter of fact, Lenny chased you around the mess hall that day, didn't he?" the DA guessed.

"Yeah, well, he didn't really chase me around. He called me a fuckin' snitch. I never did time before and I see a big guy like that coming up to me and callin' me a snitch. I know the code inside there. When you're a snitch, you're gonna get your throat slashed."

"Did he tell you what was going to happen if you didn't sign that statement?"

"No, he didn't, but I could visualize what would have happened."

"What was that?"

"God knows, strange things."

"He's a pretty strong guy, isn't he?"

"Yeah." Dellaria nodded as Lenny's face puckered into a contortion of anger.

"Nothing further," the DA announced as Hizzoner excused the witness from the stand.

95: Candace Weyant

Whenever he was about to cross-examine a witness, the prosecutor thought of what the person had been like as a youngster. As the bleached blonde approached the stand to testify for Lenny, the DA mentally walked back to her childhood, envisioning her early life as a lonely reclusive misfit, in search of acceptance and love. He understood her love for dogs. Candy could trust the happy Labrador retriever that never betrayed her.

Much like the commonwealth's reliance on its principal witness, Robert Bond, Paradiso's case rested on Candy's ability to convince the jury of his alibi. Did Lenny leave the Cardinal's Nest with Weyant and go to his apartment, or did he bring Marie to the Lynn Marsh Road? The jury would soon decide the same question. Weyant would be the final witness in the two-week trial. Closing arguments would begin twenty minutes after her testimony concluded. Lenny's lover would provide the final word, the last piece of the puzzle to the jury. The DA would have to destroy her credibility to have any chance of convicting the Quahog.

"Can you tell the jury your name please?" Schmoozer began.

She was dressed for the occasion. The pastel yellow color of her high-collared summer dress made her appear matronly beyond her years. Candy smiled wanly to the jurors, then turned to the defense table and nodded to Lenny for approval as she identified herself.

"My name is Candace Weyant."

It was one of those moments that transcended the trial. The DA for the first time fully understood the control Lenny held over his witness. It was the power of having another person take the oath, swear to tell the truth, and then lie to escape a conviction for murder. Perjury in a capital case carried a life sentence. The risk made no difference to Candy. She had given Paradiso her soul.

Lenny knew how to use it.

"Would you tell the jury where you were on the night of August 11, 1979?" Lenny's lawyer began.

As expected, and as she had done in the Connie Porter case years earlier, Candy would give the jurors a way out of convicting Paradiso. She was well rehearsed. She knew her role. Quiet, demure, she effectively offset the image of the predatory Paradiso that the prosecution's witnesses had created. The jurors craned forward to examine the witness as they listened to her testimony.

On each side of the jury box, the two noisy air conditioners hummed a losing battle against the heat of the rising morning sun.

"I took Marie to the Cardinal's Nest and then I went back to the Milanos' to pick up Lenny," Candy told the jury.

Schmoozer didn't need to ask a question.

"On the way home, Lenny and I found some papers in my car. We knew they weren't ours, so we figured they must be Marie's. We went back to the Cardinal's Nest and Lenny went inside to return them to her. He was only in there ten minutes, give or take a little," Weyant explained as the jury evaluated her speech, body language, and hand motions, asking themselves, *Can we trust her?*

"Where did you go from there?"

"We went back to Lenny's apartment on Princeton Street. It's about five minutes away. It was raining and when we were getting out of the car, we found some keys wedged in between the seats. We realized they must be Marie's, so we went back to the Cardinal's Nest a second time. I waited outside while Lenny went inside. He was in there a little bit longer, maybe fifteen minutes," the seemingly pleasant woman recounted as three of the men in the jury smiled approvingly and three of the women crossed their arms.

"What happened then?" Schmoozer obliged.

"I was outside in my car waiting when I saw Lenny and Marie leave the Cardinal's Nest at the same time. Marie walked down Maverick Street. We asked her if she wanted a ride home, but she mumbled something about having some other place to go. That's the last time I saw her," Candy stated slowly, Lenny confidently nodding in agreement with each sentence.

Paradiso wouldn't need to tell the jury his story. Candy could do it for him. Much better.

For the first time in the trial Marie's sisters reacted. With each statement from Candy they turned from the defense witness to gauge the jurors' responses. Helpless and unable to speak, their eyes filled with tears as they envisioned the case slipping away. Five years earlier their brother had been murdered on the same angry streets of East Boston. His murder remained unsolved. His killer still walked the streets. *Marie's case will be no different,* they must have thought as the witness continued.

"When we got back to Lenny's, I put on a pot of tea," Candy offered, as Hizzoner, the clerk, both lawyers, and the trooper all momentarily envisioned the Steaming Kettle across the street from the courthouse.

You could almost smell the summer rain and chamomile tea brewing as

Weyant detailed the weather on the ride from the Nest back to Lenny's apartment on Princeton Street.

"I stayed there for about a half an hour and had my tea. Then I left and drove home to Revere. I called Lenny when I got home. He always worried about me and wanted to make sure I got home safe. It must have been sometime around 2 AM when I finally got done talking to him," Candy reported enthusiastically as her nodding partner fully agreed.

There was a sinking feeling in the pit of the DA's stomach as he looked toward Drew and then back to the gallery. There was no comfort from either location.

Candy and Lenny had all of their bases covered. If the jury believed her, there was no possible way for Paradiso to have driven Marie to Conley and Daggett's. Under the pains and penalty of perjury, Candy calmly assured the jury that she was speaking with her lover at the time of Marie Iannuzzi's murder. The jurors silently nodded as Schmoozer concluded Weyant's direct testimony. It was exactly what the DA had feared: The evidentiary wind had shifted and the finger of doubt was pointing in a new direction.

David Doyle had once again become the object of the jury's suspicion. Paradiso was going to walk.

"You may cross-examine the witness, Mr. Burke," Judge Donahue said. Schmoozer shot him a smile on the way back to his seat.

It's difficult for a man to cross-examine a woman. Come on too strong and you could appear the bully and turn the jury against you. Yet the DA had known all along that if he didn't confront Candy and show she was lying, Lenny would be acquitted. He left the six pages of notes he had prepared in anticipation of Weyant's cross-examination on the prosecution table. Drew tried handing them to him, but the DA shook his friend off. He knew exactly where he was going.

It was all so clear to him.

He would ask the evil woman about the *Mala Femmena.*

"Have you ever lied to the police for Mr. Paradiso before?" the DA asked, setting the trap.

"No," Weyant responded indignantly, "I have not."

"Think about it, ma'am. I'll ask you again. Have you ever lied to the police before for Mr. Paradiso?"

"No, I haven't," Weyant calmly maintained.

"Did Mr. Paradiso own a boat called the *Mala Femmena?*"

There was a pause as the witness looked to Lenny to get her bearings. "Y-yes," she stammered softly.

"Did you and Mr. Paradiso report that boat stolen on July 26, 1981?"

It was all happening too quickly for her. "Yes," the wide-eyed witness stammered once again before Lenny's lawyer could rise.

"Objection," Schmoozer interjected.

"No, he may have the question," the judge responded over the belated objection.

"In fact, the *Mala Femmena* was never stolen, was it, Ms. Weyant?"

The irony that the boat on which Joan Webster was killed would be used to undermine the credibility of her killer's alibi witness was not lost on the DA as he waited for her response.

"No, it wasn't," the flushed witness agreed as she looked anxiously at the Quahog.

The jurors' eyes followed the witness's as the DA saw his opening.

"May I approach the witness?" the commonwealth's lawyer asked Hizzoner as he handed a copy of a document to Schmoozer.

"Yes, you may, Mr. Burke."

Weyant leaned back defensively in her seat.

"Let me show you this document, Ms. Weyant. Whose signature is that?" the DA asked as he produced a copy of the police report for the "stolen" *Mala Femmena.*

"Mine," the witness whispered.

"Really loud, please."

"It's my signature."

"I'll ask you again. Did you ever lie to the police before for Mr. Paradiso?"

"Yes I did," Weyant replied softly.

"Say it really loud, please," the prosecutor demanded.

"Yes," Weyant shouted in response, no longer demurely. One the jurors turned toward the now beet-faced witness.

"Under the pains and penalties of perjury, you put your signature on that document knowing what you said there was a blatant lie, wasn't it?"

"Yes it was," the woman in the high-necked pastel summer dress whispered in a barely audible voice.

"You've lied to the police to protect him, haven't you?"

"Yes, I have."

"And you've lied to people other than the police to protect him, too, haven't you?"

"Yes," Weyant agreed, looking toward Lenny for help.

The packed courtroom had been silent, the only sound the whirring of the air conditioners. Now the murmur of hushed voices responding to the witness's admissions filled the chamber.

"Who told you to do that?" the DA fired back as the moment built.

"He did," Weyant said, nodding toward the defendant.

"Didn't you just say, ma'am, under oath, not less than two minutes ago that you've never lied for Mr. Paradiso?"

"Yes, I did."

"That wasn't true, was it?"

"No, it wasn't."

"Who told you to do that?"

"He did," Weyant answered, pointing to her lover with a note of hesitation, signaling Lenny's domination over her.

"He did, didn't he?" the DA said as he joined the witness and pointed directly at the defendant.

"Yes."

"He tells you to do a lot of things, doesn't he, Ms. Weyant?" the DA asked, maintaining eye contact with the Quahog.

The time lapse between a question and an answer frequently gave the jury an opportunity to anticipate the response before it was given. There were ten seconds for the jury to speculate on Weyant's answer before she haltingly responded.

"Yes."

The prosecutor was poised to ask his next question of the woman he saw as soulless when Schmoozer rose.

"Excuse me, Your Honor, I think something's going on behind my back. May we approach the bench?" The judge nodded reluctantly. The request for a sidebar was a familiar means to interrupt the flow of cross-examination.

Candy was in trouble.

"Look, Mr. Rappaport, there's been no question to the witness and there's been no objection. So what's the purpose of the sidebar?" Judge Donahue reacted angrily.

"Judge, I hear nothing. Then I look behind me and see Mr. Burke staring in my client's direction," the defense attorney complained.

"He's asking a question concerning Mr. Paradiso; do you say he can't look in Mr. Paradiso's direction?"

"No, but at the same time, Judge, he spent a good ten, fifteen seconds staring at my client, and didn't ask a question, just so I couldn't object," Schmoozer added, highlighting his adversary's tactics.

"Perhaps he did that to make sure the jury knew he was talking about Mr. Paradiso," Hizzoner noted, breaking up the huddle.

"There's no doubt about that," the DA agreed as the lawyers filed back to their previous positions.

"This isn't the first time you've testified on Mr. Paradiso's behalf, is it, Ms. Weyant?" the DA continued. The jurors craned forward once again. "Tell the jury where you were on September 26, 1974."

"I don't remember," Lenny's moll lied.

"Let me try and refresh your recollection. You were seated in a witness chair under oath, much the same way you are today. Do you remember that?"

"Yes, I do," Weyant answered, suddenly recalling her appearance as a witness for Lenny in the attempted rape of Connie Porter.

"You were part of an alibi for Mr. Paradiso in a prior case in 1974, weren't you?"

"Yes, I was."

"I have nothing else for this witness," the DA said derisively, pausing long enough to make eye contact with the defendant.

"Great job," Drew said as Schmoozer rose in an attempt to undo the damage.

"That case back in 1974, do you remember what you testified to that day?" Lenny's lawyer began quietly.

"Judge, if we're going to go into that, I think it's going to open up a lot of things," the DA interrupted before the witness could respond.

"I understand. I can't control the questions that counsel asks. You're both experienced attorneys and I assume you know what you're doing," Judge Donahue answered from the bench as Schmoozer pressed ahead with a different question.

"You told the jury that you've lied to the police on prior occasions for Mr. Paradiso?"

"Yes."

"What was the document you were shown? What did that relate to?"

"An insurance claim for a boat," Weyant nonchalantly explained with a tone of everyday occurrence.

"Was the boat stolen?"

"No."

"Do you know what happened to the boat?"

"I believe it was sunk by Mr. Paradiso," Weyant casually surmised as though she hadn't been present.

"So you took part in an insurance fraud?"

"Yes," Candy readily admitted.

"Ma'am, do you know what Mr. Paradiso is charged with today?"

"Yes, rape and murder."

"Would you lie for him in a murder or rape case?" Schmoozer asked, drawing the narrow distinction.

"No."

"Are you lying for him today?"

"No, I'm not," Candy said, shaking her head in rhythm with Lenny.

"No further questions," the defense counsel concluded as he cast an anxious glance to the jury enclosure.

"I'll see counsel at the sidebar," Hizzoner announced without a request from either side.

"The question to the witness was, 'Would she lie in a murder or rape case.' She said no. That opens up —" the judge began.

Lenny's defense attorney interrupted. "I —"

The man in black wasn't listening.

"I'm making a ruling. I'm not asking for arguments. Your question opens up that area for Mr. Burke on re-cross. Now, that's my ruling," the judge said abruptly.

The jury was interested to see what the DA would do on his second round of cross-examination. He needed to end the case on a strong note.

"So, it's fair to say, ma'am, you'd lie for Mr. Paradiso for money?" the DA asked on re-cross.

"Yes."

"You'd lie for him in little crimes, right?"

"Yes."

"But you wouldn't lie to keep him out of jail?" the DA asked incredulously.

"Not for murder," Candace Weyant answered weakly, drawing the line on the limits of her deception.

96: Closing Arguments

There's an electricity surrounding every closing argument in every murder case. A crowded courtroom filled with the anxious family and friends of the defendant on one side, and the desperate relatives of the victim on the other. The tension and drama of a life lost and another held in the balance of the jury. Murder cases are won and lost in final argument. The wrong word, the wrong phrase, a failed attempt at humor, poor posture, bad breath, poor eye contact, a lack of conviction or certainty.

There are a million ways to lose a murder case.

The closing argument is the ultimate high-stakes game of life and death. Screw up and a killer walks. The prosecution always goes last. They have the burden of proof and of persuasion.

Schmoozer began by thanking the jurors for their patience, advising them about the burden of proof, and then offering a detailed summary of each witness's testimony and what it meant. The DA sat motionless, staring straight ahead. The wait, and the weight of his responsibilities, were unbearable. He listened anxiously as Lenny's lawyer wailed about the injustice of two convicted killers maligning his client.

"You folks are too smart, too sophisticated to let those two cons pull the wool over your eyes," Schmoozer told them. "Consider Pisa's and Bond's characters. Think about what their motivation is to come in here and say what they had to say. Pisa was found guilty of first-degree murder. He was sentenced to death. His jury could have recommended leniency. They chose not to. Do you want to rely on that kind of person?" Lenny's lawyer asked rhetorically as the jury weighed their options.

There was a straight-line logic to everything Schmoozer said. He got you from point A to point B really quickly. His words would be difficult to overcome.

"And what about Bond? He gets paroled for manslaughter and a couple months later he's charged with another murder. That's the person the commonwealth wants you to rely on to convict Mr. Paradiso. I'll tell you what happened. Bond learned about Paradiso's case at Charles Street Jail, filled in the blanks, and then turned it around on my client," the defense lawyer decreed as his client stuck out his lower lip, nodding in agreement.

The DA longed to interrupt but was limited to shaking his head in mild disagreement.

"Let me tell you why Bond's story doesn't make sense. You heard Marie had her panty hose on underneath her red leotard. They found her without the panty hose. How can you take the panty hose off without removing the leotard? Does that make sense to you? That's why there was no rape in this case," Schmoozer explained, displaying the red leotard for the jury to examine.

The jurors listened intently.

"There was no rape in this case, and if there was no rape, that throws Mr. Paradiso's motive right out the window."

It had been half an hour since Schmoozer started his closing argument. He was exhausted, mentally and physically. Still, he pressed on.

"You heard the medical examiner tell you there were no injuries to the victim's genitalia and no overt signs of rape," Schmoozer added, building momentum. "Even though sperm cells were found in the victim's vagina, the police never performed any tests to determine the blood type of the depositor."

Lenny's lawyer paused long enough to look at the prosecution table as if to say, *How come the police never did a semen test?*

When he turned back to the jury, Schmoozer didn't disappoint.

"Maybe Mr. Burke can explain to you why the police never did a semen test?" he asked the jury as four jurors raised their eyebrows and turned to look at the DA, who sat motionless, chewing the inside of his cheek.

God, how he hated the son of a bitch.

"And while we're at it, what could have been found from Marie's fingernails? We'll never know because the police never checked her nails, did they?"

For the first time in the ten days of trial, the DA could feel sweat forming on the back of his neck. He struggled to calm his breathing and the racing of his mind.

I'm going to lose this case. Oh God. I'm going to lose this case, the darker side of his mind screamed as he silently fought for self-control.

"So what's Bond's motive for testifying? He says he doesn't want to see Doyle go down for something he didn't do. Just like Bond, wrongly convicted. Let me ask you. Do you really believe Bobby Bond thinks one second about David Doyle? Or do you think he didn't want to go back to twenty-three-hour lockdown in Ten Block?"

He's right. Bond's lying. The jury knows it too. The DA's resolve dissipated into the stale air of the crowded courtroom.

"Do you really want to believe Bobby Bond and Tony Pisa? Do you?" Schmoozer implored the jury.

The DA prayed no one saw him shake his head.

"And what about Doyle? The scratches, the physical fights he had with Marie. You know Marie moved out of their apartment a couple of months earlier, after Doyle put his hands around Marie's throat. You know Doyle was embarrassed the day of the wedding. Ask yourselves, who really has the motive, the rage, the drug haze he was in to commit this crime? Think about the threats to David Dellaria, putting a knife to his throat and beating him within an inch of his life after Dellaria went to the police. Even the police told Dellaria to seek a complaint for attempted murder," Schmoozer said, alternating his voice from a roar to a whisper, convincing, seducing the jury.

Schmoozer's adversary sat motionless, outwardly still. Internally wishing Rappaport's closing would end, simultaneously dreading its conclusion. The DA knew it would signal the need for him to speak.

"You heard how the commonwealth attempted to link my client to Conley and Daggett's. Well, if Mr. Paradiso had something to hide, he's not going to invite his parole officer to the scene of the murder, is he?" Rappaport asked the jury as they considered the possibilities.

The logic seemed inescapable, irrefutable.

"You also heard the government talk about how nervous Mr. Paradiso was. Of course he's nervous when the cops questioned him; everyone knew he was on parole, you'd be nervous, too, folks."

There was a rhythm, a cadence to his voice, as Schmoozer ticked off the list of talking points he knew the prosecution couldn't counter. "We never denied Mr. Paradiso left the bar at the same time as Marie, but I ask you to keep in mind it was Mr. Doyle who had beaten and tried to strangle Marie a month earlier."

When he was finished, Lenny's lawyer smiled at the jury with an expression of satisfaction and calmly, passionately, asked them to acquit his client. In the fifty-five minutes he spoke, Schmoozer never mentioned the name of his chief witness, Candy Weyant.

"Mr. Burke, you may proceed for the commonwealth," the judge intoned dispassionately.

— — —

As he rose, the prosecutor's legs went weak and his mouth went dry. There was no water and no place to turn. The case hung in the balance of what he said. The jurors wanted to be convinced. They needed to see the case through his eyes. This was the moment he had both lived for and dreaded the last three years. For a moment he doubted he could convince twelve strangers that today was July 20 let alone that the man staring at his back was Marie's killer.

He glanced at his large friend, who knew there was nothing he could do to help at this moment. Drew simply smiled, nodded as he clenched his right hand in a symbol of strength, and mouthed the words, "You can do it."

The DA carefully placed the yellow legal pad of notes on the table in front of him. He knew they were no use to him now. He turned to look at Marie's sisters seated in the front row of the crowded audience and instinctively understood that they were praying. The Iannuzzis smiled back as they held hands and waited. He turned from them, briefly looked into the defendant's dark eyes, and then turned to face the jury.

He was scared.

"It's a tremendous service you have performed," the commonwealth's lawyer began.

"What you do here defines our system of justice. When we talk about justice, people automatically assume that it means a fair trial for the defendant. Naturally, it's important to make sure the defendant receives a fair trial, but justice wields a double-edged sword. There is another person who had certain rights as well."

The DA struggled to keep his voice even, calm, slow, and deliberate. While he spoke, his eyes slowly tracked from left to right as he made direct eye contact with each of the jurors. Once he was certain all the jurors' eyes were on his, the lawyer began to speak once again.

"In this case, Marie Iannuzzi had the right to grow old and die a natural death. Her right to live, to marry, to have children, and to be a comfort to her family. All of those rights were taken from her. They were stolen away on a damp, rainy night five years ago. They were taken away from Marie in a brutal and sadistic way by a murderer of some cunning."

As he spoke the words *by a murderer of some cunning* the DA turned his body away from the jurors and moved slowly toward defense counsel's table. He stared directly at the Quahog, raised his right hand with his finger fully extended, and pointed it at Marie's killer. There wasn't another sound in the courtroom as each of the players held their breath.

Lenny glared back with a look of hate as his lower jaw moved imperceptibly under the weight of his grinding teeth. From the corner of his eye the DA could see Drew shift his eyes from his friend to Lenny and back. The jurors did the same, watching the struggle play out before them.

Satisfied with the moment, the DA turned back to the jury.

"So, you are here as ordinary citizens, taken from your day-to-day life and asked to wrestle with the incredible body of evidence that's been presented in this case. You are asked to make resolution of what happened on the night of August 12, 1979. You, and you alone, decide who and what to believe," he said, empowering the jury.

The prosecutor asked the jury to visualize a trusting young woman in a red dress being slapped, choked, and punched by the muscular defendant who wanted "to commit a crime of passion." He held up the red leotard Iannuzzi was wearing beneath her dress and stretched the material to show how a rape could have occurred without removing the piece of clothing. He told the jury no bruises were found in the victim's genital area because Paradiso had choked Marie into unconsciousness and then raped her. The prosecutor reminded the jurors, "The victim's panty hose and shoes were missing."

"You heard Bobby Bond tell you when Marie came to, she was startled, and Lenny strangled her with her scarf as her body gasped for air. Bond told you the defendant found Marie's shoes and stockings in Weyant's car the next day and laughed as he discarded them before Candy saw them."

As he spoke, the jury slowly began to settle under the rhythm of his voice and the tone of his argument.

"This case isn't just about whether you believe Bobby Bond or Tony Pisa. Ask yourselves, who has the real motive to lie, to fabricate a story to you?"

The prosecutor briefly turned to look at the bleached blonde seated in the courtroom gallery and then asked the jury to consider why no mention was made of Candy Weyant's testimony in the defendant's closing argument. What had been Paradiso's rock-solid alibi turned into his Achilles' heel.

"The person who has the greatest motive to lie, who has in fact admitted lying to you on the stand this very day, is Candy Weyant, his girlfriend," the DA said as he once again pointed toward the defendant's dark eyes.

"She's the person who held the key to this case for so long, because Candy Weyant knows today, as she knew then, she is lying to protect Lenny Paradiso."

As the prosecutor spoke, Weyant gathered her umbrella and purse, stood, and walked quickly, but not quietly, out of the courtroom. The heavy oak door closed with a thud as her blond hair disappeared from view in the courtroom door's small glass window. With the exception of the defendant, everyone in the courtroom turned to watch Candy leave. The speaker stopped momentarily as the jurors returned their attention from her departure to his closing.

"Candy is the one person who has the motive to deceive you, to lie to you, to try and convince you about the critical time period when Paradiso is seen leaving the bar with Marie Iannuzzi. She wants you to believe she was with Paradiso, but Candy knows she wasn't there."

Two of the jurors nodded as he spoke. The others sat listening stoically with their arms crossed. He knew they still needed convincing as he pressed ahead.

"The only person that stands between this man and conviction is Candy Weyant. She told you, 'I only lie for him in little cases. I'd lie for him for money, for the insurance, but I wouldn't lie to keep him out of jail.' Do you believe that? She admitted to committing perjury, but would have you believe that she's sitting out in her car that night while Lenny's inside the Cardinal's Nest with some voluptuous, attractive, vulnerable girl for half an hour," the lawyer said. Another of the jurors uncrossed her arms.

"In every lie there is a kernel of truth. The truth contained within their lie is, Marie wanted to go back to the house in Saugus to apologize to the Milanos. That's how Lenny convinced her to get in the car with him. What happens after that is exactly what Bobby Bond said. He told you how Paradiso strangled Marie, discarded her lifeless body, and then tried to conceal the blood evidence," the DA said as two jurors unconsciously placed their right hands beneath their necks. It was eighty-six degrees, cloudy, with a threat of rain outside. The noisy air-conditioning had been turned off at the beginning of Schmoozer's closing more than two hours ago, and the packed courtroom was stifling. The lawyer's mind drifted briefly to the route up Heartbreak Hill and just as quickly returned to the murder scene.

"Paradiso preyed on Marie because she was beautiful, drunk, and vulnerable. He took her to Conley and Daggett's because it was deserted, secluded, and a perfect place for a murder." As he spoke the prosecutor knew the case rested on whether the jury believed Candy.

"Leonard Paradiso is a criminally sophisticated person who knew that with no witnesses it's difficult to prove a murder case. Ask yourselves, what's his state of mind? He knows there's no witness to the murder, but people have seen him leave the bar with this girl and now she's dead. Paradiso knows he's got to come up with an alibi. The police aren't gonna just buy what he says. Who does Lenny rely on? Good old Candy, his girlfriend of long standing. The same person who previously testified for him in another case."

There was a pause as the DA slowed to catch his breath.

"I know it's difficult for you to try to resolve all of the factual issues in this case. You alone decide who has told you the truth. Nothing is ever perfectly clear, but in this case the commonwealth has established beyond a reasonable doubt that the person who killed Marie Iannuzzi is seated directly behind me. David Doyle didn't murder Marie. Leonard Paradiso did. Now you know it, too."

As the words *beyond a reasonable doubt* echoed, the DA thought of the original Webster case and wished Joan's parents had stayed for his closing. This trial would be his only chance to convict Paradiso.

He was almost done.

"When he was arrested at Weyant's home in Revere, Trooper Palombo said to the defendant, 'You don't seem surprised to see us.' Mr. Paradiso told the trooper he'd been waiting for him for three years. Marie Iannuzzi's family has been waiting for five years for some measure of justice for the murder of their daughter. Marie will wait forever." The DA turned toward the victim's family in the gallery. "Ladies and gentlemen of this jury, in good conscience and good faith, I ask you to find Leonard Paradiso guilty of the rape and murder of Marie Iannuzzi."

Burke pointed to the defendant's dark eyes of death one final time and said, "The only thing that stands between freedom for this man and a conviction is Candy Weyant."

The DA could hear Drew's body squirm in his seat as the judge told the jury the burden was on the commonwealth to prove beyond a reasonable doubt that the defendant was guilty of the murder and rape charges made against him.

"What then is proof beyond a reasonable doubt?" Hizzoner asked the jurors rhetorically as he straightened his horn-rims and began to read from a legal tome written in 1850. Judge Donahue was a traditionalist who preferred the exact language taken from the original Webster case. The same brief paragraphs of jury instructions were the foundation of a legal system that had guided juries for more than one hundred and thirty years.

"It is a term often used, probably pretty well understood, but not easily defined. It is not mere possible doubt; because everything relating to human affairs, and depending on fallible evidence, is open to some possible or imaginary doubt. It is that state of the case, which, after the entire comparison and consideration of all the evidence, leaves the minds of jurors in that condition that they cannot say they feel an abiding conviction, to a moral certainty, of the truth of the charges.

"The burden of proof is upon the prosecutor," the judge continued, turning his gaze from the document toward the DA.

"All the presumptions of law independent of evidence are in favor of innocence; and every person is presumed to be innocent until he is proven guilty," Judge Donahue recited. He directed his eyes toward defense table. Lenny smiled in acknowledgment of something he didn't truly understand.

The Quahog rapidly nodded in agreement with Hizzoner nonetheless.

"If upon such proof there is reasonable doubt remaining, the accused is entitled to the benefit of an acquittal," the jurist said evenly. Lenny kept nodding. The courtroom looked toward the jurors' box, perhaps hoping for some indication of their thinking.

Whatever was going through their minds, none of them displayed any emotion. It was at this point in every case that the DA felt himself a failure. He never knew what the jury was thinking. He never knew whether he'd made believers out of them or led the victim's family down a road of quiet desperation, only to be victims once again.

The definition of reasonable doubt *keeps us all safe. This jury will know the truth,* the prosecutor said quietly to calm and reassure himself as Drew's chair creaked from the anxious shifting of his body. He turned back to listen as Judge Donahue continued.

"For it is not sufficient to establish a probability, though a strong one arising from the doctrine of chances, that the fact charged is more likely to be true than the contrary; but the evidence must establish the truth of the fact to a reasonable and moral certainty; a certainty that convinces and directs the understanding, and satisfies the reason and judgment of those who are bound to act conscientiously upon it. This is what we take to be proof beyond reasonable doubt," the judge concluded as he, too, turned to the wooden enclosure, looking for a sign from the rapt jurors.

There was none.

"This jury's never gonna convict Lenny after hearing the judge's instruction on reasonable doubt," Drew whispered, swallowing hard as his complexion colored to a thin chalky white.

The creaking of his chair broke the silence as the trooper turned his large frame to Paradiso, who smiled and mouthed "fuck youse."

"All rise," Jack Gillen told the audience as Judge Donahue left the bench for his chambers and the jurors were led upstairs to Room 8M to begin their deliberations.

Once the case finally went to the jury, the DA felt a sense of relief. Years of work were suddenly compacted into hours of deliberation and then into the finality of the forelady reading a two-minute verdict. There was nothing more he could do. Nothing but pray and wait. He turned from the prosecution table to see the deliveryman from Dandelions hand three pots of coffee, twenty-five sodas, and two huge plastic-wrapped platters of deli sandwiches to Jack Gillen, who promptly brought the collection upstairs for the jurors.

The jury would remain isolated for the remainder of the day without reaching a verdict. At five o'clock, they were taken from the courthouse by bus and sequestered overnight at their anonymous motel. The next morning they were brought back to the courtroom at nine to start the deliberation process once again.

After the jury was sent back to their deliberation room, Hizzoner invited the two lawyers into his chambers.

"You two have had a busy couple of weeks. Tell me, gentlemen, how did you spend the evening last night waiting for our jury to come back?"

"I always cook on Friday nights," Schmoozer began. "I went home and made a huge pot of potato and lentil soup for my wife and kids."

"How about you, Mr. Burke?" the judge asked. He fired up a large Panama and exhaled the heavy scent of cigar smoke into the tense atmosphere of the powder-blue room.

"I called the Websters in New Jersey. Then I went home, played the piano for a while, and went out for a run," the DA offered as he smiled and read the large sign situated prominently on the jurist's desk.

SMOKING PERMITTED, it said.

"Oh really, I love the piano. What kind of music do you play?" the man who also read Shakespeare and loved gardening wanted to know.

"'The Shadow of Your Smile,' 'As Time Goes By.' Schmaltzy songs like that," the DA answered politely. With a glance at the clock, he realized the jury had been deliberating for more than eight hours.

"He's self-taught, Your Honor. Let me guess. 'The Shadow of Your Smile' reminds you of Joan Webster," Schmoozer offered partly in jest, but partly from having come to know his adversary.

"How'd you know that?" the DA asked, surprised.

"Is that where we're gonna go next, Tim?" Lenny's lawyer wanted to know.

Before the prosecutor could answer, there was a knock on the door. A large court officer with a serious look on his face poked his head inside the room.

"The jury's got a question," the court officer announced to the group as he walked into the lobby with a folded piece of lined notepaper.

It took the judge all of a minute to read the question, digest it, remove his glasses, and quietly say, "They've asked me to instruct them again on the difference between first- and second-degree murder."

The DA smiled broadly and clenched his fist. Schmoozer joined him with the same smile and the same motion. Both lawyers turned to Hizzoner, who in turn nodded toward the defense attorney.

"What are you smilin' for, Steve? The question means they're gonna convict him on either one or the other. It's either a first or second degree," the prosecutor said.

Rappaport shook his head. "Should I tell him, Your Honor?"

"You probably ought to," Judge Donahue deadpanned as he instructed the court officer to bring the jury back into the courtroom.

Lenny's lawyer began to explain his smile. "The last murder case I tried was about six months ago. It was with Judge Donahue. The jury had the very same question. They wanted to know the difference between first- and second-degree murder. The judge told them and they came back fifteen minutes later with a not-guilty verdict."

The DA looked to Hizzoner for confirmation.

"It's true," Judge Donahue said as he took the last puff on his cigar and donned his black robe.

The DA swallowed hard, wanting to puke. The possibility of losing the case had always been there, but he never allowed his mind to accept it until that moment.

"Not this case, not this case, not Paradiso," he mumbled to himself as he stumbled out into the empty courtroom.

"What's the matter?" Drew asked his friend as he dejectedly returned to the prosecution table.

"The jury's got a question on the difference between first- and second-degree murder."

"No kidding. That's great, isn't it?" Ponytail said, giving the same clenched-fist response.

"Yeah, that's what I thought, too," the DA said haltingly. He told Schmoozer's story to his friend.

"Don't tell me this sick bastard's gonna walk?" Drew said loudly as Lenny creased his lips with his tongue, bobbing his head for the trooper's benefit.

There wasn't time to answer Drew's question as the jury single-filed back into the courtroom for the judge's instructions. Both lawyers positioned their bodies and craned their necks, hoping to make eye contact with an advocate for their respective sides. Nothing. It was maddening.

"Nobody's smiling," Drew said as he turned to look at Mr. Peepers, the lone exception, who nodded and glanced at Lenny's lawyer as he passed by.

The entire panel of jurors was expressionless as they listened to the court's instructions. The DA searched each face for a sign, a hidden suggestion, some indication to tell him what they were thinking. When the judge finished half an hour later, the jurors retraced their steps to the deliberation room, where the court officer dutifully told them to bang on the door when they had reached a verdict.

"Did the judge have to keep telling the jury so much about reasonable doubt?" Drew asked with a sense of frustration at the end of the jury's instructions.

"Yeah, actually he did. It's part of the process to make sure Lenny gets a fair trial. You know where the language about reasonable doubt comes from, don't you?" the prosecutor asked in an effort to distract them both.

"The old Webster case, right?"

"Yeah. I promise you, Drew, if we don't get him on this case, we'll get him on the new Webster case."

The two men walked from Courtroom 808 into the large lobby corridor, where Marie's sisters stood softly crying.

"We've got to find Joan's body first," Drew replied, his voice low, as the Iannuzzi family gathered around them; the two Isaacs stood nearby.

"No matter what happens, I just want you to know I'm happy I called you that day," Kathy Leonti said to the DA as she wiped her eyes, took his hand, and tried to smile. "I know you were waiting for a call on that other case you were working on. The mother and two children. Whatever happened to it?"

"It's coming up for trial this fall," the prosecutor told her. The group spoke briefly and then returned to the courtroom to finish the wait.

The worst part of any trial is the wait for the jury to reach a verdict. You're always thinking of something else you coulda or shoulda done. Something else to say in your closing. A question you didn't ask on cross or one too many on direct. It was an agony of self-doubt and fear of failure. The DA was good at it.

"You always get like this. Ya know that?" Drew reminded his friend.

"Like what?"

"Like you think you suck and you're the worst lawyer in the building, just because the jury doesn't come back with a guilty verdict in the first hour," Ponytail said.

The DA wanted to thank him for his kind words, but just at that moment one of the jurors banged hard three times on the deliberation room door.

"They must have a verdict," the large court officer said as he quickly walked up the stairs, only to reappear ten seconds later with another note for the judge.

"They've got another question," he said with a shared sense of frustration. The judge summoned the two lawyers back into his smoke-filled powder-blue chambers.

"They want to know if you can rape a dead person," Judge Donahue announced to Schmoozer and the DA as he retrieved one of the tan-colored law books from the shelf behind him.

"I am quite sure the answer is no," the DA offered, to which the judge and Schmoozer shrugged and huddled, reading over the open page.

"You're right. I'll tell them that and allow them to resume their deliberations," Hizzoner announced.

Schmoozer nodded and said softly, "This jury's all over the lot. What the hell are they thinking?"

"I think it's anybody's guess at this point," the DA responded, hesitant to make a prediction that could come back to haunt him.

It was a Saturday, and Lenny's trial was the only show in town. The gallery was dotted with small groups of interested parties. The news cameras were there, of course, as were the print media, the Iannuzzis, the Three Amigos, the two Isaacs, Mr. Leary, Steve Broce, and a pretty woman quietly seated alone in the corner of the courtroom.

Dressed in a white linen suit and raven-haired, she looked about thirty and wore an innocent smile, a small engagement ring on her left hand, and a scarlet lace scarf wrapped around her neck.

"Who do you think she is?" the DA said to Ponytail as the jury filed back into the courtroom, past the Quahog's icy stare and into their seats.

"I dunno. She looks familiar. Like someone we should know," Drew responded as Paradiso turned and glared at the woman in white.

She returned the killer's stare.

The judge gave the jurors the answer to their question, reminded them once again about the burden of proof beyond a reasonable doubt, and sent them back to their deliberation room.

"Did any of them look at you?" Drew wanted to know when the heavy door closed behind the last juror.

"None of them, you?"

"Nope."

The wait was akin to a wake. All the normal topics of conversation had long ago been hashed and rehashed and finally exhausted. All that remained were silent, anxious people, listening to the whir of the air conditioners and the din of their own thoughts. The jury had been out for more than twelve hours in all when the heavy sound of a fist striking a door three times came from inside the deliberation room door, echoing through the courtroom.

"They've got a verdict," the court officer exclaimed as he quickly made for the staircase.

At that moment the DA wanted to run, afraid to face defeat. The prosecutor turned to his friend to say something, but it was too late. He could hear the jurors' footsteps on the stairs. As he turned to the gallery, the woman in white linen smiled her innocent smile and nodded to the lawyer.

The jurors solemnly entered the courtroom, made their way to the wooden enclosure, and stood while the suddenly full courtroom stilled in anticipation. The forelady in the gray business suit and matching ascot held the two-page verdict in her trembling hands, awaiting the judge's arrival.

— — —

"All rise," the court officer's voice boomed as Hizzoner left his chambers, took his seat, and fixed his gaze upon the woman holding the papers. The audience stood near their seats, watching the Quahog face the jury of his peers.

"Ladies and gentlemen of the jury, have you reached a verdict?" Judge Donahue inquired quietly.

"Yes, we have, Your Honor," the woman in seat number seven responded. She handed the verdict slip to the clerk, who in turn passed it to the judge. The judge read it word for word, made certain it had been signed, and returned it to the clerk, who handed the slip back to the forelady.

Drew reached up to gently tug on the DA's coat sleeve as the clerk instructed the defendant and the jurors to remain standing and for everyone else in the courtroom to take their seats. The prosecutor did as he was told, turning one final time toward the gallery to see the woman in white linen.

"What say you, Madam Forelady, to the indictments charging the defendant

Leonard J. Paradiso with murder and rape, is he guilty or not guilty?" the clerk asked.

The moment of truth had finally arrived.

In Glen Ridge, New Jersey, the parents of Joan Webster silently sat in their living room waiting for the call.

After the verdict, the prosecutor left the courtroom, spoke quietly to the Iannuzzi family, and headed to Room 603. He sat alone at his desk where the tattered gray file of the triple stared back at him.

On the radio, Don Henley sang "Heart of the Matter."

The lawyer closed his eyes long enough to consider the singer's question of "How can love survive in such a graceless age?"

He placed the receiver to his ear and slowly dialed the phone.

"Guilty," the DA told Joan's parents as the sound of a muffled cry ended the call.

Epilogue

On July 25, 1984, Lenny "the Quahog" Paradiso was sentenced to life imprisonment for the murder of Marie Iannuzzi. At the request of the prosecution, Judge Roger Donahue imposed an additional eighteen-to-twenty-year sentence for Paradiso's conviction of assault with intent to rape, to be served from and after the life sentence. Both sentences were ordered to be served after the completion of Paradiso's six-to-fifteen-year term for the attempted rape of Connie Porter.

– – –

On October 9, 1984, Antonio Gomes was tried before Judge James Donoghue for the murders of Basilisa Melendez and her two children, Johanna and Kenneth.

– – –

In December 1984 a hearing was held before Judge James McGuire to request a surgical search of Paradiso's left index finger. Judge McGuire authorized an X-ray and surgery on Paradiso's hand. Paradiso appealed to the Supreme Judicial Court, where an injunction issued by Justice Ruth Abrams prohibited the surgical search of Paradiso's finger.

– – –

In June 1985 Leonard Paradiso filed a civil lawsuit against the author for defamation. Paradiso alleged that the accusations made concerning his participation in the murder of Joan Webster held him up to public scorn and ridicule. At his deposition, Paradiso exercised his Fifth Amendment privilege against self-incrimination more than one hundred times, refusing to answer any questions regarding his role in the disappearance of Joan Webster. Paradiso's civil suit was subsequently dismissed. In a written decision the court found Paradiso to be "libel proof," stating Paradiso's reputation in the community was so poor that nothing could be said to defame him.

– – –

On November 1, 1985, Paradiso was convicted in federal district court for submitting a fraudulent bankruptcy claim involving the theft of the *Mala Femmena*. Judge Richard Sterns imposed a ten-year sentence.

— — —

On August 14, 1986, Paradiso was convicted for the attempted rape of Janet McCarthy near Winthrop Avenue in Revere. He was given another eighteen-to-twenty-year sentence, to be served from and after his previous sentence.

— — —

Eight years after her disappearance from Logan Airport, the body of Joan Webster was discovered north of Boston in a shallow grave in Hamilton, Massachusetts. The cause of death was listed as a fractured skull in the same location where Paradiso told Robert Bond he hit his victim. Like the Webster case of 1850, investigators identified Joan Webster by matching her dental records to teeth from the jawbone found at the scene.

— — —

Robert Bond was retried following the reversal of his original conviction for the murder of Mary Foreman. He was found guilty of second-degree murder.

— — —

Candy Weyant still lives on Crescent Avenue in Revere.

— — —

Leonard Paradiso remains incarcerated. He is eligible for parole on October 17, 2028. He will be eighty-six years old.

— — —

On July 4, 1998, Trooper Andrew Palombo was killed in a motorcycle accident in the city of Lynn. The choir sang "Danny Boy" at his funeral.

Author's Note

I started writing this book after Terry and George Webster visited my home in 2005. Twenty-three years after their daughter's disappearance, they still carried the pain of her unresolved death. The Websters' told me they had become active supporters of Parents of Murdered Children, Inc. (POMC), a national organization that provides advocacy and emotional support to survivors of homicide victims. As members of POMC, they talked about the need for the victim's family to know as much as possible about the death of their family member. As the prosecutor of the Paradiso case, I thought they could benefit by having an account of everything that was done and learned about their daughter's killer.

This book is based on actual police reports, grand jury minutes, parole records, trial and motion hearing transcripts, newspaper articles, notes from witness interviews, and my personal memory and recollections of the events as they occurred. Historical information was gleaned from many sources. A degree of dramatization and poetic license is taken in re-creating the scenes, but each is based upon the actual occurrence of the events depicted. In some instances, the content of transcripts and conversations have been condensed to move the story line forward, and two elements of the story, the attempt to get permission to surgically search Paradiso's left finger and my conversation with FBI agent Steve Broce at the Fairview Inn, are taken out of chronological order. Otherwise, the storyline follows the actual timeline of the occurrence of events.

Personal interviews were conducted with *Boston Herald* reporter Beverly Ford, former Detective Sergeant Carmen Tammaro, former trooper Jack Nasuti, Boston police Sergeant John Doris, Paradiso's former attorney Stephen Rappaport, and attorneys Judd Carhart, Paul Leary, and Carol Ball, all three of whom are currently sitting judges in the Commonwealth of Massachusetts.

I want to personally thank Connie Porter, Patti Bono, and Janet McCarthy as well as the many, many other witness in this investigation for having the courage to testify. The names of two other victims in this case have been changed to protect their identities; both Doreen Kennedy and Jennifer Lawson are pseudonyms. Neither of these women testified against Paradiso, but they did provide the details of their assaults through interviews with the police or the author.

Appreciation

No investigation of this magnitude can be brought to a trial, much less conviction, without the cooperation and diligent effort of literally hundreds of unsung law enforcement personnel; their hard work brought resolution to the many victims whose lives were shattered by Lenny Paradiso.

I would like to personally thank the men and women of the Massachusetts State Police and the Boston Police, the past and current members of the Essex and Suffolk County District Attorneys' offices, and the Saugus, Andover, and Revere police departments. There are many individuals who are not named in this book, but without their dedication, Paradiso would not have been convicted. A special thank you to assistant district attorney Ellen Donohue and investigator Anthony Pascucci for their day-to-day support; and thanks again to Carmenooch, Lt. Dennis Marks, Lt. Dean Bennett, Tpr. William McGreal, Tpr. Rick Fraelick, and Tpr. Carl Sjoberg, Boston police detective Steve Murphy, the Three Amigos with Irish accents, Lt. Larry Murphy, as well as the Harvard University police department for their cooperation and investigative skills.

To my friend, FBI agent Steve Broce, thanks for your incredible willingness to help, and to agent Sly Rutherford, a special appreciation for sifting through the mud brought up in the *Mala Femmena*.

To my friend and adviser, Beverly Ford, you have inspired me. To all of my unnamed reviewers and unpaid editors — especially Amelia Burke, Sheila Flynn, Carol Fierimonte, and Dorothea "Bear" Doar — thank you for your intellect and advice.

And to my wife, Sally, and my children — Jordan, Jared, Jake, and Courtney — your love and encouragement has enabled me to sit at my desk typing for sixteen hours a day (that and a ham and cheese sandwich). Thank you for your patience.

Finally, to my friend Drew, thank you being a part of my life.